Rome's Third Samnite War, 298–290 BC

Dedication

To Janet, Joe, Katie and Rich

Rome's Third Samnite War, 298–290 BC

The Last Stand of the Linen Legion

Mike Roberts

Pen & Sword
MILITARY

First published in Great Britain in 2020 by
Pen & Sword Military
An imprint of
Pen & Sword Books Ltd
Yorkshire – Philadelphia

Copyright © Mike Roberts 2020

ISBN 978 1 52674 408 1

The right of Mike Roberts to be identified as Author of this work has been asserted by him in accordance with the Copyright, Designs and Patents Act 1988.

A CIP catalogue record for this book is
available from the British Library.

All rights reserved. No part of this book may be reproduced or transmitted in any form or by any means, electronic or mechanical including photocopying, recording or by any information storage and retrieval system, without permission from the Publisher in writing.

Printed and bound in the UK by TJ International Ltd, Padstow, Cornwall.

Pen & Sword Books Limited incorporates the imprints of Atlas, Archaeology, Aviation, Discovery, Family History, Fiction, History, Maritime, Military, Military Classics, Politics, Select, Transport, True Crime, Air World, Frontline Publishing, Leo Cooper, Remember When, Seaforth Publishing, The Praetorian Press, Wharncliffe Local History, Wharncliffe Transport, Wharncliffe True Crime and White Owl.

For a complete list of Pen & Sword titles please contact

PEN & SWORD BOOKS LIMITED
47 Church Street, Barnsley, South Yorkshire, S70 2AS, England
E-mail: enquiries@pen-and-sword.co.uk
Website: www.pen-and-sword.co.uk

Or

PEN AND SWORD BOOKS
1950 Lawrence Rd, Havertown, PA 19083, USA
E-mail: Uspen-and-sword@casematepublishers.com
Website: www.penandswordbooks.com

Contents

Introduction		ix
Chapter 1	A City on a River	1
Chapter 2	Into Italy	17
Chapter 3	Another Fine Mess	32
Chapter 4	Into the Wild Wood	58
Chapter 5	A Samnite Pause	82
Chapter 6	Early Stages	113
Chapter 7	A Man and His Road	135
Chapter 8	Sentinum	153
Chapter 9	The Last Stand of the Linen Legion	187
Chapter 10	The Last Campaigns	233
Epilogue		256
Notes		284
Bibliography		289
Index		293

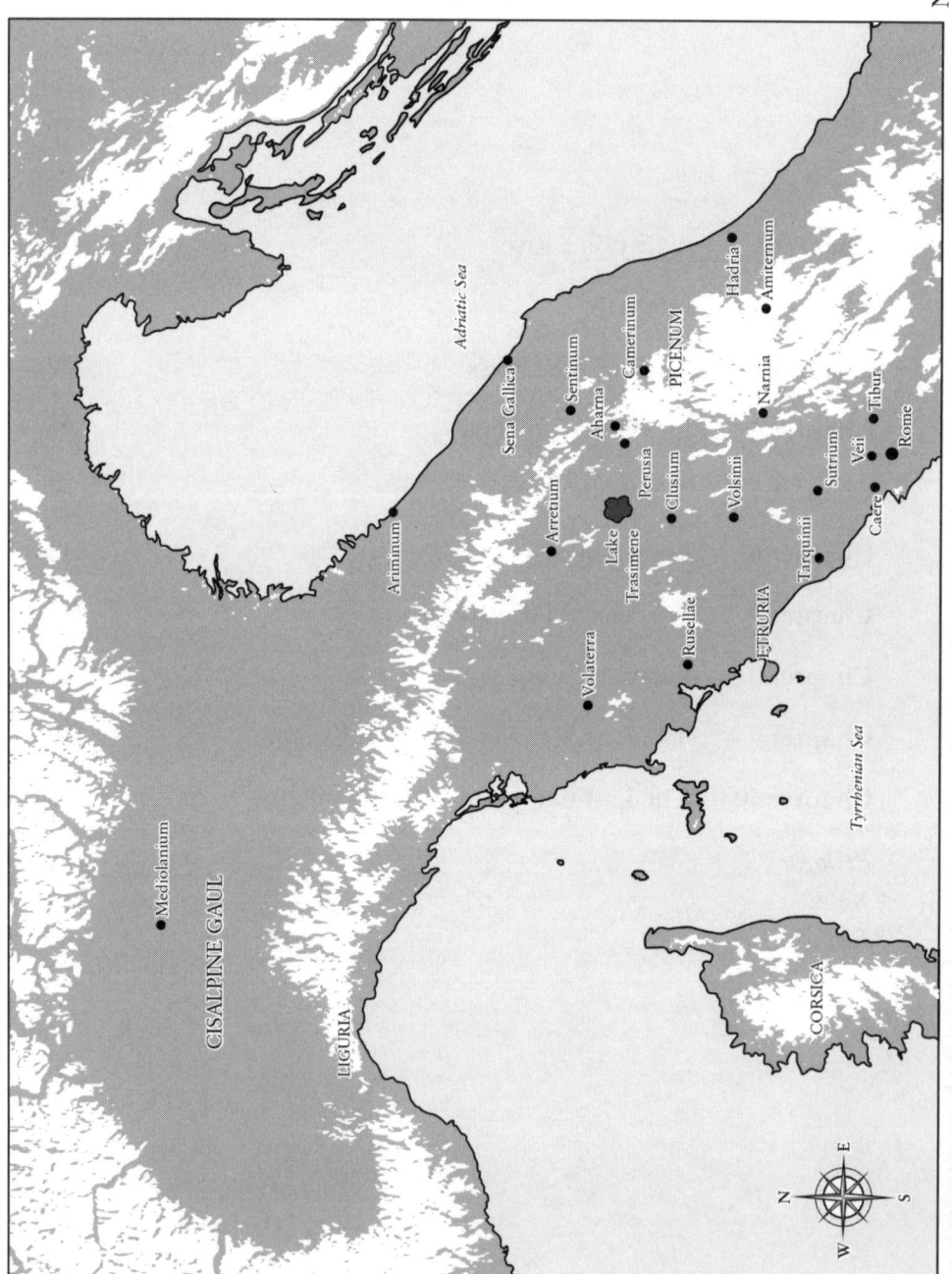

Northern Italy.

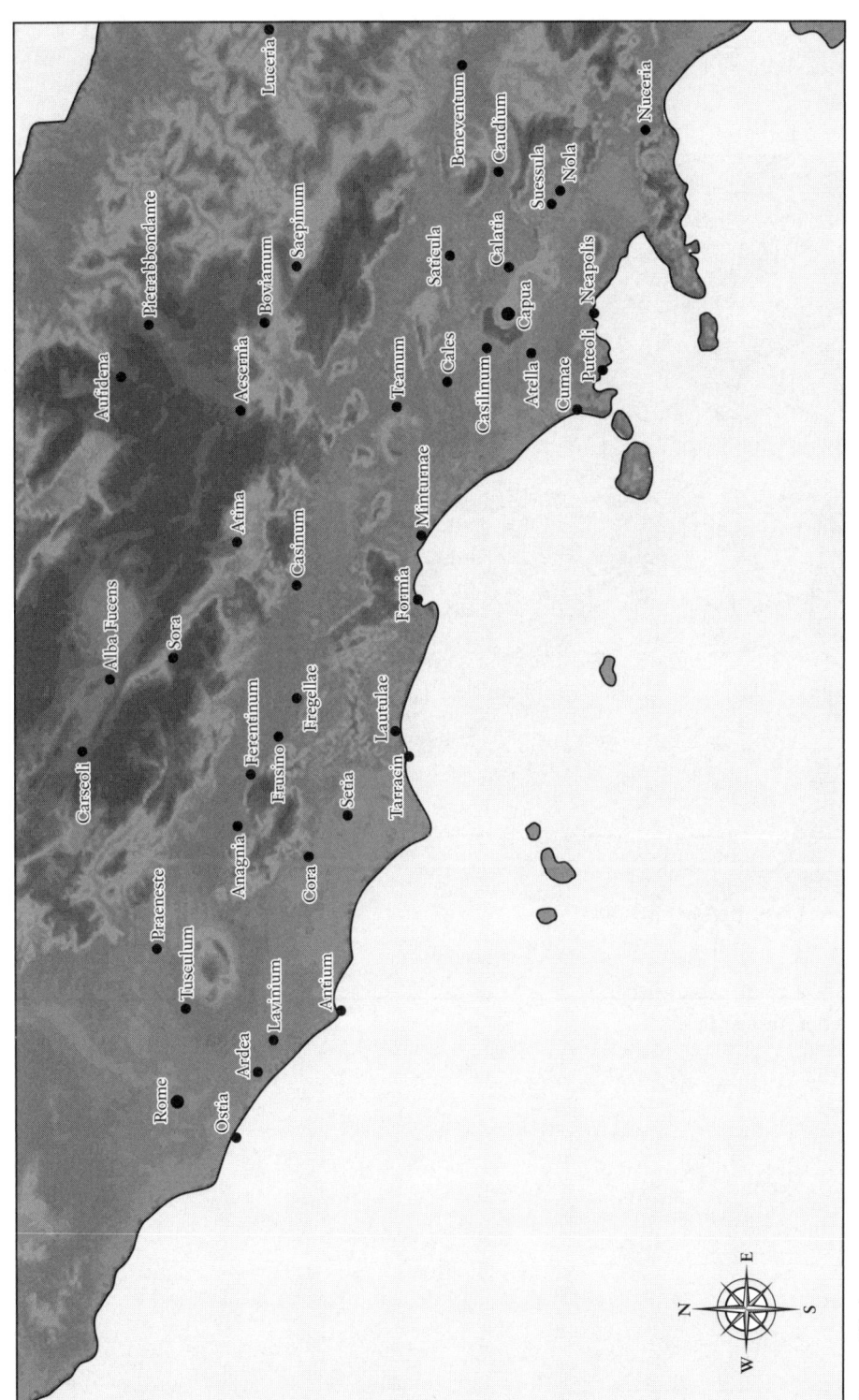

Central Italy.

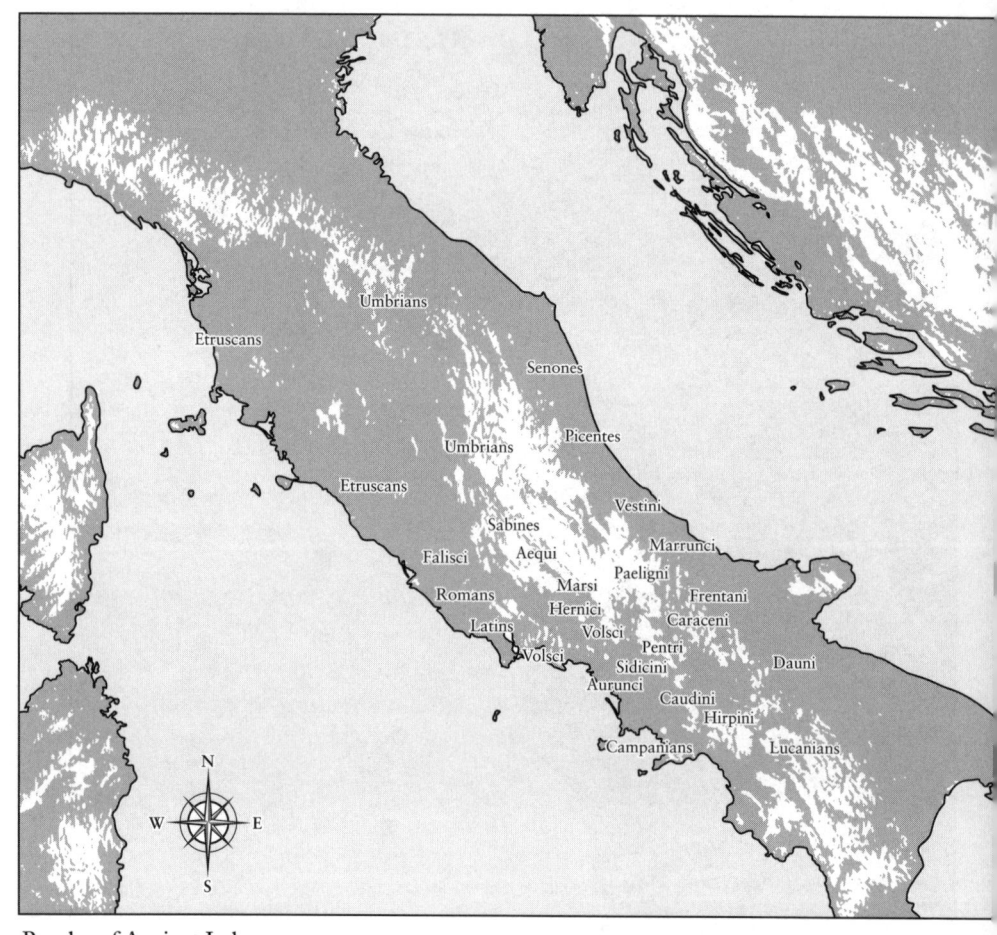

Peoples of Ancient Italy.

Introduction

'In fifty years, however, under the leadership of two generations of the Fabii and Papirii, the Romans so thoroughly subdued and conquered this people and so demolished the very ruins of their cities that to-day one looks round to see where Samnium is on Samnite territory, and it is difficult to imagine how there can have been material for twenty-four triumphs over them. Yet a most notable and signal defeat was sustained at the hands of this nation at the Caudine Forks in the consulship of Veturius and Postumius. The Roman army having been entrapped by an ambush in that defile and being unable to escape.'
Lucius Annaeus Florus, *The Two Books of the Epitome,*
extracted from Titus Livius.

One of the great events of Roman history is claimed to have occurred in a place gratifyingly accessible to the modern visitor. The road from Naples out of ancient Campania going east towards Benevento and then on to Apulia grandly advertises itself as the modern version of the Appian Way. The valley that opens for its entry is guarded on its southern lip by a foursquare Norman castle with towers at each angle and on the other side by the Castle of Maddaloni that winds delightfully up the side of the hill beneath which the town itself nestles. Continuous and scruffy habitations, communities running into each other, follow the road into the Caudine valley where pretty green foothills run off towards the far-off peaks of the Apennines, where snow sparkles in patches under spring sunshine. A village is soon reached by drivers on the old highway coming round a bend that is named as Forchia, or the forks and an information board standing beside the highway, though it would mean little to anybody not looking for the place. Turning off, the traveller can find a parking spot in a quiet village square where a pedestrian street rises between the commonplace village houses and shops of the region. It's a puff up the cobblestones, past a church where young locals happily humour a foreigner looking for the memorial that commemorates the great event that took place here in ancient times. A couple of hundred paces into town the path opens out, with a park and tennis courts on the left fronted by an open-air café, with a few patrons enjoying the afternoon warmth. These people finally directed the author to what would have been obvious, had he been more observant. Over the road in among the bushes and trees stands a rough stela (an inscribed stone pillar or column) with a picture carved into it. The style was primitive on this clearly reasonably modern monument and difficult to interpret from a distance, but up close it was possible to observe some ancient warriors holding a structure of spears under which another figure was bending to pass through. The event commemorated by this little-visited monument is one of the great disasters experienced by the young Roman Republic in the year 321.

Here the main army of the city, led by both its consuls, was trapped while invading the heartland of an inveterate enemy in the second great war against the Samnites. Perhaps 20,000 men had marched in a body from Campania, invading the lands of the Caudine Samnites, when they were inveigled in a ruse by the cunning defenders. The Samnites sent soldiers claiming to be deserters into the path of the intruders, knowing they would be captured, primed with intelligence that their main army was not nearby but had marched east to attack the Roman stronghold of Luceria in Apulia, on the Adriatic side of the Apennines. Convinced, the Roman command, without any reconnaissance at all, pressed on along the direct route that would take them through Samnite country to reach the threatened town before the enemy could take it. However, before the long lines of marching men and animals had gone far down the Caudium valley they found them themselves faced by the very enemy army they assumed to be attacking Luceria. They were dug in behind stout wooden barricades that blocked further progress along the valley floor. Because to assault these would be necessarily bloody and probably unsuccessful, the invaders turned about to withdraw the way they had come. Unfortunately they had not returned many miles when they discovered another force, also dug in behind a solid barricade, blocking their way. Unable to move in either direction, the Romans were in a quandary; any attempts that might have been made to break through in either direction were futile. With the army only carrying a limited amount of supplies and with no one available to come to their rescue, all that time could bring was starvation. It was a deadly trap and the Samnite intention was that none should escape.

These were the circumstances that saw the two senior magistrates of Rome, consuls who between them wielded for a year the authority of the old kings, not only surrendered with their men, but accepting that to save their lives, they would submit to going under the yoke. This meant that each man, stripped of armour, weapons and all but a tunic to cover his nakedness, bent down to pass under an arch made from spears, two upright and another tied together between them. Nor was this awful, humiliating disgrace all. As part of the convention of surrender, a treaty was concluded that returned to the Samnites most of the places they had lost to Rome in the preceding wars. Also as the humiliated soldiers and their generals returned to Rome to report on these dreadful events, they left 600 Roman eques, well-born knights, as hostages for their good faith.

The problems with the record detailed here are considerable regarding both the campaign and its aftermath. What is patently clear from what we learn about this encounter is that the terrain just does not fit. The Caudine valley, which leads in a few miles to the modern Montesarchio with its castle sitting under the great rock of Mount Taburno on one side and beautiful, verdant, forested high hills on the other, is not somewhere such a trap could be sprung. While Forchia, where events are claimed to have occurred, may lie in a noticeable valley, it will not tally with the story we are hearing. It would certainly be possible to block the road, as it is suggested the Samnites did both behind and in front of the invading Roman army, but this would not have acted as an effective trap. The slopes on either side may be steep and imposing along the road between Forchia and Arpaia where the passage is tightest, but they are far from impassable and to walk up them and out would be possible even for someone as unfit and aged as the author, given plenty of time and numerous rest stops, but still it could be done. So it is impossible that the young fit men of the legions, accustomed to marching many miles of difficult terrain, would have had any trouble at all in ascending to the ridge line and over, leaving the snare so carefully prepared empty of its prey. This remains true all along the road where all evidence tells us this debacle occurred. More than this, there is a real question mark over where and how the Samnites might have constructed their barricades. How could they have had time to stop up the western end of the defile before the Romans came barrelling back at them, to have blocked this wide passageway before their antagonists returned to force their way through?[1]

Much ink has been spilled on this matter over centuries of Roman scholarship. To make the account of Livy, our main source for these years work, there are suggestions that the action took place quite some way away from Forchia, where there was a real gorge that could have trapped the Romans like eels in a fyke net (fish trap). Yet while these propositions are clearly possible, none have real evidence to support them, particularly as these places mostly seem implausible as the roads an army of invasion might take. Equally if not more contentious than the issue of situation has been the debate over what occurred once the humiliated Romans reached home and how the City fathers decided to deal with articles of the treaty to which their magistrates had agreed. This is not the place to go into the details of these complicated matters, but the nub is around whether they reneged on the treaty and continued the war or that the agreement held, bringing the war to an end for several years, with the Romans withdrawing from the posts, like Cales, Fregellae and Luceria, that they had previously established in Samnite loyal country and handing them over to the victors.

This catastrophe was recorded extensively in the centuries that came after; from Cicero in works of philosophy, to historians like Appian and Eutropius, to a hotchpotch of collectables by Aulus Gellius and even the output of the fourth-century AD Christian bishop Paulus Orosius. In this not exhaustive list the picture painted by Livy of Rome's legions falling into a cunning trap is by no means always corroborated. The sources are at variance; some even resist the imperative to put down such setbacks to the enemy not playing by the rules, contending that the surrender probably followed a fair fight in the open field. However, the Caudine forks, though they occurred some twenty years before the meat of our story begins, are a sequence of events that highlight important issues with all our sources. Most particularly Livy, on whom we depend for most of the detail, who by becoming the gold standard for Rome's story ensured that so many of those who came before were allowed to fade away and those who came after just blindly followed his line. This man also wrote, at the beginning of his history, an account of the age of kings and the first two centuries of the Republic that is built on very shifting sands. Much of what was known of these early times was a semi-legendary build-up of oral traditions that were mined extensively and fairly uncritically once history began to be written. Family and state archives existed but were less and less dependable the further back they went. Also, even if the idea that all previous records were lost in the Gallic sack is now far from completely accepted,[2] much cannot be depended upon and chronological errors occurred that forced Livy to use his imagination to fill the gaps.

Myth and mystery do begin to be pushed back in the fourth century when a Roman reality was beginning to emerge. Yet even then, only a few generations before Rome's first historian was born, there was little firm ground. Was the conflict with Veii really any more real history than the siege of Troy? Did on either occasion Greek and Roman armies surround the enemies' walls and wage a ten-year war to bring them down? Certainly some sort of struggle was fought out, but most likely on both occasions it amounted to not much more than annual raiding across the Aegean for the Greeks and across the Tiber for the Romans. Can we describe what we have as history, where there is very little that is accurate in terms of chronology, action or even military detail? Also in the case of Veii, archaeological evidence does not even support the contention central to the Roman tradition: that it was trashed and the people massacred or enslaved. Indeed, it seems that the buildings on the promontory where the city stood were continuously inhabited with no layers of ash to show that a brutal enemy had entered and burned it down.

It is even possible to argue that a figure such as Camillus, by tradition virtually the second founder of the city,[3] might not be much less mythical than Romulus. Aristotle, a contemporary Greek who knew about the sack of Rome at the beginning of the fourth century, does not mention this man who is claimed to be both present and significant at the end of the fifth century and for the first forty years of the next. Even Diodorus and Polybius, Greeks writers active several centuries later who give considerable details concerning Rome in this period, have very little to say on this putative giant. The claim by many is that he was at the heart of so many great events; the man who finally conquered Veii, who defeated the Gauls and retrieved from them the loot they had taken from Rome. Five times dictator, a multiple triumpher and holder of the consular tribunate. The man appears ubiquitous to an almost impossible extent. It seems far-fetched that one individual could have done so much and even many of those convinced of his historicity accept that there must have been exaggeration of his role and that perhaps there were a number of different characters involved, maybe with family connections. His was a name that could comfortingly connect so many great actions of the heroic Republic in some of its most desperate hours.

However, as the fourth century turns into the third century, a sea change does seem to have occurred. The period of the Samnite Wars is when real history struggles to emerge; a complex time certainly, but at least one where there are incontrovertible realities to hang the story around. There are contemporary or near-contemporary Greeks Duris, Timaeus and Aristotle who we are beginning to hear from, and not long afterwards Roman historians put pen to paper. The first of these, Quintus Fabius Pictor born in the second quarter of the third century, would have met people who were active in the period of the Third Samnite War and were youngsters when Appius Claudius was censor; a connection that would allow real memories to at least shape what was written down. Soon after the analyst tradition from the second century gave a structure that was to some degree consistent, if very far from objective. From 300 chronology tightens up with the existence of a full and accurate list of consulships. Later in the third century even numbers start to become dependable. For a time sixty-five years after the end of the Third Samnite War, Polybius, probably using figures finally derived from the city archives, can record in accurate numbers the military potential of Italian peoples allied to Rome. However, if the period of the Third Samnite War shows signs of coming into focus, the difference should not be exaggerated. Not really until the Pyrrhic War of the 270s can we be confident in chronology and content in matters concerning the Italian peninsula. More particularly we unfortunately lose the Greek historian Diodorus, who for the last quarter of the fourth century up until the year 302 could be used to test and clarify where our other main source wanders way off the rails, despite a bewildering inclination to locate almost all Roman

Samnite fighting in Apulia. Yet this should not depress those confronting this epoch; after all, prior to the High Middle Ages there are really very few periods where reliable accounts shine a comprehensive light. Will Durant's contention that history is mostly guesswork bolstered by prejudice is surely appropriate for most of the ancient world. In the story of Rome there are only a few islands of in-depth reporting; around the Hannibalic Wars, the early wars against the Hellenistic kings and the age of Sulla, Pompey and Caesar at the very end of the Republic. Any of the histories we depend on were bound to have been constructed by pulling together threads, many of which may be very far from robust, when every contention can almost always find itself flatly contradicted; a reality that means the story left by Roman chroniclers can sometimes feel like the content is as much like fable as actuality.

Many have come to serious study of Rome from the epic penned by Gibbon, loving the style and story while puzzling over why the great edifice that stood for so many centuries finally fell in a rush of barbarian bustling and civil bloodletting. Reasons range from suggestions of a decline of belligerence due to the increasing dominance of Christianity to economic critiques that see an overweight bureaucracy and military crushing the life out of an agricultural landscape that could not bear the tax burden needed to sustain it. Yet this analysis of the fourth- and fifth-century AD tribulations has its pitfalls, with evidence from the fourth century AD that some places in the Levant experienced some of their most productive years, with rural populations on the increase. However, while the interest in the Empire's decline and fall is understandable, what can never be forgotten is that the really remarkable feature of the state was its longevity, even if we just take it down to the fall of the Western Empire in 475, but if we continue with Gibbon through the Byzantine years to 1452, then it is an almost impossibly long-lived polity. Other real terrestrial giants of ancient, medieval and even pre-modern times – the Persians, Mongols, Ottoman, Spanish or English – just don't even compare. Even if we accept, with devotees of Cliodynamics,[4] that the Roman Empire, just like any other agrarian-based super-state, was delineated by cyclical wheels within wheels, a very interesting take that still cannot overshadow the fact that this Rome, starting to show imperial inclinations in the third century BC, lasted an extraordinarily long time.

Civilizations had grown up round the Mediterranean basin like weeds, so it would have been a prescient man indeed who could have conceived what would develop from the human seeds planted around some insignificant hills in central Italy. The great inland sea had retained its current shape for thousands of years when travellers on the beautiful blue expanse might, on approaching the mouth of the River Tiber, have seen the slight indication of smoke on the horizon, showing the presence of people dwelling 16 miles up the river. The question of how Rome rose to take up such a huge chunk of Western man's chronicled narrative is at least of equal significance as to how it crumbled; how from a shaky infancy and youth it emerged to attain a Methuselah-like maturity. There is inevitably a desire, with hindsight, to see the rise of Rome as inexorable, as with almost any historical process where our records come mainly from the winning side, but this should be resisted. Its situation certainly had advantages: the lowest good crossing of the still-navigable Tiber allowing easy transit from Etruria down through to the rich lands of Campania and the Greek south, access to salt – so important in a pre-refrigeration world – a defensible site on its seven hills and good agricultural land to sustain a booming population. Signs of greatness are claimed as coming early as Rome of the kings is touted as becoming the dominant place in Latium. However, equally this is only part of a story of a place frequently subject to Etruscan neighbours and that, after an internal revolution, had to fight for a century and a half just to drive invading Aequi and Volsci hill folk back into the Apennines or into the Pontine Marshes. Then also to make inroads over their frontier against their closest Etruscan neighbour Veii while achieving a presence in the direction of Campania that brought them up against the might of the Samnites. These struggles might have shown a glimmer of what was to come, but surely Rome was not unique. There must have been other candidates who might have succeeded in dominating Italy: an Etruscan place or even a league of such cities, a coastal Greek enclave or an inland metropolis like Capua, raising rich crops on volcanic soil; they clearly might have been rivals for peninsular hegemony. Indeed, could Italy not have remained divided as she was for most of her history in almost the whole period after the fall of Rome? A battleground of rival powers based in the north at Milan or Turin, in Tuscany at Florence or Pisa, further south at Rome and Naples or Venice on the Adriatic and outside the peninsula as well. So if the rise of the Tiber town to greatness was not a law of nature, it becomes possible to make a case that had she been kept within the bounds of Latium, then that tipping-point would not have arisen that allowed her, with manpower resources drawn from the central Apennines, Campania, Apulia and parts of Etruria as well, to make herself first the dominant power on the mainland, and then to spread out onto first the nearby islands of Sardinia, Corsica and Sicily and finally across the whole of the middle sea.

Historians have long appreciated the implications of the defeat of Hannibal, but perhaps not so much the end of Samnite dreams. The great nineteenth-century German polymath Theodor Mommsen considers that about 330, soon after the last sparks of independence had been crushed out of the Latins and Volsci and significant swaths of colonists had considerably expanded the territory directly controlled by the Republic, is the time that Rome alone had become too great to be opposed by just one other Italian power. Yet even if this is accepted, what makes the period after the fourth century drew its final breaths still so important is that this almost decade of war from 298 to 290 was almost certainly the last opportunity for the progress of Roman expansion to have been either stopped or delayed, even by a combination of peninsular peoples. This is not just a self-serving exaggeration of the significance of this author's subject; the attention of any interested observer is bound to be drawn to the years between 298 and 290. A different result in the Third Samnite War might have provided a buffer that could have stopped the runaway train of Rome's rush to Empire. An alternative victor at Sentinum followed by advances by the Samnites up the Liris and Volturnus valleys into Campania and a resurrected Etruscan and Umbrian military effort might have been enough to significantly constrain a Roman power, even backed by those Latins and others who perennially provided her with powerful auxiliaries to support the legions. That population of citizens, Latins and allies wrested from her control after defeat, would not then have been available to mobilize against first their conquerors then after that Lucanians, Bruttians and Greek cities like Tarentum, with the regal Hellenistic condottiere she invited in to aid her. So at least a generation's delay in Rome's rise to Italian predominance could have meant that when she hurried into conflict with Carthage over Sicily, that enemy could have been already led by a family of Barcid's headed by Hannibal, who would have been able to command the resources of that city's African and island empires, perhaps with a Spanish appendage too, undamaged by dreadful defeat in the first Punic War. With the initial edge of the Carthaginian maritime expertise and the military talent shown at Trebbia, Lake Trasimene and Cannae available to her army, it is easy to imagine an outcome in which the Romans failed to register a convincing win. Then the Italian power, restrained by a rival to her south, even if she had made an impact across the Adriatic into the Greek and Levantine realms, surely would not have come to dominate the world of Alexander's successor kingdoms in the way she actually did between the victory in Africa in 202 and that at Magnesia ad Sipylum in Lydia in 290.

This is not a counter-factual that should be discounted out of hand. After all, that Rome came to cover the world from Scotland to Mesopotamia was not pre-ordained, nor indeed that it should not end up adding the lands of the Germans or other north and east European peoples to the Empire. There might be explanations geographic, political, economic and human for how much of the globe came within the Latin fold, but it could certainly have been different, and a much less powerful Rome at the end of the third century BC might have had considerably less of an impact, meaning that Europe and the Middle East would have looked very different for the next millennium. With a Roman state that was perhaps considerably smaller, maybe sharing the Mediterranean with rivals in Africa and Asia that she had never been strong enough to completely suppress, history might have been shaped differently and our own world quite dissimilar as a result. Would the spread of monotheistic religions been substantially different without a mega-state available to facilitate the astounding success of an almost absolute and organized Catholic church? Would different national organizations have arisen in Iberia, Gaul and Britain if the Roman titan had not grown so vast and ambitious that it was able and wanted to absorb them? Though equally to claim such epoch-busting possibilities really might not be necessary at all, as finally where the Roman border went may have an influence in modern times on the language we speak and the details of the laws we follow, but it has surely not been the defining factor between people living in Dresden and Copenhagen and those living in Paris and Milan in terms of either disparity or similarity. Much else has gone under the bridge and made a difference.

Chapter One

A City on a River

'Arms, and the man I sing, who, forc'd by fate,
And haughty Juno's unrelenting hate,
Expell'd and exil'd, left the Trojan shore.
Long labors, both by sea and land, he bore,
And in the doubtful war, before he won
The Latian realm, and built the destin'd town;
His banish'd gods restor'd to rites divine,
And settled sure succession in his line,
From whence the race of Alban fathers come,
And the long glories of majestic Rome.'

The *Aeneid*, Virgil
John Dryden

The Greek biographer Plutarch has a basket of stories regarding how the city of Rome, established on the lowest crossing-point of the Tiber, got its name.[1] A situation bang on commercial routes that ran north-south from Etruria into Latium and Campania and west along the river to the sea and east into the mountains, ensuring the booming growth of a community of farmers hewing out a future, with access to crucial salt deposits and a sideline in banditry, if the early legends are to be credited. A place where a competent headman developed into a regal tyrant, as the villages growing on the hills above the marshy river meadows filled the land between and coalesced into a unified urban entity. Human habitation is, in fact, shown in the archaeological records back to the very late second millennium and some communal life was certainly operational by the time of the city's legendary foundation in the eighth century. In fable, the place was born in blood when Romulus assassinated his brother and then much later the fratricide himself was butchered by his closest men, with each carrying a small part of his carcass away in the folds of their clothing so he was never seen again and the credulous were appeased by the story that he had ascended to the heavens in a night of dramatic thunder. Abduction had been central in this age of heroes past, remembered in marriage ceremony by carrying the bride over the threshold, a memory of violence against the Sabine women. Also treachery, with the story of Tarpeia letting the invading Sabines into the capital for all the rich rings they carried on their left arms, but perishing when in recompense they threw not just their bracelets but their shields as well in a mound on top of her.[2] Well before gladiatorial bloodbaths in the arena were de rigueur, bloody duelling with enemy champions was a favourite way to reputation, and the greatest of all accomplishments was winning the Spolia Opima, when a commanding general killed his opposite number in combat and stripped his corpse to dedicate these arms to Jupiter. Such an honour was first awarded to Romulus for killing Acron, king of the Caeninenses, who was looking for revenge after the Sabine rape, then later to Cornelius Cossus for killing Tolumnius, a king of Veii, and the third not until late in the 200s, the only occasion in historic times, when Marcus Claudius Marcellus downed a king of the Celtic Gaesatae.

Yet if a penchant for the gory remained, much else had changed in the 500-odd years since the traditional foundation. By the end of the fourth century nearly 7 miles of Tufa walls nestled up against the river, near where the Tiber island split the muddy currents of the watercourse surrounding the city, and perhaps two surfaced roads, apart from the normal cart tracks, led away into a long domesticated countryside. Where outside of a few suburban gardens and overspill habitations, the fields spread for miles, dotted with individual farmsteads and hamlets of a population, most of whom still lived off the land. However, by now the Romans were much more than the agricultural denizens of a large market town, with little interest in trade, manufacture or acquiring maritime muscle. Certainly not isolated or culturally backward, like so much of Italy they had felt the influence of Hellenic and Hellenistic cultures of the Eastern Mediterranean, funnelled through the Greek colonies long established along the peninsula's coast or midwifed through their Etruscan neighbours. A trail of pottery finds clearly indicates these influences spreading west and moulding the indigenous cultures developing on the Italian mainland.

They had taken to eating and drinking on coaches rather than traditional benches; statues of Pythagoras had been set up in the city, Greek coins copied and a portent-fixated people, looking for sources of legitimacy from a foreign pantheon, had for centuries plundered the Greeks for deities. Even if it would be some time before it became the fashion for the elite to have their sons educated in the tongue that was the lingua franca in a wider world, the influence was beginning to show in names chosen, a key cultural indicator in any age. There was a Philo, from the Greek Philip, who was a key man in fourth-century Rome, and it is not impossible that some of his radicalism may have been influenced by Greek ideas of democracy circulating at that time. There were bronze statues showing by the end of the fourth century, many reverencing the same humanized Olympians they had absorbed into their ritual tradition hundreds of years before. Such hefty effigies could be seen of Jupiter on top of his temple where only an earthenware one had stood before and another of Hercules was in place by 305.[3] However, it was not just gods and heroes: there were sculptures of the founder twins being suckled by the wolf and even equestrian statues of Rome's own heroes who had won her battles in centuries of war.[4] There were craftsmen and artists aplenty of sufficient talent to produce classy frescoes, a wonderful bronze head credited as the insurgent Brutus and an engraved bronze casket of the highest workmanship found at Praeneste. While sculptors might not yet have peppered the place with statues of muscular men and goddesses in pleated gowns, stonemasons would in a few generations, following Hellenistic patterns, be capable of producing the kind of Tufa sarcophagus made for a Scipio who will feature in our story. Yet despite taking so much from them, there was still and would remain huge suspicion of these men from the south and east. Like most societies, contradiction was at the heart of much of their attitudes and if paranoia about being swamped by foreign cultures made no sense for a people who had taken so much from others, still it was real. Xenophobia as a birthright, shown by a distaste for oleaginous Greeks, remained a common motif.

Though the Law of the Twelve Tables introduced in the 450s indicates little concern with trade or industry, this admittedly fragile evidence is hardly valid for 150 years later when commerce certainly was flourishing. Archaeology shows that pottery manufacture was up and running and by 300 there were exports of black glazed ware of Roman provenance found as far off as Spain and North Africa. For the first time, late in the fourth century, we know of Roman-controlled ports and harbours that were bustling with vessels, maritime and military, and the rowers and marines who worked them. A small maritime defence force had been constructed in the expansive year of 311 and only a little while later we learn of the earliest example of an amphibious expedition in the Republican period.[5] The first half of the fourth century had seen Ostia flourishing, colonists sent to Sardinia and friendship established with places as distant as Massilia. Rome was looking out, and beyond coastal colonies there was a settlement on the Pontine Islands. It was a world where some might even hope of a briny future; after all, Athens had not started much nearer the sea and she had achieved one of the greatest maritime empires of ancient times. It was a time when coins circulated; most coming from Magana Graecia and Campania, with examples found from Neapoli minted in 326 and another from 310, with a head of Mars, most likely of Campanian provenance. Soon, in an effort to fund impressive infrastructure investment, Rome would be minting her own specie out of the booty of war, with regular issues circulating soon after the end of the Pyrrhic Wars. Wealth did not just finance roads and aqueducts, but temples too. Between 302 and 264 the place was a sanctified building site with at least fourteen shrines erected, showing the benefits of a victory dividend, while the establishment of a sanctuary to the Greek god of healing established on Tiber Island in 291 shows a community looking to connect to the high-status world of the Hellenistic East. Not that this was in the least new: Tarquinius Superbus had long before sent to the Oracle at Delphi to discover the import of a snake appearing out of a wooden pillar of his great temple to Jupiter then being constructed on the Capitoline hill and after the triumph over Veii spoils were dedicated at the great Greek cult centre.

So merchants growing fat, examining bills of particulars and with local coinage running through their fingers showed an economy on the move, but still it was the groups of Patricians, landed nobles, with their town houses on the Palatine, that counted. This was 'nob hill', a place for winners since Romulus stood there while Remus occupied the Aventine looking at the sky to spot the flight of birds that would mean they had the gods' approval to found the city. There the elite wandered when not at their country estates or making house calls in their stints back home from war to rally friends and persuade waverers to support their electoral or policy projects. While this was the power neighbourhood, all glitz and glamour, most of the common people lived in districts that had grown in uninhibited chaos, where even the inhabitants could get lost in the stew of alleys that ran off the few thoroughfares as, after all, one-year officials did not have much time for town planning. This Rome was not the megacity of late Republican and Imperial times, but still there were shanties and high-built apartments enough; fires and collapsing blocks would already have been a terror. Communities were created at crossroads and in slum quarters to cater for those who could not enjoy the theatre of high-toned communal ritual. High-density housing was broken by open spaces in the valleys between the hills, where the Forum was situated or the great expanse of the Circus Maximus, seating a populace who had loved to bet on the chariot races since the days of the kings. Gladiatorial combat was not yet practised, but would soon be learned, becoming popular in the late third century, taken from the long-held practices to honour the dead at funeral celebrations in Campania, Samnium and perhaps Etruria too.

Rome in 300 was shabby and labyrinthine, mainly a city of bricks and timber with terracotta statues; they did not use concrete, and monumentalism was as yet not the style. Not a site that if dug up millennia later would have impressed in the ways the wonderful jumble of ruins of a later Rome did. The place would have reeked of the country. The world the Romans inhabited was close to the ground and a symphony of odours from animals and people must have ascended out of choked streets, while smoke rose skywards from cooking fires and sometimes from flash conflagrations encouraged by rubbish-filled streets, and throughout was the city noise. It would be another 200 years before the levels of luxury would reach almost modern levels for the elite and life was slow. Winter closed in these urban communities because it ended sea travel with many fewer people journeying, bringing the goods and gossip that did so much to brighten life, but changes were under way. It was a community becoming gradually more slave-dependent and population growth was fuelled by imported slaves buying their freedom. Indeed, this had been going on so long that in 312 the censor could be pilloried for bringing the descendants of such freed men into not just the citizen body, but the Senate as well. The fourth century had equally seen an increase of servile labour in the country, on both the great estates and middling farms.

The city itself was the centre of a polity that around 321 may have had well over 150,000 and by 290 there were 272,000 registered citizens,[6] but what were the numbers actually thronging the streets? Population statistics are notoriously difficult at this time, but if the earlier figure was an accurate estimate of the citizen body, then women, children, slaves, freedmen and foreigners would have raised it to near half a million. However, the numbers of those who lived in or close around the Servian walls would have been much less. Many tens of thousands certainly, perhaps as high as 80,000 depending on the season, as sowing and harvest time would see the estate-owners out managing their fields and those without property tramping the country lanes in search of paid employment. This population had grown apace in half a century. It is possible that the city itself contained little more than 30,000 people in 350, but by 300 this had more than doubled and could have reached 90,000 by 270, the sort of numbers that required the building of the first two aqueducts by that date, but certainly not many more than that in what was still an essentially agrarian society. There may have been people making a living in trade and industry but only a small proportion and certainly not the huge numbers employed in that way and in the service industries that would be the pattern of the Imperial centuries.

It is claimed that the great metropolis of the High Empire reached 1 million inhabitants and an Augustine inscription that has 330,000 citizens actually domiciled in Rome certainly makes this number not improbable. This was the absolute metropolis of an empire that at its height is estimated to contain 75 million, a quarter of the world's population. It was the most populous city in the Western world until 1800 when London reached these kinds of numbers, but the Rome of 300 was not such an entity. It would have been far more comparable to the English capital at the end of the fourteenth century and in the first half of the fifteenth; a place recovering from bouts of plague, where Wat Tyler ruffled feathers and Dick Whittington went to make his fortune. Certainly bigger than anywhere nearby, economically and socially complex but not extraordinarily larger than its neighbours.[7]

These Romans were ritual-bound folk; they considered the flights of birds always had great import and peered at the entrails of animals to discover the future. We lack much insight into the minds of this people for whom any kind of rational inclination was trumped by deep superstitions and fear of sorcery. Ominous portents would ensure that the deepest search must be made to find out what pious practice had failed to be fully honoured and, in extremis, consulting the Sibylline books to discover what was required to compensate for the failure. Retaining a reverence for things they had known before the arrival of the humanized gods of Greece, a vaunted distaste for change was surely real and when things ceased to be relevant they might be kept as comforting furniture, while the new was adapted to look like it had always been there. So in thrall to tradition, a history was concocted of a double kingship with Romulus and a Sabine counterpart to give some depth to the idea of a dual consulship that emerged with the formation of the Republic. This Roman personality we encounter is of course largely that of the elite; after all, it is them from who we hear and not the country rube, despite aspirations to some rural idyll of the fat and opulent imagining themselves as ploughmen, beekeepers or shepherds. These men who started like their counterparts in most polities as thugs and robbers soon constructed an identity wrapped up in pious self-sacrifice and patriotic intent.

These patricians (literally the famous) who dominated so much of Rome's story had a relationship with the City itself that was both complicated and changed over time. In the centuries after the founding and growth under half-mythical monarchs and even after these rulers had been removed, the situation might be instructively imagined as not unlike some frontier town in a Hollywood Western. The most powerful actors were that group of wealthy ranchers who lived on their grand farmsteads, running herds of cattle, aided by family and crowds of hired cowboys. These, like the great patrician clans in the Roman orbit, were rich and powerful because of their ownership of large estates and like them, though based outside of town, they wanted to have influence in and if possible dominate the urban environment too. The cattle baron wanted to occupy or control the important civic posts like sheriff and mayor, just as the patricians vied to fill the various magistracies, consular tribune, consul and praetorships that were available in Rome's early days. In each era they hoped to ensure a community where their interests were protected and they would be able to utilize metropolitan manpower and economic resources for their own benefit. Cattle barons might organize raids against rivals or local indigenous peoples off their own bat, just as patricians might mount their own campaigns with no particular sign of support or control from the city administration. Examples from semi-legendary days abound: when Coriolanus attacked some Volsci with just his own clients and during the war with Veii in 477 when a Fabii army of 300 men, family retainers and clients was ambushed and butchered when pursuing a herd of cattle at what is grandly termed the Battle of the Cremera. That this is undoubtedly a homage to the Spartan 300 at Thermopylae does not make it the less indicative that these old grandees could and would follow their own policies and carry out their own operations. Particularly instructive is the story of Brutus marching on Rome to depose Tarquin with supporters from Collatia. This place, 8 miles north-east of Rome, was where the patrician Lucius Tarquinius Collatinus had his powerbase, and after his wife Lucretia was raped by King Tarquin's son, it was the young men there who mobilized in revenge, only recruiting revolutionaries at Rome after they arrived there to depose the king. Yet equally these landed magnates might co-operate with the City authorities, particularly to face a common foe. Just as the cattle-rancher and his men would join up with a local posse to confront dangerous bandits or raiding Apaches, so would the patricians lead their clan forces in tandem with the Roman levy to face an outbreak of marauding Aequi or Volsci or to take on the armies of Latin or Etruscan cities.

In these years these clan warlords were far from ineluctably connected to the City. On occasions they might arrive from outside; after all, most Roman kings were Sabine or Etruscan incomers, powerful clan leaders who were able to offer protection to the City in return for gaining a lifetime of regal imperium. There is a tablet found at Lyon, attributed to the Emperor Claudius, that tells the story of Servilus Tullius coming from Etruria with his war band and establishing himself on the Caeliian Hill, named for his earlier commander for whom he fought in Etruria, on the way to the Roman throne.[8] Sometimes these strongmen might withdraw from the City's orbit altogether, aligning with other communities around Latium if it suited their interests; a new orthodoxy that explains why, in the early centuries, great figures from the patrician families are so often described as being in exile and on occasions taking the field against their compatriots. Camillus is a classic of this floating kind of power; his connections with Tusculum were well-known and he is accredited at a key moment in exile in ancient Ardea, halfway to Anzio, but this was most likely him just moving his interests into the ambit of an equally ancient place, the capital of the Rutuli, who even get a name check in the *Aeneid*.

This was an outline that mutated over the centuries, particularly as Rome grew in power and population. If the land-owning elite had, when Rome was a place of modest proportions, wanted influence and access to position to push their own interests, at some stage their commitment to the community firmed up and winning the great magistracies became their raison d'être. Understandable enough: if being mayor of Dodge City was an advantageous sideline, winning the same office in New York City could be the whole interest of anyone, however rich and powerful they might be and however many interests they might have outside the city limits. This was a process that had become virtually complete through the fourth century. So by the time the Samnite Wars flared, it was at the head of national armies and through occupying the most significant Roman magistracies that the great would increase the power, reputation and wealth of their clan. Where before they showed off their wealth in grand funerary arrangements, now they could think of beautifying a city to which they were fully committed with egoistic projects ranging from temple-building to erecting equestrian statues. Not that the tensions between being clan chief or representative of Rome were ever completely resolved, which might suggest a context for a continuation of ad hoc and haphazard Roman foreign policy until well after the Hannibalic War and perhaps even the final denouement of a Republic, where shared restraint collapsed in a world of warlord competition. Equally though, this could just be the blurring of the line between war as culture and war as policy that pervades the history of most peoples.

A process christened the 'conflict of the orders' that flared in the fifth century was surely part of the developments just described; that so many of the early tribal designations mirrored clan names is no coincidence.

It showed that the members, clients and other followers of the great families were beginning to commit to Roman residence and what has been traditionally designated as the 'closing of the patriciate' reflects the same changes; a firming-up of the relationship of previously mobile power families with the growing might of Rome. Such changes inevitably caused the kind of tension that was later interpreted as a straight contest between the patricians and plebs and that required significant constitutional adjustment to ensure against destructive civil strife. The creation of the tribunes of the plebs was just such a mechanism to facilitate the integration between the old settlers and long influential but fluid interests who were now settling in a much more permanent way.

The Rome of 300 that was about to face one of its greatest military tests in the Third Samnite War was apparently a city on the brink of resolving this 'conflict of the orders' that had bedevilled its politics almost since the birth of the Republic. Class conflict was endemic in almost all complex ancient societies, but in the Roman polity it was exhibited in a particular way. The patricians who had dumped the kings had themselves been motivated by the desire to inherit the power, patronage and glory that adhered to the throne, but to share with those lower down the social order was never their intent and eventually this became something the wealthier plebeians were not prepared to stomach. So the commons were mobilized and the claim is that the impact of their threatening to desert their patrician overlords and set up an alternative state on a number of occasions in the fifth and fourth centuries moved along key reforms. In these early centuries the number of high offices to aspire to were few indeed and the demands to sit at the top table and enjoy the benefits of office and influence from the growing number of affluent Romans who had no patrician pedigree was the root. So the disruption was about access to the posts that would bring wealth and prestige.

The picture is of plebeian strike action with most of the non-patrician citizen body climbing Monte Sacro or the Aventine and creating a kind of soviet in embryo, threatening to construct a polity of their own that would work in their own interest, not in that of their patrician oppressors. Yet it is difficult to really envisage every man laying down tools to congregate on a local eminence; after all, they would have had homes, farms, shops, warehouses and factories to look after. There was a tradition common to many ancient societies in which a voice of the commons developed in the context of their inherent power as the most numerous component of a nation in arms. In Rome yeoman farmers working their land with just family and a handful of servants and slaves provided the backbone of the military levy. Depending on their means, they would muster with fine armour or just shield and spear but whichever, a people in arms always had a potential for influence in the ancient world. In Greece this might vary from the sophisticated democracy of Athens to the tribal assemblies of the Aetolians, but at root it was the people who would fill the ranks, wanting a say in the two key matters of moment: should they go to war, and if so, who should lead them? From the start they retained the potential of political value. Even during the kingly war games described in the *Iliad*, the ignoble squaddie Thersites[9] might voice an opinion in the presence of nobles and princes, even if he got a cuffing for his pains at the hands of Odysseus, and even the most autocratic rulers had to take some note of those who bled for the patria. Those who fought had to be considered, whether it be a medieval king lending an ear to the gripes of his barons and knights or praetorians selling the imperial crown to the highest bidder in second-century Imperial Rome. History is full of the extraordinary progress that can be made by the people in arms in the most difficult circumstances, whether it be the new model army being the first to rid its country of monarchy as early as the seventeenth century or the soldier soviets in Tsarist Russia leading a movement that offered a glimmer of light in a world weltering in pointless bloodletting; a near-universal tendency that would surely have been some of what happened at old Rome, however much the details might be fantasy.

Therefore that from the fourth century plebeian muscle had been flexed mainly by refusing to muster in arms should be no surprise, though earlier other strategies had existed to pressure the patrician elite to consent to changes that would allow others to partake of at least some crumbs from the power table. Three secessions are claimed in the fifth century and the struggle had seen progress, with new officers being created to broaden who might reach the heights; to allow some plebeian admittance to high office and influence in the law courts; and authorizing popular assemblies that were clearly capable of exercising real influence and creating tribunes of the plebs empowered to voice popular complaint. The fourth century saw its share of disturbances too. There is something like a Catiline conspiracy 300 years beforehand, with a claim that a man called Marcus Manlius Capitolinus, possessed of an alluring reputation for defending the Capitol, after being aroused by irate geese, against Brennus' Gauls, was executed for trying to exploit the complaints of the commons to establish a one-man rule. Then on another occasion in 342, when after campaigning near Capua, the soldiers, who had been frustrated by their commanders in an attempt to take over that town, on the march back home descended into mutiny, demanding further alleviation of the conditions of the plebeian classes. However, progress was not straightforward; hierarchy might be paramount and legality crucial but people mattered too, and though rules were revered, that did not stop them being bent. A meretricious ruling elite to whom chicanery came naturally, bending so as not to break but frustrating reformers at every turn by their manipulation of political processes, by gerrymandering and vote-rigging, ensured that money did not just speak but swore as well. Rural citizens were for a long time effectively disenfranchised by a refusal to allow voting on market days, which were the few occasions when they would be in town. On another occasion, for a period of twenty solid years, though one consul was technically allowed to be plebeian, none ever made it until patrician exclusivity was punctured when a rule was introduced that no one could hold the same magistracy again except after an interval of ten years. Eventually the results showed in the appearance of several important new men; a plebeian consul even won a battle against the Gauls despite the patrician claims that only they had the sanctified credibility to ensure success in war. If some solutions seemed to have been found, exclusive patrician membership of the religious colleges, institutions with 700 years of active life before them, was something they were prepared to defend to the bitter end. History looked set to repeat itself in the 280s when there was the last threat of plebeian secession. All the problems had clearly not gone away, but a victorious Rome, having come through a purging fire of conflict, apparently was able to resolve enough of the issues. The men who fought the battle and won the wars would get at least some of their due, albeit after the commons had this time climbed the Janiculum Hill to ensure a plebeian dictator could push through an edict which gave decisions the people's assemblies voted through the force of law, even without the ratification of the Senate.

* * *

What kind of polity had really developed at Rome by the end of the fourth century is notoriously challenging. There is usually a core of truth, even at the heart of the most bizarre legends. There were active volcanoes in Latium around 1,000, so perhaps the portentous raining stones reported occasionally by Livy may be not just fantasy but something from deep within folk memory. This probably applies to the story of early Rome, that some sort of truth can be perceived through a tangle of myth, even if the desire to own somebody else's Hellenic past is palpable, as it was in the whole Italian world. If Homer had invented heroes, the Romans had fallen for the idea hook, line and sinker, and mythology could be adapted and adopted as required to fill in a background pedigree for any community that wanted to avoid the slur of being arrivistes. If the whole story of Aeneas that would sprinkle ancient credibility on much later generations, as Virgil described the hero's journey to Italy in the time of Augustus, even by 300 many Romans, happy to be immigrants, already sensationally considered themselves as having a blood connection from the rapine of Mars himself and showy antecedents from the horse lords of Troy.

Yet the picture we have of the Romans in the first centuries of the Republican era is deeply anachronistic; a construct of the first century BC created by the likes of Livy, Cicero and Varro, men intrigued by the past of their homeland just as it was turning into an empire. The descriptions we have of the administrative, assembly and magisterial organization, of the tribes, curias, centuries, consuls, consular tribunes and praetors could have virtually nothing to do with Rome of the seventh, sixth and fifth centuries and possibly not even relate much to the political arrangements of the fourth and third. The town on the seven hills was really for many centuries a far less significant place than the histories we have suggest, and the political analysis we have actually reflects the Rome of the first century. In the 500s it was hardly more significant than Gabii or Ardea that archaeology has shown to be pretty small communities at this time and their portrayal of warfare is nothing like the probable reality, with continuation of indecisive campaigning, low-level raiding and cattle-rustling posturing as grand strategy and decisive combat. Also the great surges of reform and other developments in the polity reveal as much about concerns and events of the first century as the third or fourth.

Despite this flair for reinventing history, there is still something to be learned from these sources that would have been relevant to city life two to three centuries before. After all, these later antiquarians were not fools and specifically Livy had by this time a more detailed and relevant story to tell when recorded human memory and improved records were available to him. Surely some of what we learn can be projected back a couple of hundred years; for the elite, politics had always been an infection, almost impossible to shake off, and their ambition was shameless, with patricians trumpeting the antiquity of their lineages and their personal achievements. Anything was better than loss of face: they were prepared to do almost anything to suppress those who offended them; all about a religion of family and state with an almost Chinese reverence for ancestors and reputation, with approval of their peers in the citizen body being all that mattered. Vitriol was deep and class hatred passionate, but still somehow they ensured it was many centuries before the state descended into civil violence. Certainly by 300, if not in the time of the kings and the first century of the Republic, some things were sufficiently alike. The great patrician notables and their plebeian cohorts would not have been such different beasts from those who competed for power in Caesar's day and the constitutional arrangements and legal framework of the first century certainly existed in embryo. If it would be a long time before all roads led to Rome, that time would eventually arrive.

However, if the 'conflict of the orders' that is claimed as being so central to the years from the founding of the Republic to the end of the Samnite Wars, did not necessarily develop quite as we are told, still the key issues were there. They were bound to be. So many things can be reasonably assumed to be not far off the mark about the people who were showing themselves as a potential peninsular hegemon in a time of change. As the town grew and more land was brought under the plough and the beginnings of trade and manufacture showed, new families grew wealthy, winning their own retainers and clients and becoming sufficiently influential that ambitions grew to feed at the same bowl as the older clans. These were men whose talents also needed to be tapped, in an age when Rome was fighting wars on many fronts and who could politically mobilize the commons from whom they had emerged and who had discontents that could be manipulated, and these plebeians in the fourth century found themselves with an increasingly disadvantaged component. There was an increase in the Roman proletariat, people who were not members of the yeoman farmer backbone who peopled the legions. These urban poor, with no land to speak of, were becoming a significant enough constituency that we will find Appius Claudius specifically appealing to them during his censorship. This was at the very beginnings of the trend that would see soldiers' farms failing while they spent more time on campaign, with dispossessed veterans and their families moving to the city after being bought out by victorious generals flush with loot eager to invest in larger slave-worked estates. It would take two centuries for the Gracchi to arise, but the problem that spawned them was already in gestation.

The matter of how an entrenched landed elite responded to the growth of new people with new money has been one of the perennial features of political life through to modern times. There is a particularly smug tradition purveyed by British historians that sees the ability of this island's ruling class to incorporate new money, made in manufacture and trade, as so superior to their European cousins, stumbling through bloody revolutions to achieve a lesser outcome. Such an analysis conveniently sidelines a seventeenth century in which the British people became the first Europeans to behead their monarch, where a toxic cocktail of national and civil war raged and the whole country was wracked by grim sectarianism. The efforts to ensure a share of the prizes at the top table have in many places gone along with other efforts to gain access to legal recourse from a ruling elite disinclined to allow it. Rome was no different, as most citizens might not have the wherewithal to make the bond needed to take a case to court, so codifying the Law of the Twelve Tables may have meant little to them, yet still prosperous farmers and other non-patricians of means would have benefited. Also just before the turn of the fourth century an old colleague of Appius Claudius published the dates of the legal calendar that, to the huge distress of a reactionary rearguard, was important in affording access to the law for those middling folk with sufficient wherewithal to both want and be able to utilize it.

If these events concerned those with coin in their purses, the other great issue of debt bondage impacted further down the social scale. Debt incurred by farmers trying to cover lean years and its awful outcome, bondage, was central in creating social tension in many ancient societies. This Damoclean sword hanging over the common people had been a moving force in Athenian political life that pushed it towards democracy, as ambitious aristos, possibly as far back as the misty times of Solon, used the issue to mobilize an increasingly economically desperate but politically confident people against their rivals; that it was a crucial engine in Rome should be no surprise. Horror stories of class oppression, frequently featuring the abuse of young people forced into servitude by debt and war-scarred soldiers showing the marks of whips on their backs, were commonplace and incensed the crowds against patrician usurers. While progress had been made, in 342 it was still a cause of deep resentment when an army mutiny blew the lid off a pot of troubles. Answers began to be discovered in exactly the period of the last two Samnite Wars; an end to debt bondage was registered in 326 after which only property could be taken in recompense for default. Slaves captured in war were now around in sufficient numbers to take up the slack, making the onerous and hated procedure of enslaving free Romans unnecessary, and those impecunious citizens who had often been the shock troops of trouble could be given lands in the country annexed from defeated enemies or in the new colonies where the win-win situation was that they could also gain the property to be available to fill ranks of the legions. The magistrates and Senate were the driving force, not only in treaty-making and strategy but in redistribution of land in colonies, who gave an ideological underpinning for the nobility, that they who had held imperium knew how to direct a war, to provide continuity and expertise. So in what historically is seen as the end of the 'conflict of the orders' the timing is not accidental; success in war had allowed a dampening down of class fires that had warmed the previous 200 years. Hopeless disparity of wealth and power at the heart of the state could be tolerated when desperate men who might threaten the great could be paid off with other nations' land and property. 'Into Italy' had solved so many issues for so many people.

Chapter Two

Into Italy

'Either the war ought not to have been undertaken, or ought to be conducted as befits the dignity of Rome and brought to a close as soon as possible. It will certainly be brought to a close if we press on the siege, but not if we retire before we have fulfilled our hopes by the capture of Veii. Why, good heavens! if there were no other reason, the very discredit of the thing ought to inspire us with perseverance. A city was once besieged by the whole of Greece for ten years, for the sake of one woman, and at what a distance from home, how many lands and seas lay between! Are we growing tired of keeping up a siege for one year, not twenty miles off, almost within sight of the City?'

Livy 5, 4

Like Greece, for many centuries in Italy no central state had emerged; the situation had been fragmentary, with the model being either city states as the key political entities or for mountain peoples a more tribal organization. Much of this was geography, rugged hills and mountains chopping up the landscape into independent packets with only Apulia and the Po valley being to some extent exceptions. So like the people from the other side of the Adriatic, who gave them so much, from early on the Romans, like the Etruscans, their other great tutors, were people of the polis. A city that benefiting from its location was bound to become something of a power player in the world of central Italy. Indeed, it used to be accepted that the Romans had established a pretty thorough suzerainty over Latium during the centuries of royal rule, though that conclusion now seems far too simplistic. The idea that Royal Rome's dominance was rocked by regime change and the Etruscan and Latin wars that came after maybe can be better considered just other threads in a complex web of near-equal relationships that characterized Latium and south Etruria all the way to the fourth century. We get hints about the reality of these interactions from the bronze tablet that Cicero saw in the forum of a treaty with the Latins from 493.[1] This seems like an offensive/defensive alliance; regional co-operation in the face of threats from Volsci and Aequi. Yet it is not possible to assume that this was the norm; the decades after seem to show as much open warfare as diplomatic intercourse.

After a century of Republican rule the key advance at the beginning of the fourth century was the defeat of Rome's Etruscan neighbour. The eventual victory over Veii was a pivotal moment against old enemies from the other bank of the Tiber whose king had once ordered the death of a party of Roman envoys while enjoying a game of dice, even if the indicators of the takeover were somewhat more peaceful than being captured and destroyed by Roman warriors squeezing through water pipes. It was after this that they gained an edge in terms of productive land and population that began to promote them to a different league from places round about. This was a process of local asymmetry where the final conquest in 396 was always seen as crucial, when the city expanded exponentially. New tribes cultivated conquered stretches of well-drained land with a good communications network as everything just got bigger, and when included with other recently-made gains, an increase of available land by over 500 square kilometres is recorded. This victory had been the final stroke in a doubling of the ager publicus (public land often expropriated from defeated enemies) since the end of the time of the kings. In the 390s land had been taken from Capena, 16 miles north of Rome, and other Faliscans as well, with a concomitant increase in manpower through a combination of planting Roman settlers and giving citizenship to those defeated people who were not enslaved. This was a burgeoning Rome now fully in control of the north-south trade routes whose potential was not even radically eroded by the Gallic interruption. If the fourth century in Latium seemed initially about political fragmentation, it ended with clear Roman dominance; an expansion of real estate that was both becoming a way of printing money for the senatorial elite who exploited it massively, though illegally, for their own interests with nobody able to stop them, while still leaving enough to sustain an increase in the plebeian farmer class, with four new voting tribes[2] of citizens created in 387. Rome expanded to take over much of the trans-Tiber country that had previously been a resource for her enemies and the territory won pushed their frontier to the foot of the Ciminian mountains. Also, by blunting Tarquinii aggression and the establishing of a stout frontier around Sutrium and Nepet (modern-day Nepi) in the 380s, they freed up resources to allow them to press on south.

The Servian walls, built over years in the late 380s and 370s, surrounded a Rome that was the largest, most powerful community in central Italy. Friends sticking by her after the Gallic sack had been important: Caere, Ardea, Tusculum and Aricia stood firm at this difficult time, though some later on fought against the increasingly powerful, threatening and overweening neighbour. Other allies like the Latins and Hernici on occasions reneged on their commitment to provide troops, but this backsliding was not too alarming after a fifth century that had generally seen local rivals declining in power. The Volsci in the Pontine region were largely a spent force by the beginning of the fourth century and the establishment of colonies at Satricum and Setia, on annexed land in the 380s, indicated how the marsh country had come under Roman sway. Soon it was Veii all over again, an almost complete takeover, and by mid-century soldiers and transplanted Romans were in place to defend new stolen acres. That other old foe, the Aequi, had been pretty much pushed up the Anio, back into their hillside homes, and were hardly able to defend themselves when they suffered from Roman attention not that long after the Gallic incursion. Towns like Tibur and Praeneste who before had been able to compete almost as equals could now only act against the expanding Republic in confederate unity.

Attaining local dominance was a matter of endless, decade-consuming fighting with few decisive encounters and of course for many this Roman enlargement was far from agreeable. Many neighbours, even old colonies like Velitrae and Circeii, joined the Volsci in resistance, with abundant battling round Satricum between 386 and 346 and more than one siege of Velitrae during the same time frame. Ten years of repeated triumphs recorded between 362 and 352 confirm aggressive expansion in the middle century, with the Hernici suffering the loss of Ferentinum and Tibur and Praeneste, Rome's strongest opponents in Latium, pretty much succumbing by 354, ceding land and breaking up their local league. A real re-imposition of influence was clear by this time, with allies stumping up troops again and two more tribes, the Pomptina and Publilia, established at around this time. The taking of Sora in 345 showed Roman reach was even beginning to impact the inland Volsci in their Apennine valleys, while the Aurunci suffered too, as Rome set her eyes on Campanian riches. Two treaties entered into in 354 with Samnium and Carthage in 348 show not only that they were rubbing up against the mountain men in the Liris valley, but the terms in the latter definitely indicated that they had established an over-lordship of a good part of Latium. So by the middle of the fourth century the Republic's influence over her immediate neighbours had been etched even deeper. Once again she was head of the Latin League and, unlike in the old days, leadership no longer alternated between Rome and other Latin cities. Now it was always a Roman in charge reporting on league matters to the Senate; something that so ruffled feathers that it was part of the motivation behind the last great Latin revolt in the early 330s. Even before this last burst of independence had been suppressed, Roman power had been felt well beyond Latium.

History is frequently an account of routes regularly cut by rivers, travelled by traders, soldiers and emigrants, and this despite the corollary that most people prior to the twentieth century never moved much further than the nearest market town. For the Romans their eventual predominance in Latium opened up Italy in all directions. The eventual expiration of Tibur as an independent power allowed movement up the Anio, just as the digestion of Veii territory saw them in control of both sides of the Tiber valley as it turned north. However, it was south that the fourth century really discovered an imperial dynamic in the policy of the recovering Republic, a direction where during this period the first Roman roads began to snake out to ensure an all-weather infrastructure connecting the fortress colonies planted along the way during the fourth century.

These places were something very different from those established in the regnal and early Republican years. Those earlier communities had generally been independent centres largely established to allow landless Romans to start a new life, often as prestige projects of the great patrician families with as much an eye to their own interests as to those of Rome. Places that, like their Greek equivalents, were seldom dependent on or directed by the mother city. From the fourth century on it was different.

These later townships were specifically strategic, much more military and frontier posts; places on an axis of advance, river crossings, ports and passes and only secondarily useful as new homes for the urban poor and to advance the prestige and following of their founders. The citizen colonies of Ostia, Minturnae, Antium and Tarracina were planted on the sea coast with trifling numbers, maybe 300, with small plots to work. They were essentially coastguards, links forged in a chain covering territory that by late in the century reached almost down to the Bay of Naples, while the Latin or mixed settlements were larger, comprising between 2,300 and 6,000 adult males and generally located inland, securing landward routes, and because of their size eventually acting as more dynamic agents of Romanization.

The settling of Roman citizens at Antium in 338 advertised the drive to control a coast road that headed as far south as Tarracina, where another strongpoint was established in the same year or the next. This expansion was mirrored inland along the line of the Latin way, following the fertile country of the upper Tolerus River (modern-day Saco), down to where it veers south-east to reach the Liris at Fregellae. This traced the route where the modern Autostrada del Sole runs, where by 328 a Latin colony had been placed at the river junction to hold fast close to the frontier with the Samnites, a people who had already probably fought one war with Rome and would soon fight another. Some security in the north and extra muscle from farmer soldiers billeted on purloined land allowed the Romans' gaze to rise far beyond Latium. Linking the way to a new field of operations in Campania Cales, a Latin colony guarding where the road from Rome swung inland to cross the Volturnus, was established in 334 or 335 and would be a model for many later places settled during this epoch of peninsular expansion. After that came strongholds in Campania like Suessula and Volsci, places like Fundi and Formiae and Acerrae added in 332, all peopled by citizens without franchise. These colonies that Rome established in the second half of the century were key and it seems likely that between 334 and 263 this pulse of colonization had involved something like 70,000 men.

This migration to new towns, as well as the establishment of rural tribes in the country connected by them, meant an increase in the human pool available to the Republic that would be crucial. It was these expanded resources that meant the Tiber city could recover from such blows as the Caudine disaster, the bloody defeat at Lautulae and many more in these stressful years of conflict. The end game for this expanding polity, after the period of the Samnite War and the large-scale settlement at the beginning of the third century, was that the Republic had become a much greater and more dominant entity. The lands either owned privately by Roman citizens or publicly by the state that amounted to some 5,500 square kilometres in 338 had by 264 increased to approximately 27,000; a fivefold growth in real estate that was matched by an expansion of the population from perhaps 400,000 to nearly 1 million, ending with Rome controlling about 20 per cent of the land and 30 per cent of the population of Italy by the middle of the third century.

The new hegemon that emerged phoenix-like from a traumatic Gallic trashing turned out a different sort of master, with a genius for requisitioning and redefinition. Nothing was forever un-Roman; everything could be incorporated, not just other people's lands but their customs and their gods as well. Rome showed not only a sensitivity to the religious sensibilities of those she encountered but other attitudes that differed markedly from many imperialists before. The idea of inclusion had shown from the start when Sabine immigrants had been incorporated, even furnishing great patrician clans like the Claudii and the Valerii who would make such a contribution to the city's story. From the early years of the Republic, the way servile members of the population were treated was indicative: manumitted slaves, most probably having helpfully suggested to their master that a lump sum and not having to look after them in old age was a win-win situation, or at least their descendants could become part of the citizen body in a manner that just was not seen in most ancient societies. As for the conquered, as Cicero puts it, 'When the victory is won, we should spare those who have not been blood-thirsty and barbarous in their warfare. For instance, our forefathers actually admitted to full rights of citizenship the Tusculans, Aequians, Volscians, Sabines, and Hernicians, but they razed Carthage and Numantia to the ground.'[3]

Like Cicero, others also understood, who could conceive that it was more agency than structure. The secret had been inclusion and Velleius Paterculus, in his *Roman History*, lovingly lists both the dispatch of colonists and those other peoples who were admitted as new citizens. The process was not generally immediate though; at Capua 1,600 local knights were made honorary Roman citizens very soon after the two places entered into an alliance. Usually there were intermediate steps where peoples, not necessarily ethnically Latin, were given Latin rights that permitted trade, intermarriage and migration or Roman citizenship without the right to vote. Even if those involved were not happy about their initial limited inclusion, this was a process that soon saw many of these communities fully incorporated into the citizen body and organized into voting tribes, all enabling a great expansion of the pool from which the Republic could draw its legions. It was a marvel, in their efforts to impose a thread of order on a peninsular tapestry, how the Romans made compacts between widely divergent peoples; how within fluid situations along a continuum they moved from asymmetric alliance to hegemony and beyond to complete domination. Yet there could be bumps along the road; inducements and threats might be used in a unipolar world. Even with a place like Caere, which was tight friends with Rome in the worst hours after the Gallic sack and had some kind of reciprocal citizenship deal, still bloody conflict is reported in the 350s, showing that the place remained alarmingly independent until after defeat when they were incorporated into the citizen body with lesser rights. Even then, this treatment led to revolts on more than one occasion before 273, when the inhabitants were assimilated as full Roman citizens.

Other old enemies, instead of being absorbed, were allowed to retain domestic independence while becoming subservient allies. Usually the leagues to which they belonged were dissolved and each place entered into bilateral agreements with the Republic,[4] giving up any sort of independent foreign policy and providing Rome with auxiliary troops. However, unlike in so many earlier and indeed later examples of imperialism, no demeaning tribute in gold was demanded and the connections made with local elites meant, in most allied communities, that there were significant factions who, far from being alienated, saw their interests as tightly tied to that of their new hegemon. By the mid-third century Rome had treaties with 150 Italian communities,[5] many of whom they had defeated in war; allies who provided military aid, a kind of tribute by the back door that was experienced as far less oppressive to those concerned, particularly when the allied elites could profit from Rome's victories. It is no coincidence that in the two Social Wars (wars against the allies) for which we have details, those involving Rome broke out because their allies felt themselves excluded from a political entity of which they wanted full membership, while two centuries earlier the participants in the second Athenian League only wanted to depart an association they perceived as becoming impossibly despotic.

* * *

The thundering hooves of the four horsemen – conquest, pestilence, famine and war – were never far away from the Roman consciousness at the end of the fourth and beginning of the third century. After all, the Gauls had conquered the city less than a century before, and Romans were not a healthy lot at the best of times: small, perennially racked by diarrhoea, hit by malarial outbreaks every five to eight years and occasionally stricken by plagues that could carry off considerable proportions of the population. Food shortage was an ever-present threat; it was mentioned by Livy in 299,[6] a problem that required the great man Fabius Rullianus to take up the post of aedile to resolve. It would be another century before the Italian islands could be regularly called on to help feed the city and even longer before the wheat fields of Africa were available to quench the growing maw that was the Roman populace. Of course, war was always also there. The doors of the temple of Janus being closed was incredibly unusual. Warfare was almost as enduring as the seasons that dominated fighting in ancient times, with a campaign usually taking place from spring planting until the early autumn cereal harvest. Like the city itself, the methods of waging war were in a state of flux that changed over the centuries of conflict from legendary beginnings with an army divided into five classes of infantry established by King Servius Tullius to something recognizable from the high years of the Republic.

The army that spearheaded Rome's rise to Latin dominance was, like the city, altered by the Veii epic. It was not just events which fell out at the beginning of the century that were crucial in Rome becoming the great central Italian power; the siege is traditionally connected, perhaps erroneously but still significantly, with the first payments made to Roman troops. A period of intensive warfare stimulated an arrangement in which patrician war bands and the city levy was first given some sort of reimbursement to compensate for being away longer from the family farm or other business. It was almost certainly an evolutionary process rather than a single decision to reimburse the troops that is recorded, but still real changes were happening at this time. The details are confused but this war saw the army making a far more sustained effort than the usual rustling and looting of earlier times. So a property tax 'tributum', probably instituted at the end of the fifth century, was part of this development. Paid in kind or in uncoined metal, it would be raised as and when needed, and with booty won and indemnities imposed on defeated enemies could sustain increasing pressure on the public purse. Generals might hand wartime winnings to the state that could then be used to refund taxpayers or be distributed as windfalls directly to the troops, but this was a real development in a Roman community that was now prepared to directly fund much longer-lasting campaigns. The aim of making war pay for itself was common to most states in many eras but not often achieved and Rome was no exception, yet high and low might still hope to get rich from the disposal of booty, slaves and land. So it is hardly surprising, with increased military resources to call on, particularly after the Great Latin War of 338, that Rome continued showing bellicose. Dispatching armies of legionaries whose growing reputation for solid follow-through and effectiveness would eventually make them the most successful soldiers in the ancient Mediterranean.

Half a century before the Veii triumph, the motivation for instituting the post of censor was surely primarily about assessing the potential for military service in a community wanting to regularize its fighting capacity. The chaos of military magistracies that characterize this time could also reflect the impact, as the municipality became a more significant provider of armed might and indeed a tendency to mutiny indicative of the difficulties experienced in merging city and clan-based militaries. What was the institution like, which had been welded for war over centuries? The nature of the army that fought the Samnite Wars can only really be guessed at, but certainly it was not a professional army, though it had already evolved into an extraordinarily tough fighting machine for which a couple of generations later we get a detailed and reliable description.

The legionaries of the High Republic are familiarly described by the Greek historian Polybius: an army fighting a pivotal war against Hannibal that consisted mainly of armoured foot soldiers, troops whose discipline was instilled by a fearsome group of junior officers leading the basic organizational group, a century of something around eighty soldiers. Two of these centuries made up a maniple, the key tactical unit of the Roman battle line. The soldiers threw heavy metal-shanked javelins and fought hand-to-hand with a short sword. A heavy infantry core was divided into three types. The first line, called hastati, were peopled by the youngest men in their late teens and early twenties, tyros with few if any campaigns under their belts. These were seconded by the principes, men in their prime – late twenties and early thirties – who had certainly seen fighting before and perhaps plenty of it, and finally the triarii – veterans, many in their forties – were the solid dependable base of the legionary formation. This third battle line of these legions still carried, even in the early second century, a long stabbing spear and acted as a final line of defence when the men in front of them had been used up and a solid last rampart of veterans was required, showing a hedgehog of pikes to stave off a rampant enemy. As age and experience were what defined where a soldier deployed, so this also generally reflected relative affluence and this showed with young hastati, less well-equipped with defensive armour than their seniors and with the triarii the best protected of all.

However, it had not always been this way. In the age of kings and the early Republic, the armed forces that fought the city's wars had consisted of combinations of patrician war bands and the levies raised from the city population. The way they fought is not at all clear, though a long-accepted tradition suggests the Greek-style phalanx: a tight body of shield- and spear-armed combatants, transmitted like so much else through the Etruscans, was the pattern of these years. Something supported by finds of round hoplite shields with fastenings suggestive of the Argive grip that is considered the key to this formation.[7] Other burial finds in Latium and Etruria in the period also include heavy javelins, bronze body armour, swords and axes indicative of a more heroic model of individual combat, with the written evidence that points to numbers of warriors being equipped with long body shields or smaller targets, giving the lie to the phalanx hypothesis. Certainly the kind of fighting that went on during much of the sixth, fifth and fourth centuries consisted of cattle-rustling and looting, not something that can easily be accomplished by the use of solid inflexible infantry formations. Indeed not so much had changed even by the end of the fourth century when a major battle with the Samnites was joined in 311 as the Romans, looking for profit and perhaps the rare pleasures of a barbecue, tried to scoop up a herd of enemy cattle and even in 302 when an army was almost tempted into an ambush near Rusellae by the Etruscans herding their livestock in front of their piquets.

A few generations after the Republic's formation, with the beginning of the fourth century, things begin to come into focus and we discover there had been significant developments. The population of central Italy had been growing and land becoming much more actively worked, with larger towns now able to sustain themselves on the back of this new productivity; more complex, cohesive communities requiring the law codes and embryo bureaucracies evidenced in Rome by the emergence of the quaestors. Land itself became more valued, something that places like Rome were determined to acquire by warfare, whereas in earlier times the aim had generally not gone much beyond grabbing movable loot and rustling herds of beasts from their neighbours. In those days the need to possess the land was less pressing; after all, their animals could crop the grass with no deeds of ownership.

If the early centuries saw much combat of a Homeric style, with loose groups of men variously armed following a leader mounted on horseback or even in a chariot, methods would certainly have developed. What superseded these earliest tactical configurations in an age where permanent conquest was becoming of the essence is difficult to say. Probably it was something like fighting in a shield wall. There are pictorial and historical hints supporting this proposition that saw men of different income groups formed together, probably lining up with the heaviest-armoured in the front rank; possibly akin to the archaic Greek formations, with light armed missile-men integrated in the main body, throwing or firing at the enemy from the protection of their heavier comrades' shields. However, recently an argument has been made[8] that much of what our sources give us is mere homage to a Greek template and that the combination of war bands and city levies continued to fight in a loose, reasonably unstructured manner that had the additional advantage that it made easier the military assimilation of the increasing number of incorporated and allied peoples that joined the cause in the course of the fourth century.

Reasonable conjecture suggests that from the beginning of the 300s, almost 200 years before the Hannibalic War, Roman tactics had morphed from being based on a pack of spear and shield men to something much more like the army that is so well described by Polybius. Explanations have never been lacking as to how this happened; indeed, discussion was ripe enough even in ancient days. Plutarch, in his biography of Romulus, reports the Romans giving up their Argive bucklers for long Sabine ones, though also claiming Camillus as the architect of change hundreds of years later, while Sallust suggests fighting the Samnites was the catalyst and others proposed the battles with the Gauls at the root. What is apparent is that it became the norm to fight in a looser formation using the pila and scutum rather than pike and pelte or spear and aspis. The progression out of a phalanx is well described by J.E. Lendon in *Soldiers and Ghosts*, whereby the younger, more adventurous warriors at the front of the body of spearmen would break off, advancing to fight aggressively and individually with similarly inclined opponents on the other side; a procedure that would better suit a warrior with javelin, body shield and sword.

Lendon paints a persuasive picture of a legionary phalanx like a mountainside disintegrating into scree along its front; a nice explanation, tidy and pleasing, regarding how the move to the maniple was the result of squaring a circle, managing a compromise between the discipline required for a formed army to function as a body capable of direction and the ingrained need to pursue *virtùs* for young men wanting to make a reputation. This showed a predilection for single combat where bravery might be exhibited, and that the sons of the political elite needed scars and decorations for valour to point to when they stood for high office later in their careers. However, there are problems with this explanation. Firstly, these kinds of duellists would not in general have come from the infantry; it was blue-blooded cavalry regiments that normally contained the young men who could expect a great political career and so needed a hero's reputation to boost their credibility. These kinds of knightly tournaments are indeed sometimes mentioned. Manlius defeating an enemy champion without permission from his father and dying for it was one, and another well-known story concerned a Roman cavalryman fighting a Campanian rival, who had been his best friend in days of peace, during the siege of Capua in the Hannibalic Wars. Officers commanding foot soldiers would also feel the imperative to shine, and of the two great Gaul-slayers, Corvus was certainly such a tribune while Torquatus, though serving in the cavalry, had jumped down from his mount to fight his duel. These were men of a different class from the plain soldiers who would never need to show their wounds or exhibit their decorations to win the votes needed to achieve high office.

Some of the young men off the farm or the city streets would no doubt have sought to make a name for themselves; they were just natural fighters who wanted the admiration of their peers and the spear cup, crowns and phalerae they could hang up in pride of place at home and on occasions were worn at public ceremonies.[9] They perhaps also hoped that a name for slaughtering the enemy might win them a captaincy; after all, at this time centurions were elected by the men who could see the benefit of such a man at their head. However, this would not have accounted for most of them; like soldiers in every age, the majority would have wanted to survive to enjoy the fruits of victory. Perhaps there was even a reluctance to spill the blood of fellow humans, something that was socially frowned on in every situation except war; run-of-the-mill fighters used their spear as much to keep the enemy at bay as to do them any lethal damage. So if Lendon's general idea is convincing to some degree, developments must still be seen in the historically-attested context of changing tactics, such as the need to face enemies like the Samnites, who themselves fought in looser formations, more often with javelins than with thrusting spears. Roman truculence may have played a part, but tactics were the key. The experience of a block of spearmen stuck in some rugged glen fighting Aequi, Volsci or Samnites falling under volleyed javelins and unable to reach their gadfly opponents with their spears must be something of the answer. The younger, lighter armoured men would be gradually delegated to adopt looser groupings, so they might reply with their own missiles, and then contact the enemy hand-to-hand. Other ideas championed at different times, e.g. that it was in combatting Gauls or Etruscans that the change was wrought, are far less convincing as surely a shield wall was highly suitable to face these two militaries. The Gauls were famous for their ferocious initial charge, with slashing overhead blows from their long swords that a steady barrier of shields would be just the ticket to counter, and the Etruscans were seen as the very people from whom the Romans had inherited the phalanx, so against this enemy the formation would have been seen as fighting fire with fire, therefore generating no great pressure for change.

That a vestige of the earlier type of soldier remained even in the 160s showed that the changeover had been a gradual process; a business of many generations, as would be the case with most technological military changes in any pre-modern age. So if the era we are describing sat somewhere in the middle of this process it seems probable that by the 290s the Roman army would have retained a larger contingent of these spearmen. In the army described by Polybius the triarii numbered about 600 men out of the whole of more than 3,000 heavy infantry, but would probably have been present in greater numbers in armies that fought in both the main Samnite Wars; at least double, if not more, early in these developments. We can assume a considerable solid formation of veteran spearman as the base of the legion with the rest organized in looser maniples of 140-odd men taking the fight to the enemy. Whether they would by this time have been divided into hastati and principes as Livy details, there is no sort of real evidence. Yet surely it would not have been so very different when a younger Republic faced its greatest test. The first lines of men who faced a bloody clash with their foes would have been the youngest: keen and agile, eager to make a name for bravery and innocent of the butchery that might be facing them. They might start with great élan, but there was always fear and panic hovering on the wing, even when their seniors of the other lines who knew what was what came in to support them. However, our main source is unfortunately pretty untrustworthy on military matters, even conflating the organization of both the pre- and post-Marian legions, describing early third-century legionary divisions sometimes as maniples and on other occasions as cohorts, an organization of more than 400 homogenous heavy pila- and sword-armed soldiers that was typical of Rome's first-century army. This lack of precision in Livy's comments is clear again when he mentions a couple of other unit types: the Rotarii and Asensi, first recorded as part of the army that fought the last great war against the Latins. The first were young and inexperienced and the latter less reliable but both, though we do not know how they were armed, were on that occasion deployed in the rear either with or behind the triarii.

What is clear, however, is that alongside the Roman legions on almost all occasions there were allied formations, ala or wings, lining up to face the foe. Most of these allies in the Third Samnite War were composed of Latins, colonists or from towns with bilateral treaties, but not exclusively. There would undoubtedly have been Hernici, Aurunci, Sidicini and Campanians making manpower contributions, as well as old Sabellian enemies who had come into the fold. Aequi and Volsci places would have sent soldiers and even people further south, if Livy is correct when he mentions Lucanian allies in a battle in 294. Hardly more than a decade after that war ended, Rome would be fighting the army of an Epirote king alongside Sabines, Umbrians, Marrucini, Paeligni, Frentani and even Dauni warriors.

On the field of battle this infantry was king, but the cavalry played its part, usually protecting the flanks but still up for an all-out assault when called upon. Indeed, the horsemen came from the elite, those rich enough to own a horse. The eques were peopled by the indelibly upper class, the kind of cavaliers who wanted to be seen to win the battles in which they fought and were unruly enough to try, whether ordered to or not. Yet the evidence of art or history does not paint them as well-armed; though they boasted a shield, it was a feeble button affair made of oxhide that deteriorated on campaign and would not be replaced by a more substantial Greek version until the experience of the wars against King Pyrrhus of Epirus in the 270s. Nor would their mounts have looked much to a modern eye, but the short, stocky beasts were still the best money could buy, as would have been the spears and swords with which they equipped themselves for personal defence. Heroes on horseback, the impact they had in battle may have been open for much discussion in recent times, but aware of their worth and defensive of their standing they certainly were.

Chapter Three

Another Fine Mess

'*And beyond these cities lies Ardea, a settlement of the Rutuli, seventy stadia inland from the sea. Near Ardea too there is a temple of Aphrodite, where the Latini hold religious festivals. But the places were devastated by the Samnitae; and although only traces of cities are left, those traces have become famous because of the sojourn which Aeneas made there and because of those sacred rites which, it is said, have been handed down from those times.*'

Strabo, *Geography*, Book V

The pages of this book are not the place for a specialist discussion on the antecedents of the Samnites and many other Italic peoples, perhaps coming from over the Alps or across the Adriatic, arriving to comingle with the indigenous inhabitants. What is certain is that peoples speaking an Oscan language had descended the glens north of Lake Fucino at just the time that Rome was divesting itself of its royal baggage. These Volsci and Aequi would provide much of the context for the Republic in the next 100 years, as they occupied country in Latium from the Pontine Marshes up to near the borders of Etruria. Roman dominance would be re-established to the extent that it had ever actually existed under her kings, but it would be hard won. If these Italian tribes offered a world of low-level conflict for the glory-hunting, cattle-rustling characters from the Tiber valley, they were not the only migratory bands on the move at this time. Others would virtually fill up the whole of central and southern Italy in the fifth century. The assertion is that many were dispersed following the rites of the sacred spring, where young men born at that time of year were dedicated to the god of war in order to get in good odour with the deities in times of trouble and, once grown, followed totemic animals to find new lands to settle. These sorts of adventurers trekked down as far as Lucania where they were well-established by the middle of the fifth century, while the Bruttians filled out the toe of Italy a century later; people who themselves were claimed to be the revolted slaves of the Lucanians.

One of the most important of these peoples were the Samnites who Mommsen called 'the Aetolians of Italy', four tribes who were very far from a closed book to the Romans, occupying the limestone spine of Italy, the south central mountain country roughly between the latitudes of Rome and Naples. Covered now by the modern regions of Abruzzo and Molise and running down over the borders into Campania, Lazio and Apulia too. Their home territory ran from the Sangro River south past the Ofanto but not reaching the sea at either side, with Mont Tifernus and the Matese massif standing at the heart and several river valleys running east down to the Adriatic and others west to the Tyrrhenian Sea. Hill country certainly, but with parts of it accessible, rolling and reasonably heavily populated, where it was possible to make a living from arable farming, as well as transhumance pasturage of sheep, pigs and even cattle for which the up to half a million people who made their homes there, like so many other Sabellians, were famous. The Caudini were the most westerly group occupying the region south of the Volturnus River around the road that leads from Campania to Benevento. They were centred on Caudium (modern-day Montesarchio), while other decent-sized places were Caiatia, Trebula, Cubulteria, Telesia, Saticula and Venafrum, some situated west of the Volturnus. South of them were the Hirpini, living among the old calderas on the road to modern Basilicata, along the Calor River, a country stretching from well beyond the Ofanto in the south to their capital where modern Benevento stands. Some other important places like Abellinum (modern-day Avellino), Compsa, Aeclanum, Trivicum and Venusia were off to the east and south-east, including the territory around Mount Vulture; wold country leading over the Apennine watershed and down to the flatlands of Apulia.

Probably the strongest, most populous and certainly the most central were the Pentri, inhabiting the country north of the Caudini, that spread out from the Matese massif in all directions, reaching up the Liris River as far as Fregellae and Sora, then down to where Interamna Lirenas would be planted, with their capital of Bovianum situated near modern-day Bojano. Other significant communities were Saepinum, Atina and

Casinum, the last having been wrested from Volsci domination early in the fourth century. The least significant of the peoples were the Caracini, inhabiting the hills and valleys around the Sangro River, centred at Cluviae and Aufidena somewhere near modern-day Castel di Sangro. They boasted a northern border with the Paeligni, and like their Pentrine cousins shared an eastern frontier with the Frentani who occupied the Adriatic shore and who Strabo contends were themselves Samnites. However, no others refer to them as such, nor did they act like it in any of the wars we are considering.

The country occupied by the Samnites was extensive and communications were difficult; a reality illustrated by skeletal remains showing there was little intermarriage with those outside their territory. Yet it was not without rich and fertile pockets; the Hirpini were known for cereal production and the manufacture of a smoky wine near Beneventum, while the Sangro valley was recognized for both arable produce and good timber. Still, much of the country was only suitable for hardscrabble farms on marginal land. There were silvery olive groves and rich brown fields that supported an affluent elite, but mostly among the lovely green slopes the less affluent lived by raising sheep, goats, chickens and growing cabbages. Indeed, though the Romans could make great claims for Samnite wealth, the fruit of brigandage or hiring out their men as mercenaries, even the horse-riding nobles were never sensationally rich compared with their counterparts in Latium, Campania and Etruria. There seems not to have been extensive slave-holding, which at least had the advantage that most men were potential warriors. Few major urban centres existed, while despite some mineral resources, trade and industry were very local affairs and during our period there is no evidence of coin production. The ninety-odd hill forts that pepper the country from the Sangro valley to Benevento are suggestive, as their inaccessible locations mean they are unlikely to have been the sites of major settlements but probably bolt holes for the communities settled on lower, less defensible terrain.

As for their customs, almost everything we have on them apart from archaeology comes via the Romans, so it is necessary to be circumspect, expecting these accounts to traduce them as strange. There are certainly well-known stories that report they had their pubic hair shaved off in barber shops in full public view,[1] were addicted to theatre and obscene language, while in warfare the trope is all about wild charges, ambushes and the use of earthworks. Some of this may well be true and there is never any feeling of overwhelming distaste as with some others of Rome's enemies. Indeed, clearly there was a level of ungrudging respect for one of the toughest enemies they ever faced, and much later Varro the polymath and chronologist, himself a Sabine, was happy to have his antecedents considered as close relatives of the Samnites.

Little is really known of the political organization of this people, who Greek sailors mention in the fourth century,[2] though making little differentiation between them and their coastal neighbours, but the orthodoxy has been that they largely lived in small settlements, *Vicus*, organized into economically self-sufficient cantons or *Pagi* that together made up the four *Touto*, tribes or peoples. That they were not polis-based is certainly suggested by the fact that only the Caudinii were named after a town and they were the most proximate to Greek influence coming in from the coast. There seems to have been a tribal leadership provided by an annually elected or appointed magistrate, the *meddix tuticus*, who looks like a war leader, judge and high priest all rolled into one. However, this kingly figure was certainly not designated as regnal; Rome was far from alone in the peninsula in seeming to have a deep suspicion of men who called themselves kings. These *Touto* were incorporated in a league of the kind that was typical of so many Sabellian people from the Campanians to the Lucanians and Bruttians, with a council hinted at in our Roman sources and at least on occasions a commander-in-chief of all the Samnite armies.[3]

In the middle fourth century, though they occupied by far the largest land area of any people in central Italy, we do not hear of the kind of large cities found in Latium, Etruria, Campania and Apulia. People might have gathered at cult centres and defended themselves in times of crisis from the considerable fortifications that dotted the countryside, but it did not mean they were much more than country rubes. Yet this is not the only opinion; others[4] see the Samnites as further along a continuum towards a real place of urban communities; that the *Vicus-Pagus* paradigm should be revised and comparisons with archaic Greece be usefully made. Like the early Hellenes, competing Samnite urban centres were important and if well short on monumental remains, still might have indulged in deep and sometimes vicious rivalries; that the investment in great walls from the fourth century could be as much to do with local conflicts as insecurities due to Roman incursions. Coin finds referencing the communities they came from certainly support the idea of urban centres having their own independent identity, though most do come from towns in the west showing the influence of the Greek cities and their Campanian neighbours. These Samnites, just like the Hellenes, could share cult centres such as Delphi in Greece that allowed a meeting space for communities that were often otherwise adversaries and they would on occasion combine together in the face of external threats, just as the Greeks momentously had during the struggle with Achaemenid Persia. However, if for most of those war years we are considering that the Samnites acted as an ethnicity, a group who joined together against an awful enemy, there are enough instances during various negotiations of different members of the league having to be individually consulted to show that Samnium did not always act like any kind of unitary state, despite all of them confronting the same existential threat.

Whatever the reality of normal communal interaction, epigraphic evidence, particularly at the national cult centre of Pietrabbondante, shows a considerable level of national consciousness existed; ideas of shared origins, descent and language, but ones that had to be negotiated with local imperatives. The Oscan word *Touto* itself might imply some kind of tribal senate or assembly that magistrates drawn from the great landed families had to consult. However, nothing much is known on how they were constituted from our sources and while archaeology helps in evidencing the existence of a leadership, what they comprised is very much up for grabs. Inscriptions found at Pietrabbondante have been used to argue both that the *Touto* corresponded to the whole nation and that it was purely local in nature; a debate complicated by the fact that things may well have changed over time, just as terminology could change. With Sabellian in the third century being synonymous with Samnites, a couple of hundred years later the designation could be used to refer to any Oscan-speaker. So all we can be sure of is that a probably fluid leadership held positions of power over regions that might have come sliding anywhere on a spectrum stretching from a single community to a whole nation.

These Samnites had not always remained satisfied with the country they occupied and had spread down from their hills to take over parts of Campania and elsewhere too, if finds in Apulia Taenum and Canusium are to be credited.[5] The Duani inhabitants on the Adriatic side of the Apennines would have inevitably felt vulnerable from nearby Samnites who in poor times or out of normal cupidity might look longingly at their fields of grain and heavy-branched orchards, the richness of which are indicated clearly by the superb tombs of the local elite found at Canusium. Other incomers who infiltrated the country to the south and west soon came under the influence of long-settled Etruscans and Greeks from the Tyrrhenian coast and, rapidly alienated from the people from whom they came, developed into separate polities with an elite emerging who aped the horse-riding Greeks and earned themselves a considerable reputation as hard-fighting cavalry. They established themselves in towns and leagues; Capua joining with Atella, Casilinum and Calatia/Nuceria associated with Alfaterni; organizations that might make common cause with the Samnites when they needed help against local rivals but were never part of the Samnite League itself.

Unfortunately for the people back home, these kinds of opportunities for expansion could have a downside as it was threats from the hill folk to their east that forced Capua to join hands with the Romans to secure their protection, events that were claimed as providing a fuse that exploded the very first Roman-Samnite War. The same was true on the other side of the Apennines too, with the Samnites pushing down into the vital region of Apulia; important, as this allowed them to control the key transhumance routes for their animals into the winter pasture in that country. Here it was particularly control of Luceria that mattered and it is no coincidence this stronghold was the centre of so much fighting. The Samnites remained an aggressive, land-hungry people that were perhaps bound to rub up against an equally expansionist Rome. The friction that bought on the First Samnite War in 343 may have commenced because of her inroads into Sidicini country and threats to Campania, but it was the Liris valley where the two peoples clashed against each other in a significant and explosive way. If the First Samnite War was small enough, it presaged a struggle that was critical in the story of Rome's rise to greatness. In Aurunci and Falernian country too, the Samnites had real ambitions if not to occupy, at least to control. So the Second Samnite War was an act of determined and calculated policy by the Romans; planting Fregellae was bound to start a conflict as it was a crucial place that commanded the line the Via Latina would follow and the route out of the valley down to the sea at Tarracina. Samnite demands after the Caudine triumph when they were best placed to make them are telling; it was a revanchist agenda that wanted rid of any enemy presence around Cales and Fregellae; intolerable Roman intrusions into regions that the Samnites regarded as their sphere of influence.

The details concerning the army of this tough warrior people of the south central Apennines are nowhere near as plentiful as those for their Roman counterparts, but something can be gleaned from both written history and archaeological finds. Certainly the tribal armies that fought the legions of the Republic and her allies were well-organized and motivated, and in terms of structure and tactics not very different from their Tiber town enemies. This is no surprise as most people of central and south Italy shared a military culture due to both similarity of origins and surroundings and the interaction and mutual adaptation arising out of constant bellicose interaction. That our Roman histories refer to legions, cohorts, maniples and military tribunes in relation to these enemies should not be made too much of, yet it is interesting that no such appellations are accredited to the Gauls or the Greeks or even much to the Etruscans. This is suggestive, as is the fact that many considered it as a given that the Roman javelin-throwing legionary deployed in an open manipular formation was at least partially learned from these very Samnite foes. 'Our ancestors, Conscript Fathers, were never deficient in conduct or courage; nor did pride prevent them from imitating the customs of other nations, if they appeared deserving of regard. Their armour, and weapons of war, they borrowed from the Samnites.'[6]

Grave goods are not as plentiful as we could wish, but finds at places like Aufidena confirm what tomb paintings in Campania and Lucania and south Italian vases show us. Though it can be assumed that much of the extravagance shown would have been restricted to the parade dress of the richer warriors, still, if close helmets with great crests and bronze wings were not perhaps for battlefield use, the combined desire to show off and intimidate probably ensured that they were close enough. Certainly broad belts to wear around the soldier's tunic at the waist were ubiquitous, leather armour with bronze fittings common and the trefoil breastplate or full cuirass would have been worn by the more affluent on campaign. Some artwork suggests grieves on both legs and a shield that might be a round hoplite type or a longer oval scutum, both of which were made of sheet wood or osier, covered with layers of leather to prevent penetration, with a metal boss in the centre. Javelins, thrusting spears, long knives and short swords completed most outfits, though there are illustrations showing battleaxes that could have been the favoured weapon of some. This was the people whose army trounced the Republic at the Caudine forks in 321 and as it turned out the tribulation they were capable of handing out was going to be demonstrated again and very soon, after the two sides came to blows.

* * *

Ardea, an ancient city whose remains can be found in modern Lazio, hardly 22 miles from Rome itself, was a place that once found itself at the centre of events during a seminal occasion in the history of Rome. Lucius Tarquinius Superbus, conspicuous in the high red boots of kingship, was besieging the town in 509 with his army when revolution broke out back home, led by a man who epitomized the Romans' idea of themselves as all grim purpose and virtue. If we believe the head attested to be him at the Capitoline Museum, which is traditionally dated to around the Third Samnite War, he certainly had a face that screamed these qualities. With a picked body of young warriors, Brutus had marched from Rome to the king's siege-lines to try to win over the army to his insurgency. However, Tarquinius Superbus, hearing what had occurred, rushed back to his capital and, missing each other on the road, discovered the gates closed against him, while Brutus found the soldiers besieging Ardea eager to join his cause. Nothing remained for the last king of Rome except, after twenty-five years on the throne, to leave with his sons for an exile's billet in Caere and unavailing struggles to regain his patrimony. Now once again this same place would come to the centre of things in a manner far less palatable to the memories of the people of the Republic. The appearance of Brutus had been a proud instance of an eternal hero showing just what a Roman was, but the sight of Samnite columns filling the roads from the south approaching the city defences advertised something that this people were much less inclined to remember with satisfaction. They had brought it on themselves, by after only a few years acting like the dreadful example of the Caudine yoke had never happened.

There is an improbable account that the Republic had bounced straight back from that disaster and made real strides in re-establishing her position in hardly more than a year; that a Roman army had defeated the Samnites at Luceria and sent 7,000 of their warriors under a Roman-constructed yoke, then fought successful campaigns between 320 and 317 in the Liris valley. This account 'bristles with absurdities' and a far more likely picture is painted by Diodorus that there was a real period of peace, during which the most that was attempted was diplomatic activity to ensure some access across the peninsula to the Adriatic coast, from Vestini country down to Apulia. Still the Romans were possessed of a belligerence that could seldom be suppressed for long and soon enough they decided that they were once again prepared to face those enemies who had rubbed their faces in the most awful *merde* only half a decade before. Possibly by 316 or definitely 315, the Caudine peace had crumbled and legions were levied and allies engaged to send a strong force on an invasion road again. By the later year Papirius Cursor and Publilius Philo, each in their fourth term as consul, had been put in charge; the same team that the Republic had turned to after the disaster at the Caudine forks. Now they were the first combination in a high command that would start leading Rome down a road that ended in another fine mess. While it is pretty certain that Papirius Cursor made the long journey with his army to Apulia to take on the Samnites fighting near Luceria, there are a couple of options for locating the other piece of aggression that rekindled the conflict.

One suggestion is that a Saticula war began, with the Romans laying formal siege to this ridgeline town lying in the hills above and north of Capua that was either Samnite itself or at the very least within their sphere of influence. This was an important enough community; after all, in 343 it is claimed as the setting of one of the first real battles of all the Samnite Wars where an invading Roman army was roughly handled. Control there would have opened another road to Campania to oppose the Samnites who were trying to make friends with previous Roman allies, places like Nola, Nuceria, Pompeii and Herculaneum. Yet despite this being a comprehensible target and mentioned by several sources, it just does not fit with the action in the Liris valley that came soon after. The second location matches this much better and looks near enough in spelling that it could have been mistaken by tired-eyed copyists. This is Satricum, a Volscian town near Fregellae, situated in the Liris valley where later events suggest the Samnites were endeavouring to strengthen their influence on the left bank and subvert that of Rome on the other side, so ensuring a base where they would be well-positioned to swoop down and assail the coastal route to Latium.

Whether Saticula or Satricum, the campaign in question was a multiple-year affair, with the attack begun in 316 and continuing on in 315. Staying in the field over the winter for the farmers and farmers' sons who made up most of the army might not be the norm, but it was far from unheard of. It turned out that this determined onslaught was the stroke that drove the Samnite League back into arms 'giving the Samnites a pretext for revolt'.[7] So by 315 at the latest, the old foes had declared against each other, Roman armies had marched and siege lines drawn ensuring that the Samnites picked up the gage and mobilized for war. Fighting round the entrenchments was hard and long-drawn-out; two major encounters are intimated with significant losses on both sides, but if where the fighting started is difficult, the same could be said for who was in command. There are options here too: Publilius Philo as the other consul for 315 apart from Papirius Cursor who is a candidate and is supported by a much later authority,[8] but our main source is probably right when he elevates Quintus Fabius Maximus Rullianus to the dictatorship to take over the army in pressing the siege.

This man would become the most celebrated war leader in not only the last decades of the Second Samnite War, but in the third conflict too. In 325 this ambitious young sprig of one of the greatest patrician families had appeared as master of horse after having done the stint of military service required to progress up the *cursus honorum*. Little is recorded of his next step, reaching the consulship in 322, but by the time he was called to the dictatorship in 315 he would surely have been a middle-aged officer of very considerable reputation and experience. In his endeavours on this occasion he was backed by his master of horse Quintus Aulius and these two, against the best efforts of brave defenders who had sortied out to fight them, brought about the final surrender of the besieged town. Matters appeared to be looking rosy for Fabius Rullianus and Rome; some other places near Saticula were taken over and in Apulia Luceria had been laid under siege, but this was all about to turn around. What had looked like a setback only caused the Samnite high command to bestir themselves in an extraordinary manner as they saw real opportunity in enemy overstretch; dispatching a field army that, reinforced from home, despite being unable to raise the siege of Saticula, they attacked, took and garrisoned a nearby ally of Rome called Plistica. More success followed: Calatia near Capua fell to Samnite arms, but it was in the Liris valley that events really went downhill for the Republic. Roman eyes were forced to that scene of action when at Sora the inhabitants, subverted by Samnite agents, rose up and, putting any Roman colonists they could find to the sword, went over to the enemy.

There must have been arguments on how to respond to these hydra-headed perils but they hardly led to much of a strategy, just a blocking stance with armies positioned to both try to protect the inland road, where the Via Latium would run and the coastal route where the Appian Way was commenced in just a few years, though some forces may have been directed down into Campania as well. Disagreeable surprise turned out to be the order of the day: the enemy, far from being blunted by the defeat at Saticula as optimists in the Roman army must have hoped, they had in fact been massing to offer a very different threat in a very different place. The Romans had spread themselves too wide and were beginning to realize it. They called back some of the men sent to Apulia to try to reverse the trend set by the butchery at Sora, but the enemy had the initiative and were preparing a real Sunday punch. Fabius Rullianus, beginning to realize the danger he faced, was planning to defend the inland road to Rome when word arrived that large Samnite combinations were coming his way. However, instead of pushing straight on, the invaders turned to head towards the sea and with the heady aroma of Roman defeat in the air, were able to recruit their strength among the Aurunci and Volsci, some of whom had long resented the presence of Latin colonies and Roman settlers on their ancestral lands. Yet if there were people in the Roman military thrown into panic with rumours growing wilder by the day, when the dictator heard about the Samnite advance he responded, marching to intercept the invaders. Getting ahead, he pushed his soldiers on to reach Lautulae, intending to make a stand where the Volscian hills, falling down to the sea, left hardly any place to pass between the mountains and the lake of Fondi.

With the two sides shaping up for battle, the defence should have had the advantage in this Thermopylae of Italy. Steep walls of rock on one side and briny lake waters on the other made the position virtually unturnable, but while they might stop up the pass, still the Roman soldiers looking over the ground where the enemy would advance against them were shaky enough. Position alone would not be sufficient and there was no Leonidas and 300 Spartans here. The most lethal factor in battle was fragile morale, the awful tendency to panic, when men despaired of success as they caught sight of the enemy's spear points and the homicidal looks in their eyes and this would be the key in this encounter when the advantage of ground was clearly insufficient against such a dangerous enemy. It is likely that with many of Rome's best soldiers off involved elsewhere, Fabius Rullianus was leading out not a few green recruits in defence of the homeland, very recently plucked from farms and workshops. Overwhelmed by the looming prospect of battle, nerves were frayed across the whole army and jittery men, who would have had little opportunity to be properly inducted, to train with each other and hardly leavened by experienced warriors, were now facing a Samnite army full of confidence who had been productively fighting together for some months. So not long after the first pulverizing contact, the dictator saw all around him the men falter, thousands and thousands first breaking, then running with many drowned in the shallows while trying to escape, but if he worried how much his reputation would suffer from his army disintegrating into splinters, for his master of horse it was worse. Leading out the cavalry arm to try to retrieve a day he scorned to survive, disinclined to face the disgrace of arriving back at Rome in company with those who had fled the field, primed for death or glory, he confronted the Samnite general himself, leading his horsemen into the battle. The report was that Quintus Aulius speared the enemy officer, unhorsing and killing him until, then in among his foes and exposed to troopers flinging their lances, the dead Samnite general's brother took an opportunity for revenge. Dragging the master of horse from his mount, the grief-stricken and enraged man dispatched him with a blow, while the Roman commander's followers also leaped from their steeds to try to protect his corpse from enemies intent on claiming its accoutrements as spoil. The Samnite horsemen responded, also dismounting, engaging in combat around the bodies of the two contending generals, each lying dead in his own gore. Eventually loyal retainers on both sides managed to preserve their leader's remains, ending a combat extraordinary for this bloodletting in the high command.

We are only left with hints of what came after, but it was far from glorious and with the defenders running from the reek of the battlefield, there was real danger for the Republic of a kind it did not often face. This had been a nadir, very far from Horatius holding the bridge and the piles of helmets with feathered plumes, shields and broken swords advertised the significance of the losses suffered on this bloody day. The Samnite army, which had triumphed at the gap of Lautulae, passed south round the headland to assault and capture the seaside post of Tarracina. From there the country was shimmering flat and easy with the roads running straight through marshy country reaching inland towards the Alban hills, or along the coast, only 70-odd miles to Rome itself. With Samnite outliers spreading over Latium, their raiding parties reached at least as far as Ardea. Here even the ancient city walls, set atop a tufa plug that can still be found, some of which date from the seventh century, could not save the people. Like so many of the vulnerable places of this region, they had long depended on Roman protection rather than the kind of communal self-defence that might have helped in this crisis. Even the people in Rome would have seen distant but still disturbing signs of danger, such as columns of smoke rising black from the far-off fields and buildings torched by the invaders, and would have asked the question, was their city open to attack?

The size of the danger was inevitably exaggerated by the refugees, filling the roads with overloaded horse-drawn wagons or handcarts piled high with all they owned, fleeing in front of invading armies that looked intent on decking triumph with triumph until ultimate victory was achieved; ominous signs of what might be Rome's own fate, a possibility reflected in the shocked and pallid faces of many of the bustling inhabitants. Yet the senior heads were calm enough as they pondered the decisions that needed to be made to confront an unfamiliar threat. Though there was only one possible policy, retreat, there was still confidence in Fabius Rullianus who was deputed to guard the roads back to the capital with what men he had saved from the army carved to pieces at the pass of Lautulae. These events had registered a real strategic setback. The Samnites had achieved the furthest advance of their arms in all the wars they ever fought with Rome, capturing Tarracina on the coast and raiding north most of the way to Ostia. This was country that had not seen conflict for years; pickings were immense and the terror caused concomitantly extensive. Many feared for Rome itself and the huge investment made in building the Servian walls only a few generations before now appeared to be money well spent, particularly when it became known that the withdrawing of Roman forces from the Liris valley had allowed the defection of Sora. The balance of the conflict must now have appeared to many to be turning the Samnites' way, as the mountain men for the first time took the main war onto enemy soil. Strategically the situation for the Republic appeared distinctly problematic; the enemy had by their incursions shattered communications with both her citizen outposts, her allies in Campania and the country to the north of that fertile patch. Secure links with other centres of Roman authority were threatened by a rampant enemy, who looked too strong to be faced in battle for some time. The invaders' presence was bound to make travelling the road to Apulia far more challenging too. Nor was this the complete picture; such was the hit to the Republic's reputation that we now hear of allies starting to desert the cause. With Rome's enemies making hay around coastal Latium within spitting distance of the eternal city, rethinking of diplomatic postures began to occur. A number of places in Aurunci territory and among the Volsci changed sides and this spirit of resistance reached not only to Campania but east of the Apennines too, where at Luceria the people again overthrew their Roman occupiers and let the Samnites in.

    Panic and terror could be the fuel for popular unrest in Rome and with faith in their rulers at a low ebb, this was a problem that could only be solved on the battlefield. Fabius Rullianus had broad shoulders and showed adamantine resolve to go with heartless brutality. If he had been at fault at Lautulae, he was disinclined to accept ownership of the disaster and had a merciless solution up his sleeve. Blaming the soldiery, once they had withdrawn to a place of safety, he showed a kind of cruelty not untypical of many of these Roman heroes. He decimated the troops who had fled from the battle: one man in every ten was chosen by lot and beheaded in front of his comrades, lined up to witness the punishment of men who failed their commander in battle. The ferocity of Roman discipline is not infrequently attested as part of what made them such determined and disciplined soldiers, though this was a high-risk policy at a time when the Republic needed every man to come to its defence, with the enemy thundering down with bloody intent into the heart of Latium itself. Yet the harsh man's handiwork may have had an impact, showing the kind of iron fortitude that might have daunted Samnite ambitions to attack Rome itself. An army that could inflict such pain on itself ought not to be underestimated, nor were they likely to be people who could be easily swatted aside when they returned, as they inevitably would, marching back down the southern highway. In fact, the influx of the invading tide soon reached its high point before ebbing again, with the invaders hardly making an effort to dig in or keep the position they had won among the Republic's neighbours. The Samnites could hardly have dreamed of an enemy reduced to rubble or even of a Rome that was strictly subservient to their power, only a rival whose wings had been thoroughly clipped. The advantage might for the moment be theirs, but in the aftermath the resource deficit would probably ensure that the pendulum would swing back again. Their best hope would be that after taking such a heavy hit in the past campaign, Rome's compacts with her steadiest partners in Latium, Campania and elsewhere might begin to crumble.

Little is completely dependable in the period that followed, except that there was in the next couple of years an effective reaction to this unprecedented Samnite reeving of Latium. Wallowing in self doubt was never the Roman way and once the dead hand of danger had for the moment gone and after the receipt of some much-needed encouragement with the news that the old war horse Papirius Cursor had managed to retake the fortress town of Luceria, the Roman response seems to have come hard and strong in the following season. The year 314 saw both consuls, travelling with the awesome trappings of imperium, bringing all the military might they could mobilize to try to right this war that had gone so awry. The best-known of the two commanders was a patrician called Gaius Sulpicius Longus, now in his third consulship and who would be made dictator in 312 to replace another great name of whom much will be heard later, Decius Mus, when he was invalided out of a campaign against the Etruscans. We also know that he had long experience of fighting the Samnites, though there is almost nothing to tell of his colleague Poetelius Libo, apart from his involvement in this adventure.

The Samnite bands that had done the damage had withdrawn south by the time these two had organized a sufficient response and their retaking control of the coast road showed the tendency of events: 'They took the field against the enemy near Tarracina and at once relieved that city from its immediate fears; then a few days later, when both sides had drawn up their armies, a hard-fought battle took place.'[9] So an important fight transpired at the seaside town of Tarracina, an old Etruscan port surrounded by marshes and near where the Appian Way would soon climb over the precipitous promontory rising behind the town. The place had seen plenty of blood spilt by Latins and Volsci before a Roman colony was established in 329 and now it would witness even more. The legions had crossed over the Pontine country to take on the Samnites and, after reassuring the threatened locals that they were once more on hand to provide security, explored the road ahead and a few days later encountered the whole enemy host waiting, formed to fight. It was in these environs that the two contestants faced each other, holding their own sides of a pass near the town. The Samnites, confident with their successes of such recent memory, took the initiative and manoeuvred their formations around to open ground where the armies could camp not far away from each other. It was a war of nerves now, skirmishing in the fields between the breastworks of each side's bivouacs, carried out between small parties, with the Romans gaining such advantage as was going. Yet the Samnites had lost their appetite for anything but victory in the recent campaigning, so in an attempt to return to winning ways they decided to risk the gamble of an open battle. A mass of glinting spear tips and shining armour showed them formed up, offering combat with their horsemen on the wings, with orders not only to do the usual job of protecting the infantry flanks but also to keep an eye on their camp, which was deemed particularly vulnerable.

The Romans too were prepared to terminate the shadow-boxing and their commanders content to listen to their officers urging them to advance to the attack. Preparations were meticulous for a set-to that would be brutal and hard fought, with their cavalry also posted out on the wings and the infantry deployed between them. The consuls divided their responsibilities, with Sulpicius Longus commanding on the right where he ordered his cavalry to 'spread out over a considerable distance' to oppose the enemy who themselves were deployed in longer lines with fewer ranks of soldiers in an attempt to outflank the Roman battle line. On the left the troops led by Poetelius Libo were drawn up in very close formation, a configuration allowed by an accession of strength, when some of the allied troops kept in reserve were introduced into the firing line straight away. These very numbers emboldened the Romans, who pushed forward on this wing with some success and as those opposing them felt the pressure, their horsemen trotted up to buttress the foot soldiers' efforts. The Samnite troopers came in on an angle, moving obliquely forward between the lines of the armies to aid their comrades, but in doing so they exposed their own flank. So the move was countered with a gashing attack by the Roman cavalry who 'charged them at the gallop, confounding the ranks and the formations of horse and foot.'

The cavalry of the Republican era have not generally been well regarded, particularly in contrast to their hugely effective infantry equivalents, but recently the suggestion has been made that this poor reputation was unwarranted,[10] and this even before they took up the Greek style of body armour and stout shield later in the third century. The evidence of this encounter is convincing, these eques and their allied peers performing bravely on this wing. The Samnite line suffered badly, unable to hold out long against an avalanche of armoured men on foot and horseback. The shock was as much psychological as physical and it seems it was far too much for the defenders caught up in the melee. The Roman commanders also showed inventive, as Sulpicius Longus rode over from his side of the fight to join his colleague on the left, where success seemed near and his contribution might tip the balance completely. His own men were yet to come to real blows against an enemy who had themselves not shown great initiative, so while most of them stood, hefting the spears in their hands and moving to ensure their armour and shields sat comfortably, he had risked collecting combatants from his uncommitted regiments to take them to help the men on the left. While these reinforcements may have been timely, able to buttress the success on Poetelius Libo's flank, unfortunately they were soon missed by the men they had left behind. There on the Roman right the Samnites had regained some aggression and charged into their ranks with real ardour, forcing them back. Their support lines were also coming into play, the officers giving the signal that brought them charging through where the ranks facing them had been pierced and threatening to rout the whole of the Roman wing. Consternation was soon prevalent among many of the sweat-soaked combatants; ranks were sundered and disordered, with a rataplan of javelins and slingshot striking shields. Nerves were badly shaken and standards drooped as the maniples were pressed back and terrified men peered behind towards the road north that might lead to safety.

The Roman military system, even this early, was intended to ensure a defence in depth guaranteed to soak up pressure, with wounded men carried to the rear and others moving up to take their place, but now, as bloody violent men erupted into their ranks, stabbing and slashing, enemies who clearly outnumbered them on this wing, it must have appeared to many that the method had failed. However, relief would come just in time, as messengers had been sent to Sulpicius Longus far off on the other side of the field. Hearing of the danger to his men he responded, returning on flying hooves with 1,200 horsemen, and with this rush of troopers charging across to support their comrades everything changed. The presence of their commander alone was enough to encourage his men to rally and once word was broadcast among the rank and file that their comrades on the other side of the battlefield had won a victory, it was enough to turn events around completely: 'Presently the Romans had begun to conquer all along the line, while the Samnites, giving up the struggle, were massacred or made prisoners, except those who fled.'[11]

So on both flanks the Samnites had suffered at the hands of a bristling throng, some of them withdrawing in formed units but with others fleeing miles on stumbling legs to avoid pursuit by men intoxicated with the stimulant of victory and amazed by what they had achieved after what had been such a closely-fought affair. Some 60 miles away, the hometown people they had been fighting for could now breathe again with relief as the invading army that had shattered their peace the year before was now turned around and retreating tattered and torn back down the road to Samnium. The cost to the Romans had been significant, but that could be forgotten in the euphoria of victory against an enemy who themselves lost almost 10,000 men and were now excluded not only from Latium but driven even further back south. The consul's success had achieved a crushing advantage and when the details were broadcast in the Senate and forum, it was enough for Sulpicius Longus to be rewarded with a triumph, marching his victorious men through the streets of the city of Rome in July 313; a celebration that they had escaped the fate that places like Capua had experienced in the past of being overrun by wild fighters from the central mountains.

Rome had been spectacularly and surprisingly relieved of danger. It was not the first and would not be the last time enemies would get into Latium to menace Rome itself, and if the danger from Gauls before and Hannibal later were more traumatic, still this had been a worrying time for many of those who survived. So now they were determined that their armies should make concrete the concept that attack was the best defence. To ensure that they would not soon have to face a similar situation again, the Republic's leadership decided they should revert to the old pattern of fighting their enemy far from Rome, confronting them along the Liris valley, around the hills of the Matese massif or on the plains of Apulia. This intent was manifest when both the consuls moved to Sora, commandeering some of Fabius Rullianus' old soldiers who had concentrated not far from the town. Time-served veterans whose minds were on their family farms or other businesses went home as new units were incorporated to bring this major two-consul army up to strength. All this made clear that such a force at this time still generally consisted of just one legion, so that any great military effort would need to involve both the top magistrates to ensure that they would, with allies, be able to field something like 18,000 men, numbers that would be required to challenge the full strength of the Samnite military.

Urgent business awaited and a major effort was required to be undertaken by men determined on the recapture of the frontier fortress, but after they descended on the town the defenders' determination ensured that the enterprise would be made very difficult by the terrain. The Arx or citadel of Sora was situated on an imposing rock rising to over 1,700ft above the bridge spanning the river around which the town had grown. An attack up the sheer cliff would be costly, but to starve the rebels out would take much longer than they could afford, allowing the Samnites to march to the rescue. The problem was only solved when a defector slipped out of town to enter the siege camp with a proposal to make. Sulpicius Longus and Poetelius Libo listened with great interest to the plan he outlined and, rubbing their hands in anticipation of advantage, took his advice that the besiegers fall back 6 miles to allow the garrison guards, with no enemy in sight, to become sloppy. Treacherous but plucky, this renegade prepared to put his money where his mouth was, led a picked assault party back towards the town and conducted them to a hideaway he knew. Secreting them in the woods below the defences, after dark he guided ten of the soldiers 'over steep and almost impassable ground up to the citadel'. Here on a rock that dominated the highest part of the town, the intruders prepared an unassailable position, with piles of missiles ready to defend themselves, while in a last fatal act the traitor rushed down into the streets screaming 'to arms' and that the enemy were already in their midst, overlooking them from their highest ramparts. Sleepy-eyed locals turned out of their beds, trying to evaluate the furore that had erupted in what had just before been a slumbering town. Panic set in after the men sent by the city officials to investigate reported what they believed was a whole army of intruders occupying a dominating eyrie from where it would be impossible to dislodge them. While householders with some fight left regarded the heights, so that eventually they might have realized how miniscule was the threat, others far more spooked considered only the possibility of escape. These grabbed what they could carry of their property and filled the streets with their families, determined to get out of a town they soon expected to be experiencing a terrible fate at the hands of a conquering army. On discovering the lower gate closed, they did not stop but broke it down, streaming into the country beyond, but with the doors flung open the Romans concealed in the grounds outside saw their chance and poured in, cutting down any citizens they came across to ensure no effective defence could be organized. Sora was an awful place for several hours of night-time darkness, with the terrified inhabitants hiding where they could and the invaders making sure they held all the strongpoints their numbers allowed, and suppressing with efficient violence anything that might turn into organized resistance.

The consuls and the rest of the army arrived as the sun came up and stayed the slaughter. The remainder of the people who surrendered to them were spared, except for the 225 who were thought to have been personally involved in killing the Roman colonists when the town went over to the Samnites. These unfortunates were dragged off in chains to trek the 70-odd miles to Rome, all as preparation for the condemned to be led shrieking into the forum, where they were scourged and beheaded and their corpses piled up in front of a vengeful crowd, many of whom would have had friends and relatives among the settlers butchered at Sora. In this season not only was this crucial place reconquered but other backsliders were reeled in too. The recapture had been a real triumph but the victors, unprepared to leave it at that, pushed down the Liris valley to secure the country of the Aurunci that had been massively unsettled by the coming and going of Samnite armies over the months since the victory at Lautulae. There was little opposition in the field against them, only defiance shown by pro-Samnite factions who had been encouraged to flex their muscles after the earlier failure of Roman arms. In three places in particular – Ausona, Minturnae and Vescia – it looked like the residents would go over to the enemy whose advent they were awaiting in eager anticipation. However, they suffered for their dalliance; as military columns force-marched into the neighbourhood, resistance was overcome with the aid of a fifth column of young nobles who killed the watchmen on the gates and let them in or murderous soldiers in civilian attire, with swords under their togas, slipped in through unguarded gates to take over the defences. There is a suggestion that this had been a mission of annihilation, that the 'people were wiped out' which, while an exaggeration, certainly shows the suppression of opposition was complete, something soon made obvious when settlers were brought in and Suessa Aurunca was established as a fortified settlement south under the cone of Roccamonfina. Nor did the Volsci get off unscathed; we do not hear of bloodshed, but a colony was established on the Pontine Islands off their coast near Gaeta, and far off to the east Luceria was taken at the first assault once an army had made the journey there, and anybody tainted by Samnite connection was mercilessly hunted down. In 313 that place too was planted as a colony for 2,500 emigrants and their dependants.

It was not just in Aurunci territory and Apulia but in sweet, bountiful Campania too that the spirit of resistance was afoot. There had always been people in Capua who had been unhappy with their visibly subservient status. Theirs might be a gilded cage but a cage nonetheless and such were the machinations of these very connected people that the ripples even reached Rome itself. A dictator called Gaius Maenius was nominated to look into the matter and though those troublemakers who were implicated committed suicide or made themselves scarce, sufficient evidence was uncovered to suggest that the shocking talk of traitors in the city was not so far off the mark. With many scared, the investigation appeared like it might get hijacked into a sort of witch hunt, with high-visibility patricians claiming that the guilty parties were plebeians trying to make waves so they would be able to guarantee greater access to political offices. The fallout affected the dictator, himself a plebeian, and his master of horse who both ended up resigning their posts and, branded traitors, being arraigned before the courts alongside Publilius Philo, one of the greatest plebeian grandees, in the dock with them. They all ended up being acquitted without a stain on their characters, but the McCarthyite atmosphere in the air indicated what kind of trauma had resulted from the recent sight of sun flashing off Samnite blades so close to the Servian walls.

* * *

In this latest pulse of the Second Roman-Samnite War the Republic's aggression had ensured the reignition of a contest that their rivals perhaps would not have chosen, inclined as they were to put their resources into expanding south. Yet it had taken just an attack on one of their cities to function as catalyst, an act of aggression that just could not be overlooked, but after the spark had lit the tinderbox, despite a Samnite army failing to raise the siege of Saticula, they had still been the core of a force that had shaken Roman central Italian hegemony to its foundations. The campaign engendered had seen a grand army of invasion advancing north into the enemy heartland, led perhaps by men of real strategic imagination. Samnium, after all, would produce just such another in a couple of decades' time, prepared to attempt what others of his people could not envisage. This activity was one of the very few occasions when they ever actually fought their war in opposition territory, ravaging the very centre of old Latium and getting within a few miles of the walls of Rome. Apart from this occasion, action usually occurred as a result of the invasions of Samnite country in response to their assaults on colonies often planted in regions that they had previously owned or at least claimed dominance over; places like the Liris valley or Luceria in Apulia, or as the consequence of a razzia conducted in localities recently annexed or friendly to Rome, usually in Campania or the country around Mount Falernus, north of the Volturnus River.

The temptation might be to explain the consistent lopsided nature of all three Samnite Wars by a disparity in resources and military strength, but this is problematic. A trustworthy Greek, after all, provides figures that suggest the contest was more equal than that, perhaps a reason why the Samnites lasted so long in contesting the might of Rome. These very credible numbers, probably sourced from Fabius Pictor, working from Roman archives, disclose the military potential of most of the peoples of Italy in the 220s a few years before the horror that was Hannibal's war was about to descend on a peninsula dominated by a Roman confederacy. They illustrate the depth of military resources that great commander would have to contend with in his astonishing enterprise. The totals quoted for the Samnites are 70,000 foot and 7,000 horse, which are almost exactly equal to those given by Polybius for the Latin allies, those bulwarks of Roman power from the century before. For our purposes what must not be forgotten is that by this time the Samnites, after defeat in three great wars and the revolt of the 280s and 270s, had lost nearly half of their agricultural land and that the best of it. So it is reasonable to assume their original military potential was almost double that recorded; that at the beginning of this belligerent series, they might have had a pool of potential recruits not far short of 140,000 infantry and more than 10,000 cavalry, making them a fearsome rival to any other state in Italy during this time. In fact, such numbers might have been expected to give them a winning margin against most.

Comparing this with Roman figures, though there are a number of issues around what we are told, ballpark figures can still be suggestive. At the beginning of the Samnite Wars in 343, the citizen body was around 150,000 and by the time of the third war perhaps as much as 250,000. As this would include the elderly, the incapable and the disinclined, it shows that at the start of these conflicts the Romans alone were at a disadvantage against their new enemy, but by the 290s they would have had the edge, not just because her citizen body had grown but because the Samnites had already lost land as a result of Roman victories in the previous two wars. Of course the Republic's armies from the start were significantly fleshed out with allies, on board since the commencement of hostilities or who had been added to the roster of Rome's friends during a half century of conflict, all of which strongly suggests that the contests covered in this book were no mismatches, despite the repeated picture of devastating success indicated by our main source.

Other chroniclers[12] understand that Rome's conflict with these hardy Apennine mountaineers was far more even than suggested by the tales of mounds of dead and captured after every victory. Yet if the figures provided certainly explain why the fighting lasted so long and was so hard-fought, it does not explain why from the start and almost all the way through, the campaigns were fought on Samnite soil or that of her allies rather than the territory of Rome and her key supporters in Latium. This was something different, though nothing much to do with any vaunted and particular bellicosity on the part of Rome. The Republic was certainly an expansionist power, with a ruling elite who gloried in the prestige, power and wealth earned from war and a commonality who were almost as eager, but this was hardly untypical. No one we know of ever gainsaid the warrior nature of the Samnites or the Gauls, who would attack their neighbours at the drop of a hat if they felt it in their interest. It was not military resources or inclination; it was something else that explains the direction of events. There were other factors at play in the epic contest; the lack of a constant organizational genius. The Samnites just did not have the structure of the Romans. The four separate Samnite tribes never had the long-term institutions to deliver a consistent strategy. Theirs was usually ad hoc, reactive behaviour, which explains why it was only on one occasion that they ever really took the fight to enemy country in a way that might have made winning the war possible. It was almost always all about defence, with very occasional outbursts of grand offensive strategy like that at the centre of the third great war.

This had much to do with geography. The Samnite League consisted of four peoples who lived in country that did not make mutual assistance easy, even when they were inclined to countenance it. It is not often recorded, but is surely probable that Hirpini regiments aided their Caudine cousins when they erupted out of their hills and valleys to ravage Campania or joined up as Pentrine armies led the way in raiding down through Falernian country to the sea. No doubt this was reciprocated; when enemies marched from Apulia to threaten the green wold country around Mount Vulture, perhaps all of the tribes contributed to the expeditionary forces that went north to fight with the Etruscans and Umbrians and certainly they would have picked up Caracini warriors as they passed through their country on the way. At the start of the wars, each of the three larger tribes would have had 40,000-plus men to call upon, so an average levy would have brought in more than 10,000 men including auxiliaries from adventurous young men recruited from the likes of the Aequi and Hernici looking for mercenary coin and the chance of booty. Inter-Sabellian co-operation we know occurred because of Roman reaction at the turn of the century, and these plus a few bands from neighbouring Samnite tribes must have meant numbers could have reached between 10,000 and 15,000, sufficient to face off equally with a one-consul army, at least until the Roman military expansion of 311. After this increase in enemy numbers the individual tribes clearly did find things more difficult, yet by mighty efforts and the mobilizing of whole league armies, they could still match the two-legion armies commonly fielded at the end of the second and in the third war, even in extremis to make a contest of it when both consuls came in high force. Yet there was still little institutional infrastructure to ensure co-operation, which would have made constructing and implementing a consistent strategy possible. It would have been exactly this that was required to ensure the fight would be taken to the enemy heartland and without it, inevitably it was in defending their own crenellated landscape or raiding along an embattled border where the Samnites showed best.

The Romans were different. There might be a frequent, venomous bubbling of class politics, rivalry between patricians and plebs and indeed mutual abhorrence among many of the families who comprised the governing elite. Still, they mostly were able to disregard interactions where coruscating attacks on one's rivals was as much the norm as ever and contrive a government that could at least do some forward planning, and they were led by magistrates whose imperium, though temporary, was sufficient to flex the military sinews of the state in repeated offensive actions. So whether it was military tribunes, dictators, consuls or praetors, desperate to find a fight where they might build a name, they led armies that were willing to follow on hard and long invasion roads, against even comparatively quite distant lands, to find glory for themselves and their families, to make money and advertise the kind of *virtùs* that every Roman claimed as the cornerstone of their character. The example was portentous; humiliation like that experienced at the Caudine forks and Lautulae might slow them down, but it would never dent their confidence in a final ability to find a way to best the foe, while always claiming a deity-endorsed intention to purge Rome's future of trial and danger.

Chapter Four

Into the Wild Wood

'*The Romans had now begun to be powerful; for a war was carried on by them against the Samnites, who hold a middle situation between Picenum, Campania, and Apulia, at the distance of nearly a hundred and thirty miles from the city. Lucius Papirius Cursor went to conduct that war with the rank of dictator, and, on returning to Rome, gave orders to Quintus Fabius Maximus, his master of the horse, whom he left in charge of the army, not to fight during his absence. He, however, seeing a favourable opportunity, commenced an engagement with great success, and utterly defeated the Samnites; he was accordingly condemned to death by the dictator, for fighting contrary to his orders, but was saved by the powerful interposition of the soldiers and people, so great a tumult having been excited against Papirius, that he was almost slain.*'

Eutropius, *Abridgement of Roman History*

If the Romans, as they were never weary of reiterating, emerged stronger after adversity, other peoples probably saw the events of 314–313 in a less positive light. Among these onlookers and one who the Romans would soon find themselves contending with in the Second Samnite War was a nation they had known for a very long time and who had had the greatest influence on their own story. These were the Etruscans, a fascinating people whose warm marital relationships can be glimpsed in beautiful sarcophagi, where sculptures show husbands and wives in convivial domestic embrace at the dinner coach. This, or even the fact that sons sometimes took their mother's name as well as their father's, might not substantiate some kind of equal opportunities society, but it certainly tells us of people who were a long way from the stern patriarchs of Rome or the misogynists of ancient Athens. This people, who built cities of beautifully painted chamber tombs, rode round in the chariots they probably introduced to the peninsula, loved bloody games, feasting and music and who worked with great artistry the copper found in Tuscany and the iron on the island of Elbe, from ancient times had been a mystery, with a tongue very different from that of their neighbours; indeed, only distantly related to Indo-European languages and that is still not completely decipherable to this day, and whose provenance was debated since histories began to be written. Herodotus claims them as immigrants from Lydia in Asia Minor, while Dionysius of Halicarnassus declares them as aboriginals whose unique culture developed under influences from the peoples living around them.

Some 300 years before the period we are considering had been a golden age, the Etruscans had been the greatest power in Italy, commanding from the Po valley down to Campania. Capua, Herculaneum and Pompeii were Etruscan foundations and in the 530s their fleets fought the Battle of Alalia in the Tyrrhenian Sea against Greeks from Phocaea and even Corsica was part of their sphere of influence for a time. While their merchants by at least the fifth century were flooding southern Gaul with wine, other of their seafarers were making a fearsome reputation for piracy. Still, the control of what were anyway disparate city states, only sometimes loosely leagued up and often falling out among themselves, was a relaxed one and eventually struggles with the Greek colony of Cumae, steeped in Sibylline magic where in the reeking mists of a sacred cave Aeneas came looking for a guide to the underworld, did not end well. Any control they had over Latium hardly survived the arrival of Aequi and Volsci peoples in that region, while the Po valley was lost when Gauls entered from over the Alps to settle its rich water meadows and the mountain valleys nearby. Yet if by 300 the Etruscans counted for considerably less, their communities still covered large swathes of country in what is now modern-day Tuscany, Umbria and northern Lazio. In the sixth century, twelve of their major towns constructed an alliance that, as the Etruscan League or Dodecapolis, interested itself mainly in economic and religious matters, but after this no steady or powerful conglomeration seems to have been at work. Certainly in the fourth and third centuries ad hoc groups would work together to raise and sustain considerable armies for years, but a tendency to cherish separate identities undoubtedly kept this rich and cultured people far weaker than they need have been. If their 'vast population'[1] could have been organized under some permanent and determined federal government, the outcome in what was the contest for the top seat in peninsular politics could have turned out very differently; a potential of league potency suggested by Livy when he mentions all twelve cantons of the league meeting at the cult centre Fanum Voltumnae to discuss going to the aid of their compatriots at Veii when the Romans were besieging the place at the beginning of the fourth century.

Of their main places, which in centuries past would have sniffed at Rome as a parvenu backwater, Caere was situated on the coastal plain not far to the north of the city. Then a few days' hard hiking would bring a traveller to Tarquinii, set high on a ridge with its amazing painted tombs; after that, another week on the road through planted hillsides to Rusellae and nearly 70 miles after that to Volaterrae. These were the major towns west of the mountains, but to the east along the Tiber valley were the great inland metropolises. Fallerii, 30-odd miles north of the Rome river crossing and east of Sutrium and Nepi, that had been planted by the Romans as Latin colonies back near the turn of the fifth century. From there to the north lived the Volsinii near where modern Orvieto stands; after which two-thirds of the way to Lake Trasimene, Clusium is discovered with an equal distance travelled slightly north of east, over hills and valleys, to get to Perusia (now Perugia), while 30 miles straight north from the lake, where the road pushes into the high Apennines, is Arretium. There were many other places too, but these were the names that cropped up most in many years of fighting.

These were a people who had given so much to Rome. Apart from sourcing several of her kings, purple-bordered togas, curule chairs, lictors and divination by entrails were all gained from this enterprising culture. Rome itself was almost an Etruscan foundation, with the beginnings of monumental architecture in the sixth century, earthwork defences and the great drain 'Cloaca Maxima', that allowed habitation in the Tiber Marshes, running between the city's hills. All were the result of either Etruscan learned or directly-applied engineering expertise. Yet if beautiful art can seem to almost introduce us to this people enjoying Tuscan dancers and sponsoring drama to appease their gods, it is much more difficult to realize a clear picture of the armies mobilized by the Etruscans. Indeed, it is probably more difficult than with any of the other combatants in this wide-ranging conflict. If we can be reasonably confident in the style of combat practised by Romans, Samnites and Gauls, with the Etruscans it is much more difficult. The orthodoxy is that the city states of Etruria went to war in a block of spear- and shield-armed warriors, much like those city states of Greece where it is thought they probably first learned the technique. The rich heart of Etruscan Italy certainly contains the kind of open country where noble cavaliers and citizen phalanxes might naturally flourish, much more so than in many parts of Greece. This is a proposition grounded, apart from written attestation, on the many finds of hoplite-style shields and pictures of the same in the numerous tombs that have for centuries been explored in so many sites in the region.

However, questions are raised by other artefacts, as along with hoplite shields what also have been found are javelin heads and more particularly what look like the longheaded iron projectiles called pila that are associated with the fighting practised by Romans and the Sabellian tribes. Also not untypical is a beautiful funerary urn found at Clusium from about 300 that shows men in what appears to be classic hoplite panoply involved in what looks like individual duels as against formed phalanx fighting, even though exactly similar scenes can be found on pottery from mainland Greece and her colonies where we know the phalanx was king. Written evidence is little help, because what we are told is just not specific enough and how accurate and time-specific it might be is very open to question. Certainly descriptions of fighting by the Etruscans in our period frequently involve the throwing of spears as a key component of combat and there is little or nothing that specifically describes them as fighting in the classic phalanx formation of the kind that occurs so frequently in contemporary Greek accounts of battle. What perhaps gets us closest to the truth, as indeed is the case with the early Roman fighting methods, is to imagine Etruscan city levies fighting as close-ranked spearmen but, as with the archaic phalanx of the Greek cities, with a considerable number of missile-men interspersed within their lines, who could either throw their javelins from the protection of their heavier-armed comrades' shields or on occasions sally out to skirmish in front of the main battle line.

* * *

In 311, while the political waters at Rome were being churned up by the militant censor Appius Claudius, of whom we will hear much more later, an old but long dormant problem resurfaced. For a while before this, the second great Samnite War had been something like a conflict on one front. Certainly other peoples had joined in at times and indeed created considerable problems. Lucanians, Apulians and other Sabellian peoples of the Abruzzi had got down their shields and buffed up their cuirasses to some effect from time to time, but still not acted as a frequent or major distraction from the task of dealing with an enemy who on more than one occasion alone seemed capable of being more than a handful for the armies of the Republic. Now, just before the beginning of the last decade of the fourth century, an old foe would materialize that brought a whole new dimension to the dispute. Storm clouds would gather to the north of Rome as the Etruscans, those long-time neighbours, prepared to take the field with armed men, intent on fighting. There had been a good deal of friction over the years and the Romans, with a good memory for such things, had never forgotten that some Etruscans had taken the opportunity of the Gallic takeover in the 380s to attack them in Veii. This left a very bad taste and the Etruscans also held a list of grievances, but the explanation for the timing of this outbreak is far from easy; after all, the last war between the two had been back in the 350s. Yet Etruscan intent to join the conflict had been clear from at least the year before, though decision-making took time, with envoys passing between the towns to ensure that the worries of those who knew what the wrath of Rome might mean were finally overcome.

Word of what was afoot was not long in reaching Rome and the appointment of Gaius Junius Bubulcus as dictator looks like a Roman response to the threat, but that man showed a disinclination to break the peace and no fighting occurred until the following campaigning season, despite the Romans already having a pretty clear idea of the extent of the menace they would be facing. It is possible that the expansion of the strength of the Roman military in 311 was both a response to this threat and an explanation; that it was only after this had been achieved that Rome's leaders felt able to vigorously engage in a war on two major fronts. For their new antagonists, the resolution to enter the war clearly gestated over time, but what in the end really told was the profoundly alarming fact that the Republic appeared to be getting close to finally defeating the Samnites, suggesting that if the Etruscans did not strike, she might become too strong to effectively oppose. Exactly who were the communities involved when the fighting unfolded is never made clear, though the claim is that when the war erupted, all the people of Etruria apart from Arretium took part. This was clearly not just going to be a sideshow and the first move came when the Volsinii backed by levies from the cities of Perusia, Cortona and Clusium banded together to attack the Latin colony at Sutrium. This foundation, situated in what had formerly been Etruscan territory between Lake di Vico and Lake di Bracciano, can be imagined to this day, with the attacking armies moiling around the well-defended walls standing as they still do above a steep escarpment. The original ancient defences can be found to the south of the town, surrounded by a necropolis of atmospheric rock-cut tombs and for the Romans, with Nepet, this place was the key to a crucial road into Etruria. It had been taken soon after the successful end of the Veii war and if they had lost it for a few years in the 380s, they had no intention that this misadventure should be repeated.

As the population of Sutrium peered out from the walls over fire-ravaged fields and burned-out farmhouses, beginning to hope of rescue, a figure was standing on an eminence nearby in early summer of 310, looking with what must have been a mix of surprise and relief at the backs of his adversaries as they broke and ran for their camp. The enemy were the Etruscans who had been interrupted while beleaguering that community, where fighting had started the year before. On that earlier occasion, to try to relieve this colony in danger, the two-time consul Quintus Aemilius Barbula had marched an army up from Rome, but though he took on the Etruscans in open battle it not only cost men but failed to break the lines that surrounded the town. Though the rest of the fighting season was then accounted for on both sides with rebuilding strength, by the following year the danger to Sutrium had become sufficient to ensure that initially both consuls were deputed to face the northern threat, but this was before Samnite activity far down among Rome's Iapygian friends[2] meant military efforts had to be divided. While his colleague went against the old enemy, taking the town of Allifae by assault, Fabius Rullianus assumed the Etruscan station where the matter of Sutrium was becoming pressing. Both sides brought up reinforcements and the new consul, after taking the reins of command, began recruiting and training the men of the new levy to add them to those remaining who had suffered the year before.

This man's career seems not to have faltered unduly, despite his involvement in the Lautulae debacle. He had always stood out among his peers as a commander of capacity and promise and now, still in his prime, well inured to the caprices of fortune, he was intending to make himself visible to properly refurbish his reputation with this fighting in the offing. The enemy had been at their task, dug in for quite some time with siege works well advanced around this key frontier post when he arrived to rescue the inhabitants, whose condition, worn down by accumulated pressure, had begun to look terminal. A few days out of Rome, passing Lake di Bracciano on the left and moving beneath the hills, Fabius Rullianus marched his army forward to again try to disturb the besiegers' activity, only to find them well-concentrated. Having had prompt word of his coming, they were primed for a fight with all the advantages. Shaping up for battle, their front showed wide and deep, indicating to the intruders that they had stirred up a real hornets' nest and that, in the broad plains south of the town, the long files of soldiers they faced indicated an opponent who considerably outnumbered them. Moving quickly to save Sutrium, Fabius Rullianus had marched with only those men immediately available, and this had not allowed time for all the allied contingents to be included in the column he had led hotfoot to help the colony's defenders.

The consul, leading his men forward, saw with consternation that it appeared they would be swamped if they faced their adversary in the open plain. So he redirected their march away and up into the hills that rise rocky and difficult in the country north of the lake. This made all the difference and the Etruscans, on pressing their attack, found a determined defender, well-placed and able to pelt them with everything they had, from the javelins and pila they ordinarily carried to the abundant rocks and stones they found on the ground they had taken up. The Etruscan attack faltered as their soldiers became disordered with missiles 'raining down on their shields and helmets'. They were unable to get in close, or if they came to hand-to-hand were unable to batter the Romans aside.

Apparently ill-equipped with missiles and with what they had making little impact, thrown uphill against a well-placed shield line, the young men of the Republic's citizen body, conscious of the presence of their comrades around them and the interlaced fence of body-length scutum to their front, never threatened to break. However, this deadlock could not last and the sight of the wavering ranks below them gave such confidence that the armoured yeomen of the Romans' front two ranks rushed forward. Now was the moment, with adrenalin pumping, terrifying war cries in their throats and momentum increased by the incline down which they were rushing, swords were drawn ready to strike anyone within reach. The sight of this cheering wave of attackers, high with anticipation of victory, was too much for the enemy, whatever their numbers. Realizing this wall of hurtling mayhem was not going to be halted, they hardly stayed to trade blows and, anticipating the coming collision with horror, most exited the battlefield pell-mell, fleeing in the direction of their camp over the prone bodies of comrades showing gaping wounds and spattered with blood.

The sight of the enemies' backs, running helter-skelter, dropping their shields and spears, even if a surprise, did not faze the Roman commander. Eager to strike before they could slip away, he determined to make the most of his unexpected victory and ordered his cavalry to cut the enemy off from the refuge of their encampment. Forcibly redirected by the thundering hooves of the pursuing horsemen, many of the routed Etruscans now sought asylum in the dark Ciminian wood that lay not far off north of the city, but far from all the running men found sanctuary without pain; some were killed before they reached the security of the trees, succumbing to the deadly endeavours of their conquerors. The material loss was great enough when their palisaded encampment was entered by the victors and a 'vast amount of plunder' revealed.

The forest where so many of the vanquished Etruscans had disappeared is described as a pretty extraordinary place, explaining why the victors paused before plunging in to pursue the fugitives. This region, the Silva Ciminia, described as 'primeval forest', was more impenetrable and fearful than the wooded ravines of Germany and it barred access from the south into more northerly parts of Etruria. Receiving its name from Mount Cimini situated in volcanic hills, 45 miles north-west of Rome,

28 miles from the Tyrrhenian coast and above what is now Lake de Vico, just north of Sutrium, the forest once spread down almost to Rome and from the great Lake di Bracciano and across to the coast at Tarquinii. Though much had been cut down to provide the fields for their farmers to till to feed the people of Veii, Faliscan Capena and other Etruscan places, in the late fourth century it was still an obstacle stretching from west of the Tiber valley in the direction of Perusia. It is difficult to believe that a region so near the cultivated centres of Rome, Veii and Tarquinii could have still at this time remained terra incognita, considering how much interaction had taken place over the centuries between the communities all around and for how long Roman merchants would have been wandering round the region. Yet the evidence of sediment layers certainly supports this, with records showing only from the third century the increase in organic deposits that would derive from the kind of erosion that would have followed full deforestation.

It was in the shadows of the looming trees at the forest's edge where a vista of hills stretched far away that a colloquy of troubled officers met for a council of war in which all the senior officers were ready to offer their thoughts about whether, as Fabius Rullianus proposed, they should press forward, whatever the dangers. Most were reluctant and a great cloud hung in the air, the 'Caudine disaster had not faded from their minds.' Yet one man did share his commander's adventurous disposition; this cheerleader for a plan that took shape was his brother or perhaps half-brother, who was deputed to lead a scouting party to find a way across the wilderness. He had apparently spent part of his childhood in the city of Caere and because of this he spoke the Etruscan language like a native which was expected to prove a boon in progressing this adventure, though it may be that familiarity with the language was common enough among a Roman elite who frequently at that time grew up with Etruscan tutors, just as they would with Greek ones in the centuries to come.

So, faced with this obstacle into which his enemies had disappeared, the consul sent his brother with just one slave, dressed as shepherds, to try to discover a practical route through the Ciminian forest, where no army had gone before. What shepherds would be doing in a deep dark wood is not explained; however, it may be best to regard this fraternal stuff as just a good tale and the reality was surely that a party of scouts was dispatched to reconnoitre the terrain and find a track where the rest of the army might be able to follow. These pathfinders returned with good news: an open road was before them. So the resolution was taken and, leaving the relieved citizens of Sutrium behind, the armed column swiftly ascended the hills, heading for the Silvan depths. Oak, beech, fir and chestnut created a dark canopy overspreading deep-cut gullies and rocky outcrops that for many lowland farmers in the Roman ranks must have been a place of terror and panic. The wild wood through which the legionaries toiled would have been the most direct route along the western flank of Apennine outliers. Passing where the modern community of Fabrica di Roma now stands, the country rose high enough for them to be able to view a great swathe of Etruscan territory below to the west, confirming the veracity of the description in our main account. Now, as the leafy canopy closed over their passage, the hardship of the way was at least relieved by the shade of the trees and the cool of the higher country as they climbed to penetrate far into the forest. Finally they reached their destination after following a route the Via Amerina would later take, running direct from Sutrium via Todi, famous for a late-fifth or early-fourth-century statue of Mars found there in 1835, and on to Perusia.

The story of the passage of the Ciminian forest puzzles at first, partly because Livy had no real idea about the feature, and the contention that the route to Perusia was cut off by an impenetrable woodland just does not seem plausible. The Romans would have known the road up the Tiber valley well, no doubt trading along it for generations, but Fabius Rullianus knew that to take the conventional route, the long way round up the river valley, would have been fraught with danger. He had no intention of committing a symmetrical error by attacking along that way as there were many places that might be hostile and could block a narrow road against an invading army and beyond that, a battered but still considerable Etruscan army would be left untrammelled, sitting on his supply lines and granted the run of the border country between Sutrium and Rome itself. By the time he was approaching Clusium, enemy armies could be banging on the door where the Romans would have very little in the way of armed strength to oppose them. They might be trashing the lands of Rome's Faliscan friends, enslaving Roman citizens living in the Veii country, the acquisition of which had been so key to the Republic's growth a century before, or even threatening to find a way across the Tiber into Latium. Such reasoning meant that despite the fabulous accounts of the dangers of the terrain, it was the strategy to cross it directly that was adopted.

Not that this is the only puzzle. Another outcome of this first incursion into the wild Ciminian waste was that Fabius Rullianus' brother, while scouting the country, encountered emissaries from Camerinum and initiated an alliance with them. This is odd because this Umbrian town, whose occupants may have settled there several hundred years before after having been driven out of Clusium by the Etruscans, is far to the east of the forest, over the Tiber and then beyond, deep into the Apennines, almost to where these mountains commence to run down towards the Adriatic. The town is north of Sabine country and a long way east of Perusia, so it is highly unlikely that it was Fabius Rullianus' surveyors marking a path through the woods that instigated this friendship, but if it was another Roman party, pushing over mountains that reach up to 6,000ft, who established cordial relations, they did a good job. This alliance would continue well into the period of the Third Samnite War.

By pushing along the paths the scouts had located the Roman invaders, pairs of feet pounding the road to overcome what nature had thrown in their way, only to discover they had another serious war on their hands. After a surprise arrival in a locality where they had not been seen in significant arms before, they found themselves involved in a series of encounters against Etrurians and Umbrians who, hackles raised, had mobilized in very substantial numbers. After the intruders settled somewhere short of Perusia, in behind solid breastworks on rising ground, a huge confederate army assembled in front of their camp. Determined to stake their fortunes on a single cast, they offered battle to these invaders in their midst. While the contest was first refused, the assailants were so eager to engage that as a westering sun sank, far from returning to their own bivouac, they stayed put instead. From their temporary lines in front of the Romans' wooden walls, they sent for their rations so they could recoup their strength ready to assault the enemy, either that night or the next day. Then as they settled down on his doorstep, with no ramparts of their own for protection, the Roman commander, demonstrating an intelligence none could dispute, decided on a ploy that is pretty well unique in the annals of ancient warfare.

Fabius Rullianus had already shown he would dare to do the unexpected and now he had high hopes of capitalizing on the overconfident stance of his adversaries. They were on home soil, present in great numbers and intent on showing the intruder the error of his ways, seeming to have very little regard for the threat posed by a consular army, despite its recent victory over an Etruscan enemy at Sutrium, and he intended to make them pay for this unwarranted assurance. So in the very early hours of the morning, after his men had fed and enjoyed several hours of sleep, he ordered them out to make ready to fight. Meanwhile their servants, equipped with picks, had during the hours of darkness pulled down the palisades and filled in the fosse outside the earthworks. All was done with as little noise as possible, hoping not to give any warning to the enemy deep in slumber only several hundred yards to their front. So, just before the morning sun rose, the soldiers, armed, ready and prepared for the dawn, were able to push forward all along the perimeter of the camp. Over their own filled-in ditches, they passed undisrupted and raging down into the masses of unsuspecting enemy outside. These were in no defensive position at all and many were still asleep; few sentries had been posted and even those who had been roused by the sounds of an attacking army and were trying to arm themselves were soon overrun by their assailants. These attackers had been able to reach them in just a very few moments, because rather than having to debouch slowly through the gates of their camp, they had been able to cross the ground to their target fully deployed in long solid lines. Soon, almost before light had appeared in the sky, with javelins flying about their ears the confederates, with comrades lying dead around them were no longer capable of resistance. There were pockets of defiance, men who had been able to lace on their helmets, grab their shields and show some kind of broken battle line, but these groups were too small to sustain themselves as their flanks were bound to be open, exposed to the tide of attackers sweeping on around them. It was over almost before it began. A debacle ensued and again as in the contest outside Sutrium, many of the vanquished men headed for the woods, with their attackers slashing and stabbing at their backs rather than falling back to their camp in the plain. Thus it was too late when they tried to man the defences; they just did not have the combatants left when the victorious Romans arrived to assault their walls. There was no need for much in the way of tactics or even organization in this enterprise; Fabius Rullianus' men just walked through the gates, taking captives and plunder as they liked.

The assertion that in battling this enemy they had inflicted 60,000 dead and apprehended on top of the captured standards piled at the feet of the consul is patently absurd; after all, many of the roughly awoken men with just tunics and footwear would have easily outstripped any pursuit by armoured warriors, finding refuge in familiar country and defended places where compatriots arranged their entry and succour. Yet still the truth of the encounter was that this first battle in these recently-penetrated lands was a considerable Roman success. Diodorus even reports the capture of an unknown place called Castola at this time. A modest enough result for their efforts, but time would show the profits from this adventure would amount to considerably more than just the capture of one small town. Such, in fact, was the intruders' impact that the locals decided they were, at least for the moment, far too tough to handle and deputations from Perusia, Arretium and Cortona, major towns in the Lake Trasimene region, came looking for a truce.

Before this substantial triumph became common knowledge at a Rome agog for the latest reports, there was plenty of deep disquiet. Darkening news ensured mutterings, when it was first heard that the consul and his army had disappeared into the depths of the wild Ciminian wood, that such escapades could only lead to disaster. The apprehension was that Fabius Rullianus had been reckless, preparing to risk thousands of their soldiers in a gamble that might well fail. But while it is a little difficult to fully credit that many but the most credulous and ill-informed had great concerns about an army getting lost in the wilderness, much more understandable would be the anxiety that his precipitate action would involve Rome in a foreign policy blunder; a brand-new war with a new people, and those who were afraid had been proved right. Little had been heard of these Umbrians as an enemy before, but after this they are counted a consistent foe, well into the period we are considering in detail. Though repeated battling with fractious Etruscans remained important, there is no doubt that one of the most significant features of the years after the Ciminian woods had been penetrated was that the Romans, by intruding so effectively in this part of the world, had found another enemy to fight.

Who were these people who Fabius Rullianus' activity had added as another antagonist to a lengthening list of Rome's enemies? The Umbrians were an Italic people who lived in defensible hilltop towns; some long-standing communities settled since the ninth century. They were not quite the sophisticated urbanites like their Etruscan cousins, whose influence among them was strong; many remained pastoralists or peasant farmers occupying a *Vicus-Pagus* paradigm and having more in common with the likes of the Samnites. They built similar defensive hill forts and possibly had an analogous political organization, though really there are only hints of some national religious offices. One of the most ancient races of Italy, they had once occupied a much more extensive patrimony. Dionysius calls the Umbrians 'a great and ancient people'[3] who once occupied a much greater area than they did at the time we are considering. Pliny[4] informs us that the Etruscans drove them out and occupied 300 of their towns, places like Chianciano and Clusium nearly 50 miles south-east of modern Siena, that itself contains traces of Umbrian habitation dating to the seventh or eighth centuries.

They had not long since been pushed out of the northern plains and off the Adriatic coast by the Gauls, but remained a substantial power inhabiting country that was considerably more extensive than the modern region that bears their name, occupying places like Gubbio north of Perugia and further east, Nocera Umbra, Sentinum and Camerinum and north to Sarsina in the mountains and the valleys that flow into the Adriatic. They also inhabited extensive country along both the Adriatic side of the Apennines and reaching west almost to the Tiber valley and south to the Nera as far as Ocriculum in the south. Owning a frontier with the Sabine country to the south-east, their occupation of the Nera basin round Terni is substantiated by the presence of a nearby necropolis of almost 3,000 tombs.

* * *

While Fabius Rullianus was up north in 310 knocking about old Etruscan and mint new Umbrian enemies, an ex-consul-led delegation of senators reached his camp after days on the road from Rome. The capacity for these folk to reach him easily showed that clearly there must have been a less demanding way to get to this part of the world, as it is difficult to imagine these exquisites risking a just-opened route through the wild tangle of the Ciminian wood. The reason for their arrival was that while he had been doing well enough in his war, the consul allocated the Samnium front had come unstuck, suffering a defeat, probably not far from Allifae as he is recorded as taking this place earlier. In this affray, casualties were not only suffered among his officers and men, but he himself fell wounded; events that, combined with the earlier talk of a Ciminian forest disaster, caused a sufficient stir in the capital to suggest that the defeat by the Samnites was on a considerably grander scale than is allowed by our main account. Enough, in fact, for the city fathers to wheel out the veteran Papirius Cursor, a man whose reputation alone was sufficient to face so severe a crisis. The problem was that installing him as a dictator required one of the standing consuls to instigate the process and with one hors de combat and confined to camp with his beaten men, it meant that Fabius Rullianus was the only candidate for the job. Unfortunately, animosity between him and the man proposed as dictator was deep and went back a long way.

Papirius Cursor is first noticed years before in 340 or 339 when appointed master of horse to another Lucius Papirius called Crassus, though on this occasion apparently nobody saw much action as their army spent most of the campaigning season occupying a camp in the Volsci country, down by the coast where Anzio now sits. In 325 he was himself appointed dictator and that he was master of horse some fifteen years before suggests that by then he was well into middle age, as might be expected of someone selected to save the state in crisis when one of the elected consuls was detained on his sick bed. While the still fit consul took a swipe at the Vestini, Papirius Cursor led his army south to confront the Samnites. After a while he was recalled to Rome to supervise some sacred ceremonial, directing that the young Fabius Rullianus, his master of horse, should stay clear of adventure while he was absent; a stricture that the young officer, determined to make an immediate splash, swiftly breached when he dealt the enemy a considerable blow, if not two if some traditions are to be believed.

When Papirius Cursor returned to his army's camp, he did so demanding a Manlian disposition, that the man who had disobeyed his orders should suffer a fatal penalty, just as Manlius Torquatus' son had before battle for duelling with an enemy against his father's and commander's edicts. The subject of his ire, however, mobilized the men he had led to victory to plead his case. Fabius Rullianus declared to his soldiers that the man who threatened him was motivated by jealousy over their success and that if he managed to wreak his will on him, he would soon do the same against the military tribunes and other officers who had followed the master of horse into battle. A head-to-head occurred, with the present threat of the lictors standing behind the dictator with him prepared to order them on, while Fabius Rullianus slipped back into the ranks of his men, looking for a demonstration of comradeship; the promised protection he had drawn from them against a superior who clearly saw his actions as the most flagrant breach of discipline. A pantomime of pleading and threats of mutiny was played out with Fabius Rullianus' youth being stressed as mitigation, a deadlock that finally ended with nightfall, only to recommence on the following day with the defendant ordered to come before the dictator once again. With a fair idea of what would happen if he did so, the accused fled the camp, returning to Rome to try to mobilize the kind of support that only a scion of a great old patrician family could. His father had been consul three times and dictator as well, and was soon mustering the kind of clout this gave him on his son's behalf. It is high drama reported, as the young commander began to make his case to the Senate, when Papirius Cursor himself arrived from the army with a cavalry escort, determined to re-arrest the absconder.

There were pleas and counter-pleas, a shadow-play of interests, but as the Fabii lobby failed to gain traction in this arena, they called on the tribunes of the plebs to take the case to the people. There by the rostra, where the beaks of ships taken from Antium in 338 decorated the platform, the arguments were presented again, until the deadlock was broken when, with the din of popular support ringing in his ears, the master of horse threw himself on the mercy of the dictator. Now even that intransigent man, seeing how unpopular the destruction of his subordinate would be, reluctantly permitted him to live, though the reprieved man was refused the opportunity to take up his duties again, as Papirius Cursor returned to lead his disgruntled army on campaign. Despite all this internal strife, the outcome of the year's fighting was sufficiently successful to force a truce on the Samnite enemy, despite the initial reluctance of the legionaries to fight for their unpopular leader. Neither of the two principals in this altercation was anywhere near done in terms of their careers and the incident did little to halt the rise to greatness of Fabius Rullianus, making consul for the first time in 322, and if he progressed, Papirius Cursor, despite his unpopularity with the rank and file, retained a sufficient reputation. It was, after all, he who in the wake of the Caudine disaster, 'as the people were disgusted with all the magistrates', was called on again as consul to dig the Republic out of the mire.

This was the history that looked like it might now make the appointment of Papirius Cursor as dictator again to salvage the Samnite front not straightforward at all. The worried envoys in Fabius Rullianus' camp certainly did not have an easy time of it, having to face a clearly furious consul as they outlined that they wanted him to sponsor this hated enemy. He had neither forgotten nor forgiven and, stomping away without a word, it must have appeared that the long trip to northern Etruria was going to be a waste of time for the senatorial delegation as they found their beds for the night. However, Fabius Rullianus showed himself capable of doing what was right for the general good, despite the fact that he 'dismissed them without making any reply or alluding to what he had done, so that it was clearly seen what agony his great heart was suppressing.'[5] He took satisfaction from drawing out the drama, not confirming the dictator's nomination until midnight, which was the customary hour anyway. So on the emissaries' return to Rome, Papirius Cursor was able to lead out a new levy, troops raised when the fear about what could have happened to the army entering the Ciminian wood was at its height.

The task undertaken by the dictator turned out tough enough, not helped by a deeply apprehensive home folk, who worried that the first voting group who had confirmed his position had been the same that had the privilege in the years Rome had fallen to the Gauls and the Caudine peace had been imposed. A reprise of religious rites assuaged concerns sufficiently to allow the dictator to first name Gaius Junius Bubulcus as his master of horse and then take command. After this, as raw bands of recruits, brushing the farm soil from their clothing, had been instructed in the basics of their drill, he marched to join the veterans that the consul

Gaius Marcius Rutulus had been commanding at Longula, a Volscian town not far from Samnium. There, cautious and cunning, he was unprepared to take head on the enemy army he found opposing him. The experience of defeat must have taken the edge off the belligerence of most of the men he found on his arrival; a condition not immediately rectified by the appearance of what were still green troops that he had brought to back them up. The campaign petered out for the moment, with both sides looking across at each other from the permanent camps they had built to house themselves, though the veteran dictator could at least feel that he had re-established this front, where the depleted army of a wounded consul previously looked like it would not be up to the task of stemming the tide. Now the future, in his capable hands, could be anticipated as being pregnant with hope and promise.

If they were content that Fabius Rullianus had put the national interest above personal spite in the matter of Papirius Cursor, his compatriots could with good reason complain of the other returns on his endeavours. The big picture in respect of this hero's actions was that apart from putting the wind up them when he disappeared into the Ciminian forest, he had stirred up in the Umbrians an enemy who brought a new energy to the efforts of the Republic's opponents in the northern war. Even in this year of 310, these fresh antagonists gave more trouble to a Roman commander needing to face not only them but the Etruscans, who were making a special effort too. The latter people had raised a kind of 'sacred band' on the Theban model,[6] some sort of holy pairing of warriors to spearhead their army in combat. These had an impact, when it came to blows, near Lake Vadimo in the Tiber valley. This encounter near modern-day Orte that sits high on a cliff east of Viterbo on the road to Rome was ferocious; a confrontation in which neither side bothered with their missiles but got straight down to venomous sword-work. Etruscan steadiness came as something of a surprise as 'the Romans had to contend not with the Etruscans they had beaten so often but with some new race', yet in the end they went down in defeat. Though victory was only finally achieved by the Roman eques and the Latin cavalry dismounting and joining an engagement in which both sides' infantry were utterly exhausted.

As these events coincided with another major effort by the Samnites, the pressure to retain the man on the spot increased and Fabius Rullianus, bringing back the wreaths of victory from regions where Roman arms had not reached before, so impressed the home town crowd that in this testing time his tenure of command was prolonged. In the following fighting season he returned north to perpetrate real wreckage in the country around Perusia, eager to chastise the men who, despite having pretended to bend the knee and make a thirty-year truce, had proceeded to break it as soon as the legions had left their vicinity. These inconstant folk now found this nemesis arrived under their walls after swatting off the men they had put in the field. This time the Romans were less prepared for their trust to be abused, so when the citizens surrendered they left a garrison in control while dispatching the chastened Perusian delegates to Rome to finalize the details of their capitulation. Their trust in Fabius Rullianus more than vindicated, once he reached home a triumph was awarded, despite him having only had proconsular imperium during the fighting. Nor was this his only cause for satisfaction, as he discovered his achievements were appreciated considerably more by both his peers and the man in the street than even those racked up by Papirius Cursor, the dictator he had sponsored and who had earned his own triumph for dispatching a Samnite army shining in silver and gold.

The veteran marshal had encountered Samnites who had not been inactive, calling on every resource to field an army not just numerous but also equipped with gold and silver inlaid shields and high plumed helmets to intimidate their enemies. Papirius Cursor, however, had used his time well, exercising recruits and boosting the morale of the veterans so that when it came to battle, they were not just up for a fight but looking forward to the loot they would garner from such a glistening, showy foe. When they took the field, the dictator led on the right wing and the master of horse the left, while Marcus Valerius commanded the right wing cavalry and Decius Mus, fast becoming a fixture in the high command, the same on the left. The master of horse broke through first and this encouraged the men under the commander-in-chief, while on both flanks the cavalry replicated the achievements of their footslogging comrades. Indeed, they heaped even more pain when ordered forward, disposing of the enemy horse to their fronts before turning obliquely in to attack the flanks of the enemy centre. This was beyond sustaining and the gorgeous enemy could stand no longer, turning tail and legging it for a camp that only offered a very temporary refuge, as with evening coming down, it was captured and burned to the ground; a memorable victory followed by as memorable a celebration, where the people lining the streets of Rome goggled at the mass of bullion looted from the enemy dead and captured. However, the kudos received by Papirius Cursor for this achievement was diluted by it having to be portioned out with famous subordinates. For these Romans, on such occasions, if there were big names in a commander's military entourage there was always a danger of having to share the limelight.

Fabius Rullianus' popularity was exhibited again in 308 when he was elected to the consulship, despite a law that should have ensured a ten-year gap between the same man holding the office. With him in the other consular chair was Decius Mus who himself had sat there only four years before; two men who were to repeatedly crop up in tandem in the years to come. This is a pattern that was not at all unusual at this time; after the law was passed back in the 360s that called for one consul to be chosen from a plebeian family, a double ticket seems to have become almost the norm, suggesting discreet deals being cut between powerful men to share possession of the two highest honours. Nothing in Roman politics was necessarily for ever, but these arrangements could certainly last, even if there was a hint of tension. Was Decius Mus feeling that he had to play second fiddle to his partner at the root of trouble in 295 when he resisted Fabius Rullianus claiming patrician privilege to pick the Etrurian front for himself rather than their missions being decided by lot? Yet even if rifts occurred, three times these two were consuls together; that apart from when their commands were prorogued so they continued in the field. In 304 they both became censors, a term of office in which, after putting out feelers, they found sufficient support to overturn some bruising reforms that had deeply worried their conservative constituency.

So it was long-time colleagues who drew lots in the new campaigning season to determine responsibilities, with Decius Mus given the Erutrian front while Fabius Rullianus faced a Samnite threat that had not seemed significantly dented, despite the claims of great victories declared the previous year. Decius Mus, on marching north, found that initially, while the Umbrians remained cowed by his colleague's earlier successes, other, older, nearer enemies were bent on making a fight of it. He pressured the

Tarquinii into a forty-year truce, whose conditions included delivering sufficient grain to feed his army for the task ahead. This turned out to be an attack on the Volsinii further inland, up by Lake Bolsena. Here the Romans took some fortresses to deny refuge to their opponent's troops while they set the entire country in flames, until the local people put up such a squeal that their leaders made overtures, offering a year's pay for the men and two tunics each as the price of a year's cessation. However, this was but the preamble as the Umbrians, despite previous maulings, now burst out in belligerence again. The suggestion is they had been little touched by 'the disasters' of war so far and were less cautious of the Romans than many of their neighbours. So, putting in the field as many warriors as they could mobilize, they pushed through to the country of their Etruscan cousins and called on that people, who had so recently felt the lash of Roman ire, to have another go at the old antagonist. We do not know what response they got but their own confidence was such that, with the large numbers they themselves had raised and whoever of the Etruscans were prepared to join them, they set off on the high road to Roman territory. These people are described by Polybius as capable of fielding 20,000 men on Rome's behalf in 225 when a Gallic invasion threatened, so it might be in this kind of strength that they came south to strike at the enemy heartland, confident enough to leave the army under Decius Mus on their lines of communication. However, that man reacted swiftly; receiving news of the threat he stole a march, leading his legions down from Volsinii country at a breakneck pace, only calling a halt to camp when he neared Pupinia. There, north of the Anio, which flows into the Tiber upriver from Rome, he hoped to get further intelligence on the northern invaders' whereabouts and intentions.

This impending danger threw a real scare into the populace at Rome; the Umbrians, who Fabius Rullianus had added to a lengthening list of enemies, being particularly dreaded because they were little known and spoke an unfamiliar and sinister dialect. Their imminent arrival provoked memories in people's minds of the unmitigated disaster that the Gauls had inflicted, nearly a century ago, when appearing from that very same direction. In fact, when the clouds of rumour dissipated in Decius Mus' camp, it became clear they had not advanced as far as had been feared. Solid news sifted from reports received from spies and scouts relieved some worries, except that it soon became clear they were still intent on invasion once they had made further efforts to gather their strength for the enterprise. Decius Mus, though, had been successful in implanting himself between the Umbrian threat and Rome itself and, with some security restored, the Republic's response was emphatic. Word was swiftly sent south recalling the other consul from Samnium and directing him north with his army to assist in what had begun to look like the Republic's most important war.

This reaction in itself made a difference, as information was collated that put the invaders halted near Mevania halfway between Spoletum and Perusia. They had retraced their steps on realizing they were now facing both consuls with their armies and were encamped, waiting only 15 or so miles south of the latter place. However, when it came to a fight they were pleased to discover that only one consul was approaching; that it was just Fabius Rullianus who had returned to his old stomping ground deputed to chase these Umbrian wolves back to their lair. On dogging his adversaries' steps to their position along the River Timia (modern-day Topino), the Romans found their opponents active, despite there being defeatists in the camp, claiming that prudence demanded they should return home to defend their own communities, but these voices of doom had not won out and more bellicose councils had been listened to. These Etruscan and Umbrian confederate chanceries could be erratic at times, lurching between belligerence on one hand or giving way to extreme caution on another, but now confidence was so high that it was agreed to try to throw the Romans off their stroke by attacking while the legionaries were busy at work erecting their camp defences. The impact of the grand attack was immediate; a surprise that cut Fabius Rullianus short in his speech to his troops, though it eventually did little to disorder them as they took up their regular formations. Showing rocklike and catching their assailants breaching the breastworks, the impact was devastating; disordered by climbing in and out of the defensive ditch, the Umbrian lines were ruptured in short order.

In fields that are now shadowed by almost complete medieval town walls, the defenders showed the rugged form they so often did under Fabius Rullianus; a fearsome collision, with men shoving hard with their shoulders behind their shields and smashing the bosses into their enemies' faces. Sweating in heavy armour, the attackers tried to raise themselves out of the half-dug ditch to force a breach in the line of body-length shields in front of them. Swords swung hard as warriors on both sides tried to find the openings in their enemies' armoured carapace; trying to stab over the top of shields into a foeman's face, or slash at an exposed calf or where javelins had stuck into a shield and made it unmanoeuvrable, direct a blow at the exposed torso or head. Many men on both sides were practised in this style of warfare over years of fighting not just each other but local rivals too, but the attackers had put all their efforts in what they hoped would be a knockout first strike, and when it failed they seemed to have little left. They were disordered by the dug-up ground they had crossed to get at their enemy and it was they who found their flanks exposed, where there was no comrade to protect them and enemies were able to hit them unexpectedly. Casualties mounted, even among their best-armoured, most experienced fighters who had led the charge, and it was not too long before the Romans gained the advantage and their opponents were throwing down their arms. It was soon all confusion in the Umbrian ranks as they crumbled and men tried to slip away, stumbling past still fighting comrades in the hope of reaching safety, or finding themselves being butchered where they stood or dragged off with their standards to be presented trussed and captive at the Roman general's feet. The defenders had stood resolute and they reaped the advantage.

After this bloody day the Umbrian leadership had a decision pressed on them as they processed the news coming from their commanders on the battlefield. Their vulnerability lay nakedly revealed; that the intruders could move at will around their territory and the armies they were able to collect were just too overmatched to fight it out. While the invaders harried the country and their people sought sanctuary where they could, only one solution was available to them. They had to bite the bullet and emissaries were not long in arriving at the Roman camp, where the victorious soldiers were enjoying spending what money they had made from plunder and the sale of their captives. All the communities that had fielded men in the invading army would have expected a mailed fist to be exposed when terms of peace were agreed, but what they were forced to give up is not revealed. There would certainly have been ransoms to be provided to fund the release of the better sort and perhaps the kind of tribute in grain and clothing that belligerent Etruscans were often forced to divulge in similar circumstances.

This was the last we hear of these new adversaries for the moment and Fabius Rullianus could certainly make the claim that if he stirred up this particular wasps' nest, he had also provided the solution. Yet that was but part of the story; the Umbrians had shown in a couple of years' fighting that they were a menace and the future would show in just over a decade that when Rome had to face many of her enemies in concert, they would be among them, though the man who had already caused them so much pain would again be on hand to take up the perilous assignment of facing the threat, grown old in the service of Rome but still prepared and still capable of fulfilling his duty.

Chapter Five

A Samnite Pause

'They advanced through Etruria, the Etruscans too uniting with them, and, after collecting a quantity of booty, retired quite safely from the Roman territory, but, on reaching home, fell out with each other about division of the spoil and succeeded in destroying the greater part of their own forces and of the booty itself. This is quite a common event among the Gauls, when they have appropriated their neighbour's property, chiefly owing to their inordinate drinking and surfeiting. Four years later the Gauls made a league with the Samnites, and engaging the Romans in the territory of Camerinum inflicted on them considerable loss.'

Polybius, *The Histories*

Lake Fucino, an ancient blue Cyclops eye nestled in the dramatic green mountains of the central Italian peninsula is no longer the third-largest body of water in Italy, behind lakes Garda and Maggiore. East of Rome, the valley of the Anio was the natural route towards this body of water that sat exactly in the middle of the Italian leg where, despite it now being drained, the large patch of very level terrain leaves no doubt as to what it once was. North of the fertile basin and fish-rich waters lived the Aequi, driven back into the mountains by Latin and Roman efforts in the past two centuries. Further up from them, situated between the Latins and the Umbrians, on the west of the Apennine watershed and much of whose lands was near the Tiber valley, were found the Sabines, people who had known and indeed intermixed with the Romans from the city's beginning, legend even proposing that they lived on the Capitoline Hill while the original Romans occupied the Palatine. The southern shore of the lake was home to the Marsi, while to the east, as the high Apennines fell off, the Paeligni were situated. This country, washed by the Adriatic, was home to other peoples. The Marrucini lived below the River Aternus that ran east to meet the sea where modern Pescara stands, and north of the waterway dwelt the Vestini and even further up the coast the Picentes. South of the Marrucini were the Frentani, who occupied hilly but fertile lands crossed by rivers coming out of the high Samnite country inland. The Tifernus River made a southern limit with Apulia and the modern-day Sangro a northern boundary, cutting through to a coastline that was remarkable for its few natural harbours, apart from anchorages in river mouths.

A concerted push by Rome in the direction of this lake region had been confirmed in 307 when a road, the Via Valeria, was begun, driving east towards the town of Tibur, as the first step in winding down river beds and through rugged ravines that would take it to the Adriatic Sea. This enterprise had been pushing up the agenda of the Republic's foreign relations concerns since well before peace was made between the Romans and Samnites in 304. So if Rome was banging on the door of Samnium, launching yearly campaigns against the Pentri and perhaps other members of the league, an impression is definitely given that the Tibur town elite had by that time other important irons in the fire. In the two years after emissaries first passed between the warring powers in 306 to reopen diplomatic conversations, the only success that warranted a triumphal celebration was that scored against the Hernici and most particularly the citizens of Anagnia. A conflict gestated after a victory by Fabius Rullianus at Allifae in 307 when he sent the Samnites captives under the yoke, enslaved 7,000 of their allies but sent any Hernici he found in arms to Rome, who were distributed to the Latin cities to be kept under guard after being interrogated as to whether they had been conscripted or fought as volunteers. These people, living along the Tolerus River valley south-east of Latium, were not Latins but they were near enough, so the hurt was as if a relative had turned on them. They had been members of the Latin League on occasions and if this had meant they had joined in the last great revolt against the Republic in the 340s, that still decades later their young men would happily sign up to kill Romans was a blow. That collusion, it was pretty certain, was indicated by the fact of recent Samnite successes at Calatia and Sora, the latter not being far to the south-east of Hernici territory. So when it became clear that any plea for clemency for captives who had been dragged from the battlefield in chains would receive short shrift, the Hernici assembly gathered at Anagnia, where the leaders of all the towns except Aletrium, Ferentinum and Verulae announced their intention to mobilize against the Republic.

Both consuls were deputed to overwhelm these troublemakers, who initially gave the tremulous folk back in Rome a bit of a shock by occupying fortified sites between the two invading armies and curtailing communications between them, but if nerves were shaken there was no need as it turned out; no presage of pronounced resistance. Once the invaders got themselves organized, they drove the enemy army out of their three encampments. Assaulted and crushed, they begged for a truce that, though granted, only signified an outcome that saw the denizens of their westernmost territory around Anagnia incorporated as Roman citizens, without suffrage, losing their independence and no longer allowed to maintain associations with anyone except Rome. Nor was this the end, as Frusinum, south-west of Sora, was not long after punished by the execution of their leaders and loss of a third of their land on the grounds that they had encouraged their compatriots in rebellion. The Hernici towns that had remained loyal were left alone and allowed to reject these adjustments, removing any doubt that imposition of citizenship without suffrage was as often as not judged a chastisement by those concerned.

So while a hiatus in the Romano-Samnite epic was inaugurated, this quiet was not reflected on other fronts. Certainly a Samnite pause meant nothing of peace and tranquillity for some famous names who would be kept very busy before the next major conflict overtook events, much of whose activity in the six years when the two great enemies were at peace occurred in the very centre of the peninsula. The year 304 would see events kick off with the Romans throwing their weight around against a close neighbour who was hardly a power any more; even our main source shows surprise that they should, in such a weakened condition, chance their arm against his people. In the time of the later kings and the early Republic, contests with the Aequi and the Volsci had been core activities, but the most recent conflict with the former had been way back in 388. Now, however, Roman military motion hardly skipped a beat; the same army with which the consul Publius Sempronius had just browbeaten the Samnites into terms was directed to again make war on the Aequi. The other consul came too, so this near neighbour was going to really feel the lash of Roman aggression over the next few years as a spluttering fire of resistance was kept alight.

Roman motivation was part deep resentment against those who they considered had transgressed as much as the Hernici when they allowed Samnite recruitment among their young menfolk in the last conflict. This was on top of what had become, over decades of conflict, a sense of mission that they had the exceptional qualities to not just be the greatest power in central Italy but to rule the rest as well. Obfuscating coarse ambition as noble idealism was a talent they shared with plenty of others in history. In these circumstances the wretched Aequi had little option other than war; they were not going to accept the imposition of Roman citizenship without suffrage short of a fight any more than the Hernici, but these people determined to die in harness while fighting for the right to survive were hardly a player by then. Their military muscle was wasted from years of peace, so it was a poorly-formed, ill-led levy that the Roman army, having taken a 40-mile pathway to enter Aequi country, discovered as they marched to within a few miles of their camp. Now with the enemy on their doorstep, they found they had no heart for open battle, so they dispersed, aiming to garrison their strong places and hoping to achieve something from behind stone walls. Publius Sempronius advanced unfazed, probing routes down rivers and glens and though it took fifty days, the contention is that between thirty-one and forty towns or hill forts were taken.[1] The imposition of this concatenation of woes was sufficient for the perpetrator to gain a triumph, though time would show even this blitzkrieg had far from totally suppressed the Aequi national spirit. On top of this, with the local status quo looking very fragile, these events threw such a scare into the Marsi, Paeligni, Marrucini and Frentani that, looking for at least temporary security, they fell over themselves to sign treaties with Rome.

Nor was it these people alone who wanted to be on the good side of the menacing Republic. In 302 we learn that the Vestini came into the fold as allies of the expanding polity. These people had, by the end of the fourth century, become reasonably familiar to strategists among the Roman elite, who hoped control there would be part of stopping potential enemies to the north and south joining up against them. It may seem anachronistic to assume this kind of strategic thinking, imposing backwards a sort of imagination that comes from our far greater familiarity with the physical shape of the Italian peninsula. Were the Romans really aware of the threat of Gauls, Etruscans, Umbrians and Samnites linking up in a threatening coalition? Did they really have that sort of picture in their mind, or were there many more dark zones of ignorance on the map? Was it not perhaps more that they were just regularizing to their advantage, in the normal way, settling relations with these people they had come across over the past few generations? Though such strategic thinking had certainly been shown before, in the earlier Samnite wars the Romans had made great efforts to achieve a power base in Apulia, making friends and taking hostages where they could. Indeed, there is a suggestion[2] that this was the root cause of the Second Samnite War, that even by the 320s the Samnites feared encirclement. Later in that war there was a real intent to come at this old antagonist from all round, from the north down the Liris valley, from the west out of Campania and from Apulia in the east. The establishment of a military post at Luceria had always been a part of this militarily well-thought-out project; they understood its strategic importance, as did their antagonist who made repeated efforts to stop them from digging in there.

The suppression of the Aequi appeared shaky when the Romans sowed more seeds of contention in 303 as they planted a fortified settlement of 6,000 Latins at Alba Fucens on the north shore of the lake. It turned out too much and the locals rose against this canker in their midst, desperately attacking the newly-built defences. Despite two consuls being on hand, the need to deal with these desperate Aequi, who popular opinion thought had been thoroughly subjugated more than a year before, caused a call to go out for Gaius Junius Bubulcus. This three-time consul and veteran of much Samnite fighting was made dictator and with Marcus Titinius as master of horse he steered an army down into enemy country where more places on the upper Anio were taken and annexed. After this, with his armies pressing down winding mountain paths to find and engage the opposition, he had little difficulty in overwhelming any remnants of defiance. Indeed, crushing his unhappy victims is claimed as the work of just a week, though it must have taken enough of a battle to shove these reprobates back into their place that we find the fasti recording his triumph in high summer 302. Yet this was still far from job done. It did not take long before, despite their main forces being scattered, the Aequi showed they were prepared to continue resistance, despite the suffering it brought. Confrontations continued, blazing into real fighting during 300–299, even though since 303 the Romans could easily reach their enemy's heartland, not just up the Anio but along the Liris valley from the new colony of Sora too. Despite the assertions that these outbreaks were of no consequence, they must have been much more than a police action, as the old hero Valerius Corvus was commissioned to deal with them, while his considerably less distinguished consular colleague was tasked with a major offensive in Etruria.

This Marcus Valerius Corvus Calenus – the last name celebrated his capture of Cales in 335 – was another super heavyweight of the period who, like Papirius Cursor, had been around almost as long as the wars themselves. Indeed, his adult life comprised seventy of the most significant years of Roman history. He had made his name even before the epic conflict with the Samnites began and died after it ended and as one of those great Roman duellists he first won repute against the Gauls. It is always this enemy, whether it be Torquatus earlier or Marcellus, that great warrior of the Hannibalic Wars who early in his career won the *spolia opima*, rivalling the legendary Romulus himself, when at the head of his own army he defeated and personally killed the king of the Gallic army he was facing. It was the size of these Celts, their fearsome aspect and tendency to fight buck naked that disturbed the Romans and made them the quintessential enemy:

> Two armed men were left by themselves in the midst, like gladiators more than soldiers, and by no means evenly matched, to judge from outward show. One had a body extraordinary for its size, and resplendent in a coat of shifting hues and armour painted and chased with gold: the other was of a middling stature for a soldier, and his arms were but indifferent to look at.[3]

They represented an existential threat in the way the Etruscans or even the Samnites never could. The Romans loved these stories, fitting as they did perfectly into the picture of the little man facing off against a hulking foe, seeing something central about themselves in the mirror of a David and Goliath tale. It was a special feeling, defending civilization against these barbarians, to contend with these outsized northerners with their long hair limed into stiff white spikes, and besting them was the path to enduring glory.

Having won a reputation and a name in individual combat, Valerius Corvus reached the consulship at an almost unbelievably young age of 23, but urgent business against Volsci did not allow him to bask in the pleasure of reaching so high so soon, though his achievements against them allowed the recording of his first triumph in 346. Apart from being instinctively brave, he also possessed something of the common touch; this patrician was not just happy to mingle with his soldiers as they competed in athletic competitions when off duty, but was involved in pushing reforms that would benefit the common people in the 'conflict of the orders'. He was also the man who talked down the mutineers of 342 as they marched on Rome, threatening a show of naked violence. So these campaigns undertaken about the turn of the century were to be enlivened by a character for whom Aequi, Marsi, Etruscans or Samnites had just been more enemies to pummel, in a life that is implausibly claimed as being 100 years. The existence of these vigorous old veterans, with military careers lasting more than fifty or sometimes even seventy years, does at times stretch credibility, though it should be remembered that there were contemporaries in the Greek world who matched even their robust and belligerent longevity. Among Alexander the Great's marshals, who battled for supremacy after his death, the greatest died in battle while leading his armies at Ipsus in central Anatolia at 80 years of age. Apart from this Antigonus Monophthalmus, two others, Lysimachus and Seleucus Nicator, are even claimed as fighting hand-to-hand at the head of their armies when both were in their eighth decade and if the duel itself may be hyperbole, that they were leading their fighting men at such an advanced age is the report of all the sources. Indeed, the man who most accurately recorded their deeds, Hieronymus of Cardia, was supposed to have died at 100 years of age while still active at the court of Antigonus Gonatus, king of Macedonia, the son of that same old warlord who had perished at the battle of Ipsus.

It was always going to be difficult, even with a commander of Valerius Corvus' qualities, to completely quell the Aequi. They were desperate people, fighting to the end in wild mountain glens, making it believable that some of them hung on until 299, particularly as they soon found themselves not alone in this struggle in the high hills of central Italy. Another near neighbour had reacted when Roman power showed itself too intrusive, as tidings arrived in 302 that 4,000 colonists were being dispatched to establish Carseoli at a site halfway between Alba Fucens and the town of Tibur. The chronology as so often here is confusing, as Livy mentions its foundation taking place four years later, so it may have been hearing of the project to plant this fortress as much as anything that stirred up another people who looked inevitably booked for trouble as the Romans pushed across the peninsula. The ground staked out for settlement apparently included Marsi territory, which is also odd as Carseoli, when established, occupied Aequi land, but perhaps it was close enough to their borders to cause concern. So this people, veering violently in policy, decided their alliance with Rome was not working for them, repudiated it and instead mobilized their fighters to stop the intruders from occupying their just distributed homesteads. This in 301 meant war, despite the recent olive branches exchanged with the Republic. So Valerius Corvus, as dictator, took charge of an invasion force to deal with this outbreak. Hope flickered for the Marsi only until the advent of the invaders in arms, when any resistance was crushed in battle and the remnants of the beaten army found themselves besieged in the towns of Milionia, Plestina and Fresilia. The chastened hill men, without hope of relief, entreated the invaders for peace and found what was imposed was bitter indeed. Rome was pitiless when it came to these particular troublesome neighbours; more of their land was annexed and the previous ascendancy of the Republic re-imposed with baleful intent.

Much of this aggressive action, handing out bloody noses and dismembering territory of folk who seemed little of a threat at all, had been a function of the desire to ensure there would be settlers and military posts in the country where the Via Valeria would pass, though there was another aspect of these road wars that is quite eye-catching. The continued threats and opportunities that transpired in the few years just before and after the turn of the century were the context in a confusing sequence in the executive merry-go-round of Roman politics. Despite being no longer at war with the Samnites, the evidence we have suggests that the Republic's leaders felt it necessary to initiate the repeated use of emergency measures. We now perceive an orgy of dictatorships which surely indicates tribulation that might not have been expected after signing off on a peace with their most powerful foe. So despite these not being years of great disaster or even critical fighting, evidence still suggests the Roman populace could be scared witless by trouble among their mountain neighbours. To all appearances two dictators were appointed in 302 and both these two – Junius Bubulcus and Valerius Corvus – are reported as triumphing respectively in the years 302 and 301, though the consular fasti argue for Valerius Corvus being dictator in 301. Is this credible? The idea of having two dictators in one year is not impossible and certainly these officers were not just appointed to face extreme danger; they sometimes were in demand to oversee elections, hammer nails into panels in temple walls or other arcane procedures. However, that the men appointed were veteran commanders certainly is suggestive of perceived military necessity. So the sequence remains troublesome, particularly as 301 may be one of the dictator years interposed to pad out Varronian chronology, and anyway reeks of the kind of exaggeration that has long known to be an issue for those drawing on the annalist Valerius Antias,[4] a man known not to be any sort of balanced chronicler, intent on burnishing the family name of the Valerii, however much it played fast and loose with the truth.

This flurry of special appointments arose just before a new century when the Romans took to addressing problems in different ways, a pattern of change that was almost certainly interrelated, even if we are not told so. The office of dictator after this time largely goes into retirement and it is decades before the office is resuscitated and then only on a couple of occasions during those Punic Wars that occupied almost the whole second half of the third century. The ad hoc was no longer sufficient when the threat to the state was almost constant and significant, so the Republic found other ways to ensure that her armies would be led by experienced and competent men. After this time the need to have one man at the helm was hardly felt at all, and we certainly no longer hear of those apparently contradictory arrangements where both consuls and a dictator shared command of the armies. The years ahead would see experienced generals kept on through forms of reiteration or as senior subordinates that ensured know-how and consistency at command level, while a Senate already coalescing into the body so familiar from the high Republic could lend strategic direction.

The operations that filled the year after the Samnite peace might have looked like disparate, unconnected activity but it was not. No doubt there was serendipity as well as intent, but there can be little question that in this time the Romans were digging in. The effect was that in less than half a century Roman possession had been made concrete in key parts of central Italy. Between 332 and 299 six new tribes had been added to the citizen rolls, the end of a process that was crucial in the Republic's capacity to hold on where her armies had conquered and her peacemakers had annexed. Two of these – the Aniensis and Teretina – were organized in the area north of the Volturnus that had been taken from the Aurunci in 314 and in the upper Anio where the Aequi had been losing land to her neighbour for generations and where now the west end of the corridor leading across the whole of Italy was completely incorporated into the state, while colonies held the middle section and alliances forged with other Sabellian tribes kept the country leading to the Adriatic secure.

Twenty years earlier settler communities had been given tribal status in both the middle Liris valley and the Agger Falernus in fine wine-growing country above the Volturnus River just north of Campania; many conjured out of expats who could enjoy a yeoman lifestyle on lands taken from previous owners who had the misfortune to rouse the Republic's ire. Running their farms and taking lead roles in their districts, they would have already done much to ensure local security. Defences would have been built and town watches organized, while some of the migrants would have been veterans who could provide a real iron core for the army reserves raised for local defence. When enemy armies came boiling out of the nearby hills to tear up their farms and estates, these planters might not have been able to face them in battle but they could at least secure the most important posts to wait in garrison for the enemy to retire or for armies sent from Rome to come to their rescue. So unless the foe came in such force and with such determination that they could cope with this first line of defence, they would make little permanent impact. The Romans had also been pinning down the edges of their fabric of power by the planting of a number of colonies. Cales had been established in

334 by 2,500 men from the city proletariat, Latins and other allies, and Fregellae in 328, Suessa Aurunca in 313 and Interamna Lirenas in 312, showing a leadership determined on putting sinew into the recently-won suzerainty, not only upriver from the capital but south and down the coast as well.

If the people who saw the Via Valeria snaking their way did not like this further example of Roman energy and ambition, they were not the only unhappy Italians sniffing the air with disquiet, concerned about what their neighbour's burgeoning power would mean to them. As the tentacles of her power had spread, so had her potential troubles. Real Roman influence among the ancient communities of Etruria and Umbria is difficult to quantify at this time. We certainly know that the Faliscan people not far north of the Tiber and the Volsinii near Lake Bolsena continued to be troublesome and could hardly be considered part of any Roman confederation, though up the Tiber valley they were safely posted at Sutrium, where they seem to have had a colony installed since the 380s. This place held open the road to central Etruria, while since Fabius Rullianus penetrated the Ciminian forests they also had other allies in Umbria. The people of Camerinum stayed solid friends in all the coming travails and there clearly were pro-Roman factions in charge in places as far north as Arretium, where something of a class war erupted at this time with the commons rising against the ruling family who, from the information we have, look very like Roman protégés.

Despite a much-burnished self-image of fortitude in the face of peril, the Roman public was as jumpy as anybody else when desperate rumour ruled. It took little to draw anxious men congregating in the forum to wait for news from the front. The troubles with the Marsi were already making people nervous when another cause for concern sent shock waves into every corner of city life. A real threat to the Republic's position in the north had arisen when the dictator Valerius Corvus, just returned from dealing with the Marsi, commenced an Etrurian campaign that did not go well from the beginning. The commander was almost immediately recalled to the city to take the auspices, but whatever was foretold by the flying birds or thunder and lightning from the heavens, the upshot in the field was far from auspicious. In the absence of the old veteran, his master of horse almost supervised a disaster. He had allowed his men to get sloppy; clearly no proper reconnaissance had kept him abreast of enemy movements and when he led out part of the army to forage in the countryside they were pounced upon, some standards were captured and a good many men killed before the rest, running for their lives, got back to the safety of their camp.

The response was apparently immediate, ensuring that first Rome itself was put on high alert, with legal business halted, weapons stockpiled and guards organized at the city gates, while Valerius Corvus hurried back to confront the enemy. He might have been in his eighth decade, but this old fighter was going to show he could still pull up trees in his second stint as dictator after an interim of almost forty years. In fact, when he arrived among the defeated army he found things not in such bad shape as he expected, with the camp broken up and withdrawn into a more defensible position and the soldiers who had disgraced themselves being disciplined by having to bivouac outside the ramparts with no tents to cover them. The rest of the men, taking the point, were eager to prove themselves by getting straight back at the enemy. Valerius Corvus, taking charge, pushed forward, striking deep into enemy territory well up into coastal Etruria to near Rusellae in the neighbourhood of modern-day Grosseto. The Etruscan army that had given such trouble to the master of horse was disinclined to allow the intruders to create a desert in the heart of their country, so they followed hard on the dictator's heels, and once close by, they 'attempted an attack by ambush'. However, Valerius Corvus, keeping his men in good order, saw off these bushwhackers, driving them back to their camp and through it and out over earthworks that crumbled under the press of the Etruscans trying to escape. Many got off to safety but they had suffered enough and, bargaining desperately for their lives, they offered a year's pay to the soldiers and grain supplies as well, to be allowed to send emissaries to Rome under conditions of truce, that was eventually extended to two years, by a Roman administration not prepared to countenance full peace terms.[5]

At a beetling overhang above the Nar, where the river had cut a narrow gorge in the geographical centre of Italy, stood Nequinum in a region that had seen the footprint of cavemen in the oldest times and is noted as a significant community since 600. While Valerius Corvus, elected consul for the fifth time in 300, made a last foray against the Aequi hold-outs, his colleague Quintus Appuleius Pansa was deputed to deal with this Umbrian border stronghold, and it was his endeavours that kicked off a continuous two-year campaign. The plan was simple to snap up this strategic place, but the approaches were steep and difficult and from the beginning it was clear that to besiege it would be time-consuming and hazardous, though having friends at Ocriculum helped. This south Umbrian frontier town had concluded an alliance with Rome in 308 while many other of their compatriots were suffering defeat at the hands of Fabius Rullianus. They were olive farmers and not inclined to countenance the root-and-branch destruction of their priceless groves that would undoubtedly have occurred if they aligned themselves with their fighting brethren. So instead they came to terms and now the invaders reaped the benefit, as these new friends put their *oppidum* (fortified settlement), 9 miles south of Nequinum, at their service as a base. After the Romans passed on to the attack they discovered what a hard nut they had to crack, a reality suggested by fine late medieval fortifications topping naturally formidable defensive positions. How soon it took to become clear that the struggle would go into the next consul's tenure is not known, but as winter approached and Appuleius Pansa's term of office had almost concluded he had only been able to set up his siege lines and blockade the place. It became apparent, as the men tried to make themselves comfortable in the siege lines near the River Nar, that any conclusion would have to await the arrival of the next year's commander.

This was becoming a major effort and the following fighting season saw both the new consuls, Marcus Fulvius Paetus and Titus Manlius Torquatus, take up the burden on this Umbrian front. It was a weary affair for both sides with the Romans encamped below the town, well dug in but able to make little headway against walls they found almost impossible to get up to. They were reduced to the expedient of trying to tunnel under the walls, always a frustrating business, but at least after blocking every bolthole, the blockade they had clamped over the routes into the place started to bite, leaving the townsfolk despairing of relief as famine loomed. Some of the weaker links among the locals who lived right up by the walls, gaunt from hunger and in despair at the outcome, tried to at least save themselves. They dug a tunnel from one of their houses under the defences, crawled out hungry and filthy, and approached the besiegers with a promise to let them in. To ensure against a trap, two scouts were sent back with one of the defectors, while the other was kept as hostage. On finding the proposition genuine, 300 besiegers went down the passageway during the night and on arriving, overcame the guard at the nearest gate and let the rest of the attacking army into a helpless town.

The impact of the arrival of the whole enemy force in their midst completely shattered any inclination to resistance on behalf of the defenders, who fled or surrendered leaving Nequinum in Roman hands. This had been a substantial undertaking, taking a significant fortress that controlled a route that invaders had so often taken in the past. Apart from acting as a defensive bulwark, it could function as a forward station for Roman armies looking to expand into Umbria and northern Etruria. So now it was no question of some peace where the inhabitants could get away with submission and tribute; it was going to be annexation, as settlers were dispatched to set up a colony on the site that was renamed Narnia. This settlement, implanted where Nequinum had stood, where now the broken wreck of an Augustine bridge steps out to cross the gorge, had taken two fighting seasons to establish but at least from after 299 there would be another lock, along with Sutrium and Nepi, on the Tiber route into the heart of Etruria. The Romans had had to fight in this part of the world many times over in the past decades, but time would tell that from then on, here at least, few threats would materialize in the future.

* * *

Two names, Corvus and Torquatus, advertised the sanguine intercourse that had defined Rome's relations with a people we have already had cause to mention. There is a great story, though perhaps one with not much veracity, about how these Gauls who trashed Rome came into central Italy; a tale beginning with heady romance but one that would lead to a traumatic encounter between a people new to the Italian world and the city of Rome, that in 100 years of Republican regime had established itself as the most important place in Latium. It commenced with action around the Etruscan city of Clusium, a place that had been significantly involved in Roman politics on a number of occasions before. Legend has it that Lars Porcena, a king of the city, led a confederation that attempted to re-impose the rule of the Roman King Tarquinius Superbus over the town on the Tiber. The first attempt at reinstatement had gone awry after the Battle of Silva Arsia, but with the entrance of Lars Porsena this interference became dangerously effective, with the city besieged and only with help of friendly neighbours ensuring she did not have to bend the knee again to regal authority. However, hostages still had to be handed over to Lars Porsena and recently-acquired land returned to the Etruscans of Veii. The first-century AD historian Tacitus makes it clear that there was another tradition, where Rome actually fell and after a short period of Etruscan domination, proceeded to the full installation of a Republican constitution. Some 100 years after this, lascivious intrigues in the royal house of Clusium had lit a powder train. The city's aging ruler had given his son in trust to a man called Aruns to be his guardian, but when his charge grew to manhood he repaid his foster father by seducing his wife. Unable to gain redress against a scion of the royal house, the cuckolded husband fermented an awful revenge. Travelling to the Gauls as a merchant selling olives, figs and wine, as well as making money he persuaded them that they could easily take over the lands where these wondrous goods were produced, that Clusium would be just the ticket as a new home for these peerless fighters who could easily overcome any local resistance.

Yet who were these blond boys looking for a drink and who liked the vintage on offer over the mountains? Their history in general is taxing, but what is sure is that these people adversely affected the Roman psyche in a way few others did. The blood of those old senators slaughtered in the sack of the 380s had long been washed away, and even more reality shouts that the Gauls never provided the test that was provided by the Samnites or even the Etruscans; they did not have the numbers, the perseverance or the proximity, but still it was in the mind that it mattered. These blue-eyed northerners with heavy pendant mustachios had been around for generations arriving from north of the Alps in the sixth and fifth centuries, but their advent into what was named for them as Cisalpine Gaul is not easy to understand, with even archaeology hardly helping at all. There are no finds definitively showing their presence in the Po valley before the fifth century, but then burials found of different societies north and south of the Alps can look extremely similar.

Diodorus claims them as being created when Hercules inseminated a big-boned Celtic beauty whose offspring Galates carved out a major territory from which the whole of the people took their name.[6] He thought alcohol was behind developments from the beginning:

> As a consequence those Gauls who are deprived of these fruits make a drink out of barley which they call zythos or beer, and they also drink the water with which they cleanse their honeycombs. The Gauls are exceedingly addicted to the use of wine and fill themselves with the wine which is brought into their country by merchants, drinking it unmixed, and since they partake of this drink without moderation by reason of their craving for it, when they are drunken they fall into a stupor or a state of madness.[7]

A race of drunkards envisaged spitting bombast in deep, harsh voices when not enjoying the lyric poetry of their bards. Tall, pale and muscled with hair lime-water washed so 'that their appearance is like that of Satyrs and Pans, since the treatment of their hair makes it so heavy and coarse that it differs in no respect from the mane of horses.'[8] They sang and boasted of their own and their ancestors' deeds before single combat and practised head-hunting, embalming those of their 'most distinguished' enemies to be kept in chests as prized heirlooms. Apparently a belief in reincarnation encouraged them to be lethally quarrelsome with each other and unheedingly daring when facing their enemies.

A tall story passed down the generations was that approximately at the beginning of the sixth century, when Lucius Tarquinius Priscus was king of Rome, another monarch called Ambigatus ruled a Gallic people who had become too numerous for their lands to sustain them. To solve the problem of overpopulation, he sent two of his sister's sons, Bellovesus and Segovesus, to win new territory for his landless subjects. The latter was deputed to go to Germany, while the former led the Arverni, Senones, Aedui, Ambarri, Carnutes and Aulerci peoples into Italy:

> They themselves crossed the Alps through the Taurine passes and the pass of the Duria; routed the Etruscans in battle not far from the River Ticinus, and learning that they were encamped in what

was called the country of the Insubres, who bore the same name as an Haeduan canton, they regarded it as a place of good omen, and founded a city there which they called Mediolanium.[9]

It would have taken a while for these intruders to fully push down the Po valley, establishing staging posts of power along the road, to the Adriatic littoral where the local Umbrians found themselves overrun. Also we learn that it was the Senones, who may have been related to the Gallic people who lived just south-east of Paris in Caesar's time, who settled down east of the Apennines by the sea. In fact, they were probably not established fully until around 400 after many more of them arrived, again traversing the Alps and passing through where their cousins, the Insubres and Boii, had settled in the Po valley before making hard miles to help chivvy the East Umbrians out of their Adriatic holdings. The territory they alighted in stretched from modern-day Forli to Sena Gallica which they founded as their headquarters. These were the last wave; late-comers who to find a homeland progressed almost as far down as Ancona where Greeks from Syracuse would soon found a colony.

If much of this background is legendary what does seem pretty definite is that in the 380s a band of these Senones was on the move from the Adriatic over the Apennines, crashing through Etruria and into the Tiber valley. Led by a warlord remembered as Brennus, they arrived outside Clusium,[10] not a people on the move but mainly young men, mercenary warriors without their families, either already hired and on their way to war or going south in the hope of finding employment, probably in the armies of Dionysius I of Syracuse in Sicily, who was at the time campaigning in the south of Italy. Their numbers must have amounted to several thousands or they would not have been able to confront first the forces of Clusium, then the Romans, but much more and they would have surely have been too expensive for any putative employers in Magna Graecia. These Celts might have been discounted soldiers for hire, but still the likes of Syracuse could not have afforded great hordes of them on top of the outlay they were having to make on not only native forces but their navy as well.

It is conceivable that they wanted land to settle in Etruria, but much more likely they were just demanding money with menaces to succour them as they marched south. Whichever it was, their arrival determined the Etruscans to ask for help from Rome and the story is they responded by sending three brothers of the Fabii family to try to talk the Gauls out of this unwarranted aggression. However, instead of calling for cool heads all round, the siblings joined in with the Etruscans in fighting off the invaders, one dealing a death blow with a spear through the side of a significant Gallic chief. As if this was not enough, when these characters returned home, instead of being reprimanded for failing to act as neutral arbitrators, they were elected to the highest office, proceedings that so incensed the Senones that they dropped everything to exact revenge. This activity around Clusium could all be nonsense; it may all be just an explanation of why the Gauls arrived when they did and was also nicely suggestive of Rome's role as defender of Italy against these wild outsiders. What is certain is that Brennus and his freebooters would have needed little excuse to plunder Rome if the opportunity offered itself.

It was high summer as Rome suffered a trauma that burned itself into the people's common consciousness for centuries to come. Firstly the Battle of the Allia, fought on 18 July, that remained a cursed day throughout Roman history, was bad enough. As the Roman army, cobbled together at short notice, had hurried 11 miles up the left bank of the Tiber to where the Allia tributary joined, there they found the Gallic army already arrived and crowding to the attack. The Roman commander would receive criticism for failing to build a defended camp prior to fighting that might have provided a bolt hole for his men after their army quit the field, but it had been a rush with no time for auspices or speeches of encouragement before they faced a fierce assault that they were not able to resist for long. The onslaught by the best of the Gallic warriors against what were the weaker links in the defenders' line was short and dreadful, so when the Roman reserve was driven from the hill they occupied, the main body disintegrated too. Few were killed in battle but the aftermath was different; the units on the left near the river stampeded in panic and those not overwhelmed on the banks dived in to escape, only to be showered with javelins, dying at once or wounded, weighed down with their armour and carried off to their death by the current. Others were cut down, unable to escape in the disorder, but many were luckier, managing to find a crossing-point, most likely the bridge at Fidenae, and get off to the defended post of Veii. Others, straggling back to the city that they had not been able to save, could at least provide a garrison for the Capitol.

Stunned by such an overwhelming success, the victors at first suspected a trick and hesitated in pursuit, but after what they had achieved sank in they stripped the dead and prepared to push on. Then these dangerous men barrelled into the ill-defended city through the Colline Gate – the place had no stone walls at this time – in the wake of those of the routed legionaries who had not made it to Veii. The taking of Rome is undisputedly historical, mentioned by the likes of Aristotle and Theopompus, though the Capitol, unless Quintus Ennius the poet is to be believed, remained untaken. Despite this bedrock, the details of what transpired next are extremely problematical. The Capitoline geese saving the citadel is proverbial, but more significant is that the defenders paid a ransom, sending envoys to offer 1,000 pounds in gold to persuade their tormentors to depart their home. Equally the versions of what happened to the intruders and the ransom they had extorted are multifarious. Strabo suggests not only that the people of Caere took in numerous refugees including the vestal virgins carrying the sacred fire that was freighted with the very soul of the polity, but also that their army defeated Brennus's men as they were traversing Sabine country, something for which the Romans showed little gratitude, so that by his own day the place was a ruin with fewer people living there than in the curative hot springs nearby. Others either have it that the Gauls were paid off, departing with their ill-gotten gains, or that Furius Camillus, in one of many apocryphal stories associated with him, returning from exile, rallied the homefolk, defeated the invaders in battle and took back the ransom money. Suetonius in his biography of Tiberius even has it that the Gallic band safely made their way back north and only centuries later was the gold recovered when the Romans invaded either the Po valley or Gaul itself.

What the real damage was during the sack is just as challenging; archaeology has not revealed a burn level of the appropriate age to substantiate a world turned upside-down, though later Roman citizens clearly believed that many of the archives collected before the fall of the city were lost, so that they considered any retelling of events before that time must be suspect, leaving so much before as just unsubstantial story and myth. What is certain is that the shame of the defeat was real enough, lasting for centuries to come and ensuring that the rumblings of people on the move north of the Alps would always reverberate in the streets of Rome. The loss of face as these northerners made whoopee in its streets tested their already fragile credibility as local hegemon. It was not long before this erosion of their position showed. Praeneste had been an important member of the Latin League even when Alba Longa headed that confederation, but by the turn of the fourth century had thrown in her lot with Rome instead. After the Senones had done their worst, this neighbour was found in the ranks of those lined up against the Republic as she struggled to recapture her position of pre-eminence in the decades before strife with Samnium took centre stage. Praeneste was far from being alone, as the Tiburtines, a number of Volscian towns and even some of Rome's own colonies turned against the ambitious people that had suffered so. It was a struggle, but the Romans were eventually able to re-establish dominance, creating a base for the takeover of all central Italy. So perhaps there had been exaggeration, that few men really fell on the Alia, that when the Gauls defeated the legions sent out to stop their terrifying progress most of the army was able to get away to Veii. If a few old greybeard senators were hacked down, even the Capitol taken and the intruders took all that was easily removable, apart from that Roman life and potential power was perhaps not so massively affected.

For more than forty years after these adventures the Gauls hovered, sometimes playing a considerable part in the goings-on at the heart of the peninsula. The first time after Brennus's attack that they are noticed again is in 384 when a Gallic force was involved as part of Dionysius 1 of Syracuse's attack on Pyrgi, the port of Caere, but the enterprise turned out badly when a defending army caught the Gauls on the hop and worsted them in combat. There may have been trouble in 367 when Furius Camillus is attested as being called on to see Gallic intruders off, but it was in the cauldron of a Tibur war that these bold warriors really could not be kept out. From 361, almost certainly as mercenaries, they were employed to beef up that Sabine town's arms in a desperate fight between close neighbours. This community was situated in the elbow of the Anio River and from its high defensible eminence, where water cascaded below two small temples to Vesta and the Sibyl of Tibur, through what is now the modern Villa Gregoriana, it would have been possible to see smoke hazing the air above the city of Rome 20 miles away.

Where these soldiers for hire came from we are not sure. Polybius seems to think they had been recruited in the north, either in Cisalpine country or that they were freebooting warriors from Gaul itself. All of this is possible as we know that they were widely utilized by Greek cities in Sicily and south Italy, so they might have marched either from Magna Graecia or the north to join their new employers, who needed all the help they could get against a resurgent Rome. Near what is now the Parco di Villa Ada where the Via Salaria led across the Anio, the Gauls camped just over the other side of the bridge from the Roman army. This third milestone on salt road where the defenders encamped provided the stage for the victory of Titus Manlius Torquatus in an individual combat against an enemy champion; a reverse that apparently so traumatized the defeated man's comrades that they upped sticks and returned up the Anio to Tibur. Then, after being resupplied by these generous friends, the whole of them decamped for Campania. The new season of 360 saw their return from the fat southern country, ready once more to earn the pay on offer from the treasurers at Tibur. Again, like the year before, they took the fight right to Rome, approaching the Colline Gate when the defending soldiers turned them round and forced a retreat again. Fading back up the Anio towards Tibur, they only just managed to evade another Roman army that had been encamped near the town, sent there to occupy the Tiburtine levy. The locals came out from behind the protection of their walls to help face this onslaught, ensuring that most gained safety within the city precincts. The fact that, despite this less than distinguished performance, the Roman commander still claimed a triumph is reported as causing considerable merriment among their antagonists.

The war ground on; 359 saw raids and counter-raids by the neighbours, but the Gauls were little involved until the subsequent year when they are heard of at Praeneste, now participating as an ally of Tibur. Coming up from the south, having again wintered in Campania, they encamped at a place called Pedum, a little south of their employer's city. In response a dictator was appointed to organize a counter-thrust against these intruders encamped so threateningly proximate. This man, Gaius

Sulpicius Peticus, was in luck as the Latins, looking for an insurance policy against the continuing presence in their bailiwick of a bunch of destructive Gauls, stumped up their troop contribution. Knowing that time was on his side, the dictator decided to wait and let the enemy run out of supplies rather than stake everything on a battle, but this did not suit his soldiers' mood at all. They clamoured round his tent, deploring this unprecedented docility and demanding to go into action. Under pressure he agreed, but not before hatching a tactical plan to leave 1,000 men hidden behind a nearby hill, many of them muleteers mounted on their own animals to trip an ambush when the battle was under way, though this is a story so often told it should hardly be uncritically accepted.

Whatever the exact details, the Gauls suffered sufficiently so that after 357 the war slowed down and they are no longer mentioned as playing any part when it recommenced in earnest. Without their support the Tiburtine forces were unable to hold out long against their aggressive neighbour. Three more years saw them, their satellite towns and Praeneste forced to terms. The Gauls came back again in a few years, appearing in Latium in 350, though this time it was just stand-alone brigandage until in the following years they hooked up with a Greek fleet that might well have been part of a project undertaken by a Syracusan employer. The numbers are claimed as suspiciously huge, but they were certainly sufficiently confident to camp in the heart of Latium where a plebeian consul tried to beard them in their lair after his patrician colleague, a Scipio, was taken ill. He assembled a four-legion levy, picking particularly the younger men, their elders being left in reserve in case of defeat, with their arms and armour taken from the temple of Mars outside the Porta Capena, while standards were bought forward by quaestors who had drawn them from the treasury. This well-procured force shattered and rolled back the intruders onto an eminence called the Alban citadel, where Monte Cavo now rises above Lake Albano. The victory, however stirringly reported, was insufficient to rid them of these raiders, who happily wintered in the defensible terrain they occupied. The next season, 349–348, they showed themselves little depleted and completely disinclined to keep their heads down. The only people who in fact turned out able to tame these marauders were not the prematurely jubilant men of Rome but a bunch of rival brigands, Greek pirates infesting the seas around Antium and the mouth of the Tiber who, on encountering the Gauls, administered a bloody nose to these competitors in the quest for the riches of the region.

A determination by the Latins to no longer stump up troops to aid legionary armies consistently failing to eradicate the upsurge of large-scale banditry that had broken out on both the land and the sea at least brought out the best in the Republican leadership. It inspired even greater efforts, with ten legions – surely an exaggeration – being raised and another Camillus, the son of a great father, deputed to the task of handling the intruders. He took four of these regiments into the Pontine district to constrain the Gauls while a praetor took an equal number to guard against the Greeks, with two remaining in reserve at Rome. This is the occasion when Marcus Valerius, the other great duellist of the era alongside Manlius Torquatus, made his name. Facing a huge and heavily-armoured Gallic champion between the opposing battle lines, he managed to down his man with the assistance of a raven that landed on his rival's helmet, scratching at his eyes, and furnishing the new hero with the nickname Corvus that he would carry through many decades to come. The contest of the armies soon followed the pattern of the duel, with the Gauls fleeing headlong and scattering about the country before re-forming to march south to Apulia and Magna Graecia.

Years later in 330 there was another scare. While at war with the people of Privernum, north of Terracina and their allies at Fondi, the whole Roman army was advancing to the attack when they received word of a great Gallic horde in the offing. A new consul assembled an army at Veii to face the threat, but then nothing happened. So it transpired that as the epic contests with the Samnites, Umbrians and Etruscans unfolded, no reality of Gallic fury ever arose to compound the already sufficient terrors touching the tenants of Roman lands. The fourth of those nations that would combine for the climatic events of the 290s was off in the wings, not even a peripheral threat as the Romans faced the last great revolt by the Latins, or for the first two Samnite Wars and rounds of troubles in Etruria and Umbria. They were nothing of a distraction as these crucial developments transpired in that very centre of the peninsula, proximate to the nucleus of the Republican polity.

* * *

Of the men who had ruffled Umbrian feathers around Nequinum, which led to the establishment of Narnia, one had a very famous name. He was the son of a hero of one of the great Roman stories, of civic *virtùs* triumphing over family sentiment and who was also an even more famous Gaul butcher than Valerius Corvus. He had killed his Gallic giant in the war of 361, stripping his body of not just his arms and armour but a huge gold torch from which he got his cognomen. Yet he really caught the imagination when, before battle against the Latin League, in 340 he had his son executed for disobeying orders and indulging in a duel with a Latin champion; Homeric stuff that had not received praise from the stern parent as the need for absolute discipline in the ranks had trumped any paternal feelings. This had been more than forty years earlier and now the brother of the youngster who suffered was himself about to come to a sticky end. After the Nequinum victory he was dispatched again to take the war to Etruria and the story was that he had hardly led his soldiers over the border when he fell from his horse after indulging in vigorous cavalry exercises and died of his injuries. However, this account probably hides something; after all, the death of a consul was in this period, surprisingly considering the constant campaigning, a very infrequent occurrence. Not until the Hannibalic Wars eighty years later did that terrible general oversee an extreme and brutal culling of Roman magistrates at the highest level, so at this time a consul actually being killed on campaign surely suggests a considerable military setback that Livy and his sources were unhappy about recognizing. Roman accounts were always prone to mask defeat under the guise of accident, and would have been reluctant to admit the reality behind the loss of one of their consuls. This particularly would be true as these events were connected to an awful threat. The Gauls were back; the same people who had left such a shadow on the Roman psyche in the past and the likelihood is that it was they combined with Rome's Etruscan and Umbrian enemies who had defeated and killed the consul.

It was movements in the remote margins of the world north of the Alps that were at the root of a returning menace in a new century. Earlier terrors might have had time to be dissipated for the occupants of Italy, but from transalpine Gauls new freebooters were coming over the mountains in 299, looking for advantage. Whether this meant land or loot, their cousins already settled in Cisalpine Gaul were concerned what their arrival might mean. Persuaded or paid off, the newcomers passed through the Po River country, attracting a few of the more adventurous of the Gauls established there to join their ranks on the way, making it into Etruria. Here they joined up with armed men of local city levies and plundered their way through into Roman territory until, happy with what they had procured, withdrew laden with booty. That they then fell out over their ill-gotten gains may be true or just that was what was expected of barbarians who showed 'undisciplined habits of drinking and gorging themselves'. This raid, whether accurate in detail or not, advertised thrillingly the presence of a wild and dangerous people returning to the Roman orbit, a presence that had so often before presaged portentous and dangerous developments.

So if the Gauls had not been back for forty years, when they ventured south again it was with a bang, instigating the kind of threat that Rome had not seen for many years. Their return around 299 had coincided with a world outside Rome that was peopled with worried folk. As the century turned, the Romans appeared to many to be just getting everywhere in mainland Italy. Their armies had won battles near Perusia and made friends with towns even further north; they had completed the establishment of a key stronghold in northern Apulia at Luceria and made treaties of alliance with many other places in that region. In Campania, the elites in Capua, at Nola and elsewhere were their firm friends and both the coastal and inland areas between there and Rome were peppered with their colonies, while around the Bay of Naples were Greek towns that now mostly saw their futures as totally committed to the Roman cause. Such an influence was held tight by the new road leading south from the capital, facilitating communications with rich Campania, allowing not just merchants but most importantly armies to get to that crucial borderland in double-quick time, when those down in south Italy who did not mean the Republic well threatened. Also in what is now Abruzzo, most of the Sabellian tribes there had been suppressed and driving through their lands the Via Valeria clearly headed towards the Adriatic.

Now with ferocious Gallic warriors churning around north central Italy, much must have seemed to be up for grabs by those who feared the expanding Republic. Whether the Etruscans were being threatened to extort money and land by the newcomers or were hiring them as mercenaries is not crystal clear. Certainly after the raid on Rome they were content to be paid off by their allies, who had to dig deep into their war chest to ensure their fields and cities were left unmolested, but this was only going to relieve the shadowing menace for a season. The Senones, who had settled along the Adriatic east of Italy's limestone spine, and the raiders from over the Alps who may well have wintered among them or along the banks of the Po had no intention of leaving it at that. If their intention was to act again in confederation with Rome's northern enemies, then a very real threat had only been postponed. Indeed, as this people had, less than 100 years before, crushed the legions in battle and taken Rome itself, if they now came mob-handed as the auxiliaries of the Etrurians and Umbrians the result could be catastrophic. Roman hegemony, so hard won and recently established in this region, could well be in the balance.

That the attitude of Rome's northern Italian neighbours would remain belligerent despite past defeats was not difficult to predict. The Umbrians were outraged by the presence of the Roman colony at Narnia, sitting four-square on country they used to control, with its very raison d'être being to exercise control over the people living near the Tiber valley, just as Rome's long-term alliance with the folk from Camerinum ensured a presence on the eastern side of the Apennines. This, apart from memories of when the Romans had garrisons installed at Perusia, meant they could be expected to join any anti-Roman axis available. That many Etruscan communities would involve themselves was not in doubt either. The ambassadors of those already fighting Rome had been circulating round the other major places to try to coordinate military efforts and the promise that the Gauls might be joining as confederates was a massive tonic to the process.

However, before this diplomatic activity came to fruition, the death of the consul Manlius Torquatus was the warrant for a last hurrah for the veteran marshal Valerius Corvus. These Romans loved an ancient hero, as is repeatedly evinced in these pages. The fight to the death that gave him his nickname was portentous for his long life and now, in response to the fatality, he was swiftly elected as replacement consul to take up the gage, sent north and linking up with the grieving legions in Etruria. It is asserted that just his presence was sufficient to intimidate the enemy, who refused offers of combat and quailed behind their city walls for the remainder of the fighting season while the Romans had a free hand to wreck all the enemy country they could reach, although the reality might well have been that those in the Etruscan councils had determined to keep their powder dry until the putative Etruscan, Umbrian and Gallic confederacy could be made operational.

* * *

There had been plenty of interaction between Rome and the vast orbit of a wider world over the years. Her merchants had explored Gaul and Iberia, the state itself had contracted several treaties with Carthage and envoys may have reached the court of Alexander at Babylon just before the great man's death. So late in 301 news would certainly have reached ports on the Adriatic coast of Italy and registered with many other peoples around the peninsula that the greatest Hellenistic king had died in climactic battle on the plains of central Anatolia at the venerable age of 80. However, if the fate of the eastern Mediterranean and West Asian world was up in the air, things looked very different in central Italy. Despite the fact that only nine decades earlier Rome's streets had run with the blood of their elders and the town's rafters echoed to the cries of Gallic conquerors, since then they had established a putative hegemony running from Sutrium and Narnia in the north as far as Campania and Apulia in the south and deep into the centre of the Italian leg around Lake Fucino.

Yet this too would not remain untested and waves from this wider world to the east would play a part as a trigger in the third and climactic conflict between Rome and Samnium. The Republic had been involved in Apulia and Lucania before and was well-informed on Magna Graecia, the region around the heel, toe and sole of the Italian boot where Hellenes, from both the Greek islands and the mainland, had settled after leaving home, feeling the pressure of overpopulation or the threat of enemies menacing their borders. Croton, Locris, Thurii, Heraclea and Rhegium were some of the most famous but Tarentum was the greatest and by far the most crucial player in the sequence that unfolded. The rulers of this town had long had concerns about what went on near their northern borders, even offering arbitration between the warring parties in the Second Roman-Samnite War when fighting developed around Luceria. Their attitude had been aggressive, suggesting they would come in to help the side that accepted their adjudication against the one that refused. If on this occasion it turned out to be little more than hot air, later it would be this city that would be at the centre of a chain of events that brought Roman-Samnite relations to the brink.

There was a tradition of hiring in Balkan mercenary leaders to fight the wars of this people who were themselves more inclined to make money from seaborne commerce than to fight their own battles. They often tapped up Epirote or Spartan royalty to bring over bespoke armies to deal with their local Italian enemies and in 303 they got involved with just such a man from over the water. Cleonymus was a Greek prince from one of the kingly houses of Sparta in the Peloponnese; though the second son of King Cleomenes II, this did not ensure succession once his father died in 309/308. He was of 'a violent and arbitrary temper', characteristics which were apparently too much even for his notoriously bellicose homefolk, allowing a cousin called Areus to inherit that Spartan crown traditionally worn by one of the Agiad line. What he had done to gain such a damaging reputation is not recorded, but a taster is given from many years later in 272. By that time he had married a lady called Chilonis, a Eurypontid from the other Spartan royal line, but she had a fancy for the son of Areus, the very man who had deprived him of his hereditary rights years before. This double humiliation was just too much for a dangerous personality and was the rationale behind his inducing that other adventurer, Pyrrhus of Epirus, to invade the Peloponnese and set him up as ruler of Sparta as part of an overall plan to establish that king's suzerainty over all the country below the isthmus of Corinth.[11]

This quarrelsome man had, when younger, been looking to carve out a kingdom to which he felt his pedigree entitled him when the Tarentines called him west across the Ionian Sea. They were hoping to utilize those military qualities that were assumed to be in the DNA of the Spartan elite against their perennial Lucanian foes. The details of his adventure starting in 303 are opaque, but first fighting for the Tarentines, then on his own account, this soldier of fortune caused a real stir in south-eastern Italy. Arriving with 5,000 professional Greek fighters, soon bolstered by 22,000 Tarentine horse and foot, he made friends with other players in Magna Graecia as well as the Messapians, the tribe occupying Italy's heel. If these numbers Cleonymus committed to the field appeared good, they were a pretty heterogeneous bunch, though still sufficiently threatening that the Lucanians hardly put up a fight before folding, with some even joining in with the Spartan when he pitched into Metapontum, a city state located west down the coast from Tarentum.

This was destabilizing stuff in a complex of south Italian sovereignties and was almost certainly part of what encouraged the Samnites to look south to make up for their loss of influence in the centre of the peninsula. Years of wars with Rome, despite having their quota of victories, still had in the long term seen a diminution in comparative power and spheres of influence of these two rivals. So when this difficult time for Lucanians, threatened by Tarentine and Spartan intruders, was advertised in the whole region, it was almost ineluctable that the leaders in Bovianum, Caudium and Maleventum were bound to begin to consider what advantage they might reap. So it is no surprise that within the next couple of years Samnite armies filled a power vacuum appearing in Lucanian country, demanding a submission and adherence that might soon mean that local men and money could be weighed in the balance when the inevitable next encounter with the Roman Republic supervened.

The Lucanians were as proud and independent as their Samnite cousins and despite these menaces emanating from beyond their northern borders, not long after Cleonymus had battered them from the other direction, they were still prepared to fight. Yet they hardly had the resources left and in a number of encounters, events fell out so badly that 'having lost many districts already and being in danger of losing all the rest of their land',[12] despair drove policy and the Lucanians found themselves with little option but to throw themselves on the mercy of a people who had in the past showed they were able to handle the aggressive hill men who were encamped deep in their territory. Unfortunately the history of their relations with Rome had not always been friendly, as we learn they had themselves broken a treaty with that power not that long before. Yet it seems with the Samnites threatening to lay their country in ashes, there were no other choices and envoys were dispatched on the road to the Tiber town, accompanied by the sons of the leaders of all the foremost Lucanian communities brought along as hostages to show how complete their determination was to keep faith if the Romans would ride to the rescue.

These envoys found a receptive audience among a Roman establishment already concerned about what their old rivals from the Samnite confederation were up to: 'The power of that nation, which had already become great, and promised to become greater still if, upon the subjugation of the Lucanians and, because of them, of their neighbours, the barbarian tribes adjoining them.'[13] The recrudescent confederation might reinforce itself sufficiently in terms of wealth and manpower to be able again to go head-to-head on near equal terms in another round. It was not just fear of a potential enemy, rejuvenated by newly-acquired Lucanian resources, but they had also just heard from the Picentes, who controlled an important stretch of the Adriatic coast, about proposals the Samnites had made for an alliance. That would allow these potential enemies to open easy communications with the Umbrians, Etruscans and Celts to the obvious detriment of Rome. The reception was apparently such that the Senate and other assemblies, with no dissention, prepared to stand by these new associates, whatever the consequences might be. Showing serious purpose, the Senate chose some of their most experienced and credible members as ambassadors to demand that the Samnites return the country they had misappropriated from the Lucanians and also agree to refrain from any further aggressive action against them.

So a delegation followed an accustomed road to the heart of Samnite country. These visitors, sporting their distinctive heavy, woollen formal outfits, hoped to make an impression of blunt, severe and notable consequence. Considering brusque forthrightness as trumping diplomatic language, they intended the recipients of their messages should have no doubt about the seriousness of their purpose. However, whatever the credibility of the emissaries and the details of the message they delivered, it cut no ice with the people who received their protestations, considering them far from real advocates of peace nor just intent on implementing their obligations to an ally. The spirit of the Samnites is well-captured by Dionysius: 'That they had not made the peace on the understanding that they were to count no one as their friend or enemy unless the Romans should bid them to do so.'[14] The mountain men saw the requirements voiced by the envoys as showing they were just looking for an excuse to declare war, so they were prepared to argue the toss, reminding their visitors that the Lucanians had very recently been their enemies and that this rushing to aid them was a transparent ploy to find a loophole, a way out of the treaty Samnium and Rome had so recently signed with each other. They recognized that they were faced with either kowtowing or going to war and, unprepared for the former, the emissaries from the Republic were driven out without ceremony. This was a defiant statement of intent that went hand-in-hand with officers circulating to alert the authorities all over Samnium of the need to raise men and funds for the coming conflict.

The drive to war had become irresistible, but if a kerfuffle in the lower peninsula had been the spark, there is a concern that the whole thing is so like the story of the First Samnite War with Capua calling in the Romans in extremis, one wonders if it was the complete picture. Any war for a nation wanting to instigate bellicose relations with the Republic was bound to be a long odds contest. The short shrift received by the Hernici and the Aquae in just the past couple of years showed this, and this was bound to have given pause to policy-makers, even among those who had not already accepted Roman hegemony as a foregone conclusion. There was going to have to be a context for such a decision and indeed there was. Much was transpiring at the commencement of the new century that would ensure fighting would range over great swathes of the peninsula, involving people who lived both to the far north as well as to the deep south of the pugnacious polity nestling on the banks of the Tiber. The factors discussed in the Samnite councils before the decision to go to war was taken would have included developments in Etruria, Umbria and beyond that might even up the chances in any conflict. Much must have hung on them believing that these antagonists could well end up as crucial partners in the coming challenge; hope and anxiety, a heady mixture that it can be assumed had its influence.

Chapter Six

Early Stages

> '*Fabius Rullus Maximus, when in Samnium in his fourth consulship, having vainly essayed in every way to break through the line of the enemy, finally withdrew the hastati from the ranks and sent them round with his lieutenant Scipio, under instructions to seize a hill from which they could rush down upon the rear of the enemy. When this had been done, the courage of the Romans rose, and the Samnites, fleeing in terror, were cut to pieces.*'
>
> Sextus Julius Frontinus, *Stratagems*, Book II, 4 2

There is a fine tufa sarcophagus set among the treasures of the Vestibolo Quadrato of the Museo Pio-Clementino in the Vatican complex, one of the very first of its kind ever found. Appropriately its occupant was from a family that would be central to Roman epic and was one of the first names to emerge in the Third Samnite War. He was the patrician Lucius Cornelius Scipio Barbatus who, though a sprig of one of the great families that had produced Roman leaders since the end of the fifth century and the great-grandfather of Scipio Africanus, had not been heard of much before. However, he would, like his colleague, continue in important military roles during most of this latest conflict just started in smoke and blood. Reaching the consul's seat for the only time, though censor in later life, this man saw considerable action. Famed for the unusual habit of sporting a beard, a number of successes on the battlefields were impressed on his tomb: 'He captured Taurasia Cisauna in Samnium – he subdued all of Lucania and led off hostages.' These places, though the names are not always possible to identify, were almost certainly somewhere on the Apulian-Samnite borderlands. Indeed, they could be in country north of Beneventum that was later used during turbulent times in the 180s to forcibly settle 47,000 defeated Ligurians and became known as Ligures Baebiani.

These blows registered in stone were among the first to indicate that for the third time relations between Roman and the Samnite League had broken down sufficiently for war to be the only option. It had been hardly six years since they had laid down their arms, but the reality was that war was surely inevitable. The road to peace and co-operation was never really open against people who the Samnites were convinced were bent on their destruction. The unrelenting bellicosity exhibited by the people from the city on the banks of the Tiber, if real enough, was not untypical. Many if not most ancient polities expanded at the cost of their neighbours if they had the power to do so,[1] but aggression had certainly been there, happily staking the chance of success against ruin. War could bring both glory and wealth, an irresistible combination, and if it might be risky, then life was always a violent, chancy business and many Romans showed themselves prepared to take the gamble on a regular basis. However much of a feat it would be to take on the Samnites again, on top of a list of other enemies, there was no sign of any shirking. So members of the college of fetials from the best families occupying lifetime positions, distinctive in woollen fillets round their heads and wearing sacred robes, carried out the rituals that the Romans considered profoundly important in persuading themselves that they were entering upon a just war. Thirty or thirty-three days' grace were given after the formula had been broadcast before, if the recipients were obdurate, 'It was customary for the Fetial to carry to the enemies' frontiers a blood-smeared spear tipped with iron or burnt at the end. With these words he hurled his spear into their territory.'[2]

The mention of Lucania on Scipio's memorial makes sense; after all, the spark for the third great war between Rome and the Samnite nation was ignited in that country. The world in which these old foes operated was expanding and fighting would now consistently take place in a larger arena than had usually been the case in the fourth century. Defeat or victory would hang on events in places that had only been familiar to many Romans for a few generations. The most important battlefield would be more than 150 hard miles north of the city in Umbria, not somewhere in Latium, while another crucial front would be contested in Apulia and around Mount Vulture. Not that there had not been bloodshed in these places before, but these were adventures; participation in which sometimes caused great concern among the people in Rome. In the last decades of the fourth and into the third century, the clouds of war would cover the peninsula from Cisalpine Gaul down to where the Dauni inhabited the wide plains of the south-east and even southern Greeks on the peninsula's coastal instep could be involved.

However, as with everything in this first year of war, appearances can be deceptive. In the season's fighting, other testimony suggests an alternative for Scipio that leads this patrician searching for enemies far away from objectives in Samnium or Lucania into the northern reaches of modern-day Tuscany, though with no mention at all of what might have happened to the dust-choked marchers who followed in his train on the journey there. They are described as arriving at Volaterrae above the Era valley where a town had existed since Villanovan times and Etruscan walls still exist, with a lovely gate boasting images of Hellenistic Dioscuri (the twin deities Castor and Pollux), suggesting influence from the south and east in this prosperous community. This is hardly surprising in the heart of wide, rich agricultural country where an amazing Medici fortress now houses incarcerated criminals and a Roman theatre can still be seen. In its environs a ferocious battle is depicted, commencing when the intruders accidentally ran into columns of the enemy and ending, after a full day's combat, in a drawn match as the shadows of twilight deepened over the battlefield. Yet if this was a stalemate, it was a bloody one and only the Romans were up for further fighting on the following day. So when the enemy, unprepared to go again, quit the field, the Romans were able to walk through their camp gate and loot everything left behind, taking 'vast amounts of plunder for it was a permanent post and had been hastily abandoned'.

A discrepancy in the sources should not necessarily make us turn up our noses at the evidence we get in this period, but much of this just does not ring true as the question posed is why a Roman army had marched so far north, through Etruria, to a place well over 170 miles from Rome with no mention of the response of the people on the way. This particularly applies as the next we hear of the same invasion force, it had fallen back into the territory of the Faliscans, not far north of the Republic's frontiers. From there they ravaged the lands of any hostile Etruscan they could get at, with the inhabitants and the garrisons cringing behind their walls, too terrified to make any defence at all, only looking down as flames licked upwards and fire crackled around the farms and hamlets that dotted the countryside. Clearly this had all been a very considerable razzia, but suggestions of a great victory against a considerable enemy army are surely unlikely. Also no triumphal fasti recognizes these Etruscan successes; a lack of evidence that contributes still further to the muddle.

The story is no simpler with the other consul. The evidence we have as 298 came round was that there were few cautious voices among Rome's wise heads and not only Scipio Barbatus but his consular colleague were prepared and determined to take the war to an enemy they knew so well. This other general was Gnaeus Fulvius Centumalus, a high-status plebeian who is first noticed serving in 302 as an officer under the dictator Valerius Corvus and was one of the many experienced soldiers who were kept on in army command during this war. By the time of his consulship he might have been about 40 years of age and, with plenty of militarily successful plebeian consuls as role models, he was eager to make a name for himself. However, the flaw once again is that the sources place him on multiple fronts, warring with both the Caracini and the Pentri as well as down on the borders of Lucania. Understandable efforts are made to start his war with a bang, with violence erupting into the forested defiles of Samnium, as his invading army is claimed as pressing into enemy territory, bringing a defending force to bay near Bovianum and roundly defeating it before moving on to take that town by assault. With the storming of the walls of the capital of the Pentri as practically the first act of the campaign, that was followed by his pushing on to capture a place called Aufidena. The question here is always how much of this is propaganda, because our main source is always declaring that Bovianum, one of the most important Samnite cities, was captured, despite very soon after being clearly back in enemy hands once more. Suspicions must arise at the report of an enemy capital falling so early in the fighting in what would be a near decade-long war, particularly as there may be more confusion here; an echo of the same success reported for a different Fulvius in 305.

The location of his second success, ancient Samnite Aufidena, a Caraceni settlement in the upper valley of the Sagrus, can be identified with a number of sites within a few miles of each other. Castel di Sangro, with its dominant rock and traces of polygonal walls, is generally thought to be the most likely prospect, but there is a place down the valley with traces of defences and a nearby Samnite necropolis from the period that is actually still called Alfedena. Whichever it was, Fulvius Centumalus' success in taking it, combined with whatever he had achieved before, was sufficient for this tyro commander to win a triumph for the blows he had struck first time out in army command, although confusingly the triumphal fasti that record these victories show him rewarded for success not just over the Samnites but against Etrurians as well. These archives can be as problematic as so much else during this period, but it is possible that in this case they are accurate and it had not been Scipio Barbatus but his colleague who had turned the screw on the locals around Volaterrae and other parts of Etruria in 298. Yet there is even more that confounds any attempt to peer behind the veil in that there also exists a book of stratagems written by a first-century AD Roman, a general and civil engineer who campaigned in Wales and Yorkshire in his time, that seems to have Fulvius Centumalus fighting down in Lucania in this year.[3] This might fit with the idea of him battling Rome's enemies around Aufidena as it is a believable sequence that after this success he could have marched down the Sangro valley en route to the Adriatic before turning south down the coast road; a very practical route through Frentani territory that would have led to Luceria in Apulia, a strong Roman post where he could base himself for a Lucanian campaign. The evidence for both consuls is thus suggestive of significant activity in or near that country, which after all had been the *casus belli* (cause for war) that brought Roman Samnite relations to the point of all-out conflict. It surely would have been sound strategy for the Republic's leaders to have sent major forces there, both to help their new friends and utilize them in operations against the southern and eastern borders of enemy country.

This confusion in the first fighting season of the war at the centre of this work is perhaps an appropriate warning, hinting at flaws in respect of what is more detailed stuff to come. To make sense of almost all ancient history is to follow Indiana Jones across a rickety jungle bridge, with the lianas that hold it up either failing under natural stress or being hacked away by people with sharp and apposite arguments. For every proposition there is an opposite, and indeed often another as well, that has almost as much validity, not infrequently propounded by an author with either a personal stake or wracked by a very particular rivalry, but this is the process itself. Nor does this apply just to ancient history; all that we read telling of the past is open to question; an opinion, sometimes valid and useful but not the only one. With the period we are studying, it is almost the very paucity of sources that defines the attempt. Indeed, from 301 we do not even have Diodorus to corroborate or undermine our main contributor, and though there are other voices from even later, they are usually derivative and give only snapshots rather than delivering a continuous story.

* * *

For almost half a century there had been a rule in place at Rome that a magistrate should only hold the same office again after ten years had elapsed, but it had been honoured as much in the breach as the observance when the times demanded. Now these current times were looking to be considerably upgraded in terms of menace, particularly as those in charge in Etruria, after being berated by popular opinion for failing to sign up the Gauls as auxiliaries, upped their game in what was perceived to be a crucial round of fighting. The Samnites also realized that they would have to make much greater efforts than had been the case when they failed to significantly reinforce a military that had been just intending to fight brush fires in Lucania. So now, as the critical conflict entered its second season, serious principals were called for at Rome; men who had shown over and over that they could win battles and take fortresses against any number of the peoples with whom they had been at war in the past thirty years. The Republic had turned to the immense experience of the old man Valerius Corvus in the years just before this latest Samnite war began, but if this relic of a bygone age had perhaps become just too decrepit to continue, once bloodshed was fully started in this latest conflict they continued to show an exactly similar inclination.

In the next campaign the ground is firmer as we try to understand what occurred just as two veterans of the greatest renown, Fabius Rullianus and Decius Mus, were called upon. To the former, whatever the regulations said, indulgence could be extended. The decimation after Lautulae long forgotten, he was honoured and respected now, so where else would Rome look for leadership? The predominance of the Fabii was getting near enough to those very first decades of the Republic when the family had provided a consul in most years in the 480s. There was no Athenian ostracism to curb the over-mighty available at Rome; a circumstance that ensured the rest of the noble families, always suspicious of greatness, would try to subvert such authority. This imperative can be perceived when rivals tried to keep Fabius Rullianus from the highest office in 299, though he still managed to end up as curule aedile, claiming that year there was not a real war for him to get his teeth into. This man was without real peer in the core years of this Samnite War; the head of a family that was tightening its grip. Now he and Decius Mus were not only made consuls in 297, only five years since their last stint, they were also kept on in the highest commands in an almost unprecedented manner for the following three years, one of them even remaining central to great events for some time after. These generals, however much a brave and tenacious enemy might try to check or divert them, were going to make real progress in establishing hegemony up north into Etruria and Umbria, east across to the country of the Aequi, Marsi and further to the Adriatic, south into Volscian country, Campania, Apulia and Lucania.

Decius Mus was a plebeian who had been consul first in 312 and may have claimed a triumph over the Samnites in the following year. In 308, again as consul, he had shown himself an able partner for Fabius Rullianus in battering Umbrians and Etruscans, but this veteran did not just have his own past glories, it was the credit that attached to the name of his father that really mattered. This earlier Decius Mus, like his offspring, had a penchant for stealing the limelight when, like his son, in the fight against the Samnites' glittering army in 308, he had also garnered what success was going in one of the very first battles of the earliest Samnite War. Yet this was not his greatest claim to fame; that had transpired when this man, one of the first plebeian consuls, saved an army in battle in the year 340 by sacrificing his life; a pious self-immolation that made him legend, performed in a crisis in the life of the state when Rome was imperilled by a revolt of the Latin League.

Fabius Rullianus and Decius Mus, who had been at the heart of the Republic's military efforts for the past couple of decades, would continue in a new century. The former was first called on to accept nomination for the consulship and take command, though there is a suggestion that initially he was reluctant to accept the duty and indeed not unreasonably pointed out that it was making a mockery of the law to elect him again so soon after his last consulship five years before. This might be the trope of hesitancy to accept great power that can be found in ancient sources from Perdiccas, the successor of Alexander the Great, to Tiberius, Rome's second emperor and even Theodosius the Great; still, the fact was that this old warrior had been around a long time. In 297 he would surely have been over 60, so perhaps it is believable that he would not necessarily have relished more hard campaigning. As it turned out, any reservations scarcely mattered and were soon overcome. So with his own place secured, Fabius pressed for his old partner Decius Mus to be elected at his side.

It was settled and the decision to march was taken. Then, as the weather became warm enough for the campaigning season to begin, these two drew lots to see who should take on the Etruscans and who the Samnites. However, it turned out that the former were in far less combative mood than had been imagined, though plenty of trouble was anticipated against the latter, a reality that further calls into question claims of great victories at Bovianum in the previous year. After orders were issued and the levies gathered from the city and its surroundings, nearby colonies and allies, the fresh armies assembled with the best arms and armour each fighting man could afford. Both consuls, it was agreed, would be dispatched against the southern enemy, though once mobilized they took their separate ways to pick up more loyal allies to flesh out their ranks and confuse the enemy as to where they might deliver their Sunday punch. Fabius took his men, eager to enjoy the success they expected under this great warrior, down the valley where the Latin Way would go and the modern motorway to Naples now runs, passing communities crowded onto defensible hills, many of which had been independent Latin or Volsci places which over time had been incorporated into the Republic's sphere of influence, before branching off to Sora. This was a place that had settled down under Roman rule after years of contention between Romans, Volscians and Samnites. It was almost safe now, despite many of the inhabitants boasting Volsci antecedents, and the town had been repeatedly taken and lost in the Samnite Wars between 345 and 305.

The old township sat under a mountain reef in a bowl of fine green hills with the River Liris making a natural moat, a handsome place which still boasts both ancient polygonal walls and later medieval defences that was annexed and colonized in 303 and would now provide an ideal advanced base not just for Fabius Rullianus but many others in the years to come. Below its defences an animated scene played out in the early summer of 297 with sheepskin tents raised and defences dug by men who had laid aside their mail shirts or bronze pectorals, while cavalry mounts and baggage animals lapped the water murmuring at the river's edge. A full consular army of two legions with equivalent allied contingent, at the start of the fighting season with little attrition having occurred, perhaps would have numbered near 18,000 men, enough not only to give plenty of headaches to a badgered commissariat but also to cause exasperation and damage even in friendly territory, though no doubt soldiers' money filling the pockets of local entrepreneurs would have provided some compensation. So there would have been mixed feelings at the sight of the column of men and animals eventually moving out, marching past the city and east down the river towards the Colli a Volturno, where green sward mountains covered in deep, dark woods rise up on either side of a route leading towards the heart of enemy country.

Decius Mus, at the head of a similar-sized force, had come as quickly as he could but by a different route to join up with his fellow consul. Travelling directly south from Rome, he had initially set up base at Taenum Sidicinum, modern-day Teano. From there he had pushed his men through the country of the Sidicini. This people occupied the Liris valley back up to Fregellae, having according to Strabo taken over these lands from the Opici and played a central role at the beginning of the conflict between Rome and the Samnites. The story is (though there are those who think the whole sequence is invented to justify Rome breaking her treaty with the Samnites), that in 343 the Samnites had a thrash at them, an act of aggression that then sparked a war with the Campanians into which the Republic was drawn. This expansion of the struggle saw the arrival of an army high above Capua on Mount Tifata, setting the scene that saw the locals give themselves up to Rome for protection. Thus was ignited the first fighting between what were to become the two greatest central Italian rivals. These same Sidicini were also involved in the great turnover of alliances after the First Samnite War. Again the claim is that they too tried to surrender themselves to Roman protection, but on being rejected they joined up with those Latins who, with many Campanians, had rallied in a last great revolt against Roman dominion.

Decius Mus' route was familiar where the people were friendly enough; living cheek by jowl with the Samnite threat, some Sidicini would have welcomed the security offered by the presence of a consular army. The forces under Fabius Rullianus coming along the road from Sora, pressing past Atina towards the country round Aesernia, modern-day Isernia, joined hands with their comrades when they discovered them coming out from under the cone of Roccamonfina west of the Matese massif. The two consuls had worked well together in the past and now it was just as well as they were deep within enemy territory. Needing to make an impact, they allowed their soldiers off the leash to lay the land in ashes, permitting them full range to the animosity they felt against an enemy who they considered had breached a sacred accord by going to war. Despite the intolerable provocation of wrecking and looting that the locals repeatedly reported to the Pentrine authorities in hope of succour, they showed disinclination to face a two-consul-strength army. They just would not have been able to put in the field anything near the 36,000-plus men the invaders could, so shrinking from the prospect of these fearsome numbers and preferring to live to fight another day, they faded back into the hills, shoring up their position and waiting to see if missteps by the enemy might allow them to take advantage.

Soon enough, with tens of thousands of mouths to feed, supply demands became a major headache and with so many animals and men together fouling the water, dysentery would become almost inevitable. So this, together with the other claims made on the Romans' resources, ensured that their field strength could not be kept together. Stresses in the south, where the war had been detonated the year before, could never be long ignored and soon Decius Mus was called down there to continue the struggle on the Lucanian front, a circumstance that meant, with one army departed and with only Fabius Rullianus left facing them, the defenders were now prepared to consider taking on the intruders. So determined to triumph or at least to die in arms, now the odds were more acceptable, the decision was made to advance and confront the invaders.

Those troops that had been mobilized to protect the people of the Pentri acted, moving into a remote valley in the hills near the invading army. The region is described as 'near Tifernum', most probably not far from where the modern-day Biferno River rises in the mountains. It is clear from what we hear of the response to this move that the Romans had learned much from the Battle of Saticula and the Caudine forks disasters fought in the First and Second Samnite Wars. The legions in the kind of treacherous country where they had suffered so before had long-practised tactics to respond to the kind of ambushes laid by the fleet-footed mountain men with whom they found themselves in contention. So when scouts reported that the steep country around them was far from empty, in fact teeming with hostile soldiers, Fabius Rullianus ordered the baggage train to be placed with a small guard out of harm's way, while most of the fighting men were arranged in a protective square, a formation they endeavoured to retain as they advanced along the winding road to make contact with the enemy.

This obvious preparedness on the part of the invaders almost immediately yielded benefits when the route opened out sufficiently to allow an orthodox encounter. The Samnites, realizing they would not be able to entrap the enemy or come at them from higher ground, moved eagerly down the slope, looking to coordinate their deployment as they formed up on the level, challenging the Romans to open combat. Numbers are as usual not easy, but there is no reason to think Fabius Rullianus would not still have had command of most of a complete consular army, not much under 18,000 men fit for duty, particularly as with the Etruscans quiet there were no great demands on the Republic's manpower elsewhere. How many men the Samnites deployed we have no idea, but once the maniples marched out with standards to their fronts and the two sides came together, the outcome suggests at least they had sufficient men to make a real contest of it. They were facing a challenge worthy of their mettle and even after bloodletting aplenty and ferocious assaults by the enemy legionaries, the Samnites held their ground in a convincing fashion. With the defenders holding firm and progress hardly discernible at all, in the command group around the commander consultation was frantic as the old man's son offered to try to make the difference by leading the cavalry into the fray. This was a new generation trying to make an impression and Fabius Maximus Gurges, of whom we will hear much later, and Marcus Valerius, kin of the celebrated Corvus, were dashing young noblemen who, acting as tribunes, accompanied the consul into the forward ranks of their horsemen.

It is clear that the place where the battle was fought, though more open than the road they had been travelling, was still pinched in and the infantry lines occupied the whole of the valley floor. In these circumstances the cavalry, geed up by their general's strictures, could not attack out on the wings, but had to wait for the foot soldiers to disengage and then passing through their footslogging comrades, make a rush at the enemy line. They hoped to clear a way through, to break them up with the weight of snorting animals and shrieking men. However, the defenders had prepared their position carefully and the assault not only failed in its intended purpose, with attackers thrown back from a stout line of spears, but the Roman infantry, who had been critically disrupted by the horsemen moving through their ranks, looked like they might be defeated too. The scene was terrible; masses of desperate men and beasts hardly able to advance, yet finding no way out, with the ranks of their own compatriots pressing behind them and enemy javelins fizzing by. What had begun well enough for Fabius Rullianus now began to look like it might end in a fully-fledged disaster as the consul himself surveyed the extraordinary scrimmage that had been the upshot of his latest gambit. Matters were only salvaged when, as the officers prayed for a miracle, the soldiers from the reserve lines rushed forward to stabilize the front and a ploy put into action at the same time as the horsemen began their charge had the desired effect.

Scipio Barbatus, retained in command from the year before and now a legate in Fabius Rullianus' army, had acted and what he did made the difference. He had surveyed the ground and found a way to scale the hills guarding the enemy's flank and at the head of the hastati from the first legion he moved. Using the mountains to try to hide their passage, the men had zigzagged in ascent before breasting the foliage to descend over the edge of the slopes that constrained the battlefield and their arrival on the Samnite flank was enough to rock the enemy's will to resist. All this is a common enough trope in the portrayal of the fighting in these wars, but still there is something here that suggests that in this case it could well be genuine. These hastati were the front line of the legions, heavy infantry organized as described by Polybius and though this configuration might not have come into its full form for some decades after this period, still the legions of the 290s were unlikely to have been structured very differently as the practice of dividing men by age and relative affluence goes way back into the Roman past. What this clearly indicates is that those soldiers chosen to make the flank march were the youngest men, in their very late teens or early twenties, who did not have the wherewithal for heavy defensive armour; just the sort that would be needed to climb, agile and swift and still be full of energy when, after sweating up under a blistering summer sun, they came around and over the rocky slopes that hemmed in the enemy flank.

Our account has it that when these men appeared, the consul and his men began shouting that it was Decius Mus' army come to their rescue. On hearing this, the Samnite defences that had long held firm were filled with 'panic and dread' and hardly stayed to defend against the new attack. Many in the chaos of battle turned in disarray to disperse into the glens and gullies of the mountains behind them. Though victory was the result, that the newcomers were thought to be the army of Decius Mus is very improbable as surely Scipio's detachment would have been noticed and the clash of metal heard as they mounted up by the sides of the valley to take up their position? In fact, that the Romans could send such a strong task force out of the main line clearly showed that the Samnites were outnumbered as they manifestly did not have men available to respond when the new threat materialized; an imbalance in numbers that probably explains the outcome of the fight as much as any tricky manoeuvring. Whatever the reason, the Samnite commanders felt the situation sufficiently dangerous that they decided to cut their losses and order the men still holding on in their battle line to fall back from the fight as best they could and retire into the hills in their rear. Gratefully, the victors paused on a ground where the enemy dead lay thick, though interwoven with plenty of Roman corpses as well. That the outcome is recorded as resulting in fewer casualties than would normally be expected is telling. Instead of the usual tens of thousands claimed in the battles of previous wars, hardly more than 4,000 are declared as Samnite casualties with 23 standards taken. As there is no evidence that their camp was captured, this suggests that the defenders, if driven from the field, were able, on home ground, to avoid the kind of terrible bloodletting that might have been anticipated in the pursuit phase of such an encounter.

Still the intention on the Roman side was to exploit a battlefield victory and as a matter of urgency. So, after resting his men, tending his casualties, stripping the enemy and disposing of his captives, Fabius Rullianus marched his army forward to plunge like a knife into the heart of Samnium. Soon rumours of the defeat were filtering through the countryside and locals realized the Romans were more than just drawing near; they had arrived and were intent on an orgy of destruction. Starting from the site of the battle, the victors 'ranged over the land in different areas and destroyed everything'. The light troops, cavalry and some heavy infantry separated into detachments to spread the devastation as widely as possible, while the remainder concentrated to offer protection to any who might be threatened and ensure the army a secure night's sleep by constructing a ditch and palisade encampment. The raiders entered habitations where there were numerous signs of the recent and disordered departure of the owners, many of whom peered on from their hiding-places in the nearest rocky tree line as all they owned went up in smoke. These superstitious intruders were usually wary of disturbing the rural Lares (guardians of fields and boundaries), but now Mars the god of war trumped these lesser spirits and anyway they knew they would be far away by the time they could gather sufficient malevolence to take revenge. Farms and hamlets were torched and locals who were too slow on their feet were dragged off in chains by men who had learned to hate the mountain folk of Samnium over generations of war. They were at this wrecking business for most of the fighting season, until it must have seemed that a black, dirty cloud of belching smoke covered the whole region, visible to almost all the occupants of the Pentri. During a period of four months Fabius Rullianus' men camped in eighty-six different locations in the crenellated landscape that was the core of Samnium, making a wasteland of a large swathe of country. There is no list of towns taken in what was, for the most part, a destructive and wide-ranging razzia, though a place called Cimetra fell to assault, but its location is unknown and never mentioned again, surely indicating that it was of no great significance.

While Fabius Rullianus was winding up encounters that showed how terrible it was to fight the Romans, his colleague had concentrated his endeavours to the south-east of the Samnite heartland. To achieve his intention of augmenting the Republic's position in Apulia and Lucania would have involved his men in a good few days' hard slog down the Biferno River valley that drained into the Adriatic Sea. This was through the centre of enemy country, but the Romans were in real strength so the journey would not have represented too much of a problem, before they turned onto the well-travelled road to the key military post of Luceria in northern Apulia. Once arrived, much of the activity undertaken by his army was directed to the country round Venusia, though one episode shows that the intruders ranged a good way up the road from there as well, over the high wold country peopled by the Hirpini, towards Malaventum where fighting took place on the approaches to the town. Near where modern-day Benevento now stands on the Calor River, the consul fell in with an army of Apulians dispatched to reinforce the Samnites who were facing Fabius Rullianus. Discovered in column of march, Decius Mus blocked their way, a convergence that brought them to battle and ended with the Apulians being driven off in a bloody rout. These adversaries had not made much of a contest of it, so now, with no dread of these particular adversaries, the consul ceased to concern himself with dangers emanating from the eastern flank of the Apennines and instead continued to make headway in tearing up the lands of the Hirpini.

This heavyweight terrorizing of these southern Samnites, and perhaps even those Lucanians who still held to the anti-Roman cause, took up the rest of the fighting season as any armed defenders in these regions sought sanctuary behind their town walls; a considerable five months, during which time Decius Mus set up his camp on forty-five different sites. From the oppressive heat of July and August to the sharp days of autumn they criss-crossed the country in a caravan of smashing demolition, even continuing in the field for at least part of the winter. Yet however many gutted ruins bore witness to their passage, however many fields and barns were burned, and however many groves of trees hacked down, this was not a conquest in any meaningful sense. Roman sources were never reluctant to claim success for their compatriots in these kinds of operations, so no mention of towns being taken should give us pause, particularly as it is also probable that when Decius Mus was recharged with command for the following year, his men were by that time back in the safety of Apulia or friendly Lucania, where weary men could recuperate far better than deep in what was still enemy-controlled territory. The lack of triumphs recorded is also indicative of the truth that it had been only approximate success, that despite the battle at Tifernum and the widespread effects of two consular armies marching deep into Samnite country, the people back home saw none of these achievements as decisive. Yet what could not be denied is that both the consuls had been devastatingly efficient in pursuing a tried and tested strategy that was at the heart of much conflict from the Trojan War right up to modern times. The ruin they caused both chipped at the economic base of an enemy, whose livelihood was overwhelmingly dependent on agriculture and had the crucial side advantage of at least partly making the war pay for itself from the provender and other valuables that the marauders were able to retrieve before leaving burning husks of buildings to mark the passage of every plundering party, activity whose importance was recognized by a citizen body, many of whom had indulged in such behaviour in their own military days. This ensured that there was no lack of future confidence in the two veterans who had been in charge in 297. They both would be retained in command in the next fighting season, and even if the former at least initially was required to return to Rome to oversee elections, Decius Mus took up the slack, showing from the beginning a determination to turn from career looting to hard-handed occupation.

The men making the decisions in Samnite councils, as they turned away from these worrying exhibitions of Roman reach, would have realized their enemy was developing institutions that allowed her military muscle to be exerted for a longer time and further away from home. By finding constitutional arrangements that enabled them to continue utilizing the talents of their most experienced officers and fielding armies that were prepared to spend more than one season away from home, they were gaining an increasing edge. So it was no coincidence that, particularly after 296–95, the use of extraordinary commands and prorogations became far more usual. So the retention of Fabius Rullianus and Decius Mus in command of their armies for a further six months to keep up pressure on the suffering Samnite country was becoming a pattern. However, it would be no lack of enterprise or patriotism on the Samnites' part that meant the Romans would be allowed so much freedom in this second incursion, when Decius Mus found himself again encountering a foe disinclined to come out to fight. The Samnites were faced with the desperate realization of how much their situation had deteriorated from previous rounds of combat now that the Samnite League lands were regularly being squeezed from east and west, with a shatter belt spreading round their heartland. Picking over the details of their strategic options, they would have realized the rot had begun to set in, even since 314 once Luceria was firmly established under Roman control. Standing on the site of modern-day Lucera, a place most notable for its splendid Hohenstaufen castle, built where the old acropolis once stood and home in the thirteenth century AD to Saracen auxiliaries uprooted from Sicily and intended by Emperor Frederick II to overawe troublesome subjects in this part of his vast patrimony. The fortress occupied by Roman garrisons, above which colonists' fields radiated out from the inhabited outcrop, was just as important as the one that can still be seen today, acting as a vital foothold on the eastern flank of the Apennines. With this place securely held and with friends among many of the Apulians and Lucanians, Roman armies could continuously exert pressure, up from the eastern plains, through the valleys of modern-day Cervaro, Carapelle and Ofanto and into the hills of the Hirpini. Easily reaching the country around Mount Vulture, they could then make hay even before they founded a solid military base at Venusia, built on the remains of another Samnite town, that would be crucial in the Romans holding onto power in this region, not just against local enemies but other even more dangerous adversaries over generations to come.

Decius Mus' army, still based somewhere in Apulia, did not let the grass grow once the season became clement enough for campaigning. He led his men first west up into the Apennines again, attacking and taking a place in north-eastern Hirpini called Murgantia by a ferocious assault, with success achieved after only one day. More than 2,000 defenders were driven off the walls and penned in the centre of the town and, with columns of attackers pressing forward down the streets, there was no escape. Finally surrounded and wavering, massively outnumbered and with many wounded, the garrison laid down their arms, preferring servitude to annihilation and handing over to the victors 'an immense amount of plunder'. It is speculation, but the place where these Samnites fought and lost was most likely modern-day Baselice Morcone in the hills between Benevento and Campobasso in East Pentri, though an alternative case can certainly be made for a district called Le Murge on the road from Venusia to Bari.

The Roman commander was in a hurry and, worried about the cupidity of men who had spent half a year looting, he urged them to quickly sell what booty they had acquired, trains of captives as well as other valuables, to the traders following the army, so light-shod they could push on to further success and the plunder it would bring. Heading south into Hirpini country, things were bleak indeed for any habitations in their path. Thousands and thousands of men, armed and eager, spread far and wide with horse-borne outriders leading the way, herding terrified country folk into the depths of tree-covered glens or the hill fort refuges that dotted the country. Soon in a region where they had wrought so much damage the year before, the intruders reached Romulea, the next community that was going to feel the lash of Roman wrath. The route travelled to approach this next place had been south-east of modern-day Benevento and west of Mount Vulture. The target may well have been modern-day Bisaccia, 10 miles west of Melfi, that is marked as 'sub-romula' on later 'itineraria'.[4] It looks like this town was not well walled as the attackers did not even have to bother with opening trenches or bringing forward engines of any kind. Decius Mus' men, eager for more after their recent taste of easy profits, rushed forward and drove on in an immediate all-out frontal assault, not even reconnoitring for weak spots, never mind setting up siege machines. All they needed, as they hurled themselves forward, were the scaling ladders carried to the walls, with waves of soldiers pouring up until the garrison was forced back and breaches opened at the 'nearest points'. Legionaries, once the walls were taken, streamed down from the battlements, surging through the streets until the whole place was 'captured and sacked' with a claim of piles of dead and 6,000 disconsolate prisoners corralled ready for transportation in the centre of the market place.

Even after this, there was little or no let-up for the troops. As Decius Mus watched over his men warming themselves around their camp fires against the evening chill, far from content to leave it at that, he decided there would be no time to award battlefield decorations or revel in the victories so far. They were hurried on towards Ferentinum, where the defenders made more of a fight of it. This place, while it cannot be absolutely identified, could well be near Lavello in Apulia, a very old habitation peopled by Daunians before the Romans took over and renamed it Forentum. This community was situated in a position of great natural strength, built high up on a ridge in pancake-flat country, difficult to approach with formidable walls. Yet despite this, a ferocious defence was overcome by a Roman army now well accustomed to success, but a titbit we are given suggests that this was not the whole story and that despite the weight of numbers, it actually turned out a very hard nut to crack. Taking some time to conclude the enterprise without doubt took a good deal out of the men, as this is the last mention of significant action in this campaigning season. After this there was no more rampaging into the enemies' country, though at least the soldiers were well rewarded for their latest efforts with plenty of booty after they had completed the usual massacre of thousands 'round the walls'.

Something had become clear as the campaign of 296 flamed out. After the war had raged for two years, events had shown the actions of the contenders in a very different light from what had been the case earlier in the epic sequence of conflicts between Rome and Samnium. This was that the war of attrition the Romans were waging must, in the end, be successful unless an alternative approach could be found. In that year Decius Mus, acting as proconsul, had declared to his officers that the enemy was no longer prepared to fight it out in open battle. He had trumpeted to his soldiers that the men they had been warring with for so long had given up any hope of contending on the field of battle; that all they would do now was defend their cities where they had the benefit of defensive walls. So he and his followers could, without danger, concentrate on real conquests: 'Why don't we attack cities and walled towns? There is no army now to protect Samnium.'[5] Yet if this picture of unfettered opportunity was not without some veracity, what this experienced officer was asserting with such emphasis was far from the whole story.

Opportunity combined with desperation was going to make the next year one of the most significant in the history of ancient Italy as the

Samnite leaders decided not to fight it out toe-to-toe along the usual lines since such a policy would be playing into Roman hands. Yet while they withdrew some of their armies from the field, they also prepared to move in a different strategic direction. There is a suggestion that the Samnites' perceived incapacity was the result of Fabius Rullianus and Decius Mus beating their armies back and ravaging their country, but this portent of enfeeblement is at most only partly true. Another factor was that there was a man with a plan. This was Gellius Egnatius who, if he was no fabulist and had accepted that the Samnites alone must eventually succumb to greater resources that the Romans could mobilize, was still no defeatist. A real war leader had emerged, determined to set the agenda rather than respond to Roman aggression as so often in the past. We unfortunately know virtually nothing about this man, only that his was a well-matured project, showing the fertility of the Samnite supremo's mind. He was a man of soaring self-belief who knew that timid reticence would get him or his people nowhere. Few characters in this period could remotely rival his decisive imagination to take the fight to the enemy in a different place, in tandem with people who knew that Roman expansion was a threat to them all. The man who proposed it was no model of a primitive hill chief; he was a charismatic leader, unorthodox and resourceful and must have possessed the golden tongue of a Samnite, Demosthenes or Cicero, to have convinced the league's senior leadership to accept that thousands and thousands of that dwindling resource, the Samnite warrior, would be heading over the northern horizon rather than defending a Patria in jeopardy.

Gellius Egnatius recognized the awful inevitability of carrying on in the same old way and had decided that only by approaching Rome's enemies in the north could he initiate an axis of anti-Roman powers; a grand coalition of her perennial enemies that might yield significant and enduring results. Only time would tell if he could pull off what his imagination had composed, though lavish preparations would ensure the effort would not fail through being under-resourced. Not one to hedge his bets, Gellius Egnatius knew to make his play he would have to outflank Rome's central Italian powerbase, to pass by their holdings and those of their friends and allies, directing his steps north across the area of modern-day Abruzzo to appear in Etruscan country in arms with the largest force the Samnite League could muster in this crisis for so many of Rome's enemies. It is not just the parenting of this idea. Was it, with so many of their men marching north, that the Samnites could no longer compete at home? Or was it because resistance along their own borders was clearly not working that was itself the motivation for radical thinking? We do not know. Nor is the timing of this move without its complications. Certainly it had to have been either in Fabius Rullianus' and Decius Mus' own consular year or their prorogued term in the next that all this transpired. It was definitely on the watch of these two old boys that these seminal developments occurred and they signally failed to even try to stop them. It had been while they roiled in the enemy heartland that the coup was executed. The exact road taken by Gellius Egnatius and his men is unknown, but it would have taken several weeks for them to pass through the country of the Paeligni, Vestini and Picentes. That they came through unscathed was reported by dust-coated riders bringing news to Rome that the old enemy were playing for high stakes, having travelled the back roads of the peninsula to reach potential allies in the north. The fact that, prepared to commit almost everything to the northern strategy, they swiftly combined with the armies mobilized by these powers is shown by the reaction of the new consuls, when not long into the campaigning season, Appius Claudius' and Volumnius Flamma's movements indicated that the threat from the north was already appreciated by the long heads among the Tiber town establishment.

The very presence of these Samnites in the cities of Etruria and Umbria and the camps of the Gauls had made the war in the north a much more serious matter than could have been predicted by what had appeared an indecisive front during 298 and 297. Neither the Etruscans or Umbrians had been such a tough opponent in the last few years, but still they had been persistent. Though despised as peculiar and exotic for their unmanly uxoriousness and for paying up in bullion and garments when Roman armies appeared razing their countryside, still the Etruscans, both proximate and very numerous, were never shy of taking up arms as soon as the time was propitious. The Umbrians, a newer enemy, comprised plenty of hardy hill men among their numbers and, conversing in strange accents, they undoubtedly worried the Romans. These, apart from other enemies in the wings, would force the men who sat in the consular seat in the mid-290s to confront a blossoming confederacy; one that would provide a test for the Republic which would need all its resources to pass. A perilous situation that had been challenging enough in 296, though it represented not much more than half the potential military might of the new coalition, would eventually draw both consuls into decisive action against a much greater threat.

Chapter Seven

A Man and His Road

'... *attacked by Rome's army and unable to remain in the field with their own army facing up to the Romans, the Samnites decided to leave the towns in Samnium guarded and pass with their entire army into Etruria.*'
Discourses on Livy, Niccolò Machiavelli, Chapter 44

There is a Eulogium (Museum of Roman Civilization) put up by the Emperor Augustus listing the achievements of one of the characters who bestrode this period:

censor, consul twice, interrex three times, praetor twice, curule aedile twice, quaestor, military tribune three times. He captured many towns from the Samnites and he laid waste to the army of the Sabines and the Etruscans. He prohibited peace from being made with Pyrrhus the king. In his censorship he paved the Via Appia and he led water into the city. He built the temple of Bellona.

The man in question had the bluest patrician blood flowing in his veins. Appius Claudius Caecus was a member of a family so frequently touched by scandal that it would be notorious after him. With Claudius Pulcher throwing sacred chickens into the sea before the Battle of Drepana in 249 and later, in the dying decades of the Republic, the family produced an infamous brother and sister pairing who were claimed to have had an incestuous relationship and certainly feuded bitterly with Cicero. Indeed, after Publius Clodius Pulcher's death, his widow Fulvia, now married to Mark Antony, brought about the great orator's demise and in revenge for his taunting of her dead husband, on being shown his decapitated head, stabbed his tongue through with golden hairpins. Nor was it just family members who came after him; there had been a long line of proud nobles before, significant figures in Rome's story, some of whom were not remembered well at all. The line, as far as we know, started with Appius Claudius Sabinus Regillensis, who is recorded migrating from his Sabine homeland with his adherents in perhaps 504, or maybe considerably before, entering the list of patricians who comprised some of the greatest families in Rome and Latium. Another family member was Appius Claudius Crassus Sabinus Regillensis, one of the most notorious of the decemvirs (member of a ten-man commission), who were designated in 451 to administer the state as a temporary expedient while a table of laws was drawn up. From a constituent assembly these ambitious men, succumbing to what was always a temptation, tried to turn themselves into a permanent government and this Appius Claudius managed to make himself a decemvir for two years running, something none of the others even tried, so if the institution remained in control, except for him the personnel changed. Demanding twelve lictors each, these men in their second annual term really began to throw their weight around, refusing to allow appeals against their decisions and leading about crowds of young patrician bravos to intimidate any opposition.

The worry was not only that this cabal of would-be oligarchs wanted to stay in power indefinitely and abolish elections, they also managed to gravely upset plebeian opinion by not only suppressing the tribunes of the plebs but also forbidding intermarriage between the orders. However, it was failures in wars against the Sabines and Aequi, with these ten would-be tyrants in the lead, that brought about their downfall as opposition arose in a Senate assembled to facilitate the war. Appius Claudius tried to suppress the resistance by hauling of a number of the senators to prison and a soldier, who proposed that elections be reinstated, was murdered on his orders. Yet despite these oppressive events, the tradition is that it was a different crisis that brought the decemvirs to their knees; a story that makes generations of distaste for the Claudii more readily understood as this Appius Claudius was not just a leading member of a detested ruling clique, he was also accused of personal abuse of power that remembers the worst days of the Tarquinii. This lecher, intent on seducing a teenage girl whose father was away at war, instigated an intrigue that would have had her reduced to the status of a slave and therefore completely unprotected from him. He arranged that it would be he himself who was sitting in judgement as the matter of the girl's standing came to court, so her father returned from camp and, knowing the outcome was a foregone conclusion, killed her as it was the only way to save his child from dishonour. After this a mutiny in the army and another plebeian secession ensured a terminal outcome to their despotism as the decemvirs were forced by the Senate to stand down. While they fled a crowd determined on a lynching, Appius Claudius himself was detained and was only saved from trial by hanging himself in prison. Later another Appius Claudius Crassus, grandson of the decemvir, in the 360s is reported as rehearsing the arguments in defence of patrician exclusivity. The case against a quota for plebeian office-holders that he made chimes almost exactly with those deployed against proposals for the same for women and ethnic minorities in our own day. A proclaimed intention to allow inclusivity is matched by an absolute rejection of the most efficient method of achieving it, and on this occasion the result was the same because though a reform was passed to allow plebeians to compete for the consulship, for years afterwards only a derisory number ever broke the glass ceiling.

Rivalries were as unforgiving among the Roman elite as anywhere in the ancient world. So for Appius Claudius Caecus, obnoxious antecedents aside, inheriting the leadership of a powerful clan, it was inevitable that honour and vanity would push him on to compete for the greatest prizes, despite the fact that his family had not been at the top table for a few generations with just one undistinguished dictatorship in the last 100 years. Yet interestingly, when he first appears it is as a champion of an opposite strand in Rome's political development. He first made a name for himself after he was established as censor in 312 before he had even become consul, despite that in the middle Republic it was usually a prerequisite to have felt the seat of the consular chair through the toga at least once before filling a post where the incumbent could have his say in not only who was part of the citizen body, but membership of the equites (knights) and who sat in the Senate. This office, which like the consulship had two occupants, had in the past decades become central in the political development of the Republic. Up until the mid fifth century the consuls had overseen the censorial roles, but after that time a special office was created that could initially only be held by patricians. It is even possible that the changes had been a rearguard action in the 'conflict of the orders', specifically designed to deny any plebeian the chance of standing for this increasingly significant magistracy. Yet this stricture did not last beyond 352, when Gaius Marcius Rutilus became the first plebeian censor and only twelve years later, a requirement was introduced to bring the censorship into line with the consulship; that one office-holder should be a plebeian and one a patrician.

This already prestigious office developed later in the fourth century when the *Lex Ovinia* ensured that it was the job of the censors to revise the list of senators, with the powers to both relegate members whose behaviour was unacceptable and create others. Before this the consuls had retained this prerogative, making the Senate effectively a selected council, there to advise and support the chief magistrates. It was perhaps in 318 that the censors accrued the crucial facility of revising the register of the Senate, so that afterwards the senior magistrates no longer had the power to ensure their own men were installed in the key advisory body of the state. Previously membership of the Senate had hung on the discretion of the executive, with no excuse of bad behaviour being required and no shame felt when senators were dropped from the rolls. With this change senators normally became members for life and could only be deselected by the censor, giving them a power base independent of magisterial sponsorship, gaining increased kudos when most time-served magistrates, if not already there, automatically entered the body. So in time this moved the Senate towards the position of almost supreme power typical of the later Republic when consuls, with too short a term of power to be able to dominate the state, largely exercised their imperium within a context of Senatorial direction. So the nobles became independent of the executive in a way they had never been in the days of the kings or the early Republic. Unshackled from the domination of consuls or consular tribunes, they found themselves set on the road that would see the Senate forming an oligarchy that created policy. Longevity inevitably meant it was they who ended up having the most important say in the direction of long-term state strategy.

As the first time we hear of this Appius Claudius is when he became censor in 312, it is reasonable to assume he did so at an uncommonly young age. Yet this did not in the least handicap this high-tone patrician from stamping his mark, taking a radical stance that ensured he would be well-remembered, often with horror, as a demagogue of genius who actively courted popular opinion, seen as a populist posturing to win favour of the great unwashed by the conservative historians from whom would come the story of these years. In fact, the claim is that his censorial colleague resigned his office 'out of shame at the shocking and invidious manner in which Appius had filled up the senatorial list',[1] championing those who previously had little clout; not only were sons of freedmen enrolled in the order of the equites and the Senate, sending shock waves through an elite disinclined to share their privileges, but the citizen lists were expanded too, entering many in the voting tribes who previously would not have been considered sufficiently entitled by pedigree or affluence. It is easy to understand the distaste of these desperate Tories when they learned that sons of ex-slaves had been allowed to serve in the highest state bodies and that voting rights were given to non-landholding men. Nor was it just this radical stance that alienated many; questions of finance were always sensitive and many considered Appius Claudius was profligate with public money,[2] spending the cash needed to commence the Appian Way and start Rome's first aqueduct without going to the Senate for their approval. On top of this he is traduced for refusing to step down from the office of censor after his allotted eighteen months.

Much of the vilification of Appius Claudius signals ingrained Roman attitudes. This family of grandees inevitably suffered from those others who felt themselves unable to grow sufficiently in the shadows they threw, men who felt diminished by the blaze of others' glory. If he was one of the great public figures in a changing city, he perhaps represented a receding past; exactly the kind of moneyed bigwig who, when required, was happy to mobilize the plebs around an anti-patrician platform to beef up his own support. Quintus Publilius Philo, a wealthy plebeian, had been a pattern of this charismatic leadership and faction impact that combined with a populace that could be mobilized to ensure four consulships, a censorship, several stints as dictator or master of horse and enduring importance for nearly forty years. Appius Claudius was a political heir of this man who was heard of no more after his acquittal trial for trying to subvert the Republic in 314. This sort had not been uncommon during the fourth century, repeatedly holding the highest office even year on year on occasions, but would decline as the Senatorial oligarchy took the driving seat after the last Samnite War. Like the type, Appius Claudius was never consistent and could be found, when not advocating for the penurious, defending an absolute patrician monopoly on the high priesthoods and on one occasion challenging the practice of a consulship being set aside for a plebeian that had long been usual practice. This was part of a tradition where the likes of Disraeli sat, that ersatz blue-blood who, while holding his nose, offered crumbs from the table of power to the lower orders who he would never have tolerated socially and whose interests were certainly never his. More than this, the radical censor was something of an intellectual, showing interest in and knowledge of Greece and its culture, even credited with writing the *Sententiae*, a book in Greek on a Greek model of aphorisms and moral sayings, the kind of stuff that would irritate a xenophobic people suspicious of clever foreigners even centuries later, never mind just as a youthful Republic was emerging into a greater world. Theodor Mommsen sees Appius Claudius as the one great personality of the era; an almost regal rule-breaker sitting large on a timeline between Tarquinius Superbus and Julius Caesar. Mixing wealth and illimitable ambition was always of the essence, but with Appius Claudius it reached new heights with a road and an aqueduct named for him left behind as part of the very fabric of an expanding polity. If much of what he had wrought was to be undone, he still would have had the consolation that he would come again and indeed in only a few years reached for and occupied the consul's chair; no more than this scion of a great patrician clan would have expected, despite the touted resistance to what is claimed as his corrupting both the citizen body and the Senate.

Yet despite the reality that Appius Claudius was trying to woo the commons with his reforms to progress his own career, there is something very suggestive about the timing of the changes he championed. A year after they were mooted we hear of the increase in the numbers of military tribunes to sixteen, which means as there were four to each legion, almost certainly at this time the army's size was virtually doubled, with consular armies frequently raised to two-legion strength, accompanied by the equivalent number of allies; this on top of moves to establish an embryo maritime arm. So the Roman army expanding in 311 would make complete sense, with Appius Claudius converting humble men, freed slaves, their descendants and the proletariat into citizens, distributing them in tribes and centuries to increase the pool of men available to join the ranks of the army. A head count of heroes primed for war was required at a moment when, pressed by the times, it was crucial to flesh out the legions after disasters like the Caudine forks and Lautulae, and when a new threat was known to be growing in Etruria. This would not have been the only source of new blood; there had been a general increase in population with geographic extension of the citizen body, but still the push for radical social surgery would have been strong to reach the numbers required. It was also not long after this time that the first monies were minted in Rome, a development that corroborates a state under pressure to mobilize its latent assets, in a period not only when the consular armies were doubling in numbers, but small strides were being made to establish a mint new marine for coastal defence and when major public works like the Appian Way had to be funded. Wages were required for soldiers, sailors and public workmen in an exponentially greater manner than in years before.

Whatever the real needs that Appius Claudius' reforms were reflecting, there remained long-standing grievances against the Claudii present in many of the histories our main source would have utilized. They are recognized as a family who had gained for themselves a reputation for reckless and impious entitlement and with Appius Claudius Caecus in particular, we must be very concerned that much of what we are getting is the very opposite of a whitewash. It was not just during his censorship that it was considered the rot had set in; every dangerous change was seen to have his fingerprints all over it. Many certainly had no doubt that he had been whispering in the ear of his old freedman Gnaeus Flavius, who when elected aedile in 304 published abroad constitutional procedures and a legal calendar that had previously been kept classified by the patrician colleges of the priests. Before this, for most citizens appealing to the law was almost impossible without running foul of unfamiliar practices and timing. Another step along a road began in 451 when people pressed for laws to be codified as some defence against arbitrary oppression by their rulers.

In fact much of what Appius Claudius enacted failed to stick, the consuls refused to accept his amended list of senators and the censors of 304 reversed much of what he had done for the new citizens recruited from the landless and the head count. Yet though the unhappiness with both the man and his clan is palpable in all that is left to us, still nothing can overshadow how considerable were the achievements of this man who is one of the first almost two-dimensional personalities that emerges in the story of Rome. He would eventually be remembered for more than the controversial stuff; for example, a conduit bringing nearly 20 million gallons of water a day into the Forum Boarium (cattle market) to slake the thirst of an expanding city and the commencement of the great road going south near the coast, sweeping past the Pontine Marshes, veering inland before it reached a spectre-haunted vent into the underworld near Lake Avernus. The first stage would reach 132 miles to Capua in Campania and then, in generations to come, would reach down into the deep south all the way to Brundisium. Not that this well-travelled country that stretched in a finger down the coast to Cumae had not had routes before, but now a real proper highway with drainage ditches on each side ensured against the kind of dust bowls in summer and morasses in winter that had been typical of these earlier byways. This extravagant investment in infrastructure was costly, but a steady water supply was clearly needed and the Appian Way meant both the potential of exploiting commercial opportunities to the south and that the legions could travel with supply trains at a speedy and dependable pace to feed a southern front that in the last decades of the fourth century and the first ones of the third was absolutely crucial, ensuring rich Campania and others of Rome's allies there could be supported against the Samnites, Lucanians or other external menaces. Last but not least, Appius Claudius could ensure the clients he had won along the route could more easily reach the city for voting on committal days.

* * *

It was in the fabric of the city life rather than on the battlefield that the legacy of this controversial and complex man lay and this showed again in 307 when for the first time he achieved the consulship. There is a suggestion that he had run for consul when censor, only to be stymied by a tribune of the plebs who contended that he couldn't stand until he

The ancient walls of Ardea.

The pass at Lautulae with medieval tower; site of a battle in 315.

South Italian horseman, fourth century, Paestum Archaeological Museum.

South Italian cavalryman's armour, Taranto Museum.

Montefortino helmets from the fourth or third century, Chieti Archaeological Museum.

Samnite warrior, castle museum, Montesarchio.

Fourth-century trefoil cuirass, Chieti Archaeological Museum.

Site of Sutrium; remains of the ancient walls.

The gardens of Villa Gregoriana in modern-day Tivoli, ancient Tibur.

Ancient Etruscan gateway in the city of Volterra at night.

Modern-day Orvieto, ancient Etruscan Chiusi.

The Appian Way inland from Gaeta.

Looking down from Mount Vairano where the Battle of Aquilonia may have taken place.

Showing the steep descent from the Matese massif, going west, that would have faced Roman armies advancing into Samnium from that direction.

Looking down on Bojano, ancient Bovianum, from the medieval castle.

The battlefield of Sentinum seen from the heights of Sassoferrato.

La Rocca in Pentri country north of Bojano.

The remains of ancient walls at Praeneste, modern-day Palestrina, where young Marius was besieged during the battle at the Colline Gate.

The cyclopean walls at Rusellae.

had resigned his office. Yet when he finally occupied the consular chair, unlike so many of his peers he made no attempt to prove his mettle in the usual way. So often the route was for a successful military man to entrench himself as a heavyweight political competitor but he on this, his first incumbency, rejected the opportunity. There was enough business on hand: a campaign against the Sallentines, tenants of the Italian heel, was available that he might have tried for, but he proved happy to allow his colleague, Volumnius Flamma Violens, to deal with these truculent southerners. This 'new man', a plebeian with no tradition of officeholding in the family, was the first of his line to reach the consulship, but this was not the only time he personally had occupied the curial chair. He had a reputation as a glad hand with his men and more than just having the common touch, he was capable too. However, his wife may not have been to traditional Roman taste as they liked their women to keep in the background and she created something of a cause célèbre when, despite herself being of patrician stock, because of her husband she was refused access to a ceremony of patrician ladies to honour female virtue, so set up an alternative altar in her own home for plebeian women. This colleague of Appius Claudius showed himself capable, winning victories, taking cities and distributing spoils to his men while he stayed content to remain in Rome, ensuring he was constantly in the thoughts of his fellow citizens, able to build on the popularity he had gained as censor.

In 296, as eyes swung north towards an imminent threat, this pair from seven years before were again elected to the consulship, this despite the fact that many wanted Fabius Rullianus to stand again. However, quite such an arrant flouting of the law that forbade consuls being elected until ten years had passed meant that putting him in on consecutive years could not be countenanced, even if this tenet had been bent so often in the past. Indeed, the two consuls of 297 would be in harness again in just over a year's time and even in Appius Claudius' consular year the need for their talents could not be gainsaid as they were kept on for six months to progress the war in Samnium. However, if the increasing need for continuity of command in this conflict was advertised by these prorogations, it was by no means all that the year 296 would bring. Something else was happening, of which the antecedents had been touted even earlier. Appius Claudius was in his prime, in between making his name as censor, progenitor of the road and aqueduct that bear his name and entering legend as a blind old senator who threw back a Greek king's offers of peace in his face, refusing to treat until he and his men had left Italian soil. As one of the two senior magistrates, on this occasion he would set out to the northern front where he nerved himself to the expected task of facing an old enemy, the Etruscans. By spring things were ready and, after basic training and provisioning, his army marched out of the city and up the Tiber valley, a well-travelled route past the outposts of Sutrium and Narnia. His force comprised two legions, the first and fourth with 12,000 allies, so they probably numbered almost 20,000 men in total, but would they be enough? Initially they moved sufficiently fast to dissuade some Etruscan cities from chancing their arm against the Republic and this despite the fact that though their leader was a charmer blessed with popular appeal, he had no great military reputation. Still, he would find his hands full on arrival as there were plenty of enemies in the field by the time the country around Perusia was reached.

Appius Claudius found the context of his efforts in unfamiliar terrain was something far more menacing than just an Etruscan war. Most campaigning was plentifully seasoned with hazards, but now finding paths through forests, passes, hills and bridges over the rivers would be more problematic than in Latium and other places where the Romans had fought so often before. Also intelligence was seeping in, discovered by spies set to the task or through the interrogation of casual travellers, of an alarming massing of coalition forces in Etruria. Samnite envoys had been criss-crossing the country to some purpose, persuading and cajoling, claiming the hour of all their doom was drawing close if they did not act in concert against Rome. So the new consul discovered that appearances had been deceptive when he anticipated a contest with a single enemy; he in fact would be the first to face the coalition engineered by Gellius Egnatius. By this time the sight of masses of Samnite warriors in their bronze accoutrements, accompanied by brimming war chests, had acted as much as any arguments to broker an alliance that by now included the Etruscans, though the presence of Gauls or Umbrians cannot be confirmed. Whatever the finer points of co-operation and who was present in the army facing the Romans, they were very well led. They manoeuvred with intelligence and only accepted battle where the occasion and terrain were propitious. So before much time slipped by, several encounters had occurred; bloodletting that began affecting the morale of the Roman troops. Self-confidence, high at first, became ragged as casualties were taken, with no real anticipation of success against numerous and fearsome foes who had clearly earmarked them for even further pain as the fighting season wore on. The worry of being bottled up was palpable, but there seemed little option but to defend themselves where they camped against the solidary effectiveness of their adversaries.

The danger was already grave enough and the news that the Gauls were intending to join armies already massed to make an impact only increased the worry. So it is no surprise that 'three analysts' are cited, claiming that Appius Claudius, fearful of disaster if he carried on in the same way, wrote a letter to Volumnius Flamma asking for his assistance. This plebeian powerhouse had already showed well in his second visit to the position of highest magistrate. He had 'already taken three fortresses in Samnium in which about three thousand of the enemy had been killed and about half as many taken prisoners',[3] and we know that busy man had made quite an impact in the south, sending a proconsul to Lucania to put down a rising of the common folk against the local nobles, who were well-connected with their Roman peers and always inclined to put class interest before the national cause. We know that when the letter arrived from Appius Claudius, Decius Mus was among the officers present in the southern encampment,[4] so this battle-hardened veteran was available to be left to stay on and wreak what havoc he could in Samnium when the consul decided to respond positively. The best part of an army that comprised the second and third legions and 15,000 allies rushed to face what had been advertised as a real emergency; a show of collegiate solidarity that ought not to have been too much of a surprise as these two had worked together before. Yet despite this warm history, alliances might buckle, twist and invert and decent relations would not survive this encounter. Appius Claudius' men, becoming frustrated by the small wars fought in the rugged ground between the opposing camps, would have heard the sound of tramping feet and marching songs coming from the south with considerable relief. Dust-covered lictors preceded the consul Volumnius Flamma as he led his army up to his colleague's bivouac, reporting that he had come in response to the dispatch calling for aid. The man on the ground appeared dumbfounded at this, claiming he had never sent out any such call, was doing fine and would be quite capable of besting the Etruscan and Samnite forces facing him without the help of this man who he now claimed to despise. The ominous silence that followed these exchanges seemed likely to presage an awful fall-out, when the officers surrounding the two consuls stepped in to defuse a situation that threatened a serious rift while they were literally in the face of the enemy. These men had influence; after all, many would have scions of great houses, young certainly, putting in their years of campaigning so they might eventually compete for the highest office, yet still not people either of the commanders would want to needlessly alienate. So the atmosphere calmed a little and while nothing had been resolved, it at least appeared that an ill-fated flare-up might have been avoided.

This ruckus continued for quite some time, with Appius Claudius making wounding cracks about his colleagues improved declamatory aptitude and that pauciloquent man snapping back, that it would be more useful to Rome if the other's military capacity had been equally upgraded. Insults flew as the man on the spot continued to declare he had been doing fine against the enemy, contending that Volumnius Flamma had come of his own accord, like a hyena on a lion's kill, to claim credit on a front where he and his army had already done all the hard work. This silly beef looked like ending with the new arrival leaving in a huff and retaking the road south, had not the senior officers in Appius Claudius' army, more prepared to accept the need for timely help, begged their commander not to turn down this opportune offer of reinforcements, while others standing in front of Volumnius Flamma implored him to put the needs of the state over his bruised personal feelings. The trouble in the Roman camp, it turned out, had been sufficient for word to reach the enemy who, perceiving an advantage, appeared in the field in front of the palisades offering battle. The outcome of this initiative was a chaotic affair. Neither party came at the contest in a thought-out manner. On the attackers' side the commander-in-chief was not even there; Gellius Egnatius had taken a few thousand of his cavalry to search for forage. The Romans, riven by division, had just come rushing from the assembly with the commanders hardly able to agree on anything, never mind integrating their regiments.

So it was all disorder as Volumnius Flamma's men arrived at the front of the battle line, first encountering the Etruscans, while Appius Claudius' soldiers came on later in time to oppose those Samnites who themselves had failed to harmonize their attack with their allies. The battle, once it came to bloodshed, was a mess of disordered encounters, with little shape or reason. The details of Appius Claudius standing in the front line, praying to Bellona and vowing a temple in the case of success, is the usual stuff, as is the suggestion that the rivalry between the two Roman armies encouraged battle-winning ferocity. Apart from these tropes, all we know is that the legionaries and their allied comrades, though initially concerned that their division and disorder might have dreadful consequences, actually overthrew the enemy, forcing them to quit the field and beat a tactical retreat all the way to their encampment. There is even a claim that they took these entrenchments, despite Gellius Egnatius returning and showing obdurate in its defence.

On this occasion the northern confederates were seen off, despite intra-consular bickering having reached new heights in the middle of the campaign; that a good number of truculent enemies had been deducted from the balance sheet was a success worth winning, despite there being no triumphal fasti to corroborate it. Yet what remained clear was that the Etruscans and the Samnites, despite this Roman battlefield advantage, continued an ever-present menace in the region of Perusia. They persisted there in considerable numbers and after being joined by the Umbrians and Gauls, which could not be long delayed, there was going to have to be a reckoning. The unthinkable seemed about to occur; a power grouping had arisen that just might crush the life out of Rome. The occasion was pregnant with hazard and later, people would recognize it as a crossroads. This was an alarming time, when unity among the leaders of Rome's armies was surely an imperative priority, but if there is any account of how or even if the bad feeling between the two victorious consuls was resolved, it is lost. Surely that their efforts had ended in at least something like a success would have helped smooth out relations, though soon enough events in Samnium ensured that these two were not together going to be able to concentrate on facing a situation where, even if their men had just showed well in combat, seemed increasingly fraught with danger. From south of Rome intelligence arrived that other

Samnites, armed and eager, had boiled out of their mountain homeland to bring pain and loss to Rome's allies, people who could reasonably expect succour from a hegemon whose claimed raison d'être was offering them protection.

The raiders had come on by Vescia situated on the left bank of the Liris, rolled by the cone of Roccamonfina, down the river near the hot springs of Suio, pouring past where in eighteen centuries a Spanish army would force the river and only chevalier Bayard's heroics at another bridge at Scauri would save the retreating French force, then on towards the coast on one side and on the other overrunning the Falernian region, famous for its fine wines, and down into northern Campania. Any ability to face the new threat was undermined by the fact that both Fabius Rullianus' and Decius Mus' prorogued imperium were about to end, thus men with generations of experience of fighting Samnites to draw on between them would be absent, while troops would also have been stripped from the locality to swell Appius' numbers at the beginning of the campaign. So once the reality was digested, that the enemy around Perusia were at least no longer immediately rampant, it was possible for Volumnius Flamma to head south, travelling fast to try to catch the plunderers before they could get away with their loot. It was a considerable distance, 200 miles across Etruria and Latium if he came by the most direct route, down the Tiber and, once over the river near Rome, picking up the path of the Latin Way, so with forced marches it would have been barely two weeks later when they arrived. The Romans may not have had the most sophisticated commissariat in the world, but it would have been sufficient to get between 15,000 and 20,000 men down the hard miles to reach the enemy. At Cales the ruin the Samnites had wrought was clear, with the sky angry red with flames, while smoke palled over farmsteads and country hamlets. Yet if this was distressing, the word that came from locals was more encouraging as these informants reported the raiders were making a dash for it but were encumbered by so much booty that their convoy could hardly keep any organized pace at all; that their leaders were even trying to encourage the men to drop some of what they carried so they might dodge the army sent to intercept them and get back home in one piece. Scouts gallantly pressing forward confirmed not only this, but also that the heavily-laden Samnite warriors were encamped not far away, installed on the banks of the Volturnus River, in preparation for fading back to Samnium. Hardly waiting to rest his footsore soldiers, Volumnius Flamma moved near enough to be within striking distance of the intruders but far enough away to not be reported to them.

Before the flush of dawn had illuminated the landscape, the consul brought up his legions to within sight of the enemy defences, but instead of attacking straight away he sent in Oscan-speaking infiltrators to see how the land lay. The information they returned with was even more encouraging. The enemy, anyway of mixed quality, were in a mess; a few men with the standards were already on the road while the baggage was just exiting the gate and most of the armed men were still in the camp. With their prey in disarray, the Romans knew an opportunity when they saw it and the legions, accompanied by their allies, trumpets blaring, fell on the retreating column showing outside the camp walls. Now it had come to fighting the raiders were not ready; many had not even donned their armour and were strung out on the road engaged in driving their rustled cattle or trailing their carts of plunder when a withering volley struck their ill-formed ranks. Now the confused defenders were torn between pressing on or returning to the safety of their ramparts. Caught in two minds, little resistance was put up either by the column on the road or even in the camp itself. Everywhere it was uproar and the turmoil was exacerbated because all along the column prisoners taken in the raids, 7,400 in all, took advantage of the panic to escape their bonds; men who then picked up what arms they could find lying around and attacked those who had only a few moments before had little concern for what they perceived as cowed and pitiable captives.

These released prisoners even managed the feat of capturing the enemy general Statius Minatius. He was riding along the ranks of the column trying to organize the lines when sufficient of these men, hefting the javelins they had found discarded on the ground, drove off his escort and grabbed the man as he sat on his horse, rushing him pinioned and surrounded into the Roman lines. This seems to have been enough for men who from the start lacked the discipline that might have allowed them to put up a fight against an orderly enemy assault and stampeded in panic. A comprehensive victory is averred with the enemy cornered and destroyed and such a haul of recovered booty that there was enough for the previous owners to reclaim what they could identify, while plenty was left over to reward the soldiers, who swiftly sold the 'spoils' to local merchants so they would not risk replicating the mistakes made by the men they had just overrun.

All this sounds uncannily like a year later when in late 295 another raiding party was caught on the road after spoiling through a similar part of the world. That Volumnius Flamma was concerned in countering this act of predation too is telling, yet enough is different, such as the involvement of Appius Claudius in the later engagement and details of the geography, to make it quite possible that there were two raids within two years in an area that was deeply susceptible to such ransacking. The lack of any triumphs in this season certainly is indicative that whatever had been achieved, the danger threatening in this part of the world was far from over, and a familiar strategy of settling colonists was unveiled to try to cover where the Samnite raid had shown weaknesses in regional defences. New fortified communities were planted at Minturnae by the mouth of the Liris, where the Appian Way crossed the river, and in the tenth century AD was a base for Saracens to terrorize central Italy for generations. Also the route taken by the most recent marauders was plugged by a colony called Sinuessa further down the coast. The establishment of these places was always a source of potential conflict back at Rome because those who arranged the land grants could garner a large client population among the colonists, but if the commissioners were eager on this occasion, they found enrolling volunteers problematic. Minturnae and Sinuessa must have appeared a long way south to potential migrants, particularly with what had just occurred in these vulnerable lands so proximate to hostile neighbours. Any prospects would have included a heightened sense of unease for people who must have expected to be transformed into guardians on perpetual outpost duty rather than finding the prosperous life of a yeoman farmer.

However, trouble with reluctant transportees soon paled as it became clear to the administration at Rome that nothing had been settled in the north, but the problem had grown with Appius Claudius again confronted by a blossoming confederacy. Words leached back that not only the Samnites and Etruscans but Umbrians and Gauls, tempted by mercenary gold, were massing in menace along the Umbrian front.

What had been just a threat the year before was now clearly becoming a very sobering reality. The commander dug in at Aharna, modern-day Civitella d'Arna, had not been reticent in airing his concerns and a number of envoys dispatched over the late summer arrived from north of the Tiber, unveiling what developments were afoot in his military district and suggesting that the hour of doom was drawing close. The Umbrians were no longer just making menacing noises, they were on hand in numbers and the same was true of the Senones. They had come up from the Adriatic shore in such force that to the north of the Roman camp near Perusia, armies were coalescing that looked like they might be capable of turning the tables in what had previously been a successful war for the Republic.

United at last, the greatest enemy coalition ever mobilized against Rome was on hand. This was a threat of such magnitude the Romans had hardly faced before, and it is no surprise that as on not a few other occasions in her history, we hear of terror in the streets, with the populace having a clear view that there was a danger of the sort they had not seen for a long time. They were used to facing both Etruscans and Samnites, and even on occasions a third party might have got involved. The Umbrians since Fabius Rullianus had penetrated the Ciminian forest had always been a potential adversary and the Sabines, Marsi, Picentini, Vestini, Marrucini, Hernici, Aurunci, Apulians, Lucanians and even Tarentines all might involve themselves on occasions, but seldom more than one at a time. Now there were four and one of them were those Gauls who were the direct descendants of the men, always perceived as awful and dangerous adversaries, who had trashed the city of Rome just under a century before. So it is little of a surprise, that as elections approached to choose the men to face this threat, thoughts turned to those considered a safe pair of hands. Volumnius Flamma, who had returned to oversee the polling, argued that the situation was sufficiently grave for the veteran Fabius Rullianus to be appointed dictator to lead all of Rome's armies against the hordes that were gathering in the north. As it turned out, despite there being few prepared to stand in his way to command, the old soldier competed in a race he knew was his to win not as dictator but as consul in the usual way. The eighteen centuries of the knights showed the way and the voters also took notice of his recommendation and that of

Volumnius Flamma as well when they chose Decius Mus to fill the other chair, while Appius Claudius, considered rock steady at the tiller of home administration, was made praetor in absentia.

The Romans had turned to experience in spades when Fabius Rullianus and Decius Mus, men with exemplary track records against the Samnites, had been made consuls in 297 and then kept on in command in 296, and they were sticking with it. They had been developing institutions to allow their power to be exerted for a longer time, further away from home, and it is no coincidence that prorogation now became far more usual. In the previous campaigning season both ex-consuls had been retained in command of their armies for a further six months and the example of these two was not all. During almost the whole of this war we find veteran generals, men with nerve and spirit, kept on in commands in a way that had very seldom been done before. The only convincing cases we know of before are Publius Philo in 326 and Fabius Rullianus himself in 307, but these seem to have been one-offs. Now they came like an avalanche; prorogation became almost the norm for the consuls of the 290s, whether it was Scipio Barbatus, Fulvius Centumalus, Appius Claudius, Volumnius Flamma or after them Curius Dentatus and Postumius Megellus. Though it would not last, the Third Samnite War was also the last hurrah of the iteration of senior magistracies. Things were normalized afterwards with the consulship being shared among a larger group and the need for experience being provided by continuing these men on in the field as proconsuls. Yet now institutions had been amended, experience mobilized and the Republic's military resources were about to be tapped in an unprecedented manner, would even such herculean efforts be enough?

Chapter Eight

Sentinum

'As when on a sounding beach the swell of the sea beats, wave after wave, before the driving of the West Wind; out on the deep at the first is it gathered in a crest, but thereafter is broken upon the land and thundereth aloud, and round about the headlands it swelleth and reareth its head, and speweth forth the salt brine: even in such wise on that day did the battalions of the Danaans move, rank after rank, without cease, into battle.'

The Iliad, Book IV

So the verdict of fate was at hand, as a babel of voices gave cacophonic cadence to the assembly of encamped warriors marshalling in north Etruria. Etruscans were there in numbers, as were the Umbrians joining with Gellius Egnatius' Samnites who had instigated their coordination, and finally there were the Gallic tones of the Senones, whose armies had at last crossed the Apennines from the Adriatic coast. It had been a massive gamble when the Samnites dispatched so many of their best fighting men north, far from their own threatened heartlands, but this alarming throw of the dice seemed to have paid off. The impact of the alliance might have taken time to be fully revealed, but now it was up and running and making its move in numbers. The Romans had only to confront a couple of the confederate allies in the past fighting season but in the new one it would not just be columns of burnished warriors from the Etruscan cities and old, purposeful and obdurate Samnite foes, who had sore feet from crossing half the peninsula and intended to make it count; these would be seconded by both Umbrians and intimidating Gauls. A vast host crowded the roads, tens of thousands of tramping feet kicked up clouds of dust that marked their progress in the hill country north of Perusia, alerting and alarming the Romans still encamped at Aharna under the consul Appius Claudius. This man, who must have felt the screw turning on him, may have recently received some good news when he heard that he had been kept on in office as praetor when the magisterial elections were carried out in Rome in the autumn of 296, but the rest of the intelligence reaching his camp would have sat much less easily.

The continuing grimness of Appius Claudius' reports had ensured that, when his consular colleague entered Rome, it was to supervise what were perceived as some of the most significant elections in the history of the city. Everybody was aware now of the potential threat emanating from the lands beyond the northern frontier, even if the exact magnitude of the armies mustering to attack were less familiar, so that inevitably at least one and probably both of the new consuls would see the war the Romans had been fighting there as the priority. One of the two great magistrates was bound to set out on the road to Perusia and the personnel involved ensured there would be a tense encounter when they arrived. The two men who had been made consuls again had a considerable history with the commander at Aharna. Fabius Rullianus and Decius Mus were bone-deep enemies of the censor of sixteen years before and had done their very best to undo his domestic reforms. These characters fared well at Livy's hands, incensed as they were by activities that not only disturbed the exclusively elite roll-call of senators but also augmented the citizen body in a most radical manner. Fabius Rullianus particularly is pictured as a just hero who would turn back this tide of corruption in the curia and the forum after their instigator had stepped down. Claiming dreadful consequences if Appius Claudius' revolution was allowed to stand, both he and his colleague were among the magistrates who in the years following, with the overwrought analysis of natural Tories, ensured that many of the reforming censors' judgements were not carried through. Particularly the senatorial lists reverted to the names that had been on them before he entered the censorship. Then in 304 both men shared the censorship themselves and consistent in opposition to contentious enactments, they revoked the changes that had been made to the tribal arrangements, repositioning the newly-enfranchised citizens in just four new urban tribes so they could not, from their domiciles in the city, dominate the rural tribes where Appius Claudius had placed them. The antagonism had by no means travelled in one direction, as Appius Claudius was noticed trying, when he was consul in 307, to stop Fabius Rullianus from being kept in command after his term of office had expired. With the other consul things went just as deep. Only five years earlier it almost seemed a further denting of patrician exclusivity was destined for grudging acceptance when two champions ranged themselves on either side of the argument; 'there was a violent confrontation between Appius Claudius and Decius Mus' over access to an expanded number of religious offices previously monopolized by the old families. For Decius Mus this was personal; he as a plebeian could not become a pontiff or auger, despite his own father being legendary for saving a Roman army by sacrificing his life in a manner that showed such non-patrician involvement was clearly acceptable to the gods.

Day and night the armourers of Rome bent hammer to anvil and the night sky was lit by sparks, while the green levies practised their drills and hefted training weapons; blisters were earned and muscles toned in a callous crash course for farmers' boys, shopkeepers and merchants' sons, who taken together were perhaps the largest proportion of the population ever required to go to war in this generation, beaten into cogs in a military machine that might face the forbidding hazard emerging in a quarter that had seldom before held such threats. There was uncertainty and foreboding in the streets as the citizens almost longed to know the worst rather than just quailing in terror in the face of the rumours of hordes of enemies coalescing beyond the horizon. After weighing the reports of the menace posed by a four-nation coalition, it was decided that it would be Fabius Rullianus who should grasp the nettle and go first to the Aharna camp. So the orders were given that would assure an interesting personal slant on events. The veteran commander who was headlining the Roman effort had clearly taken seriously the warnings about a situation that looked set to flame out of control enough to ensure celerity. He moved at breakneck speed, deliberately not taking all the men he could have, winding north up the Tiber valley with only a skeleton force, the best 4,000 foot and 600 horse available, ensuring it took less than a week to reach the ex-censor and road-builder who still had most of his army present from the previous year; men who were making great efforts to ensure they were as comfortable as they could be, sending out parties to bring in wood for fires, still very much required in the sharp weather before the start of the fighting season. Some of these soldiers, out foraging, found themselves confronted by the light-shod reinforcements coming up from Rome, marching behind the grizzled but familiar figure of Fabius Rullianus, under whom some would have served in years gone by. The tradition is that when the men told him they were out to collect firewood he, showing towering self-confidence, retorted that they had no need to search because they should burn the palisade of their camp to keep them warm as they had become too soft and settled in their permanent post. Under his new regime they would need no manmade defences to face the enemy, only their brave hearts. The incoming commander was clearly prepared to push his prerogatives, though his comments were a little unfair and the criticism implied in respect of their previous incumbent was obvious, thus making it even more certain that any intercourse between the two was bound to be extremely chilly. However, the potential for confrontation between these men, who looked formed as natural rivals, was quickly alleviated when Appius Claudius, determined to suffer no further indignities, hurried out of camp the very next day, taking the long road back to Rome.

Then, good to his word, though winter was not yet over, the army was put on the move, making camp each day in a different place in an effort to terrorize the enemy over as large an area as possible and return the soldiers to the peak of fighting fitness, capable of prompt manoeuvre. They struck out down from the hills where the Aharna camp was situated, around nearby Perusia and west to 25 miles south of Lake Trasimene to reach the neighbourhood of Clusium, where Roman walls still show in this ancient place with Villanovan roots. Called Camars in a previous existence and prosperous, set in hills and fertile farmland, it had been a powerful Etruscan place for generations, part of the twelve-city league that had dominated the region in the sixth century and intimately connected with Lars Porsena, the warlord in power when the Romans dumped their kings and whose tomb was a destination for sightseers even in ancient times.[1]

Then, with winter changing to spring, while his army bivouacked in the swamps of the River Chiana below the town, Fabius Rullianus decided to turn south. Taking the great majority of the men he had so effectively honed, he headed back to Rome. Only the second legion was left behind in the care of the competent Scipio Barbatus, somewhere in the country around Clusium, with instructions to hold tight in a place where the Romans might still hope to retain a foothold. The reason for this withdrawal is not made clear, but surely in part was just the nature of the Roman military in a period well before the Roman legionary had become the sixteen- or twenty-year stint professional of late Republican and Imperial times. The men who had followed Appius Claudius in the previous fighting season were needed back home to work their farms or run the other enterprises that formed their livelihoods. They had, after all, already spent the winter under arms and the kind of warfare Rome had been fighting in recent decades ensured that, when necessity demanded, the legions would have to be kept mobilized for several seasons, but this kind of commitment could only ever be exceptional.

Most Roman warriors saw themselves as soldiers for a season and after that would expect others to take up the burden while they resumed their old lives. Some with a predilection for fighting might stay on in the ranks with others, veterans whose skills were needed could be pressured, but there was a limit and the rulers in the Tiber city well knew it. Still, over long periods of constant warfare, expectations had become mutable and eventually periods of service would extend even more. Yet even 100 years later, when so much blood had been spilt in the contest with Carthage, still the legionary remained a farmer soldier. A man might several times in his life be called to the colours, but never became a full-time warrior. That change would only occur with the advent of an imperial project that expanded the Republic's sway outside of Italy. Then distance from home ensured that in the second century the man who took ship to Greece, Anatolia or Iberia logistically could not return to his old life for years and indeed, many would never come home at all, either leaving their bones on foreign strands or settling down to live as planted rulers and defenders of the lands they had conquered; developments that not long in the future would bring a sea change in the polity that Fabius Rullianus was now being asked to defend against an awful menace.

There are other explanations offered for the lure of the big city for the new consul. It may have been his own desire to get back to consult with the authorities in a situation where he considered the dangers were considerably greater than he had imagined when he had set out. It is also possible that he had been subject to an imperative recall from a Senate stirred up by the extravagant reports of the confederation's numbers that Appius Claudius had sent. That man in the field had been urging that both consuls with their armies would be needed to face four foes in the north, so it would be no surprise if the City fathers felt the need for a full briefing with the commanders who would end up holding the fate of Rome in their hands. The early-season campaigning between Aharna and Clusium conducted by Fabius Rullianus had turned out no more than a preamble and it was with his return to Rome that the countdown to Armageddon really got under way. Whatever the causation and sequence, once arrived he made it absolutely clear that the two legions Appius Claudius had had under his command and the 5,000-odd men he himself had brought to join them just would not be enough for the task. Knowing that most of the Republic's resources would be required, he pushed hard for both consuls to act together if the chances of success were to be maximized; that Decius Mus too must take all the men he could to join the northern war rather than heading for Samnium, or if that was not possible, then Volumnius Flamma should back him up with a 'full consular army'. He had to be persuasive as he argued for a full concentration on the Perusia front and that any inclination to worry about leaving themselves weakly defended in other places had to be resisted. Within the senatorial conclave there surely would have been powerful characters qualified by past military experience who would have pointed out the hazards of putting all their eggs in one basket. However, in the end enough of them realized that war was always full of bad choices and the one Fabius Rullianus was pressing stood the best chance of success and that the coalition of old enemies and their barbarian confederates required confrontation as soon as possible, whatever this might mean elsewhere. In fact, it was his old partner Decius Mus who ended up seconding him as the war turned into a double-consul struggle, with so much of the City's military resources focused against the impending threat.

When the talking stopped and with a heavyweight pairing prepared to shoulder the burden of an apprehensive community, the long-expected orders to advance were given to take the road that led north, but before the armies had marched far in what was going to be a monumental year, a considerable setback occurred for an officer who had done well enough since 298. The spring had seen the hirsute Scipio Barbatus holding the fort and covering the main valley route along which an invading army might move south. Encamped near Clusium with just one legion, it was he who was first to suffer from the terrible enemy who were going to make this fighting season so tense and memorable for the Republic. The Gauls were back and, in combination with so many new friends, they felt little need to restrain themselves when their scouts laid information that only a rump Roman military remained holding on in northern Etruria. Scipio Barbatus we know was not present in great strength, suggesting few allies were available to support his legionaries, so when the warning came that a horde of enemies, with the Senones at their head, were about to descend, he had to act. Between his defended camp and a nearby town was a steep hill and he swiftly decided this would make a far better place for his outgunned men to make a stand rather than on flat ground, even with a fosse and palisades from which to fight behind. Hustling his followers, he made for the top, up the track mounting the hill, but unwisely he had failed to reconnoitre the other side and as the sweating troops breasted the rise they found the enemy was already there in force. Worse than this, while ascending they had not detected another detachment coming up behind to envelop them. The numbers involved are not made clear, nor indeed if anybody else was present apart from the Gauls, though there are claims that both the Samnites and Umbrians were there and in a tactically advantageous position they made the most of it, cutting down the surrounded force to a man.

Yet this tale of extermination after a two-pronged attack is only one version; another story has the Roman commander, at the same affray, leading a successful attack against the Umbrian wing of the enemy army. His involvement had become necessary when a legate called Lucius Manlius Torquatus, perhaps the son of the man who is reported fatally falling off his horse in 299, was cut off with his men when they were caught out foraging. Scipio Barbatus, learning what was afoot, rushed to the rescue, not only saving his careless lieutenant but retaking the booty and prisoners the enemy were trying to whisk away. These stories are clearly contradictory, though it is just possible to believe that while much of the army was trapped, their commander escaped after driving off the Umbrian regiments facing him. We certainly know he is alive and accounted in action on a number of occasions well after this encounter. Nor is it just the tactical particulars of this donnybrook, but also the siting is far from completely certain. If our main source suggests Clusium as the venue, there are other claims[2] that Scipio Barbatus' second legion had been encamped in the territory of Camerinum when they were attacked, having been dispatched towards these important Umbrian allies situated to the east of the Roman post at Aharna and south of where the great battle of nations would take place later in the year.

Not the most glorious opening to this crucial campaign. That there had been a real reverse for Roman arms, if not an actual annihilation, is a conclusion supported by the dependable Polybius, who mentions them sustaining 'considerable loss' at the hands of the Gauls,[3] a circumstance that was soon advertised to the two consuls as they marched their armies up from Rome. The advanced guard encountered Gallic warriors on their sprightly mounts and this vanguard noticed immediately the grisly, severed heads they displayed of men who they might have known as comrades from the legionary ranks. Some were swinging from their saddle horns, while others were impaled, cold, white and lifeless, atop the spears the warriors carried in their hands which, along with the songs of triumph they were singing and other rodomontade, made it abundantly clear that the army the consuls hoped to meet up the road was no longer going to be worth a bean.

So it would have inevitably been with their confidence slightly dented that the two commanders led on to confront the main enemy army. Still, happily for the nervous intruders they did not encounter immediate resistance as once the victorious confederate warriors saw that they were now up against the whole might of the Roman military they pulled back north. Having integrated anything that remained of Scipio Barbatus' defeated remnant into the main host, the Romans pressed on. It would have been a long, hard journey as they tramped, column after column of armoured warriors kicking up dust along the main Tiber road, through Etruria and past Perusia to reach the wide mountain valley in east Umbria where a great battle would take place. After they had trailed across the Apennines, the Romans found themselves cheek by jowl with a huge enemy army in the 'district of Sentinum'. Here, in the valley beneath modern-day Sassoferrato, they camped 4 miles to the south, the soldiers settling down to build their fortified camps, with slaves collecting wood to provide the gates and palisades, as well as firewood, water and fodder for the animals. The high command soon learned that their foes were not only nearby but in such mammoth numbers that they had been forced to split up their contingents, with the Gauls and Samnites in one camp and the Etrurians and Umbrians in another. This information was sobering enough as, although the Romans could field decent numbers themselves, still they were far from confident that they were sufficiently strong to face the conglomeration of combatants gathered just a few miles away. Never before had a Roman army faced an enemy horde that covered so much of the land with their numbers.

Unsurprisingly, Gellius Egnatius and the other allied leaders, despite finding themselves contemplating the largest force that Rome would ever mobilize for one engagement until the Second Punic War, were far from intimidated by the size of this Roman throng. In normal times such a force might seem fearsome, but now they were outnumbered by the combined Samnites, Gauls, Etruscans and Umbrians, all anticipating their finest hour, and this confidence was reflected in their plans. The decision was made that the best way to utilize their advantage was for the Gauls and Samnites, who were camped together, to confront the enemy in open battle and once their adversary was fully committed, the Etruscans and Umbrians should sally out of their joint bivouac and overrun the enemy's encampment. The key was would the Romans come out and fight? It was surely likely, as the very size of the armies involved meant that supplying them in one place for a long time would be difficult. Logistics would force a decision. It could not be long before among the milling rank and file the question of provender would become critical; after all, it was hard to squeeze adequate meals out of a country stripped almost wholly bare by what must have amounted to nearly 1,000,000 men and animals, but before the attempt could be assayed the coalition army proved leaky. The plan was sufficiently common knowledge that three men decided they would see what the information would be worth to the other side. They slipped out at night and presented themselves at the guard post of the Roman camp and ultimately found themselves in front of the consuls, who listened to their story with great interest. The traitors got their gold and it was worth every penny; what they had revealed would save their audience's bacon, deciding them to resist the pressure to fight until they could find a way to diminish the forces facing them.

The spies' information might have confirmed the Romans' darkest forebodings when estimating the numbers opposed to them, but the answer to the question of how to sow division among the confederates was not long in coming. In this lull before the storm they decided to utilize the troops who had been left in defence of the Republic's heartland in a more proactive role. In an attempt to even up the odds, the consuls wrote to the men commanding the two armies 'not far from the city' in what was looking like the most dangerous of years. These detachments were commanded by a couple of pretty significant characters both now installed as pro-praetors. Fulvius Centumalus, consul in 298, was posted in the Faliscan country on the west bank of the Tiber, north of Veii, while Lucius Postumius Megellus had been kept near the Vatican Hill on the right-bank flood plain near the capital. If these veterans, two of the many experienced officers kept under arms in this year of decision, had first been deployed to keep the home folk safe, the consuls now demanded a more active role of their subordinates. To ensure they would not have to face all their enemies together at Sentinum, instructions directed them to march up the road towards Clusium. The consuls proved fortunate in their lieutenants as both commanders did their bit. On receiving written orders, they set about ravaging Etruscan country and making sure it got about that they were on the way to punish the Umbrians as well. There was a reaction; in no time the leaders of the Etruscan and Umbrian contingents encamped near Sentinum had to give bad news to what must have been furious and unhappy allies: that they intended to depart to defend their own people who were afraid and vulnerable, denuded as they were of troops to face the Roman invasion armies heading their way. Nobody in confederate headquarters, however annoyed they might be, had any interest in destabilizing relations and the danger that the alliance might quickly fragment if the partners started arguing the toss made any attempt at stopping them going impolitic. No patched-together coalition would stand such division.

Many in the streets of Rome, from the cream of the elite to propertyless labourers, already suffering after a nervous winter, now worried further when their city was stripped of most of their organized fighting men and inevitably there were questions about the future, a fear of being enslaved by awful foreign hordes. The issue of how they would fare if the field armies were defeated or if enemy detachments slipped past to move south inevitably caused a mood of heightened dread not typical of most of the wars fought by the Republic. Yet if the citizenry worried, at the battlefront they had good reason to hope and presently prying eyes watching the roads were able to report long columns of soldiers leaving the enemy camps heading west, up and over the limestone hills that separated them from the country around Perusia and west to Clusium; places already suffering from the attentions of Fulvius Centumalus' and Postumius Megellus' men, an occurrence of such importance that it cannot be overstated. The Battle of Sentinum was clearly 'a damn close-run thing' and if tens of thousands of Etruscan and Umbrian veterans had been there to second the Samnites and Gauls it is difficult not to believe that the Romans would have experienced at least defeat, if not disaster. Forward defence in Umbria always incorporated the risk of destruction, but the distraction had been enough and with the enemy clearly depleted, the consuls were eager to fight, not being sure how long the departed regiments might stay away.

A council of war would have gathered: Fabius Rullianus, Decius Mus and their senior men to decide on how to handle the problem of the Samnite-Senones combination with which they now had to contend. With their other foes departed, the general agreement was for action at the first opportunity. They were at the end of long attenuated lines of communication, in unfriendly country with no prospect of reinforcements and had no good reason to wait, but there were drawbacks. It had been a while since they had had success against the Gauls in battle and this unfamiliarity would show, but at least they knew what they were dealing with when it came to the men under Gellius Egnatius. Two days passed as the consuls deployed their armies, drawn up in ranks between their own camp and those of their foes, but battle was refused and apart from some skirmishing with a few javelins and slingshot flying, the deadlock continued. It was only on the third occasion that, siting their horses behind the files of men drawn up for combat, the consuls saw that the enemy too were preparing to fight, emerging behind their standards in main force, dressing their ranks and willing to put matters to the lottery of battle at last.

The confederate high command had been delaying in the hope that their allies would quickly return to again give them the edge, but realizing this was not going to happen and still full of confidence in their numbers and quality, the resolve was made to meet the enemy despite the absence of so many comrades. To knock down the Romans was the prize, so they decided to fight the battle they were bound to if they hoped to tear at the heart of an antagonist who had made so much of central Italy their own in the last few decades. Gallic horsemen, riding at the head of their army, would have been on the lookout, ensuring that the advancing Romans were soon discovered, while the scouts Gellius had posted echoed a similar warning. The confederate command, knowing two of Rome's most belligerent generals were on hand and had already offered battle, anticipated a prompt confrontation against adversaries as full of aggressive intent as themselves.

* * *

In late spring or very early summer of 295, after omens were taken, the commanders, followed by a glittering tail of staff officers in sumptuous armour, led out their armies into the dawn of a sunny day and onto a terrain of rolling fields and tumbling hills. In this impending showdown the numbers are well attested, as the consuls had commenced the campaign at the head of four legions and an even more numerous force of allies, Latins and others, while the cavalry was made up of the normal numbers of Romans and allies seconded by an elite band of 1,000 Campanian horse. The legions and allied regiments, primed for battle, would have been present in good strength. Only the attrition of a considerable march subtracted from the numbers mustered at the start of the campaign. So there would have been something around 4,000 infantry and 300 horse each for the legions, with more foot provided by the allies and double the number of cavalry, if later practice is anything to go by. The field of battle filled the wold country below the jutting rock where Sassoferrato town now stands, where the rugged beginnings of the Apennines to the east are green and well-watered to this day by

Plan of the Battle of Sentinum 295 BC

Confederate camp

Samnites

Gauls

chariots

first and third legions and allies
Scipio Barbatus   Gaius Marcius
Fabius Rullianus

Campanians

fifth and sixth legion and allies
Decius Mus

a river whose name remembers the blood that was spilt on that day. It would not have been very different 2,300 years earlier, except that the vegetation would have included vines and fruit trees throwing shadows among meadows where columns of heavy infantry trailed out of the dawn, with cavalry guards out to the front and flanks. Leaving behind the carts, pack mules and sumptuary paraphernalia that made up an army's baggage train, tens of thousands of Roman warriors stood in their ranks looking across half a mile ahead of them. The dust would have risen thick and churning, kicked up by the Earth-shaking hordes of bare, sandalled or booted enemy feet, even before they saw emerging the spike-haired Gauls howling their blood-curdling war cries, shouting and shaking their shields and spears above their heads. The Romans' resolve must surely have wavered; grim precedent ensured that the sight of the enemy ranks covering the terrain in front of them conjured up nightmares of the barbarian shattering of their home in the time of their great-grandparents. It was as daunting as anything they would ever have seen: their opponents' outlandish appearance, some naked except for a sword belt, others in rainbow plaid cloaks buckled at the shoulder, breeches or trousers and strange horned helmets, deployed in deep lines. Along their front were men with strange serpent-shaped horns showing above their heads and their horsemen stretched far out on the wing, many high-riding nobles with fine mail armour, shields and long slashing swords. Over the greensward on the other flank was a view towards the more familiar ranks of their Samnite adversaries; the whole comprising different nations cheering each other all along their line.

First contacts would have occurred not long after the haze of dawn had burned away and the sun risen on a contest that many present would have known was likely to be crucial in the life of the Roman Republic. This was a crisis, as the army of the city state on the Tiber faced probably the greatest enemy in its history so far in terms of numbers and quality of the foe. So it was appropriate that events were remembered as being presaged by beast and omens. A legend grew that between the armies in the rolling ground, in the considerable period that ancient armies took to shake out into lines, two animals appeared. A deer had been chased down from the hills by a wolf, but once they both realized they were trapped between two huge groups of noisy and dangerous men, they bounded off;

the deer towards the confederate multitudes and the wolf in the direction of the Roman position. The fates of the two were starkly different: the Gauls cut down the deer, while the legionaries facing them opened a lane for the wolf to escape, suggesting that the wolf, the emblem of Rome, would survive to prosper while the enemy, who had bloodily dispatched the avatar of the goddess Diana, would themselves only find death and destruction.

For the Romans the job of getting their lines in order was not without difficulty in undulating country with which they were not familiar and a situation where it was always possible for the ranks of farmer warriors to become confused. The manipular system was much less liable to be disrupted by rough terrain than was a phalanx, but the manoeuvring that these smaller units needed to undertake required more practice and some of the greener troops would not have been expert yet. Ahead the enemy had also stirred with the dawn as birds practised their harmonious chorus, and now in formation the glitter of helmets and spearheads showed along the Samnite line, with messengers speeding between the allies' headquarters to try to coordinate two peoples who themselves were not that familiar fighting alongside each other. All knew what they needed to do against their belligerent foes: drive them from the field and force a battered remnant to suffer the dangers that would inevitably face a defeated army in enemy country, with a long way to get back home.

Fabius Rullianus had been fighting Samnites all his life and when he weighed his options before the battle, ignorance of their psychology was not going to be a factor. So when we learn that 'Their commander knew that it was the habitual practice of both the Gauls and the Samnites to make a furious attack to begin with, and if that were successfully resisted, it was enough',[4] we might believe that it was not just a trope to barbarize these long-time foes. If this is accepted, then so can be the consul's determination to stand firm on the defence to blunt the expected onslaught; a sensible course of action to soak up all that would come their way, knowing that Samnite spirits would erode as the battle went on. So with this in mind, he confronted an old antagonist with the first and third legions on the right wing, these men taking the place of honour on the flank with the allies on their left. The right was the place for the bravest, as it was on that side that they had no shield for protection, so risked immediate destruction if the enemy caught them exposed. This was a practice that applied particularly to men lined up in a classic hoplite phalanx, but even when toting a scutum it was still a disadvantage as it was not possible to ward off a missile or a sword blow from the right without swivelling the body round and risk breaking formation.

The bronze-edged lines of Romans and allies, knowing well the kind of enemy they were facing, would have expected a ferocious charge, but unlike the Gauls, once endured, this was not all the Samnites had. Even if particularly dangerous on first contact, they would keep at the fight as they had shown so often before and the Romans would need to hold their ground and struggle their hardest to have any chance of winning. Knowledge that his men would need every advantage to endure whatever the enemy might throw at them caused Fabius Rullianus to establish a reserve commanded by the bearded man Scipio Barbatus and Gaius Marcius behind his line; a fall-back position if the Samnite assault turned out all it was cracked up to be, and if even the triarii were unable to stem the enemy tide. The numbers are unknown, but later events suggest they must have comprised several thousand men and perhaps some of his best as well.

One advantage that the consul might hope to count on was that supporting the right wing were not just the normal numbers of Roman and allied cavalry but 1,000 Campanian troopers as well. These offspring, relations and retainers of the opulent barons occupying the country inland from Neapolis were some of the best horse soldiers in Italy and we can see them in their glory in tomb paintings at Capua, Nola and Paestum: high-stepping horses, some of them even wearing armoured chamfrons and poitrails defending their head and chest, carrying riders usually considerably better protected than their Roman and Latin counterparts. Apart from fine feathered helmets, effective shields and bronze belts, pectoral defences are occasionally shown, sometimes even grieves, along with javelins, spears and slashing swords. The influence of the Greek colonies is evident here; they had fielded this sort of wealthy and well-guarded cavalier at least since the fifth century. Tarentum was particularly famous for such troopers, but more proximate places such as Neapolis and Cumae had long affected their neighbour's ways of making war.

The Roman lines moved off to the sound of the cornu, a curved trumpet, behind their standards across the pleated fields to their front. The youngsters of the hastati at the front kept silent, saving their breath for what they knew would be a gruelling physical test to come. Any battle cry would not be sounded until the instant of contact was almost upon them, when the adrenalin rush required an outlet, to not only encourage comrades but put the fear of God into the opposition. On approaching the enemy, their commanders' intention had been made clear: Fabius Rullianus held back his warriors, despite the rain of missiles hissing and rattling round their heads and thumping into their shields. The main ranks of heavy infantry did not advance; only light troops responded, perhaps Livy's rorarii, antecedents of the velites, most hurling the sheaf of light javelins they carried, with the liveliest coming to sword blows with their Samnite equivalents, but then the armoured mountain men came on with the kind of ferocious onslaught for which they were famous. They knew they had committed everything to their northern strategy and that a walloping triumph was the required dividend for this investment. The pressure was intense all along the right of the Roman battle line, missiles filled the air and many of the front-rank men came to hand-to-hand blows with those they could reach. Yet the defenders held back; those that stepped forward did so tentatively, crossing swords or thrusting with their spears to try to keep those opposite them off rather than do them real hurt. Still, as the Samnites picked up the pace and fed in their second line, the Romans found more assailants rushing at them. It took all the courage and strength of the men of the front maniples to hold their place to ensure no breaches were made through which their enemies might pour.

Battle lines shivered, bending and warping as terror gripped at the hearts of so many of the combatants. Labouring to hold their own against an increasing press, shield-to-shield ramming like goats, the participants sweated under a summer sun. Only a few moments of combat would have turned coats of mail into an almost unendurable burden and the efforts to raise a shield, particularly if enemy spears had lodged in it, became almost too much. That was when the men in the ranks behind stepped forward to offer relief, allowing their bloodied comrades to take a breath and even dress wounds they had taken. All the long morning and into the afternoon the fighting raged, with the first lines on either side wearing themselves out before the deeply-ranked men behind took over. As hastati struggled before being replaced by principes, heroes showed and those of a more human stamp too; the former chests puffed out in shining armour and blades flashing in shimmering parabolas, while the latter stared in terror at the carnage around, only looking for a way out, fear of their centurions and other officers behind them outstripping that of the enemy the only motivation for staying put. These officers were brutally attentive to anything that looked like shirking, as they had to be. In the maniple, unlike the phalanx, the soldiers were not literally pressed into place by the bodies of their comrades; there had to be something else to ensure cohesion, a ferocious discipline for which the Roman army would become justly famous. That might include a sentence of death for sleeping on guard duty and even decimation when a whole formation showed cowardice on the field of battle.

Sometime during this fighting, Fabius Rullianus decided that the decisive moment was at hand and determined on a switch of tactics. This was all about timing. When he perceived the force of the enemy attacks faltering, he rode over to the cavalry commander on the right wing and ordered this officer to lead his troopers in a turning movement, round the enemy flank, to a position where they could inflict a hammer blow against the Samnites' vulnerable side, when he would have the infantry ready to do their part:

> On the right Fabius, as I have stated, was protracting the contest. When he found that neither the battle-shout of the enemy, nor their onset, nor the discharge of their missiles were as strong as they had been at the beginning, he ordered the officers in command of the cavalry to take their squadrons round to the side of the Samnite army, ready at a given signal to deliver as fierce a flank attack as possible.[5]

The foot soldiers were reordered, standards brought to the front and officers repositioned at the head of their companies, while the units kept in reserve made ready to support whatever success might be achieved by the main line. Hefting what javelins they had to hand, the first line of both the legions and the allied formations discharged them in a shower before charging into combat. The ground between would not have taken long to cover, as in units six or eight deep, they roared their war cries that turned their foes' blood to ice and pushed forward, boots sinking into the turf or scrabbling along stony ground, heading towards waiting opponents who would have been trying to knock off any missiles that had stuck into their shields, making them difficult to manipulate in hand-to-hand fighting.

The allied horse and their Roman comrades had confronted their Samnite equivalents even as the infantry fight heated up, impeccably well-bred eques from moneyed families of Rome sporting gold rings of status alongside their peers from the Latin towns riding into battle. Their quality may have been frequently questioned, that they were the weak link in an essentially infantry army; indeed, that they often dismounted to fight because they were lacking in confidence when on horseback and as soon as possible were replaced by foreign auxiliaries who could do a better job. Yet even the largely unarmoured trooper of 295, wearing only his tunic, helmet and carrying a small round boss-less shield, a light quivering lance and sword was very far from useless. They could undertake the tasks expected, whether that be scouting, pursuit, fighting other cavalry or attacking enemy infantry on the flank in combination with their own foot soldiers, and the wars in which they had been involved for many years showed they were successful as often as not. Indeed, what is clear on this occasion is that after a heated struggle, their Samnite opponents were overrun and many riders toppled into the dust. The attack pressed them back, exposing the flank of the infantry line they had been positioned to protect.

Cavalry won battles by breaking or disrupting enemy infantry and this was the key, but like all their kind through the ages they had a tendency to engage in wild pursuit after having defeated the horsemen facing them. However, Fabius Rullianus' men were kept well in hand and the greater number soon reorganized into their squadrons and were already prepared when the signal was given for them to engage the enemy foot. As the high-riding, bloodied troopers advanced, just the sight of them threw the infantry on the Samnite flank into confusion. Attempts were made to turn against the onrushing cavaliers, to use lances and javelins to create a hedge of spear points sufficient to put off the horses and riders pressing over the grass towards their ranks. Yet it was not enough: the exposed men on the flank began to fall under the points of the Roman lances, the edges of their swords or were knocked over by the flying hooves, or just terrified, they pulled out of the line disregarding the cries of their desperate officers, moving in the direction of their camp where they hoped the walls would keep out the sanguine antagonists milling all around them.

The line collapsed from the left and those further along could do little to stop the rot as they were faced by the enemy infantry pressing in along their whole front. Exchanges of missiles had long since given way to more immediate and gory contact. Some of the defenders kept their order and fell back in a disciplined manner, keeping off any Romans who seemed inclined to bring them down, but this could only last so long. With the noise of disaster off to the left and the sight of enemies high up on their horses showing in the dust on their flank and rear, eventually it was pell-mell. The Samnite infantry did not stand, despite their strongman Gellius Egnatius and his officers riding in among the lines, appealing to a courage that they had so often exhibited in the past. With some it worked; men fought back, but too many holes had appeared and too many men were now only thinking of safety, no longer that triumph was a possibility. Yet many would not find the haven they desired inside their camp's breastworks; some squeezed through the gates, others may have somehow clambered over the walls, but the great majority had no option but to turn and try to face the pursuing enemy at 'the base of the ramparts'.

This was still not the end as the Romans wanted the camp too and the treasure it contained. In front of the ramparts there unfolded a struggle as cruel as at any stage of the battle and as many Romans lost their lives here as anywhere else. The Samnite remnants might have been in disorder, but these men who had not been crushed by the blind rush for safety were now fighting for their lives and Gellius Egnatius was there with them, with his military family in their fine raiment and shining armour. So it is no wonder that the fighting grew particularly savage, though how close the contest really was outside the camp is difficult to know; indeed, plenty of those involved would have been unclear until the whole mess unravelled. However, we do know the tradition was that as he pushed forward to join the attack, Fabius Rullianus, positioned high aboard his horse to improve his view of events and for his men to be better able to see him, vowed a temple to Jupiter Victor. This kind of enthusiastic piety, appealing to a divine presence to intervene, is not generally noticed except where the battle was in such a balance that every kind of help, both practical and supernatural, might be looked for. The Samnite stand was certainly desperate, with their braver comrades giving support by hurling missiles from the camp ramparts. They made a match of it until Roman arms shattered the life of the greatest strategist their people had produced. Among those who fell below the breastwork, slathered with sweat and blood, was Gellius Egnatius, ensuring that most of those left fighting lost heart. There was now no refuge for the defenders, and the victory on the right wing was underscored as the Romans forced the wooden walls, winning the encampment at last.

While on his flank Gellius Egnatius had made a gambler's throw for massive stakes and lost, on Decius Mus' side of the battlefield a different contest had played out. The country in which the great combat took place was not dead flat terrain; there are few such places outside of Apulia in all of south and central Italy. Here north of the Sassoferrato heights was folded country, with fields rising in slight gradients before falling down again. Still there would have been just about room for these two large armies to deploy and sufficiently expansive fields for the Gallic chariots and both sides' cavalry to manoeuvre into contact. There Decius Mus' legions, the fifth and sixth, with their allies faced the mass of Gauls, an enemy who were regularly traduced as out of control: 'as a nation they cannot command their passions', not the thinking men in control of their natures that was the hallmark of civilization. Yet that was just one side of the coin; not only was it that these fierce warriors worried them out of their wits, but they learned much from them as well. The appearance of the legions was becoming radically altered by technologies acquired from contact with the Gauls. The Montefortino helmet that was coming in at this time and by the end of the century would be the pattern of head protection was based on a Gallic model and the technique of making chain mail had derived from that people too. The period we are describing is in the middle of a process that would soon see most of Rome's heavy infantry wearing this variety of protection.

Yet the name and sight of these pale, blue-eyed, moustachioed giants was genuinely traumatic, freezing the Romans. They were, after all, these very same Senones who had overrun their home less than a century before. Defeat at their hands might mean a kind of obliteration that other enemies would not bring; merciless foes against whom every reserve of effort must be tapped to ensure they did not end up at their mercy. Such emotions explain why, as on this other flank, the Romans also did not commence the action with the kind of ferocity that they liked to think was typical of them. So the infantry contest again began on the Roman side with no great urgency, which our main source contends did not gel with their commander's approach; as a younger man he was naturally more aggressive. This claim of callowness is pretty extraordinary as Decius Mus' father died well over forty years earlier, so he had to be at least middle-aged if not teetering on the edge of elderly. What is clear is that unlike Fabius Rullianus, he had not ordered the lack of aggression among his infantry and so, displeased and frustrated, he almost immediately upped the ante and sent his whole cavalry wing forward, leading himself 'at the head of a squadron of exceptionally gallant troopers', spearheading what we can assume was a force a couple of thousand strong if numbers were similar to those in a few generations' time. So, unprepared to let the footsloggers dictate the pace, he 'summoned the young nobles to join him in a charge' and after raising a battle cry, the impact was devastating, with squadrons of lance-wielding troopers plunging into the enemy opposing them.

This Gallic horse were of high quality; like their counterparts, it was the aristocratic arm where the well-to-do in the best armour, solid shields, fine-honed spears and swords showed at their best. They had technological advantages too: their mounts wore iron shoes and the riders utilized a solid four-horned saddle that was so effective that the Romans would copy it in centuries to come. Yet despite this, they could not sustain the attack: Latin horse and Roman eques pushed them back, their beasts barrelling into their opponents and the riders thrusting and hacking until so many men fell that the disordered defenders had to pull back to regroup. As in all these kinds of cavalry fights, however, the successful attackers actually found themselves almost as mixed up and dishevelled as the enemy they had just overthrown. So now Decius Mus also had to repeatedly get his horsemen back into their places, to catch their breath and ensure gaps in the lines were filled so they might attempt further assaults; an endeavour facilitated by the fact, suggested by later evidence, that there was a ratio of about 4–1 of officers to men in the cavalry as against more like 20–1 in the infantry. In the time this took, the Gauls had also pulled themselves together, tribal leaders had rallied men who had fallen out of the line and reserve squadrons, not so far involved, were brought forward to support the bloodied men who had already been engaged.

The mechanics of what occurred when lines of cavaliers fell to fighting is never very fully described, but from similar instances reported in later ages it is possible to imagine an outcome. Charging horses will not run into each other at speed, so as often as not to avoid collision, one side broke and ran, but if this did not occur and both reached to within a sword or lance stroke, it was because they had slowed and infiltrated in between the opened-up files of men and animals opposing them, ensuring the whole broke into a series of individual duels. It was on occasions like these that the Romans had the habit of dismounting to fight. Nimble with no armour to unbalance them, they could slip down to the ground where the stability of being on foot could give them a certain advantage. Whether the enemy broke before impact or lost out in a number of individual fights, in the second assault the Romans again made progress, moiling their shaken adversaries back another time. Yet all was far from won, as behind the distressed Gallic horse the attackers now found not only lines of infantry but to their surprise a weapon of which there is no record of the Romans ever encountering before; a novelty that they had never thought to borrow from their northern enemies, chariots that stood in bristling proof of the effectiveness of surprise.

That Celtic peoples retained this weapon a long time after they had become obsolete in most people's military is well-attested. Julius Caesar, more than two centuries later, found the Britons still adept at fighting with these battle carts, like Homeric heroes in *The Iliad*, riding them into battle and swiftly being taken away by the waiting driver if the fight went against them. However, generally by the time there are written histories to dig into, the chariot had become little used in combat, though usually when they were it was not without considerable drama, particularly when scythed versions were thrown into the mix. Also the exact manner in which they functioned on the battlefield has been subject to plenty of debate, disagreements compounded by the fact that written history is pretty thin on the ground when these horse-drawn war wagons were the queens of the battlefield. Lightweight cars that could be carried on a man's back over a mountain pass with a driver and an archer balancing on leather thwarts were the business end of Egypt's new kingdom military machine. Carrying a missile-man into easy range and quickly out again was a tactic intended to disrupt the enemy's formation, and the slightly heavier, three-man versions fielded by the Hittites, Mitanni, Assyrians and others functioned similarly too. Yet there is hardly anything in the way of written detail on the encounters between the armies of this period apart from the vainglorious cant engraved into stone walls from the cataracts of the Nile to the heartland of Mesopotamia.

Making the reasonable assumption that the British vestigial remnant reflected the practice of their cousins centuries earlier, they would have functioned to bring elite warriors near enough to the enemy lines to either throw their javelins or jump down to fight hand-to-hand if it was propitious. It was the impact on morale as much as anything that counted, scaring both infantry who saw them bearing down on them or cavalry afraid of the flying machines that because of their greater stability would give their occupants an advantage over men without stirrups, sitting on saddle-cloths and holding on with only the muscles of their legs, that apart from whatever damage the animals and what they pulled might do when they crashed into them. How many of these chariots there were on this occasion is unknown, but surely they would not have been counted in more than tens or twenties, as only a few decades earlier at the Battle of Gaugamela in 331 the massive Persian Empire could only deploy 200 scythed chariots, flamboyant weaponry raised from vast feudal lands near Babylonia dedicated to their upkeep.

If the Gauls expected the introduction of their chariots to be demoralizing, they were proved right. The Roman cavalry had been in fine fettle before these Earth-shaking carts careered into their midst. They were not well protected, these young bluebloods, certainly insufficiently to give much confidence against this new-fangled weapon they were facing. Now the impact was pulverizing and these Roman knights suffered; their horses could not stand the noise made by the unfamiliar vehicles rumbling towards them accompanied by the dissonant noise of the Gallic war horns as the hulking blond spearmen on board thrust at the riders, unseating men unfamiliar with such combat. The cavalry had been bloodied twice already, the young toffs racing in, holding tight with thighs pressed hard against their mounts' blanketed flanks while their hands gripped spear and the small target. Faced with an unexpected new danger, there was no entropy, no gradual decent into disorder, but a collapse. With the Roman knights and their allied peers turned about, looking anywhere for a way of escape, in their panic many trampled through the ranks of their own infantry. The unnerved horses kicked out and their heavy bodies crushed all who stood in their way, while following after came the fearsome chariots rolling over them. Decius Mus' foot had been holding their own until then, but the impact of this disaster on the left was infectious, as standards went down in the dust in ranks broken by their own cavaliers. The enemy, thrilled with bloodlust, were not long in realizing what was happening in front of them and the Gallic chiefs did not wait to put their infantry in order for an assault. Along the whole line the warriors broke into a trot with their shields held forward and their spears raised, hoping to bowl over an enemy who looked in little condition to resist them; a line of undulating furies who, as they advanced, threw what javelins they had left and hacked with their long swords, soon drowning in blood the young soldiers of the Roman front ranks.

The Republican army facing this point of maximum danger was deployed in several lines of maniples, the one behind intended to support that in front; a formation that sacrificed breadth for depth with its three lines of armoured infantry. Now it was grimly apparent that appearances could be deceptive, that the system would not function in the way expected and it was looking horribly like they would break and that even sending in the last reserves, the veterans of the *triarii*, might not now stay the tide. So it is no surprise that, with the appreciation of this fateful moment, one man turned from the picture of his wavering army to thoughts of the great tradition of his family that stretched back to his father in a battle fought decades before. Decius Mus was looking the alarming prospect of defeat and disaster in the face and it may be that the remembrance of the act was a measure of his mood. His men, in alien country far from home, fighting in an enemy land and confronted with pale giants, leaping from their unanticipated battle cars, were truly scared, in deep need of some inspirational leadership from a man whose family had specialized in providing this very thing in desperate times past.

Decius Mus, about to enter in his finest hour was a veteran, boasting a fine sculpted corselet of bronze round his sturdy torso, a fine crest-topped helmet and conspicuous scarlet cloak. With him were priests kept ready to read the auguries, and if the account is to be believed, would do even more on this day. A group of other horsemen surrounded him too; young nobles counting off the years required of them to serve in the army as an entry qualification for high office. With these staff men he tried to stem the rout, berating those soldiers who were slipping away from the fighting line, attempting to persuade them that to run was to ensure death or capture and only by staying to fight could they endure. However, a few minutes sufficed to persuade him that they were not listening and that it would not be very long before the collapse of his wing of the army would be complete. In this desperate pass he called on the spirits of his father and determined to repeat that hero's actions from another time. His forebear had led an army in the last great Latin war, the final time these neighbours of Rome made a bid for independence. Allied with Volsci, Sidicini, Aurunci and Campanians, who occupied the country running south between the mountains where the Samnites lived and the Tyrrhenian Sea, they represented a considerable threat to the authority of a republic defended in decisive battle by the consuls Manlius Torquatus and Decius Mus.

This encounter produced two of those stories that the Romans loved to tell about themselves. The first concerns the stern, ferocious patriotism of Manlius Torquatus, who had his son executed for indulging in a duel without permission. The second tells of Decius Mus senior who, when his men were about to fold under pressure from a mob of howling Latins, decided to sacrifice his life to ensure that his army would win out. This act of *devotio* is reported as a highly formal process beginning with the general clad in a purple-trimmed toga, with a spear dedicated to Mars laid under his feet, appealing to about every god going, Roman and non-Roman alike, to afflict his enemies with 'terror, dread and death' as he devoted himself and his enemies to the powers of the underworld.

Then, after informing his co-commander of his intentions, still clad in his toga but with armour on top, he rode into the heart of his enemy's formations to fall under a shower of their missiles before his life blood ebbed away. The impact was immediate: the enemy failed to press home their advantage as the dead man's followers were revitalized and won through in a hard-fought encounter.[6]

Little is absolutely detailed about how events played out on this occasion in Umbria. There must have been preparations, that Decius Mus was primed to devote himself if things went badly, though unlike his father he does not seem to have been warned by a convenient dream. Yet if arrangements were made just in case, it must still have been a time-consuming business getting the paraphernalia and the appropriate clothing. The consul had kept his pontiff Marcus Livius Denter with him during battle, knowing he could depend on this experienced man who had been consul himself in 303. The procedure undertaken, pregnant with portentous possibility, shows what leisurely affairs these ancient battles were. There was plenty of time, while the maniples in each line threw their javelins, then came on to fight hand-to-hand. Then the hastati supported or replaced by principes from the lines behind; all the time breathing spaces being left as the battling sides drew apart to reorder their formations. There was an element of high ritual in the process of combat, just as there would be in what the consul Decius Mus was about to undertake.

The event when it occurred was an exact homage to his papa; the prayer, the dress, all followed the earlier exemplar, and 'with these imprecations upon himself and the enemy he galloped his horse into the Gallic lines, where he saw they were thickest, and threw himself on the enemy's weapons to meet his death.'[7] As the consul approached through the parting lines of his shaken soldiers, thinking with stern satisfaction that his sacrifice might save the army, the Gauls did their part, throwing their javelins at the man in odd combination toga and burnished armour bearing down on them. Whether it was these missiles that downed him or the spears and swords of the men in the front rank when he reached them, he did not survive contact. The inescapable question in all this is can we really believe what we are told of the death of the consul? The ritual magic of human sacrifice was far from unknown to the Romans in times of crisis, usually with an element of punishment attached and often not consented to, while we also know individuals and indeed groups do enter battle virtually certain that they are going to die; leaders who do not want to survive to experience the shame of defeat or the likes of the 300 Spartans and their allies at Thermopylae, determined to etch in blood a determination to not succumb in the face of a dreadful threat. From the mists of legend, even down to modern times when we can be pretty certain of the facts, this kind of thing has not been unusual, but there are aspects of this instance that are different. Firstly in most cases the key is a preparedness to die, not as in this instance that death is itself the crux; a suicide as sacrifice, a voluntary scapegoat, which is far less usual in any culture at any time. Clearly it is possible that it occurred just as described and it is not even a requisite that the father's example had to be real. Even if the *devotio* of Decius Mus senior was just a legend, this would not of necessity have made it less potent as a model for his offspring. Yet what really argues against is that this seems to be last instance of such a thing occurring; we get no repetition in the centuries after when a greater volume of written history makes the information we get more secure.

There was another Decius Mus of the next generation, who apparently contemplated a repetition of this kind of intervention at the Battle of Asculum against Pyrrhus in 279, the suggestion being that he too should follow the lodestar of family tradition. However, the attempt was not made because the Romans had been informed that the enemy had orders to not kill any officer riding at them in the distinctive *devotio* costume of toga and armour; instead, the soldiers were instructed to capture the man. As this would only give the enemy the bonus of a captive consul to no effect, any attempt was aborted. Yet this does not explain why, in so many battles in the future when the Romans were facing defeat, no commander, whether from Decius Mus' family or not, ever attempted again what in the past on the two occasions it was tried was completely successful. Were the likes of Tiberius Sempronius Longus at the Trebbia or Gaius Flaminius at Lake Trasimene, when facing defeat at the hands of Hannibal, less pious or dedicated? Possibly but possibly not, and certainly on these occasions there is no suggestion of *devotio* as an option open to them.

Yet whether supernatural or more ordinary causes were at root, the Gallic fury passed not long after this claimed act of self-sacrifice and

Roman arms began to hold their own. They no longer shrank from the fight; renewed belief and enthusiasm visited the men, commanded now by the pontiff to whom the consul had bequeathed his lictors and orders to take charge after his death and who was wildly trumpeting a victory guaranteed by the consul's martyrdom. Now again they trusted in their fortune, beginning again to exhibit the courage and ferocity that was a minimum demand and that murderous aptitude for both manoeuvre and duelling that was expected of them. So the ranks might interchange with the smoothness of a machine and new lines of fresh and eager warriors be presented to the enemy when the first rank had been exhausted; a demoralizing exercise for the Gauls facing them who just did not have the facility to ensure such a transfusion of men to keep their front ranks fighting. They were brave, skilled at arms and their long slashing swords dangerous, but did they not practise in the way the Romans did, normally expecting that their first savage charge would sweep all before them. So not long after his men had seen Decius Mus make the ultimate sacrifice:

> From this moment the battle could hardly have appeared to any man to be dependent on human strength alone. After losing their leader, a thing which generally demoralizes an army, the Romans arrested their flight and recommenced the struggle. The Gauls, especially those who were crowded round the consul's body, were discharging their missiles aimlessly and harmlessly as though bereft of their senses; some seemed paralysed, incapable of either fight or flight.[8]

With the heat oppressive and while diverse stenches assaulted every nose and terror every mind, the stress became just too much for many of the Gauls. The corollary of their famous fury, the initial charge intended to overwhelm, was also well-known; that if victory was not achieved the northern warriors tended to lose heart. Their strength was not in their staying power and now they drew back, clustering together and covering each other in a manner that is described as being similar to a testudo. This is improbable considering what occurred, but certainly they did present a tempting target to men arriving new to the fight. These were reinforcements that had been led over from the other flank. Messengers had been passing from one wing to the other during the battle and Fabius Rullianus knew that his colleague on the left was in deep trouble, desperate for succour. So, despite battle still raging on his flank, Scipio Barbatus and Gaius Marcius were ordered to pick men from the rearmost lines of the army to go to the assistance of his colleague. This may not have been the contingency for which these reserves had been held back, but it did not matter now and these officers led their men off behind the ranks of their own side and across the battlefield. Once they arrived, they soon saw the opportunity to aid their comrades. After hearing for the first time how Decius Mus had died, they directed their soldiers to pick up the many javelins that were 'lying scattered on the ground between the two armies'. Once sufficient missiles were collected, they led them forward towards an enemy who was holding stationary behind their shields. The non-noble Gauls, apart from not generally wearing armour, also often carried quite narrow long shields covering them from neck to knee, but flat and only perhaps a couple of feet wide as opposed to the curved scutum of the Romans that gave much greater all-round protection. Perhaps this was the case on this occasion because we learn that when the Romans worried them with javelins, not all stuck in their shields but some struck flesh, transfixing bodies and limbs and deeply perturbing even those who were not actually wounded: 'The closely massed ranks went down, most of them falling without having received a wound, just as though they had been struck by lightning.'[9]

Nor was this the sum of Fabius Rullianus' contribution: once he was confident the enemy to his front was finished as a fighting force and that their camp would soon be his, he released 500 of his Campanian horse, supported by the principes of the third legion. Having pushed the Samnites way back to their camp, this assault group was now in a position to fall on the rear of the Gallic hosts whose flank had been unmasked by their allies' withdrawal. So as the Romans, already reinforced by the arrival of the two legates, were pressing the front of the Gallic army, now another force emerged out of a murk of dust and fell on their rear. The Campanians, going smoothly into action, were at last in the fight and the holes they cut into the enemy formations were exploited by the heavy infantry arriving soon after, so that the enemy just could not stand it. Backpedalling did not last long before their formations were affected and a tendency to rout became apparent among a doomed battle-line frantically slipping and sliding rearwards. The ground was rolling and uneven and chariot wrecks and the corpses of horses in their traces hampered the Gallic foot in retreat as they tried to keep up a defensive front. Soon many were throwing away swords and shields as they ran over a trail of dead and wounded men left behind them, only interested in finding a place to run and hide. Many did not find anywhere to go, though at least most horsemen and plenty of the charioteers would have had the speed to make a successful exit and even the foot soldiers were lighter armed than their pursuers. So the fit and able would have stood a chance to get to the tree-covered hills where escape from the rampaging horsemen, chopping and lancing at their backs was possible.

There is no memory of a brutal chase, so it is perhaps not unreasonable to assume that on Decius Mus' wing, where we know reinforcements from the other side of the battlefield had been required to sustain the struggle, the Romans were just too used up to attempt much of a pursuit; that the northerners were bloodied but sufficiently unbowed to regroup before marching away to try to join the other splintered fragments of the coalition that had survived. While the Romans stopped to strip the dead bodies, others just tiring of the struggle threw themselves onto the ground to rest, with rasping breath and heaving chests as the cries of wounded warriors reverberated in their ears and the carrion stench of the battlefield filled their noses. Under the brilliance of stars on a summer night there was a monstrous scene of death and destruction wherever the eye rested, with thousands of men lying on the bloody field; food for the flies, long divested of anything of value and a sad sight for any victors touring the ground, even those who had not forgotten the defining fatality of the contest.

The sigh of relief heaved by the victorious Romans must have been audible all along the valley of the nearby river. They had gambled, taking on a massive coalition army far from home and succour. Defeat could have meant extirpation, a disaster to rank with the Alia, never mind the Caudine forks, but they had come through and were stunned by the scale of their deliverance. Battered and wounded but victorious with the enemy dead, captive or running and a camp secured with all the trappings of a Samnite army that had come to Umbria with its men accoutred to the very highest standard the people could afford. Valuable furnishings would have been hauled from the tents and war chests of precious plate ransacked, while fine wine and other provender in the dead commander's tent was the tangible reward for the officers and men who could at last relax, knowing that for the first time for years there was no organized enemy in this part of the world who might threaten them. Nor was this the only profit to be found among the crumpled bodies of the dead and riderless horses munching the grass, as soldiers, slaves and camp servants got to work, stripping the enemy fallen of armour, weapons, neck torques, rings ripped from fingers and other valuables. Fabius Rullianus was not one to let the gods wait for what he owed them, particularly after he learned of the bombshell that his colleague had followed his father's example in a most dramatic way. So straight after the end of the battle, while Decius Mus' body was still being hunted across the battlefield, looted enemy spoils were burned as offerings to Jupiter Victor, who had so singly done his stuff. In fact, it was not until the next day that the corpse of Decius Mus was discovered 'buried under a heap of Gauls' and indulged with the proper rites by tearful soldiers who had followed him in life and a partner who had achieved so much in tandem with the dead man over the last few decades.

An assumption that the Roman town established under the name of Sentinum was sited on the battlefield has led to real confusion. Why it should be expected that years later, after the bones of the dead had mingled with the dust, people would remember exactly where the fighting had taken place is unclear. In fact, this place where considerable archaeological work has disclosed a substantial site is set in a valley that just would not allow the sum of men involved to deploy, even at the lowest estimate of numbers. There is an argument that if the armies fought on both sides of the river, against the Samnites on one bank and facing the Gauls on the other, this might work, but apart from this being very unusual, any viewing of the site shows that still no two large armies could have faced each other where the Roman town sits. It has to be north of Sassoferrato, where the country opens out to some extent, that the encounter played out, where a river called Sanguerone, surely referencing a bloody past, flows to this day. Even here, to get extremely high numbers in it would again be necessary to have the armies fighting on both sides of the river that runs through these fields; something almost impossible because of the deep gorge cut by the stream in the soft rock such that the modern visitor looking down can hardly see the water through the steep, cavernous, overgrown banks. It might not have been so deep 2,300 years ago, but still surely it would have been sufficient an obstacle to prevent the kind of movement described when the 500 Campanians and picked reserves crossed the battlefield to aid the Roman left.

Fabius was very conscious of what had been achieved; it had been a high-stakes strategy he and Decius had played against a palpable threat but finally the Republic had been saved, and he wasted no time in basking in a glory so hard-won. Some soldiers were left to hold down Etruria, perhaps some of Decius' men, though there is evidence contradicting this, but it was certainly 'his own legions' that accompanied the victorious general as he swept into town, men on whom he could count to evidence that he had done more than enough to warrant a triumph. Their reports probably echoed numbers given as casualties that are if not utterly ridiculous still clearly exaggerated as the 25,000 discovered to have died in battle and 8,000 prisoners would together have been well over half if not three-quarters the numbers the confederates could have fielded in entirety. Also we know that apart from those whose blood had blended with the soil, at least 5,000 Samnites led by agile-minded officers got away in some sort of order. Honesty at least infuses the recording of the home team losses, where it is noted that the costs were high enough, with Decius losing 7,000 men, while casualties in Fabius' army amounted to 1,700 men.

There was no gainsaying on the occasion of this homecoming, the old veteran would have had enemies in the establishment like any of his ilk, but no one was going to want to be perceived as traducing what had been won on the green fields round Sentinum, when awful bloodshed had erupted on the banks of the Sanguerone and Rome had emerged triumphant. Appropriately the dead Decius Mus, now installed as the very pattern of a hero, was not forgotten on the day of celebration 'in the songs which the soldiers sang in the procession' rendered by happy men who had received a victory donation of 'eighty-two assēs [coins] of bronze, with cloaks and tunics, rewards not to be despised in those days', and few would have denied that it was their due.

Nor was he the only hero with whom Fabius Rullianus had to share the stage as news arrived that Fulvius Centumalus when released against Etruria had not been content to merely make a few feints to occupy as many of the enemy as possible. He for one was looking for more than just wreckage, wanting the fame of victory too. He found it, reaching so far into the territory between Clusium and Perusia that he needed to fight a full-scale battle. Encountering a major enemy force, 'he fought a brilliant action with the united forces of Perusia and Clusium' with thousands of casualties inflicted and twenty military standards taken. These must not just have comprised the local forces but also many of those who had recently left the main confederate camps over the mountains. This other veteran had chalked up a real victory, though it is easy to believe he did not play down his men's achievement. After all, this character, who had done much in the past and would do much in the future, may have resented being kept out of the glory being won so near. His colleague Postumius Megellus had also done his part, departing the marshy country round the Vatican and by threat or activity ensuring many thousands of other Etruscan or Umbrian warriors were absent from the fatal field. Whoever else wanted to horn in on the credit and if it was generally accepted that no single factor had won the day, still Fabius Rullianus had written his name in the city's military pantheon. He would never be the only show in town – that was not the Roman way – but he had certainly gained sufficient kudos that many believed it was this man, who loved a grand occasion, that instituted the parade of knights, a staged and spectacular cavalcade that took place every year on 15 July.

Chapter Nine

The Last Stand of the Linen Legion

'When Papirius Cursor, the son, in his consulship failed to win any advantage in his battle against the stubbornly resisting Samnites, he gave no intimation on his purpose to his men, but commanded Spurius Nautius to arrange to have a few auxiliary horsemen and grooms, mounted on mules and trailing branches over the ground, race down in great commotion from a hill running at an angle with the field. As soon as these came in sight, he proclaimed that his colleague was at hand, crowned with victory, and urged his men to secure for themselves the glory of the present battle before he should arrive.'

Sextus Julius Frontinus, *Stratagems*, 2 4 1

If Sentinum was a turning-point it would not necessarily have been obvious to many in the forum or streets when news of victory arrived. Reasoning in Rome at any age is opaque but what certainly influenced them now was that they had other things to think about as neighbours, friends and family members were succumbing to deadly disease. Plague struck hard in 295 and is perhaps more of a context for the following years than is generally reckoned. Certainly before modern times any human population suffered regularly from various sorts of pestilence, with heavily urbanized areas on occasions becoming virtual graveyards. In ancient Rome malaria remained endemic, despite early and considerable efforts at drainage in a metropolis that had partially developed on a swampy riverbank. Yet if sickness was ever present, when great epidemics hit they could have a real influence on the prospects of the polities that were their victims. We can see this in the time of Emperor Marcus Aurelius when the loss of life, often projected as higher than 5 million souls, particularly hitting the army, was one of the crucial factors leading to the desperate decline in the third century of the Empire. The impact on the rump Byzantine state ruled by Justinian is also well-known when the bubonic plague, as a pandemic, first reared its head in the 540s AD, spreading all over the world from Britain to Mesopotamia and perhaps killing 50 to 60 per cent of the population. It is difficult to believe that among these savage waves of infectious diseases that the 290s outbreak was in the same league, yet it was still significant in a much smaller world. A raging malady that impacted the Republic's efforts in the years after Sentinum almost certainly was one of the reasons it took the Romans an inordinately long period to fully reap the rewards that were surely available after the bloody overthrow of their four enemies. It was discriminatory too: urban areas suffered more, where people lived cheek by jowl, creating microbial and bacterial Disneylands with little in the medical armoury to counter them, while the rural mountain habitations that comprised so much of Samnium would have been less vulnerable to these invisible killers.[1]

If the Romans, with plague stalking the streets, did not fully make hay after the victories of 295, that would not have been the only factor. The effort made in the climactic year would have itself taken its toll, ensuring there would be no finishing the war at a stroke. The numbers of soldiers enrolled and the casualties suffered must have required an easing up. The task they faced, to invade the heartlands of Samnium and finish the job, was always going to be difficult and in the two earlier wars much of the fighting had been around the periphery. Many of the claims of armies invading the Pentri and capturing the capital Bovianum or occupying cities in Hernici or Caudine country were really much more likely to have been raids on the country around rather than full-scale sieges, battles and assaults. The very fact that the terms of the peace treaty of 304 were not in the least draconian showed the Samnite League, if battered, had been far from truly ruined. It had been a long way from a peace of annihilation dictated by a victor's justice.

The defenders enjoyed all the advantages in a country that was baking hot in summer but cold and harsh in winter, as at least one Roman army would find out in the coming war when it had to suffer the beginnings of a winter season there. Soldiers would not have found the going easy as they tried to enter enemy territory, using those few riparian routes that were the only ingresses into the country. There were not many valleys that pierced the walls of mountains and the roads that followed them could become either clogged with dust in the heat or quagmires in the rain. Even traversing the hills in good weather was fraught with difficulty. Any attack on the Pentri from the south had to come over the shield of the Matese massif that any traveller today can attest as being an arduous journey that takes far longer than it looks like it would on any map. Winding around country lanes where only the sight of mountain cattle with horns like beasts from the Scottish highlands and Lycra-clad locals indulging in road skiing breaks the monotony. For a Roman army having to trail for days up and over zigzagging mountain tracks, ever conscious of ambush or that even a trifling enemy force might effectively block their way, this was not something to be taken on lightly.

The locals knew all the broad drovers' roads where they took their animals into the hills in the summer and down to the lowlands in the winter, allowing them to move their forces easily, while the invaders, even if they came across them, might well have no idea where they led. This was perfect ambush country, a realm where wooded slopes overlooked every route that an invader might take, with tight gorges and craggy outcrops, sometimes occupied by fortified communities, or hilltop castles where stout defences, even if only manned by skeleton garrisons, could slow down even major armies; a rugged plateau set under limestone mountains covered with snow for much of the year, an upland wracked by centuries of earthquakes. It was a vast, natural inland stronghold, with great massifs of almost 5,000ft acting as bulwarks and jumbles of outcrops topped with cyclopean walls like towers in a castle's enceinte (enclosing wall).

So perhaps it was an understandable response, even after Sentinum, that the Romans did not follow up in full force and in confidant mean to finish off the vital enemy that they seemed to have defeated so decisively in the great coalition war. The truth was that the Samnites had been far from mortally wounded by these reverses and even Livy, despite his iteration of so many Roman successes in the previous campaigning season,[2] reports them as far from a spent force. Even if the long term would show a sea change, immediately any ideas that the fighting in north Umbria had finished the war were quashed in no uncertain fashion. The people of Perusia, for a start, still clearly nursed deep resentment and had not accepted the result of Sentinum as decisive, and once Fabius

Rullianus' army had left the area and encouraged by Samnite friends left behind, they prepared to enter the ring again. Such activity would see the old veteran return to suppress them in the same fighting season, with casualties amounting to more than 5,000 and almost 2,000 captured, who had to be ransomed at a cost of 310 assēs each. However, these Etruscan ripples were only a part as the Samnites set preparations afoot to impact on three fronts that would have been truly impressive except that much of what was planned never got off the ground. Swift action by the Romans who pressed forward to confront them forced the Samnites to concentrate their efforts. Rather than the intended scattergun approach, wise heads found they needed to focus to try to handle an enemy whose self-belief was such that even their superstitious spirits did not quail, despite stories circulating that their soldiers were being repeatedly struck by lightning, a sure sign of celestial displeasure.

However, this was the future. Even in the same season as Sentinum was fought, the Tiber town leaders had had to contend with other dangers while their consuls were covering themselves in glory up north. It had been a hell of a year and now the very emphasis on the Umbrian front was the trouble: not only were two consular armies engaged there, other detachments were committed in support too, with Postumius Megellus and Fulvius Centumalus commanding thousands of men based on the north bank of the Tiber and in Faliscan territory. Such circumstances made it hardly surprising that other Samnites endeavoured to exploit this overstretched condition, particularly when word had arrived from Etruria that Gellius Egnatius had got the Umbrians and Gauls to join the northern coalition. Then the men left behind gained confidence, looking to old habits as they contemplated the undefended state of so much of Roman and allied real estate. The kind of raid these practised plunderers contemplated took some time to organize, so it was almost certainly after Sentinum had been fought that messengers arrived in Rome reporting that an enemy was active again, far away from where the Romans had committed so much of their military. Raiding parties had come boiling out of the Pentri lands, overrunning the farmlands around Vescia, an old Aurunci place not far from the Liris valley, Formiae further north by the sea and past Minturnae, ravaging the land between the coast and the cone of Roccamonfina. Nor was it just these bands overrunning the defenders posted in that area, but others also wreaked havoc as they struck the country around Aesernia and other places high up in the hills near the valley of the Volturnus.

The man on hand to deal with this emergency turned out to be the praetor Appius Claudius, who in response ran through the gears when details became clear that the enemy were harassing a great swath of people inhabiting the very centre of the peninsula. This other times hard-luck officer learned that at least some of the men from Decius Mus' army were on the road back to Rome when this most recent bit of fire-fighting was required. These footsore survivors would have been anticipating a triumphant homecoming celebration as they entered the well-recognized country of Latium, with the population spilling out to applaud them and wine, women and song for days if not weeks. Yet with hardly a break for rest, the depleted regiments were commandeered and dispatched after a man with far less of a military reputation than their old commander. Their humour was most probably considerably improved when they learned they were to be joined by Volumnius Flamma and his men, who had been chasing Samnites round Mount Tifernus as the Sentinum campaign was being fought. These veterans were now marching up from Capua towards Cales, intending to join Appius Claudius who had arrived first to deal with the menace to a territory where not long before, two new tribes of citizens had been organized.

Volumnius Flamma, leading the other posse, joined in the chase with the second and fourth legions and their allies in tow. This army would have experienced deductions through the attrition in the preceding month's marching and fighting, but was still well able to smoke out the raiders they found in their path. Both Roman armies had considerable success in chivvying the intruders out of Aurunci territory before herding them back up the Volturnus towards the Stellate region of Campania, where the river cuts into the hills above modern-day Caserta. Though this in itself was satisfactory, it had the negative effect of forcing their detachments back together into a challenging military combination that, despite being encumbered by their ill-gotten gains, had coalesced into a considerable army and dug in among rugged hills. Here they were allowed little time for rest, as lookouts reported that both chasing armies had now combined and were pushing on swiftly. They were discovered near

Caiatia by Romans who had arrived out of the blue intent on bringing them to battle.

In the valley on the right bank of the Volturnus 200 metres below the modern-day town of Caiazzo, where both the cyclopean walls of an ancient fortress and the remains of a Lombard castle still stand, opposing sides were set to collide. Here 'the battle was fought with the utmost fury' as the legionaries, determined on payback, laboured up the slopes eager to be the first to draw their swords against the foe. They had seen plenty of evidence of the ruin the raiders had brought to their long-term friends who inhabited the country through which they had just marched and they wanted revenge. Victory attended the larger force but the claims of huge numbers of casualties are a deliberate piece of propaganda. An inclination to inflate enemies' losses was as much as anything due to the need to ensure no tarnish would accrue to the lustre of Sentinum; to paint a picture of the praetor and pro-consul realizing a victory in the Stellate region of Campania with piles of Samnite dead and thousands of prisoners to veil the embarrassing fact that they had failed to live up to the expectation that they protect their compatriots; that their foe had been able to thoroughly trash the newly-established Roman lands where two new colonies at Minturnae and Sinuessa had been planted to guard against just such inroads.

* * *

In the year after Sentinum, any efforts that were going to be made by the Republic's antagonists would be done in a context that might have been viewed as bleak indeed. It must have seemed when Gellius Egnatius had died under the walls of his camp in Umbria, so perished the hopes of Samnium. The commander who had constructed the great coalition designed to constrain the power of an enemy who had looked to be becoming invincible was no more. Not only suffering this loss of inspirational leadership, after the defeat the 5,000 survivors who had reconstituted themselves after their northern misadventure, ready for a hard road home, found people on the way hostile. As they followed winding paths through the glens and valleys of the Paeligni, living east of the lake of Fucens, they found themselves under attack. The remnant of the defeated army just wanted a safe passage but they were not going to get it. As the long line of disconsolate warriors journeyed through difficult country, local bands cut off any men who strayed from the main body and perhaps for once we can credit the numbers, as the loss of 1,000 men sounds realistic.

Somehow, superhuman efforts were made to resuscitate the cause of a battered people and spies were soon reporting in Rome that in the new season the Samnites were mobilizing three armies, one 'to return to Etruria … and resume their raids into Campania with another, while making the third ready to guard their frontiers'.[3] However, the effort of the allies in Etruria to continue the war did not in the end amount to very much, as Etruscan strategists now painted on a smaller palette, even if young bravos were always prepared to urge more rounds of fighting against the great power to the south. No longer feeling themselves a mainspring agent, although they would fight on for decades to come, it was seldom with any sort of confidence in a grand outcome.

As 294 wore on, other exertions certainly threatened to bear fruit and this while the characters who would confront a frayed if determined foe were not as celebrated as those who preceded them. Marcus Atilius Regulus did not have the antecedents, being only the second man of his line to revel in the glamour of the consulship, but still his was a coming family. They may well have hailed originally from the south as he had cousins called Atilii Calatinii, suggesting a connection with a Campanian town. Yet despite personally achieving plenty as an active participant in Rome's narrative, he was overshadowed by a son who became the seminal hero of the First Punic War, showing true Republican virtue even in the face of the disaster that followed an invasion of Africa, something about which his people could preen themselves, despite the evidence for the story being not a little suspect. The father of this more famous Marcus Atilius Regulus would now, as the year turned, emerge among what was a new tranche of imperialists filling the void left by aging marshals and taking up his consular imperium with a colleague who was far from unknown to him. When provinces were given out, as in the previous year when both the consuls had gone north, now they were directed south, drawn by news that the Samnites were making extraordinary exertions to compensate for the defeat of 295. Atilius Regulus acted swiftly, with the clear intention of offering such a threat to the enemy heartlands that they would think twice about repeating the kind of incursions they had carried out the year before, from which Rome's allies had hardly recovered, borderlands that had so recently suffered and where the colonists or allies were squealing in panic to be protected. The direction in which the consul led his men is not absolutely established but was probably the time-honoured invasion road from Sora, down towards the borders of the Pentri country and wending around the Matese massif. As outriders galloped along the road to prepare the way in friendly country, the main force followed, to be well placed to not only threaten the road to Bovianum, but also in position to guard the habitual Samnite raiding routes down both the Liris and the Volturnus River valleys.

As this latest Roman intruder approached the Samnite realm, the new leadership there responded; the men who had taken over from Gellius Egnatius showed themselves far from cowed by the presence of a large, two-legion army striding into their country. When these invaders halted behind their normal entrenchments, they did not blanch but built their own marching camp pressing up close against that of the interlopers. In fact, more than this, they soon showed that they were prepared to take the offensive once some meteorological extravagance gave them the opportunity. Though the Roman legionary of the Third Samnite War was not yet the digging machine of the later Republic and Empire years, if the chronicles of the period can be depended on at all, they were still pretty dedicated campers.[4] Before battle and possibly after every day's march, they constructed the kind of effective defences that were not dissimilar to the sort from 100 years later that are described in detail by a Greek historian who knew what he was talking about. Polybius describes ditches at least 1 metre deep, defensive banks used from the spoil dug up, all topped by wooden palisades, making a wall over 2 metres high. Inside the ramparts a space was kept before the men's tents were set up strictly according to their rank so enemies might not bombard them from outside with any hope of hitting anything, while streets led out from the centre where the commander and staff men had their quarters. The later camps were 800 metres square for a two-legionary force and there is little reason to think it would have been much different in an earlier age.

So it was this kind of edifice that would have been thrown up by the army of Atilius Regulus, but if it was an exactly normal structure that loomed out of the dark across from the Samnite lines, what turned out a little unusual was that such a mist descended over the valley where they faced each other that it was hardly possible to see even a few feet ahead. As the Romans relaxed in their animal-skin tents or huddled over their evening meal, they found the camp itself and the country around shrouded in fog. The sentries on the camp walls were as good as blind and the Samnites, realizing the exceptional circumstances might offer a chance to profit, gathered their men outside their own camp gates before setting off in the direction of the enemy. The suggestion is that this action was 'extreme foolhardiness prompted by the depths of despair', but this is clearly nonsense and in fact their promptitude in trying to take advantage shows that morale was still high in the ranks and that their ferocity and initiative had taken little of a hit from the defeat at Sentinum. To begin with the tactic worked: the attackers felt their way round to the back of the Roman camp 'in the dim twilight – what light there was being obscured by the fog',[5] where at the gate they found the guards hopelessly inattentive. The assaulting party quickly overran these piquets and before the alarm could be given, they had reached the quaestor's tent, killing the occupant. Following on, the main body came careening down the tent lines, slaughtering as they went. The confusion would have been total, with defenders struggling to don their armour menaced by shadowy figures and running for their lives, with nobody sure who was who in the mist-obscured darkness where only the dim flames of dotted camp fires showed.

The problem with such attacks in the dark was always that if the defenders were initially surprised, inevitably the attackers were bound all too soon to end up hopelessly disordered as well and this is just what happened. It in fact occurred to such an extent that the consul was able to scrape together a defence as the intruders got close to the camp centre where his own quarters lay. He improvised a line of men, made up mainly of allied soldiers from Suessa and Lucania, and while they endeavoured to hold the flood of assailants along the main road, Atilius Regulus and his officers gathered as many legionary maniples, finally raised from their inertia, as they could. These troops, learning from the noise of alarms and battle cries that the enemy was near, had armed as well as they were able before rallying round any standards and officers they could find. Eventually these survivors had formed ranks, even deploying in some order, but still nerves were frayed; this remnant of the army was far from in perfect condition, with morale dented from the knowledge that the enemy was among them, though darkness prevented them from knowing how many were attacking or where they were.

These troubled fighters were not difficult to push back and the Samnites were soon driving them down the lanes almost to the further defences and the gate that led out the other side of the camp. Atilius Regulus was trying to stir his men up now; asking if they intended, even before they had tested themselves against their opponents, to retreat so far that they left the camp, ensuring they would then have to attack the very defences they had built to regain the day. It seems improbable that this kind of stuff had much impact on men deeply afraid; much more credible is that the attackers had run out of steam, confused and lost among the enemy lines, so inevitably the effectiveness of their attacks waned. Now the defenders, granted some grace, showed on their own ground they knew how to use it. Men who had been forced along, now in the constricted space in the shadow of the walls, found that near each other they could discover comrades, standards and officers holding in good order. Arms could be distributed to those who had none and some cavalrymen even found their charges led out from the horse lines and were able to fashion a mounted arm.

It eventually became clear that the initiative had shifted. From this moment on it was the Romans who knew what they were doing; they who would have felt secure with comrades around them in their familiar formations. For the attackers the context was different and uncertain. In the deep darkness of a foggy evening they did not know where they stood and inevitably some had stopped to loot the senior officers' tents of the luxuries that they typically took on campaign, some dining off the consul's silver plate and drinking wine from gilded cups, while others gathered valuables with the intention of getting away as quickly as possible. Though we do not know who was in command, it would have taken a remarkably able and lucky general to keep his men in disciplined order and capable of pushing on through. With no such man in the offing, it was not long before the defenders, showing a teeming line of swords and spears, were pressing back and regaining, inch by inch, a camp still shrouded in the dense fog.

Once turned, the Samnites, stumbling back over bodies of both friends and foe, were never able to rally and were driven out of the position they had so recently seemed to have captured. Yet if success had begun to slip through their fingers, it is interesting to note that once the perimeters were secured, the Romans did not dare to venture outside to pursue an enemy who had given them such a fright. They had strained every sinew to regain their camp and the stress of bloody fighting in the darkness told on everybody involved, and the casualty figures leave absolutely no doubt how close they had come to disaster. These invaders of Samnium had not only been given a real scare; those hurt on their side amounted to 750 men, considerably more than the 300 Samnite casualties, showing without question that 'the Samnites daring attempt had not been unsuccessful and their spirits rose.' It had almost been a dazzling coup de main and if the success had not been total, still their achievement was made even more apparent in the days following. The Romans, despite losing less than 1,000 men, were so shocked by the aggression of an enemy who now mercilessly harried them when they tried to forage in the fields around their camp, found they could do little before this rising tide of peril. With their position untenable, they scuttled back towards Sora where the country was safer and the men could find themselves a meal without the threat of being jumped all over by a foe they were neither inclined nor primed to face again in battle.

While this poor stuff was under way the other half of the 294 consular team, far from bringing more war to his enemy's world, had been laid up in his bed. This convalescent was possessed of both a considerably greater personal reputation and family standing than his colleague. Postumius Megellus was of good old stock; his clan had always been at the forefront of the hard-line defence of patrician privileges to prevent the opening up of the political offices to the plebeians in the 'Struggle of the Orders'. Indeed, they had been big news since at least 505 when Publius Postumius Tubertus won the consulship, just after the last king was thrown out. The family had always shown that proud high-toned stuff was in the blood and this particular Postumius Megellus consistently demonstrated that he would ride rough-shod to get what he wanted. He is reported by Dionysius of Halicarnassus as a difficult, arrogant personality with few friends, and it seems the already high opinion he had of himself was only aggravated when his father died and he came into his full estate.[6] He was a maverick with a strong sense of entitlement and quite prepared to break the rules to get what he wanted, even causing an uproar by nominating himself for the consulship while standing in as interrex, an abuse of power that compounded another breach of the law that should have prohibited anyone being elected consul before ten years had elapsed since they last served. There is also an almost unique story about him, that this blue-blooded chancer took the opportunity, possibly before the campaign of 291, of a Roman commander's absolute control over his soldiers' lives. So as they passed some of his lands he instructed 2,000 of them to work on these estates and 'ordered them to cut down a thicket without axes; and for a long time he kept the men on his estate performing the tasks of labourers and slaves.'[7] Digging up vegetation to improve the yield of some of his estates was not just a blatant abuse of power for personal profit, it showed a contempt for his soldiers that cannot have gone down well with either the men in arms or popular opinion back home. The middling farmers who peopled the legions would have known hard work and built good muscle in the vineyards, wheat fields and olive groves on their own farms, but the context was everything. Then they would be directing family members, slaves and other retainers, not themselves being led in what must have seemed to them something very like chain gangs, working to line the pockets of a general who should have been dedicating all his soldiers and time to fighting the enemies of the state. Being bullied into physical work in this way must have made it very difficult for these men to imagine themselves as incarnations of Cincinnatus, fighting for the fatherland before returning to follow his plough.

However, if little cognizant of the dignity of his followers, that of his own family was different and there is no question that it had been tarnished by the man in command during the Caudine campaign in 321. This Spurius Postumius Albinus had by his failure placed himself at the head of a group of Roman military incompetents that included the likes of Varro, a man who by congesting his formation thereby lost all the benefits of manipular flexibility before he marched them into the awful meat-grinder Hannibal had prepared for him at Cannae. And Quintus Servilius Caepio who sustained even greater losses at the Battle of Arausio 100 years later when he allowed his personal feelings towards his colleagues to make him camp his men on the other side of a river, ensuring their isolation and annihilation by a horde of Cimbri and Teutones. Now this able if arrogant warrior, who would be consul three times, intended to refurbish the family name, even if he was never ever going to get close to making it loved. The best that could be said of him is that he did not discriminate, showing little respect to Romans whether high or low and giving little or no consideration to his partners in the wars he fought. First heard of as curule aedile in 307, he annoyed many of Rome's moneyed men by fining those who had improperly encroached on public pasture, a common enough transgression. His military career had not been derisory, leading an army as consul in 305 that put the final pressure on the enemy to conclude the peace that ended the Second Samnite War, and if our main source is correct he crushed a defending army near Bovianum, captured that place and had been carried in triumph to mark these achievements.[8] Also his credentials had been sufficient that in the year of crisis 295 he was made pro-praetor, unelected but with imperium, commanding one of the two armies that had been part of the key diversion drawing the Etruscans and Umbrians away from that critical combat at Sentinum.

It is possible that it was not illness alone that lay behind his delay in 294. Commotion in the north still caused concern, particularly after it became known that a party of Samnites had headed north again, entering Marsi territory on the way to encourage the Etruscans and Umbrians to further resistance. That they, in the end, probably got no further than Milonia could not have been foreseen, so this may have been a part of why Postumius Megellus was dilatory in leaving an apprehensive city to take up his burden. Not that sickness could not have been sufficient cause; mosquitoes, happily breeding in the haze rising from the Tiber Marshes, could have brought on a bout of malaria sufficient to floor him for a time before he regained the strength to get on the campaign trail by the height of summer.

News of the setbacks suffered by his colleague had not been long in reaching Rome, so Postumius Megellus, on taking command, dispatched orders to all the officers with soldiers available to march with all haste to reach Sora to reinforce Atilius Regulus trying to hold the ground between there and Samnite country. Once they had mustered in the fields below the town by the river, they pressed on to a junction with the men who had just withdrawn in alarm from the Samnite frontier. Once combined in high summer 294, the consuls sketched out their strategy before advancing and crossing the enemy border again, where an enemy command was given real pause as full reports of this convergence reached them. News of the imminent arrival of two consular armies turned out to be too much even for men who had previously had the conviction to attack a Roman camp. These formerly aggressive enemies were no fantasists; they knew that while they might have done well so far, they were just not present in sufficient numbers to face the biggest force that Rome was ever likely put in the field at this time. In light of this, the only option was to promptly pull back, even if this left their country exposed. With any hope of victory beginning to dim they receded completely, reversing their march and failing to retain any significant force on the ground; a show of weakness that allowed the two consuls' men to wreak havoc wherever they willed. It was like 297 all over again. The invaders did not have to worry about anything more than individual garrisons and it looked like they were going to be allowed a free hand for much of the remaining campaigning season.

However, it was always difficult to keep two such armies together for any length of time; providing for them would be bound to put a huge strain on supply lines, particularly as the country through which they were travelling did not produce the kind of provender they were used to when crossing the rich lands of Campania, Etruria or Latium. So with their men's stomachs rumbling and the horses' ribs beginning to show, the consuls decided on division again, hoping to make the most of necessity by putting the maximum pressure on the enemy from different directions. In the short time they had been together it had been decided that Atilius Regulus' men could be best utilized by heading for Luceria, which it was rumoured was about to be attacked by another Samnite army, while Postumius Megellus was deputed to make an attempt on a town called Milonia.[9] But once arrived there his men's initial attempts to assault the walls proved a total failure, so the impatient commander had to brush up his poliorcetic skills to match his undoubted enthusiasm. The men dug in and 'moved his protective sheds close up to the walls', shaking the ramparts with bronze-tipped rams and when a breach appeared, assault parties of battle-hardened warriors were sent forward. However, they only found themselves faced by resolute and skilfully-led defenders. It took from the fourth till the eighth hour to overcome a garrison who disputed not just the walls that the attackers swarmed over but fought street-to-street, ensuring every quarter was contested before the Romans could claim that they were finally in control. Not surprisingly the body count was high, particularly as a good few would have been civilians, combatants only in the narrowest sense.

From Milonia they pressed on to a place called Feritrum, the site of which remains a mystery, though the best guess is that it was down the main road from Sora, along the Atina road towards the heartland of the Pentri. The story here is puzzling as when the advance guard neared the walls they found the whole place deserted and no defenders to be seen. Postumius Megellus, fearing a trap would not let his men attempt an assault, instead sent a squadron of Latin cavalry to make a circuit of the walls and discover what was going on. They found the gates had been left open and flotsam on the roads out of town suggested the inhabitants had left in a hurry the night before. Even this did not fully quieten the general's nerves who, after bringing the army round to face the open entrances, sent five horsemen to explore the streets inside the walls. Only after reports that all was quiet did he grasp the nettle and introduce light armed troops while the legionaries built their camp outside. The intruders turned up a few sick or aged denizens hiding out and when these were interrogated, it was learned that the terror of the Romans' arrival had been such that a mass decamp had occurred not only at Feritrum but at other defensible places in the neighbourhood too. This final certitude allowed these other ghost towns also to be occupied without a contest.

While this was being accomplished Atilius Regulus had not stayed with his colleague, but had struck east, the destination of his army being that steady colony of Luceria after news had arrived suggesting friends of Rome there were under threat. The task he had undertaken demanded hard marching before he could have the kind of impact his colleague was having further north-east. It was a long way and if they went directly, the road would have brought them near where modern-day Campobasso stands and down the valley of the Biferno. However, the dust-soiled travellers were not destined to reach their target unmolested and on descending towards the plain surrounding Luceria, as scouts rode out to find the enemy, the general found himself again faced with a force of pugnacious Samnites in arms. The menace was real enough and as his legions trailed down from the hills, it became clear that unlike on the other side of the Apennines their antagonists were not going to relinquish the field. Fighting men on both sides steeled themselves to come to blows, knowing their courage would soon be tested in the cauldron of battle. Almost from the first encounter, ferocious combat was the order of the day, though neither side could force a breakthrough until, without great reluctance, they pulled apart. Yet if this fighting was indecisive, the Romans were unquestionably unsettled by the attitude of their foe. The way the Samnites had backed away before had given the impression that this campaign was going to be as much of a cake walk as the one undertaken by Postumius Megellus had been, so when it turned out otherwise they were alarmed. Their feelings were only compounded when the body count of the first day showed they had suffered more than the enemy. Detailed casualties are not reported, but the statement of 'how much greater' they were on the Roman side is telling; honesty that will be looked for in vain in our sources on most occasions.

Now there was a tableau of two armies that had slept badly after a nervy night spent worrying about an attack on their breastworks and who wished to disengage from each other, but because of the vagaries of the terrain could only escape by passing the other's camp. The Samnites, equally unnerved by the savagery of the combat and feeling the losses of men they just would not be able to replace after so many years of bloody war, moved first to get away. They might have succeeded had the Roman commander not showed aggressive and this despite the reports that his soldiers had hardly slept because of 'their wounds and the groans of dying men' and that if they were attacked they would be found to be ruined and hardly capable of any resistance. Initially this man had little more fortune in this encounter than during the fight in the mists, as moving among his soldiers he tried persuasion, hoping they would understand a failure to engage would inevitably mean death or dishonour. There was some class contention here, as when he declared that if they would not follow he would go without them, those who were prepared to share their commander's fate were the officers: legates, tribunes, centurions and blueblood cavalry. However, finally, despite whispers of mutiny beginning to seep through the ranks, the dissatisfaction of the men was not enough to make them actually down tools. So when their officers led towards the gate, they reluctantly armed themselves, clustered round their standards and straggled slowly into the fields outside the camp where the enemy was fast approaching.

The Samnites, finding that if they wanted away there was no option but to fight, dropped their heavy marching knapsacks in a pile around the carts that followed the army as they took up their formations, with captains to the fore, hoping that just this show might convince their foes to let them pass. When there was no great distance between the two armies they paused as the men gazed fixedly at each other, but with none of the usual signs of warriors eager to commence combat. Yet both sides knew that if they made to withdraw it would leave them vulnerable to a devastating strike from armed enemies so proximate, so it had to be forward. Even when the stalemate was broken, it was only desultory stuff that was the order of the day before Atilius Regulus finally pressed his men to a significant effort. Nerving themselves, a cavalry strike was decided upon, so these men who had at least shown willing from the start undertook an assault that far from breaking through, only encouraged an enemy who thronging forward struck where the disrupted cavalry had trampled back into their own lines, wrecking the infantry formations with the flailing hooves and careening bodies of their mounts. Seeing their opportunity, the sparring came to an end as the Romans were pressed back; breathless men who had never wanted to fight and now found themselves buffeted by not only their own retreating troopers but a reinvigorated enemy as well.

The consul, now desperate, posted what was left of his cavalry in front of the camp gate, with lances levelled and orders to kill any of their own comrades if they tried to enter. This had all the makings of a disaster except that the Samnites had no stomach for the chase, allowing the Romans to get back into some kind of fighting shape. Centurions and other officers beleboured reluctant soldiers into formation as their commander vowed a temple to Jupiter, a theological quid pro quo, if the gods would put some backbone into his men, and it turned out to be enough as the Samnites approaching the reformed lines wavered in their turn. The pendulum had swung and they now gave ground, pulling back and intent on retrieving their packs, despite the sight of enemy cavalry barrelling down to try to get round their rear while revived legionaries pressed along their front. The eventual outcome is not detailed, but what is surely certain is that any claims of Roman triumph would have sounded hollow when it became clear that the almost 8,000 casualties they had suffered were not significantly fewer than the enemy's 10,000; Pyrrhic enough, and a peculiarly bloody and perhaps incredible outcome of what had been a scrap between two very reluctant armies.

These unimpressive performances in indecisive encounters may seem strange in the year after a triumph like Sentinum. It was not just that the same people, who had demolished a four-enemy confederation, now looked far from being set on a triumphant course, but that the actions of the enemy appeared nothing like that of a defeated people. This continued Samnite bellicosity is evinced, at just this time when Atilius Regulus was trying to drive his reluctant men back into battle, by other combatants on another front. A different Samnite army showed a real intent to cut again into the heart of Rome's new-found territory in what had once been Volscian country. They poured down out of their hills heading for Interamna Lirenas, a fortified settlement planted in 312 on the route the Latin Way would take, that almost competed with Sora as the most frequently utilized Roman base in years to come, situated where the Liris met the modern-day Rio Spalla Bassa on a wide plain some miles south and below where the Monte Cassino monastery now stands proud. Though intending to turn the screw on the Roman and Latin settlers and showing that Samnite offensive spirit was far from cowed, this particular enterprise itself did not end in great success. An assault on the town failed, but this did not stop the invaders wasting the countryside and accumulating huge amounts of booty from a population surprised by their arrival. Stolen goods on the hoof and piled on carts as well as prisoners destined for the slave-trader's block were being hurried along the road when these raiders, returning home, had the bad luck to bump into Atilius Regulus on the way back from his sojourn to Luceria. He may have appeared less than sensational so far in this season's fighting, but at least in this circumstance he made the most of it when he showed on the right side of the goddess Fortuna.

We do not know what road he had taken on the way back from Luceria, but as it is probable he was himself wounded, the medical men in attendance no doubt searched for the least bone-jolting itinerary. Whichever route they found, by the time the army had crossed back over to the west flank of the Apennines with scouts leading boldly ahead, they found a highway crowded with Samnite warriors labouring under the goods they had taken from the countryside around Interamna Lirenas. The column of marauders was practically defenceless when they found their path blocked by long lines of Roman legionaries with cavalry in among them, ready to set to as soon as their commander gave the order. It was over almost before it began, with an armed tide overrunning an enemy who could hardly find a line on which to regroup. The Samnites were dispersed and dispossessed, captives rounded up and valuables that had been dropped in their efforts to get away collected. The victorious commander intended to seize the moment to take advantage with an eye to his reputation. Aiming to make friends in this important part of the world, he sent out messengers to alert the despoiled victims that they could get back their belongings by applying to his headquarters and identifying what they had lost. Whatever the satisfaction he got from the local goodwill he gleaned, it failed to carry the hoped-for weight when he got back home. Anticipating that he and his men, after trailing back and forth across the peninsula in the past year, would be welcomed with a full-blown triumph, he was in for an unpleasant surprise. When the authorities heard the reports from wearied and resentful soldiers that any success he had had was bought at too great a cost in Roman lives, they wondered whether the ultimate accolade was warranted, and on top of this was the fact that Atilius Regulus had sent the Samnites he had captured in Apulia under the yoke. This practice had not been heard of since 307 when Fabius Rullianus had humiliated his Samnite captives after battle at Allifae, while the Hernici combatants were sent to Rome to face punishment. Before that there is an improbable claim that, only a couple of years after the Caudine humiliation, a Samnite army was treated in this way near Luceria, but this is palpably an attempt to even up the record at a time when the Samnites and Romans were not even at war.

Now the consul found, whatever satisfaction he got at the humiliation of his enemies, it came back to bite him as the hometown crowd saw only the downside in that they would see none of the usual profit from ransoms or even any agreement by the defeated men not to take up arms again.

While his associate had been crossing and re-crossing the country, Postumius Megellus, deep in Samnium, had made a decent fist of the year already, but this was not the last of this active man's achievements. In a busy season, if sickness had delayed the kick-off he was not lingering now, but was determined to make up for lost time by intervening in the northern war to deliver even more pain to a host of troublesome Etruscans. The Volsinii had again become an irrepressible epicentre and he was soon sucked in, ravaging the country around Lake Bolsena and over the hills towards where Orvieto now stands on its lofty ridge, punishment that brought the local defence force out in strength. These militias formed in front of their defences in the hope that they might scare the intruders off, but the consul and his men had been doing well this year and with morale high, they took the defenders on. After battle was joined, legionaries were soon cutting the Etruscans down, so it was only the proximity of refuge behind the city's walls that meant they did not leave more than a couple of thousand lying on the battlefield. Having swatted aside this resistance, the army, leaving burning fields, groves and vines, then marched northwest over more than 70 miles of hard road to reach the next target. This was Rusellae and though days would have been required to reach it, once there not only were farms 'laid waste' in the normal way but more than 2,000 country folk were captured before they could reach the safety of their defended city, but on this occasion the town itself was captured as well. At this place, twice as far again up the coast as Tarquinii, Postumius Megellus clearly intended a real solution, but it was not going to be the usual protection racket stuff of demanding money and clothing with menaces. We do not have many examples of major towns being actually taken over, particularly when there appeared to be no intention to plant a colony, but this was exactly the unusual activity that consumed the end of the 294 fighting season. It was worth the effort; this old place on the shore of the ancient Lake Prile with its impression of ruins which can be discovered on two hills almost 200 metres high, 3 miles north-east of modern-day Grosseto, includes the foundations of Etruscan houses found under layers of Roman occupation. Villanovan from the mists of time and a friend if not a member of the twelve cities of the Etruscan confederation, its strength is attested by 2 miles of cyclopean walls that in places can still reach between 6 and 7 metres in height, maybe suggesting that this town had been a real tough nut to crack for the Romans, ensuring they had no intention of turning it back again to people who had so often turned enemy in the past.

The loss of what was a major city had its effect on the northern coalition that had been so efficiently roughed up and it is perhaps no surprise that we soon hear of envoys from the Volsinii, Perusia and Arretum being dispatched to urge an arrangement, efforts that won an agreement to a forty-year truce with the invaders camped so destructively on their land. So with clothes, grain and 5,000 assēs contributed by the people they had been fighting, a happy if used up and battered army made its way back home to Rome after their brisk campaign of pacification,[10] the soldiers and commander anticipating with relish a triumph that surely would be the only proper reward for their year of achievement, but the reality turned out to be more controversy. It is quite possible that their accomplishments were exaggerated and, whatever the essentials, there were people back in Rome who would not be beguiled just because they had taken or neutralized some Etruscan and Samnite posts. Postumius Megellus was hated, so it was hardly a jaw-dropper when, despite him having had a good war, the likes of the Fabii and plenty of others nursing vendettas showed both interested in and capable of belittling the reputation and accomplishments of a character who knew so well how to make enemies.

This consul was not just haughty but disputative too, prepared to fight his corner after criticism that not only had he delayed departing on campaign, but that he had then taken his men off to Etruria with no specific dispensation from the Senate. Postumius Megellus knew that much of the censure was personal, not just antagonists taking the opportunity to denigrate his standing, but others who were friends of Atilius Regulus trying to console their man for his disappointment by denying a triumph to his colleague. Not prepared to be kept down, the case was first argued in front of his peers, but when he was rebuffed it was rehearsed in the popular assembly where his own eloquence and the influence of friends and supporters appeared to be winning support. Yet even when the majority of the popular tribunes were mobilized to veto his triumph, he did precisely what might have been expected from this impossible man and decided to go ahead anyway. Breezing into town, he marched his army down the ceremonial route with prizes and prisoners on show, with much of the gaping populace crowding the processional route offering their tacit approval. So if both that year's headline acts had been snubbed by a Senate flexing its muscle, at least one had been prepared to flout their rulings to get something like his way.

What is noticeable is that in this epoch, how a triumph was authorized and what it entailed was not set in stone as it would be in centuries to come. Such events always mined the substratum of custom while incorporating the imperatives of the immediate and this would certainly be manifested in future disputes. Marcellus, a hero of the Hannibalic War, ended being denied a surely warranted celebration for his conquest of Syracuse in 211 and instead undertook a sort of ersatz version on the Alban Mount, 12 miles outside of Rome. Scipio Africanus was also refused a triumph a few years later after his extraordinary successes in Spain by rivals resentful of his success at so young an age. Also even in the first century Pompey the Great dealt in controversial celebrations, winning his first triumph at the outrageously young age of 24, having led great armies prior to filling any magisterial office and even trying to use elephants to pull his chariot on another occasion, while he broke records on the bonuses he gave to his soldiers and prolonged his last jamboree to two days in order to have time to show off the incredible amount of plunder he had gathered in his eastern wars of the 60s.

* * *

Now, as a radiant spring sun washed the centre of the Italian peninsula, a season of fighting was undertaken that was almost as crucial as had occurred two years before in the hills of north Umbria. Despite there remaining a suspicion here about a match with events that took place seventeen years earlier, we can still be reasonably confident of what transpired in the critical year of 293. The earlier episode saw the people of Samnium scrapping together every stash of precious metal that could be found to equip two elite units. The smiths and artisans of each community laboured to endow their warriors with shields of gold and silver, in a dazzling effort to fend off Roman thrusts into the heart of the motherland: 'They had new glittering armour made in which their troops were quite resplendent. There were two divisions; one had their shields plated with gold, the other with silver.'[11] Dreading this menace, Lucius Papirius Cursor was enrolled as dictator to take charge of dealing with this shimmering foe and after a victory in the field, the equipage of the enemy was a sight for the eyes of the crowds following his men as they marched in celebration through the streets of the capital with captured gold-inlaid shields given to decorate the banking booths in the forum and other valuable items dedicated at the temples of the gods. Much is open to question here, particularly how these mountain men would have found the amount of precious metal needed to outfit their warriors in the way described, this apart from the fact that much of the armour described is that of a Samnite-style gladiator of much later days rather than a fighting soldier. Most suggestive of all is that the time this is reported as happening was just when news would have drifted back west that this very brand of troop decoration had been carried out by the great Alexander of Macedon when his army invaded India and that in the wars that followed his death, the most famous battle-winning regiments, particularly under Eumenes of Cardia, were the Silver and Bronze Shields defined by armaments bedecked with precious metals.

This echo of what occurred sixteen years earlier is compounded by the fact that again in 293 another Papirius Cursor would be involved, this time the son of the great warrior of the Second Samnite War. We know nothing of this man before this year, but he would almost certainly have served on campaign with his father, perhaps even fighting as a very young man against Samnite warriors glistening in their precious finery. He would shine later in life too, triumphing in 272–71 against the Tarentines and other southerners after Pyrrhus left these people to Rome's tender mercies. However, if he was the offspring of one of the greatest marshals of the Republic, a patrician who was five times consul and a multiple dictator, his colleague was a plebeian and the first of his line to reach the consulship; not that Spurius Carvilius Maximus would be the last as his son became consul in both 234 and 228, while he himself celebrated a triumph against Italian tribes, again in tandem with the man who was his colleague in 293, and even reached the heights of the censorship at the start of the 280s.

The war these two would now fight against a people with their backs against the wall would centre on a place called Aquilonia. The Samnites' intelligence service would have learned early on that both Roman consuls would be coming at them in the next campaign, yet their leaders still determined that all was not yet lost and proceeded to muster a new army, calling on every able-bodied man to rally round, even threatening that those who did not heed the call or failed in the heat of battle 'should forfeit his life to Jupiter'. Their priests set up a special mustering place, 200ft square, built of wicker and hides and roofed in by linen cloth. This motif was further emphasized by savage incantations from an ancient sacred book made of the same material to underscore the hallowed nature of the oaths the recruits were required to take. The whole was orchestrated by a dignified ancient named Ovius Paccius who, trading on the memories of traditional practice, claimed that the rigmarole went back over a century to when the Samnites had planned a coup to take the city of Capua from the Etruscans, who had founded it way back in the seventh century.

The picture we get of the actual process is of young Samnite nobles climbing a steep slope before entering an arboreal sanctuary where eerie light filtered through the fabric roof as they were bullied into commitment by verses iterated in ferocious rhythm, with those reluctant to dedicate themselves to holy war being beheaded. Then these devoted warriors, stumbling out into the sunlight, were empowered to pick others to join them to live and die by this stern code; then these others, sanctified by selection, had to choose even more and so on until the total number reached 16,000 men. All this was done against a background of diabolic curses taken in the deepest secrecy in an atmosphere of naked terror at a place where the enclosed ground was covered with the bloody corpses of those who had refused the call. The warriors, when gathered, were armed with the most splendid weapons, with linen tunics and high-crested helmets 'to make them stand out amongst the rest', this 'rest' being the remainder of the army that itself numbered another 20,000 who the accounts claim were hardly inferior to the Linen Legion in terms of the quality of the personnel or their panoplies.

How much of this should be taken seriously is problematic; certainly it is likely that at this critical stage of the war the Samnites would have pulled out all the stops and dedicating sacred warriors to take a knife to the jugular of an enemy as a consecrated act was not at all unheard of in the Italian military tradition. We learned of the Etruscans recruiting a similar army before the Battle of Lake Vadimo in 310, but if the intent to give their efforts a hallowed luminosity is plausible, what should not be credited is the suggestion of awful impiety in their behaviour. The bloody corpses in the sacred grove are hokum, intended to traduce the humanity of an enemy who may have been facing an appalling crisis but who would, having already lost so many men in years of fighting, surely not murder more of their own. The accuracy of the numbers is also open to question but 36,000 might not be too much of an exaggeration for forces raised from all the tribes in this year of decision. After all, the Linen Legion and its auxiliaries would be facing an invading army led by two consuls that at full strength could well have comprised a similar if not considerably greater number. Whatever the details numerically and in terms of designation, these sacral fighters knew they would soon be charged with the fearsome obligation of fending off an existential threat to the motherland.

Effort would be matched by effort and what is of interest in the accounts of this year's activity is that a trend beginning in the description of the Sentinum campaign is continued, as we are frequently informed of the names of more of the characters taking part, even officers in subordinate positions; indeed, we even know the name of the priest who organized the induction of the Linen Legion. As had become the norm in the last few years, the Republic had ensured that many of its best commanders were kept in the field, even Postumius Megellus, who had offended so many by forcing through his triumph the year before and on leaving office was threatened with arraignment by a tribune of the plebs. Due to the need for his skills, the matter was shelved while he was made legate in Spurius Carvilius' army. We know that a Scipio was in the ranks too, certainly Barbatus who had been under arms almost since the war's commencement and Volumnius Flamma as well, who again had hardly put down his sword since pairing up again with Appius Claudius as consul in 296.

Soon enough Spurius Carvilius showed his intent and the orders to march were given. He was able to act swiftly, having taken over Atilius Regulus' already mobilized legions that having survived the Luceria fight and just rounded up the latest bunch of Samnite raiders were awaiting their new commander in camp around Interamna Lirenas. Whatever heated talk he might have heard of the new enemy troops being raised, he was confident in a powerful well-found force totalling almost 18,000 men. This invading army pressed forward, capturing a place called Amiternum while his foe was still fussing with religious ritual and hatching their plans. The only Amiternum we know of is the Sabine centre that would suffer soon enough at the hands of a different conqueror, but this place up north is by modern-day L'Aquila and unlikely to have been a target in this season. An argument has been made that it is indeed the place in question, suggesting perhaps the Sabines were active allies of the Samnites at this time, or indeed that the whole of these wars were really Sabine contests.[12] These are far-fetched theories and the most probable explanation is that either it is a mistake or there is another town in Samnium of the same name. Anyway, this was but a prequel as the son of a great father, if slower off the mark, delayed by the requirement to enrol and train the new regiments that would make up most of his army, now entered the picture.

If Spurius Carvilius' route was geographically problematic, Papirius Cursor's was more straightforward. He marched from Rome against a place called Duronia and once arrived stormed what does not sound like a heavily-defended place. Good practice for many of his green recruits, this easy success occurred most likely where there is to this day a community with the same name. Duronia with its Samnite fort is found on the Apennines' eastern flank, up from the valley of the Trigno and even in modern times is not that easy of access and is certainly not a natural route for an army pressing from Rome down into the heart of the Pentri. Yet that this was the target both consuls had chosen to strike became clear when joining hands at Sora they commenced their main campaign. Some 70-odd miles from Rome, this town was frequently the forward base for Roman incursions in the later wars against the Samnites and now while the soldiers gathered nearby, the consuls consulted on the momentous activities afoot in the heart of enemy country. At Aquilonia an irrepressible enemy was making the kind of effort that looked like it was going to demand a real combined endeavour. Having mapped out their strategy, as summer temperatures continued to rise they headed down the dusty road of invasion, destroying the countryside round Atina as they went, before dividing with Spurius Carvilius advancing towards Cominium and Papirius Cursor in the direction of the main menace massing at Aquilonia. Finding a location that fits Aquilonia and Cominium has tested many, with suggestions that could place it in Hirpinian territory not far from Venusia, or Valle de Comino near Alvito, even the Trigno valley where the reference to the capture of Duronia would make sense. Yet if Livy is to be credited at all, his references to the proximity of Bovianum and Saepinum have to count, making the rocky site of Mount Vairano between Busso and Campobasso north-east of Bojano the most likely candidate.[13]

This military co-operation between the two consuls directing their steps towards the heartland of resistance was no standard procedure. Usually the practice was for each to head in different directions intent on doing their own thing, not this remarkable coordination seldom paralleled in previous campaigns. Certainly in circumstances where both consular armies were jointly marching as one, as before Sentinum, collaboration was to be expected, but now with two separate forces synchronizing their activities, this was something special. Some 60-odd miles would have taken several days' hard marching before both prongs of this offensive reached their targets. Once arrived they camped 20 miles apart, remaining in close contact and spending more days either skirmishing in front of Aquilonia or preparing siege lines around Cominium. In advance of full-scale battle being inaugurated, Papirius Cursor wrote to his partner informing him that his plan was to attack the next day and requesting him to strike on the same schedule, so the enemy could not themselves coordinate any support between the two parts of their armies, even waiting for his messenger's return with notice of agreement to be sure of synchronicity.

Papirius Cursor was an early riser; 'in the third watch of the night' an hour or two before dawn he was up to see what his augur, who was observing the sacred chickens, would have to report. This man, picking up how unpopular he would be with the eager soldiery if he did not come back with good news, chose to disregard the fact that the birds, once released from their cages, had refused to eat and reported the omens were the very best for battle. With these preliminaries apparently satisfactorily concluded, the consul could survey the field and make his plans against an enemy snug in a camp that could be seen up ahead as the ground rose, steepening behind, and the defences of Aquilonia perceived appearing out of the morning mist, high up on a rugged tree-covered eminence.

The story that kicks off the contest entails a nephew of the consul who was in command of some cavalry. One of this Spurius Papirius' troopers reported to him that he had overheard the priests who were taking the auspices arguing about what occurred when the sacred fowls failed to consume their rations. This conscientious officer, after investigating, reported to his uncle that indeed there was a question mark over what had occurred and that the diviners had deceived him about the birds gobbling up their feed. However, knowing his army was waking for the day ready and eager, having become frustrated by the indecisive skirmishing on offer so far, the general showed a mechanistic mindset, not at all untypical of his time and people. He determined that as he had been informed by the officiating priests that the auguries had been fine, he could proceed without incurring any disfavour from the heavens; that any offence given would rebound on the head of the fraudulent priests and to ensure this outcome he ordered them to be put in the front line of the army so they could be cut down by the first javelins of the enemy as a sacrifice to propitiate any gods offended by their duplicity:

> Before the battle-shout was raised or the lines closed a chance javelin struck the pullarius and he fell in front of the standards. When this was reported to the consul he remarked, 'The gods are taking their part in the battle, the guilty man has met with his punishment.' While the consul was speaking a crow in front of him gave a loud and distinct caw. The consul welcomed the augury and declared that the gods had never more plainly manifested their presence in human affairs. He then ordered the charge to be sounded and the battle-shout to be raised.[14]

Papirius Cursor had little option; his men would not have put up with any delay as there had already been rumblings since they had arrived in

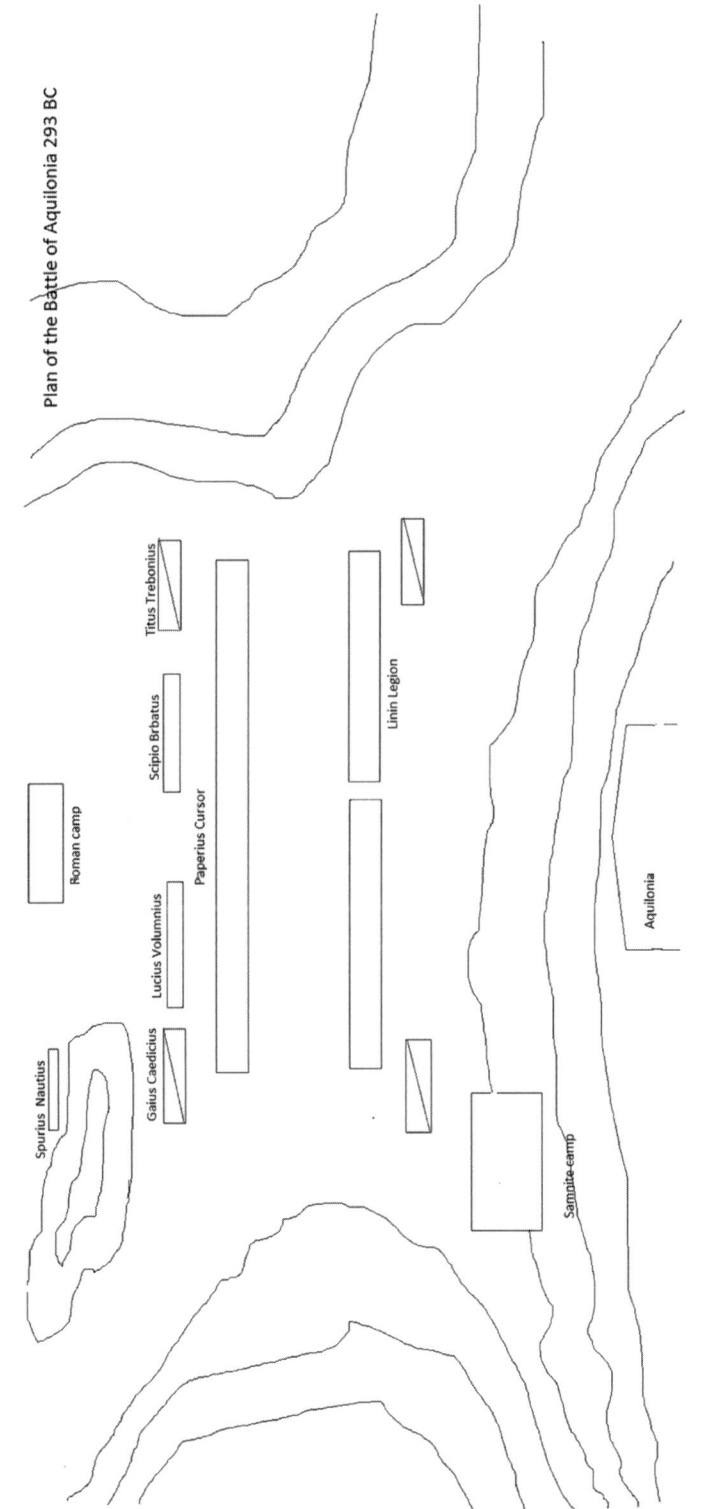

the presence of the enemy. The soldiers even had little enough sympathy with their general's meticulous planning. They wanted to be led out to battle immediately: 'Satisfied that humanly speaking they were more than a match for their foes, they clamoured with one voice to be led to battle.'[15] They resented even the fact that their general would not immediately take the plunge and had resolved to wait a day and a night until his colleague replied to his letter.

It had all been religious rigmarole so far in this crucial year, but after this events would be decided by the hands of men. Yet discounting the consuls' inspiring sangfroid, the situation remained perilous; the Romans were, after all, deep in enemy country and a reverse might soon translate into a disaster. By the time the earnest discussions in the command tent were concluded, word had arrived out of the mouths of Samnite deserters that an enemy detachment was leaving Aquilonia to reinforce those forces at Cominium, intelligence that meant this was the moment; Papirius Cursor knew he must now hurry his followers to take advantage of his adversaries' reduced condition. As the hills were touched by the rays of a new sun, the men had already bestirred themselves and made a simple breakfast of porridge, bread and olive oil, and with the help of slaves or servants, dressed themselves in whatever newly-burnished body armour they had to provide protection to their vital organs. Once equipped and refreshed, they followed their standards into the field, taking their customary places in the ranks, occupying perhaps a metre or two of space between comrades who, even if they had only known each other since they signed up, still would have built strong bonds born of shared danger. Peering between their shields, the front few ranks would have had a clear view of an old enemy emerging from their own camp and showing as a dark smear above the ground around the base of the high ground rising behind them. Emotions of those facing battle were bound to be complex, whatever the froth and bombast of those who had demanded it, and whatever is reported about the frailty of the Samnite spirit, this would not have been the experience of most of these men. They knew Rome had lost as many battles against this enemy as they had won and prior to Sentinum generally the most decisive ones as well. So there would have been fear, but also trust in their sturdy shields that covered all their body not protected by grieves and helmet. Blaring trumpets rent the air and centurions were barking orders, but these were familiar sounds, good for flagging spirits, particularly for those who were experiencing battle for the first time and affected by the sight of the enemy, coming on now sporting tall plumed helmets that made them look so much larger to the men, many of whom would have stood not much over 5ft 6in tall.

Dressing and motivating the long lines of combatants would have taken time, but there was plenty of experience for Papirius Cursor to call on and it showed in the details of the Roman array. The commander was a careful man who understood what he was up against and readied his reserves under generals who knew what they were doing. In command of the right side was Volumnius Flamma, a two-time consul in 307 and 296 and militarily active between those years as well. On the left was Scipio Barbatus, recognizable and resplendent in his beard, who had hardly been out of harness since the latest Samnite war had begun. Two legates, Gaius Caedicius and Titus Trebonius, commanded the cavalry held behind the battle line and if they had not been heard of before, now deep in this war it is reasonable to assume they would have been time-served veterans. All was orthodox so far, but the next arrangement showed that this son of a great soldier had learned some tricks at his father's knee. An officer called Spurius Nautius was designated to carry out the manoeuvre that he hoped might be decisive. He was dispatched, with the pack animals, camp followers and a contingent of more than 1,000 allied soldiers, to wait behind a nearby hill, with orders to intervene when the fight was well under way and the critical moment had arrived, the intention being they would persuade the enemy that a large and uncommitted body of reinforcements were approaching to join the battle.

As the ranks moved forward under a spread of light clouds in a summer sky, there would have been some for whom dread would have overcome any adrenalin recompense, and having heard that the men opposite, whose every spear was pointed at them, had dedicated themselves with the most sacrosanct oaths to win or die, would have badly wished they were not there. After all, their comrades had, according to the story, benefited by just such a sacred sacrifice by one man only two years before, so what might an army of similar devotees achieve, advancing to victory over a carpet of their own bloody corpses. In the loose manipular formation such men might falter except for the non-commissioned officers specifically posted at the rear of the files to ensure they had no option but to move forward with the rest. Yet the Romans we know were eager, 'exasperated against the enemy and thirsting for his blood', and as the battle lines approached light troops on both sides discharged their missiles, then pausing threw again before withdrawing back into the ranks of those following. Then it was not long before the first line of heavies, the hastati, swept forward. They were young men, probably with a small bronze pectoral protection, plumed pot helmet and scutum, who flung their heavy iron-shanked javelins before drawing swords to get in hand-to-hand.

The speed either side approached across no man's land is impossible to know; velocity is just not detailed by the historians. After all, how a soldier approached his enemy would be just too well known by everybody to need to be specified, but it would not have been anything like a run, at least not until just before impact. Even if the day was not yet scorching hot, the effort would have been too much considering the weight of their arms. Also the individual soldier who approached his enemy opposite was not a phalangite in a shield wall, who might want to barrel over the opposition. He was commencing a duel and would need to be well in control and capable of manoeuvring his shield and wielding his sword, not an easy thing to do at a run. On both sides the front few ranks would have faced javelin showers, striking helmets and shields and with a few finding vulnerable flesh, but as these had strictly a short-term impact there was no need to rush in close to get out from under a continuous rain of missiles. So the best guess would be that a steady march was kept to maintain formation, perhaps increased to a trot for the last few yards. By the time they reached within striking distance of the foe, many would have had javelins sticking into their shield and their priority would be to try to knock out these weapons hanging down from their bent metal heads because while they remained stuck, the soldier's key piece of personal protection would have been very unmanoeuvrable indeed.

The fighting was soon general along a line that might have stretched for up to a mile. It was savage and frenzied as the Samnites responded and with the morning turning into afternoon the sun heated up helmets and body armour, leaving their owners soaked in sweat and hardly able to see as they brushed away the salty droplets flooding their eyes. Even if they did not have any advantage bestowed by magic ceremonial, still the

Romans had murderous talent on their side, honed over years of warfare, drilled to fight until they could no longer lift a blade, after which they would be replaced by comrades loping forward to take their place. As with individuals, so with the maniples, that having held their position for as long as bone and sinew could stand would be replaced by more experienced detachments waiting behind, a regular refreshing of the men at the cutting edge of the carnage that ensured even if the combat raged for hours, they would hardly tire: 'The standards of the Samnites were now advancing, followed by the army in gorgeous array; even to their enemies they presented a magnificent sight.'[16] The evidence suggests these Samnites were as well-protected as their adversaries, with bronze body armour or reinforced linen cuirasses acquired from their Greek contacts. If fewer coats of mail were in evidence, it was because not many could have afforded what was always expensive armour. These men of the Linen Legion on the right side of the line in their burnished arms were strong and courageous; whose hearts swelled with god-borne purpose, yet still it was tested as these fighters made contact. Iron crushed bone, spears and shields shattered, while bronze pierced flesh in a maelstrom of horror as white powdered dust held in the air entered eyes and throats. Yet at least those at the front could release their overwhelming emotions of hate, anger and terror by striking back at the men who wanted to kill them. Four, five and more lines back they could only watch and wait with guts melting and legs shaking; a kind of stress that was difficult to bear. It was no wonder that when an army broke it was usually those who had not crossed swords who ran first.

A discordance of voices was raised in paean as metal rang against metal, followed by screams of pain when the front ranks clashed in a swell of roiling regiments. Men on both sides fell, downed in viscera and blood, making the ground slippery for those who had to carry on fighting, trying to survive at least and if possible win. The assertion is that the Samnite defence was sustained not by courage but by fear; that they only fought because of the picture they had of the bloody corpses of those who had been unwilling to enrol, lying with sacrificed animals spread in bits on the floor of the linen compound and the 'frightful curses' that they would be subject to if they did not defend their land, but as the Romans pressed along their whole battle line any suggestion of the Samnite morale being low is not credible. The first lines fought it out toe-to-toe where the fittest and most youthful warriors disputed, seeking to show well in front of their comrades and by downing several enemies even make a reputation that might go beyond their own small squad. Swords and spears stabbed and cut as long as arms had the strength to carry on. Most were fended off or shivering against the metal-bossed and rimmed shields, but enough finding unprotected limbs, torso or face. Dead and wounded on both sides covered the space between the lines as they pulled back when the sweating terror of this deadly labour became too much, and the undulating lines of duelling warriors retired to rest to be replaced by the men in the files behind.

Two veteran armies traded blow for blow with desperate savagery as 'The Romans pressed on from both wings and from the centre and cut down men who were paralysed by fear of gods and men.'[17] This does not sound like subtle military surgery, just prolonged pressure all along the battle line, though it is possible to read the Roman tactics as arraying their best troops and largest numbers on the flanks, hoping to encompass a sort of double envelopment, but if this was the intention, it was not this attempt at an eighty-year-earlier Cannae that proved the tipping-point. That decisive intervention was left to the men and animals who had been posted behind a nearby hill at the very commencement of the fight. They decided the moment had come or a signal was given and the detachment emerged; a squad made for this occasion coming over the hill with Spurius Nautius at their head. Non-combatants and auxiliaries sat upon braying donkeys and cantankerous mules, with camp servants dragging branches, all raising great clouds of dust and exhibiting all the standards they had to give the impression of numbers. With the enemy already all committed, the hope was that they would perceive them as fresh regiments about to make a definitive entry into the fray. The consul colluded in the deception, yelling that it was Furius Carvilius' army come from Comitium after having defeated the Samnites there, to encourage his own men and sow confusion when word reached the enemy.

The impact was shattering. Morale was always the key in these ancient battles, as an active chasseur called Ardant du Picq, who perished at the Battle of Mars-la-Tour in 1870 AD has amplified.[18] Now against a backdrop of long hours of slaughter and pandemonium, the Samnites heard the ominous metallic sounds of approaching antagonists followed by the appearance of terrifying silhouettes shrouded in clouds of dust and brave and committed though they were, most soon ceased to believe in the possibility of countering the new threat. So after that the question was just how long would the whole take to unravel? Papirius Cursor certainly was not going to be patient; once the enemy began to lose formations and give ground he himself led the way in exploiting the success. Knowing he needed to get his horsemen up and at them to ensure success, he belaboured his infantry officers to open up their lines so the cavalry could find space to charge and ensure the victory was comprehensive. The troopers had been well-rehearsed. The two officers, Titus Trebonius and Gaius Caedicius, had been told to look out for the consul raising his spear high above his head and at this signal to lead their men in a headlong charge against the enemy battle line. There was to be no holding back, as if all went to plan by the time the horse went in the enemy would be too shaken to sustain the onslaught. This confirms what any visit to the region in question would suggest, that in the valleys and rolling hills where most battles were fought there was not a huge amount of open terrain. Something confirmed here; that the battlefield of Aquilonia was so pinched in that there was no room on the wings for the horsemen to deploy. They were only able to charge and engage once their own infantry had got out of the way to let them pass.

The hard-boned horses and active riders in the front ranks saw the enemy open-mouthed in horror as they charged towards them. Steady infantry showing a hedge of spear points are a match for the very best of cavalry; horses will just not rush against a dangerous and unbroken obstacle, but these men fixed in this ghastly tumult were far from solid. Distraught at the sight of thousands of new enemies approaching them, their spirit was exhausted and the attackers easily drove them back and broke holes in their front, making passages for comrades to cut into the flanks and rear of the already shaken lines behind. Allied nobles from the Latin cities and Campanian towns with well-born Roman eques all piled in, ensuring no group of champions could rally their comrades in a stand that might slow down the bloody pursuit on which they were intent. With the enemy line shivered, by both the fear of a fresh enemy arriving out of the dust and the presence of caracoling cavaliers spearing into their midst, Volumnius Flamma and Scipio Barbatus threw in their infantry reserves. Breaking into a trot, these men, kept well back from the stress of the battle line, were fresh and eager, voices clear as they sang their paean and after throwing their missiles, drew swords to cut out at the blanching men in front of them. How long the fight was sustained we do not know. How long the heroes in the refulgent ranks of the Linen Legion fought is not recorded, but 'At last the dread of gods and men had yielded to a greater terror, the "linen cohorts" were routed; those who had taken the oath and those who had not alike fled; the only thing they feared now was the enemy.'[19] Now it was not a matter of pausing to catch their breath to allow them to fight on; they were breaking in horror, streaming away with their only idea being to get to the protection of friendly walls. The terrible men behind pressed home their advantage, heavy swords chopping at undefended limbs and heads from high up on horseback or lances impaling sweat-soaked, linen tunics of running men. Soon it was not just a few thousand horsemen; not long after the Roman heavy infantry got in on the deadly work where the enemy line broke in front of them. This would have started where the horsemen had crashed through, but when it became clear that the combat was lost, even the bravest of the Samnite soldiers, whether at the front and directly in deadly danger or further back in the ranks, knew that the only chance was to get out.

Papirius Cursor's tactics had inflicted dreadful damage and it was now a free-for-all, with commanding generals desperate that they had blundered and nobles on their horses frantic to get away, all hurrying in the direction of Bovianum and the Roman cavalry galloping on their tail. For the infantry this was not an option; the only bolt holes open to them were the palisaded camp or the nearby walls of Aquilonia. None of these last two groups, who reached their goals in sweating terror, were allowed time to gather themselves into ordered formations at either of these places. Volumnius Flamma had already collected his weary but victorious troops together on the right wing and led them eager from the fire of battle in the footsteps of the flying enemy towards their encampment. Evening was coming on, but the Romans were determined to complete the victory before night made further fighting difficult and they discovered little resistance along the breastworks. Any last desperate attempt at defiance was overcome and the attacking columns poured over the wooden walls or in through the gates, massacring anyone showing the slightest signs of resistance and corralling the rest of the dejected and defenceless combatants into a despondent mass of captives. However, in Aquilonia Scipio Barbatus discovered he had a considerably harder nut to crack. At the head of the other wing he found himself facing not just a ditch and wooden palisades backed by shaken defenders, but a great obstacle of huge stones fitted together in emphatic defences, dominating the ground all around the town. On these walls the routed troops had reorganized themselves and, bracing to resist, had used what time they had to raise piles of missiles, rocks, javelins and arrows to keep off the attack that they knew would soon arrive. These ramparts were also situated atop a steep hill that took some time for the attackers to scramble up to avoid completely losing their formations. The bearded commander was only too well aware of the problems he faced, knowing that only by hitting the enemy before they had properly rallied would he be able to achieve swift success.

Appealing to his men's sense of regimental pride, Scipio Barbatus demanded of them, puffing up the hill in heavy armour and rounding the spurs below the town, whether they could stand to see their comrades capturing the camp while they were 'driven back from the city gates'. The appeal worked. 'There was a universal shout of "No!"'[20] and, leading his men with shields raised above their heads against a rain of missiles, they burst through the gate that the defenders had not been able to properly close in time. As evening was turning to night they rushed the walls to form a bridgehead that would allow the men following to enter and support them. The fighting on the ramparts was as ferocious as at any time in the battle and many Romans fell there, dispatched by the weapons of desperate men. Exhausted, sweat-streaked combatants were perhaps less cautious and many soon had blood soaking their tunics as well as perspiration. The crush was awful in this desperate combat, terrified men striking and thrusting in despair as much as lethal intent, hoping for a pause when they might survive to be replaced by a comrade from behind. It was almost dark but still the consul saw what was happening and directed all the men he had to hand, including those just recalled from taking the camp, to go to his subordinates support. Late in the day though it was, he countenanced no delay and as lengthening evening shadows ended the fighting, the Romans, bivouacking on the ground they had won, were controlling the town gate and in a position from which they could not be thrown back. So with both sanctuaries, camp and town overrun, the remnants of both sets of defenders abandoned them and followed into the night in the footsteps of their cavalry in an attempt to reach Bovianum.

This, it turned out, was the first piece of something like an ancient Jena-Auerstedt moment; a rare enough occasion until at least the second half of the nineteenth century, where two battles occurred on the same day at two places a good number of miles apart, yet still very much part of the same campaign. The second encounter in this decisive season saw the other consul Spurius Carvilius confront his division of the enemy army at Cominium. He was well coached to do what had been asked; to occupy all the Samnites on his front so they could not go to the aid of their comrades fighting Papirius Cursor. As the horizon lightened, his army of veterans had left their camp to deploy outside the enemy town, surrounding the walls and ensuring the men were arranged in greater depth where the gates showed in the defences and the heaviest fighting might be expected, but before he was able to come to blows he heard that it was in fact he who would have to worry about succour reaching his enemy from the other front. A messenger arrived with news that 20 units of the enemy, each 400 strong, were on the way from the army facing Papirius Cursor. The Samnites may have courted defeat by this depletion of their numbers, but they knew these men were absolutely required on the other battlefield. Food for thought for a preoccupied commander, but he proved decisive and in response just as the signal to attack was about to be given, withdrew the first legion, nearly 5,000 allies and the cavalry from the battle line and dispatched them with Decimus Brutus Scaeva to deal with the threat that had just been flagged up. He was determined to keep these 8,000 enemies out of the Cominium battle at all costs.

With this danger covered as best it could be, the main army took up the gage against an antagonist waiting behind the city walls. This was no open field affair, so scaling ladders had been prepared and the infantry, schooled in the manoeuvre, formed a sort of testudo of shields to keep off the enemy missiles being rained down on them as they pressed towards the gates. The fighting was hard, with attackers kept back from the gates by men made sharp by desperation. They flung down missiles, javelins and heavy stones kept on the battlements for that purpose and with the Romans taking casualties, it looked like the Samnites might hold their own, until some of the assailants managed to get their ladders propped against the stonework and themselves up and over onto the battlements. There the combat was more even until the advantage turned against an enemy whose morale was dented by their failure to safeguard the viability of the stone defences that they had considered near impregnable. All around the pressure grew, with men climbing up and those approaching the gates able to push their way through to threaten the defenders on the walls from the rear. The front held for the moment but it could not last; the weight of numbers told in the end. With spears splintering and swords knocked from their hands, only when blood splattered and some fighting at last with teeth and fists did they falter.

There was no doubting the Samnites' courage; nobody was yet in defeatist mood on the ramparts, but the Romans were confident they were a match for them and it was not long before the defenders' commander decided his only option was to draw back, to make a final stand in the public space in the middle of the town. There they pulled together a line, with the officers desperately straining to raise their followers' spirits so they might construct a perimeter defence against a rampant enemy who were sweeping in down the main streets and collecting in formation opposite their own. The Roman captains were given their instruction and the lines of soldiers began their advance over thoroughfares already liberally sprinkled with corpses that shimmered with heat and carrion flies, sanguine reminders of what once had been vigorous warriors but were now just a jumble of limbs and shredded torsos. Any javelins that remained to hand were thrown before the ranks clashed, with battered swords, axes and daggers bloodied once again. In the wicked closeness of hand-to-hand combat, groggy men on both sides slithered in the gore, tripping over the dead and wounded. Still, it did not last long; the defenders quaking amid the ruins had little left to give and the accounts verify that soon, with hundreds fallen and no effective options, those who had not succumbed had slipped away or thrown down their arms and surrendered.

There had been two battles already but all still expected a third to take place somewhere on the rolling road between Aquilonia and Cominium because of the 8,000 men dispatched from the army facing Papirius Cursor, sent to the assistance of their friends at Cominium. This suggests the Samnites might have fielded a considerably smaller army than the one attacking them, as Spurius Carvilius was able to reduce his own strength before the battle by a similar number of combatants to counter the threat of these reinforcements, yet retained the confidence to throw the remainder of his men in a desperate assault on the battlements of Cominium. In fact, nothing transpired in the country between the two towns as the Samnite general commanding at Aquilonia, realizing the magnitude of the fight he had on his hands, sent messengers to recall the task force. They reached the marching men 7 miles from Cominium, when those in charge responded, turning back in accordance with their latest orders, but far from affecting events where they had come from, it meant this large body of men was unavailable for either contest. Over halfway to their objective when they turned around, the counter command not only kept them out of the fight at Cominium but meant they did not have the time to return and help their comrades at Aquilonia, who were desperate for the sound of marching feet echoing through a cloud of dust that might mean rescue.

In fact, by the time the footsore men found themselves back where they started from, darkness was descending and all that confronted them was the blackened burning remnants of their main army's camp and Aquilonia town, suffering terrible destruction at the hands of a victorious foe. These dispirited men, exhausted, threw themselves on the ground to sleep without entrenching, near where the cries of the wounded could still be heard, filling the night on the field where the battle had been fought. Still terribly tired, they were slow in stirring as morning light started to show and on being seen both by Roman cavalry ranging the country and legionaries pacing the walls of the captured town, found themselves promptly attacked and dispersed, hundreds being killed but most, after discarding their arms and baggage, reaching the temporary safety of Bovianum.

Synchronization of the two armies had been of the essence and now the consuls, happy with their work, allowed Aquilonia and Cominium to be given over to plunder, sack and flame so thoroughly that they burned down in a day. The victors inspecting the field of blood would have noted the fine apparel of the sacred warriors they had faced and recognized they had bested all their enemy could offer. Then their commanders led their soldiers off to combine in camp where they were paraded to distribute awards:

> The presence of the two armies' rewards and decorations were bestowed by both Carvilius and Papirius. Papirius had seen his men through many different actions in the open field, around their camp, under city walls, and the rewards he bestowed were well merited. Spurius Nautius, Spurius Papirius, his nephew, four centurions, and a maniple of hastati all received golden bracelets and crowns. Sp. Nautius won his for his success in the manoeuvre by which he frightened the enemy with the appearance of a large army; the young Papirius owed his reward to the work he did with his cavalry in the battle and in the following night, when he harassed the retreat of the Samnites from Aquilonia; the centurions and men of the maniple were rewarded for having been the first to seize the gate and wall of the city. All the cavalry were presented with ornaments for their helmets and silver bracelets as rewards for their brilliant work in various localities.[21]

The success had been considerable, though figures of nearly 40,000 Samnite casualties in both fatal engagements must be taken with a heavy pinch of salt as these add up to more than their whole army amounted to before the campaign began. The Samnites had been outnumbered from the start, after all, their young manhood had been bleeding out for years and recruiting sergeants had been getting near the bottom of the barrel well before this year's campaigning. Just as questionable is the idea that the enemy who had contested the Roman onslaught was timorous, kept in the battle line by the fear of their priests and the flummery that had occurred around their recruitment. This was Roman wishful thinking; the reality was that almost the last of a warrior breed had showed the kind of fight that would be expected against an invader poised to destroy the very heartland of their mountain home, and the survivors of the Linen Legion, turning from the spectacle of a flaming Aquilonia and Cominium, would undoubtedly have perceived the fate that awaited the rest of their people.

There was admin to be done as well; important enough for the commanders' reputations. Fulsome reports were dispatched back to Rome to a people whose appetites for victories could not be sated; not just to be read out at the Senate, but in front of the popular assemblies as well. The celebrations in the city went on for four days and the relief was palpable when it became clear that threatening trouble in Etruria might have made life considerably more uncomfortable if the outcomes in Samnium had been different. Once the home town administration was made aware of their success, the consuls acted to exploit it. Seeing their victories as potentially decisive, they intended to reap the rewards for themselves. There was no inclination to bequeath to the men who would take over in the following year the finishing of what they perceived as a prostrated foe. So in confident mood, full of patriotic belief in their own and their country's destiny, they departed their camp, intending to lay Samnium in ashes, until their soldiers were sufficiently enriched and the enemy forced to sue for peace. For decades they had fought this enemy, but now they could hope that these latest victories would stand as bristling proof of their supremacy.

Soon, despite the profits of victory, among the milling rank and file the question of supply was bound to become serious. After all, it was hard to squeeze adequate meals out of a country stripped almost wholly bare. So with this in mind and the desire to widen the impact of their incursions, the consuls separated. A Samnite high command who worried where they next would fix their gaze soon found out, as Papirius Cursor headed south towards Saepinum. There may have been terror in the face of these advancing hosts, but any assumption by the Romans of a quiescent foe proved premature. Saepinum, nestling in the hills in or around its citadel, the remains of whose massive defences can still be seen to this day and though the attackers might have expected a desperate defence from behind these ramparts, they would not have anticipated much else. However, there was clearly more than just a stalwart garrison; large numbers of the men defeated in the previous battles, after regrouping at Bovianum, had also ended up there. Those who had survived out of the Linen Legion, combined with the remnants from the Cominium fight and many of the 8,000 soldiers detached before battle were gathered together and would have made up a considerable and veteran force to counter the invaders.

Papirius Cursor marched deep into enemy territory, skirting the high terrain of the Matese massif looming on his right, bypassing Bovianum where so many refugees had been attracted, to take fire and sword into the country. Nearing Saepinum they were carving into the enemy's vitals and despite recent shattering setbacks, there was bound to be a response. As the Romans followed the road down the valley east from Bovianum and approached the hills behind, the defenders, far from remaining behind their walls, came out to attack the invaders on the march and, setting up in line of battle, the Samnites prepared once again to face a dangerous invader. A perilous mission surely, but long-odds bets had worked before and they hoped that just their unexpected appearance might give them an edge.

These encounters would not have amounted to full-blooded battles, more hit-and-run affairs with desperate enemies appearing out of the grey of an autumn morning, but they were frequent. The Samnites set up viscid snares and more than once attacked against a marching enemy already hindered by distance and terrain, showering them with missiles, forcing them to break stride and slow down to prevent heavy casualties. The Romans eventually reached the town itself, but even then the defenders did not give them an easy ride as they endeavoured to put the place under blockade. Having had plenty of time to refurbish the defences, they were determined still and braced for a lengthy siege, even sallying out to attack as works began to be dug around the town, interrupting things so effectively that the consul and his men became extremely exasperated with the enemy pouring out to loose their javelins at them and pounce on any groups of besiegers who strayed from their main lines. Eventually the attackers' numbers made the difference and Saepinum was fully invested, with many of the troops who had fought so well and so hard trapped inside. Nothing could now stop the consul beginning the siege proper: building his lines of circumvallation, setting up sheds and battering rams to try to weaken the walls. Yet the attackers were reluctant to spend the time it would take to starve the enemy out and when opportunities arose they attempted assaults on the ramparts, but these endeavours were inevitably costly and what happened when the town fell showed how infuriated the Romans had become at the course of events. Ultimately a wall was broken down or enough men reached the ramparts on their scaling ladders for the defence to be no longer tenable, 'after pressing the siege with spade and sword he finally effected the capture of the place',[22] and once stumbling over the broken masonry and swarming in, with defenders at their mercy, they butchered with a will. Thousands were assassinated in awful fury and only after this did the attackers tire of massacre, taking the remaining terrified men as prisoners, though how many of the casualties were combatants and how many just inhabitants unable to escape the doomed town, we have no idea.

The capture had taken time and there were signs of winter arriving as the siege reached its conclusion. The hill town which the army now occupied was hit by a snowstorm and the whole region became deeply inhospitable: 'Everything was now deep in snow and it was impossible to remain out of doors.' So in a situation where there was little chance of making further progress, the consul had to acknowledge that his term of command had come to an end, but if needs must and a new man would take over at the helm of the Samnite war the consul was determined to make an unforgettable show on returning home, one that would even outshine his own father when he triumphed in 308. At Saepinum his men had found a fabulous amount of booty 'Owing to the Samnites having stored their property in a limited number of cities.' So when they paraded in a Rome receiving them in festival mood, the troopers and foot soldiers, apart from showing off their decorations and famous Samnite leaders and their sons led along in chains, escorted transports that carried '2,533,000 bronze Aes, stated to be the proceeds of the sale of the prisoners, and 1,830 pounds of silver.'[23] Despite the trophies carried away and the destruction wrought, it still did not mean the Samnite threat was completely eradicated, and even after another season of victory, this was revealed when the army was not allowed much time to wallow in their celebrations, instead being directed to winter near Vescia to protect the Aurunci country. This posting at least had the consolation that they would be near the coast where the weather was going to be much more clement than where they had just come from. However, if they would not end up shivering in winter camp, there was still some dissatisfaction at the lack of largesse from a 'niggardly' Papirius Cursor, this despite the fact that if the norm of later times held, this was the time that pay was usually distributed to see the soldiers happily debauched through the off season.

If before the year ended one conquering army had found itself stuck in the snow, the other had ended up having to deal with a different if just as familiar antagonist, but before this Spurius Carvilius also drove to reap the harvest of the double victory of Aquilonia and Cominium. There is an itinery of conquest that includes places called Velia, Palumbinum and Herculaneum and at the last of these he had to fight a regular battle where the Roman losses were considerable, after which his followers, refractory from exhaustion and with a hard winter drawing on, pressed for the end of the fighting. The mystery here is where these places were, as the only towns we know of with these names are down in Campania and even further south on the Lucanian coast. Although it is not impossible that they had pressed on this far from the heart of the fighting in the Pentri country, it is still not probable.[24]

Certainly the subsequent appearance of this active new man is nowhere near any part of Samnium, never mind Lucania. It was old foes in Etruria that received his attention after the two consuls, taking a break from the fighting front, reunited back at Rome and drew lots on who should respond to the new trouble. The exact details of the events that pulled attention north are difficult, but undoubtedly a number of Etruscan communities had broken out and envoys from Rome's allies came complaining that they were putting pressure on them to revolt too. This threat was compounded when the Faliscans joined in, though this people who had been friends of Rome for a good long time were at least given the full treatment, with fetials sent to warn them off before formal war was declared. We know it was very late in the fighting season when the national security advisors in the Senate oversaw the choice of who should front the mission, because when Spurius Carvilius' army heard that he had been allocated the Etruscan War, their cheering filled the air, deeply relieved that they were not to be returned to continue the reiving of a damaged enemy in a snowbound Samnium. However, their leader's feelings may have been less ecstatic over being pulled from the throat of an enemy who was surely at last gasp. Still, it hardly affected his commitment to duty as he made a strike at a place called Troilum. This seemed like easy prey, as even before fighting began, 470 local moneybags ransomed their freedom, after which he captured the town by assault, killing or capturing all who remained unredeemed. In the wake of this success there was more fighting and we know the Romans 'carried five forts, positions of great natural strength', with the garrisons suffering 4,000 casualties in the sequence. The numbers do not suggest the places were large, but this exertion was sufficient to pressure the Faliscan leaders to reconsider their rash decision to turn against Rome, and they must have felt themselves lucky when a truce was secured at the cost of stumping up a year's pay for the invading army as well as 100,000 assēs of bronze as a lump sum. While victory was attending Roman arms both north and south, still there remained a lingering question as to whether total success was finally within reach.

Chapter Ten

The Last Campaigns

> '... when Curius, with his own hands, would lay upon his modest hearth the simple herbs he had gathered in his little garden – herbs scoffed at nowadays by the dirty ditcher who works in chains, and remembers the savour of tripe in the reeking cookshop.'
>
> Juvenal, 11 78

Six years of the Third Samnite War are chronicled with masses of dramatic detail, but unfortunately after 293, when a breakthrough was on the cards, this is no longer the state of affairs. We are down to the bare bones with our main source enduring in a very slight epitome, leaving us only able to make a stab at constructing some sense of events from Zonaras, Polyaenus, Eutropius, Paulus Orosius and others. Even if, frustratingly, all we have has justly been seen as the scouring of a few poor-quality minds and coming mostly from even later than those of the Augustine period, the picture is not so much more obscure than on plenty of other occasions in the history of Rome. We know for certain that the Linen Legion had bled profusely and Roman armies were more than ever before primed to ramble at will over most of Samnium. The agonal years looked like they had arrived for good. Disaster was stalking the Samnite League with its lands eroded at the edges over decades of war, like a seashore that had looked so stable for so long but as the tide rolled in was being undercut, becoming so much less than it had been. Yet still it was far from the end, and while the Hirpini had been harried to the bone in the years before Sentinum, in 293 the Pentri had been the scene of a devastating action. So while they licked their wounds, now it was the turn of the Caudine communities to feel the lash. Zonaras certainly asserted that Samnite pillaging of Campania in 292 brought proceedings to a head in that region; something supported by the involvement of the great Gaius Pontius whose family hailed from there and would be apprehended while active in defence of his motherland.

If a name from history was significant for the Samnites, so it was with their opponents. On the Roman side as the year before had featured the offspring of one of Rome's greatest marshals from an earlier age, so this one saw a son of the grandest man of this era take centre stage, but this time the father would be required to involve himself personally in the struggle against the Republic's enemies. Quintus Fabius Maximus Gurges was the progeny of the hero who had penetrated the Ciminian forest, then reached even greater heights as the surviving victor of the climactic Battle of Sentinum, but a strong odour of the disreputable hung about him in his youth as a dissolute lifestyle won him the epithet 'Gurges the glutton'.[1] However, by the time he became curule aedile in 295 he had changed his ways and, like so many reprobates turned upstanding citizen, was even harder than most on his watch on rule-breakers. Indeed, it is reported that he loved fining moneyed matrons who had been enjoying the good life with men other than their husbands, then using the funds garnered to boost a newly-discovered reputation for piety by founding a temple to Venus near the Circus Maximus. His was a flawed career, never to match that of his father, that eminent man who did so much to win the Samnite War, yet he would still end up a pretty significant figure, occupying the consulship not just in 292 but in 276 and 265 as well during a period when such multiple tenancy was less the pattern, and ending fatally injured in a Volscian faction squabble during his last incumbency.

Clearly by 292 time, the great healer, had sufficiently dimmed any remaining reputation for dissipation for him to win his first consulship. Getting[2] the top job at a very young age, the father's very considerable influence was clearly at work. The magic of his name alone was a boon, even if the idea that from the beginning the old man going to war on his staff was never really going to be part of the package. Indeed, Fabius senior made it abundantly clear that he was not going to get involved, so his son could garner all the glory that was expected to be won in a triumphant campaign. So in combination with Brutus Scaeva, who had done well in the battles of 293, Fabius Gurges took up the commission of finishing off the people they had been fighting so long. However, as was often the case in these years, the two senior magistrates could not immediately concentrate all their efforts against the great enemy, as

Etruria remained a concern and Brutus Scaeva, backed by the proconsul Spurius Carvilius, kept in post from the year before, had to be swiftly dispatched north to knock heads together.

Still Fabius Gurges' principal focus was on what was happening in the other direction. This new consul, long on rank but not necessarily on intelligence or experience, learning that enemy forces were ranging out of their hills into prosperous Campania and plundering in great style, took the high road south. After passing the River Volturnus, the army came in sight of the rich country with telltale trails of smoke showing above farms and villages and discovered advance parties of enemy soldiers who fled at the very sight of the new arrivals. Only a thumping triumph would do for this son of such a father, so Fabius Gurges followed up, driving the invaders back through much-fought-over country along what would become the line of the Appian Way up towards Caudium, and in his impatience for action he showed inexperience. The suggestion is definitely that it was the man in charge who was at fault; who, thinking the whole Samnite army was now in flight and in a hurry to score a major success, sent his men rushing forward. Now in this territory, where they had so famously come unstuck in 321, another confident Roman had arrived and it did not turn out lucky for him either.

Fabius Gurges, having failed to send scouts ahead and only intent on bagging as many freebooters as he could, walked into a trap with his eyes closed, reaping the whirlwind as the enemy got lucky. Having unwisely marched for miles, probably under a blistering southern sun, his men were tired at the commencement as most of these unfortunates were suckered into a lethal snare hardly in any sort of formation, while the Samnite army had stayed alert, concentrated to support their raiding parties and eager to take on the disorderly horde they learned was heading down the road towards them. The resulting battle was in the balance only a short time as the sound of clashing lines reverberated across the sun-scorched fields, Samnites tearing into the loose Roman formations, so they had to draw on all their reserves of strength to hold the line. Even the few regiments who were kept well in hand by the consul, once engaged were shaken by what had happened to their comrades and outnumbered with so much of their army already routed. Only the arrival of night, when eventually both sides pulled apart, saved the sagging Roman ranks from a real disaster. In terms of casualties it had been far from a massacre, but as for morale the contest had ended very badly for the tyro commander, though there is a curious story that it had been Fabius Gurges' father's reputation that saved the day: 'And they would certainly have perished on the following day but for the fact that the Samnites, believing Fabius' father was near at hand, felt afraid and withdrew.'[3] Yet still it was bad enough. A trial had been set and he had failed it, as the Romans, for whom rigorous discipline was an article of faith, were forced to withdraw from the scene in disorder and slink back across the border. To compound matters, they found their baggage and the doctors had been left far in the rear, so little organized help was on hand, leaving large numbers of wounded, who needed tending and transport to carry them off, without succour; a cognizance of pain that showed in later traditions which report that they had suffered a really substantial reverse.

An enemy the Romans continually censured for their barbaric, disorganized approach to battle and who were supposed to be on the edge of defeat had turned the screw, ensuring that the eager young man who had expected to roll them over had failed completely and ended up causing the deaths of many of his followers. Fabius Gurges soon realized, knowing his family did not lack for enemies, that many back home would be preparing a difficult reception for him. The mood in Rome was already grim since earlier in the year; signs of discontent with complaints about the raising of a war tax that suggest a population resentful at being stung for the bill for a struggle that appeared never-ending. So it would have come as no surprise when after three days, well-born stragglers on good horses, ahead of the other retreating units of the army reached Rome with accounts, strewn with personal self-justification, of a reverse they discovered had cost the Republic 3,000 good men;[4] that once the Senate assembled in the bright painted portico of some temple, the Papirii, the Claudii and the rest were soon eager to rub salt in the wounds of their traditional Fabii rivals. Unscrupulous to be sure, using a national nightmare to push personal agendas, but this behaviour, sanctioned by centuries of clan rivalry, soon gained traction as Fabius Gurges discovered his peers raging against him. Be-toga'd bigwigs rallied their clients, while tame orators roused the commons until the furore was such that it seemed the young man, who had done so badly in his first time in command, might be recalled, if not worse. There is more than one account of what fell out in a poisonous public space, where men openly jeered at the consul who had failed. The resentment around the needless losses in battle would have been compounded by the fact that many families were already facing repeated bereavement caused by the severity of the plague raging at this time. Yet what is finally apparent is that this was one more occasion when the Fabii rallied round, just when many of the senatorial grandees were primed for the head of one of their number. Ties of loyalty were always a tightly-woven fabric and the father and the family had saved Fabius senior's bacon when Papirius Cursor was after his blood in 325 and now that man, even against the backdrop of a Senate roaring its disapproval, came through to work the same trick for his own son. Fabius Gurges may have returned to Rome to fight his corner or Fabius Rullianus took up his case in his absence, but whichever it was they had to contend with real anger over a campaign performance that was claimed as a complete fiasco, with debates in front of the people's assemblies as to what punishment was warranted for this hard-luck commander who had put the state in peril and threatened his family with the basilisk stare of dishonour.

The ignominy felt by the young commander was compounded by the fact that it was unusual indeed to suggest a general should be treated in this way in mid-campaign by the folks back home. It was not just the impact on his own career that was in the balance, but the reputation of his kin as well. One of the great Roman clans was involved and they could not countenance the humiliation and the unravelling of dignity and authority that might come with it. So when the greatest living Fabii put his credibility on the line, the mood music gradually altered. The victor of Sentinum disposed of sufficient clout even in these circumstances; there were plenty who wanted to stay on the good side of this best-connected man staking his reputation and that of his forebears as well in an impassioned plea against significant censure. He maintained that his son's youth should argue for clemency and if the people were afraid for the future, knowing that his own military reputation would ensure confidence, he offered to turn a hand himself, to join the consul's army and guide his actions from a subordinate position. There are no accounts of his speech on this day but it must have been stirring; a figure of legendary repute putting a compelling case on the line to save his son.

So, donning his gorgeous breastplate and plume-decked helmet, Fabius Rullianus left to join his offspring at the front, who even if he keenly felt the humiliation of having a parent so publicly pull his chestnuts from the fire, knew he had to swallow the indignity as the alternative was worse. The older man flung himself into the war with enthusiasm and the effect of their teaming up seems to have been almost immediate in restoring the glory so tarnished by the earlier rout. Presumably the old veteran came with a reinforcement boost too, to ensure the morale of the already recovering army was given a further fillip; sufficient, in fact, that they swiftly felt buoyant enough to get back on the invasion road. Energy and self-assurance restored by his father's presence, Fabius Gurges prepared to show the brute facts of overwhelming resources that were almost bound to see his side victorious in the end. The new high command showed well as they found an enemy not only led by their own veteran commander but who were in resilient spirits after their recent success and scorned anything except recourse to another open battle. Both sides lined up for a second round in the year's contest and at least a few details are known. Paulus Orosius in *Against the Pagans* describes a family at war with Fabius Gurges leading from the front in a brutal assault, hoping that a showing of élan would trump his other faults; aggression that again almost led to disaster, as he found himself assaulted on all sides by blood-flecked enemies headed by Gaius Pontius himself, only to be rescued when the older Fabius astride his warhorse charged into the fray, followed by the rest of the battle line.

Desperate bravery and grim determination won the day and ensured the Samnites took a beating. Their line, made up of almost the very last military resources that a desperate people could find, eventually crumbled, with the surviving men fleeing to a camp that itself was soon captured. This was a sweet moment; a scene in which Fabius Gurges' and his father's exultant faces would have shown lit by the camp fires as their men settled down for a night of well-earned rest. Virtually nothing is known about the childhood and youth of most ancient historical figures and not much about the private and family life of even the greatest; a lack of insight that is certainly the case with the individuals we are considering in these years. So even if these Fabii, father and son, went out of their way to champion each other, we have no real idea if this is suggestive of personal closeness. Whatever their personal feelings, they could now exalt with the pendulum swinging their way and they would not be reticent in exploiting it. The family combination not only claimed an unbelievably exterminatory 20,000 enemy men killed and 4,000 captured, but also pushed on with the campaign, indeed accomplishing a sufficient number of conquests in the rest of the year's fighting for the earlier setback to be forgotten, particularly when wagons piled with plunder were driven before their army into Rome, sufficient not only to fill the state coffers but to reward the soldiery as well, resulting in Fabius Gurges receiving the ultimate recognition of a triumph. Enough of a coup already, with villains becoming heroes, this reversal of fortunes was topped off when during the triumphal parade the captives on show included the Samnite hero who had hurt the Romans so badly at the Caudine forks in the Second Samnite War. That had been nearly thirty years earlier, so it was an old Gaius Pontius borne down by chains who graced the hometown spectacle before his final demise on the headsman's block,[5] a real satisfaction to the crowd that followed the cavalcade, to wipe away a stain that had long disfigured the city's escutcheon. Apart from this, with the young consul leading the cavalcade, taking pride of place in the entourage was old Fabius, veteran of so many Samnite triumphs of his own; a spectacle that would have an echo in the Hannibalic War when Fabius Maximus 'the delayer' acted as subordinate to his son and also followed behind him in triumphal parade.

This campaign that ended with Rome in party mood and the streets thronged in scenes of joy and celebration is, like so much from our Roman sources, difficult. The trope of a defeat almost immediately followed by a return bout that ends in victory is just too frequently trotted out to be accepted without question. On this occasion the early reverse is assuredly believable, but not perhaps the complete victory coming after in compensation. Nothing was altered at a stroke and two more years of war shows the suggestion that Pontius' capture finally finished off the Samnites is clearly wrongheaded.[6] What, however, is striking is that what almost happened to Fabius Gurges was a taste of developments under way over the period we are describing. This era is generally considered to be when the dominant role of the nobility was truly established; an oligarchy of rich families, patrician and plebeian alike, organized as a permanent Senate, becoming the guiding hand in the policies of the Republic; a body that would have sufficient authority even to remove a commander with consular imperium who had failed to deliver the goods in the field in a manner that had not been in the least common in the decades and centuries before. When the norm had been that if a consul on campaign fell short, was killed or injured, a dictator could be called on, but one who must himself be nominated by one of the elected consuls. The men who led armies to disaster at Caudium or Lautulae may not have been showered in roses by the crowds back home, but we hear of no movement to have them removed from office in this earlier time. A sea change had occurred and a Senate, fully established by an independent censor and freed from the tyranny of yearly magistrates, could begin to flex its muscles and eventually would end in contention for a Mediterranean empire, feeling their authority even against great patrician names that a century before were still almost a power unto themselves. Not that withdrawing imperium became a popular pattern; future disasters tended to be blamed on failure to properly appease the gods or the ill-discipline of the soldiers. The city's leaders were always reluctant to activate this kind of radical disposal as it could come back to bite any of them or theirs when they might also suffer disaster in the city's wars.

Yet now a triumphant Fabius Gurges, milking the glory while his father stood back out of the limelight, found himself in such good odour that despite his consular term of office drawing to a close, his command was prolonged into the following year, so he was able to take advantage and continue the systematic lashing of enemy country that had occupied the end of the last fighting season. To keep up the pressure he led his men around the south-eastern end of the rampart of mountains that was the Matese range and towards the important centre at Cominium Ocritum. He opened siege works against the town, but just as the defenders were beginning to feel the pinch, this man who had previously been threatened with ill-usage by armchair compatriots now found himself actually suffering at the hands of a military colleague. In his second year of command, with a veteran force behind him, he must have felt that the ripe fruit of complete and final victory might be his when a bitter rival arrived to dash the cup from his lips. He was relieved of his command by Postumius Megellus, one of the consuls elected for the year 291. The reason for this cursory removal was, some suggest, because he was vulnerable after his father had left the army and the memory of his previous failure was remembered against him. Yet this is not convincing, as this was a man who had just ridden through Rome in triumph and his military repute remained sufficiently impressive in later years for him to receive the highest command again in 276 when Rome was facing the second eruption of King Pyrrhus of Epirus onto the peninsular scene.

There needed to be no perceived weakness in the position of the younger Fabius; the spiteful new man on the scene would have acted so whoever he had to replace. Nor indeed need there have been bad blood between the two, though it is certainly reported.[7] It was just the way Postumius Megellus was; this man whose attitude inspired a rare dislike in his fellow citizens. Even on this occasion, just before taking the field he had showed profound disrespect towards his colleague in front of the Senate when he mobilized his considerable political influence to ensure he was given what seemed the plum post of taking on the Samnites in the campaign just determined upon. On his arrival at the siege lines this intractable man, determined to assert his predominance over a personal rival in the most insensitive manner, chastening Fabius Gurges by dismissing him from his command in writing, and if he was 'not willing to give up command voluntarily, to force him by arms to do so'. This was against the direct orders of the Senate:

> And to the envoys sent by the senators to demand that he should not hinder the proconsul from remaining in the camp nor act in opposition to their decrees he gave a haughty answer worthy of a tyrant, declaring that the senate did not govern him, so long as he was consul, but that he governed the senate.[8]

So it was settled and having sent Fabius Gurges packing, he took control of the siege, aiming to secure all the credit for its conquest for himself, and whatever divisions this might have created at command level among those loyal to their old general, the men were sufficiently motivated and happy to obey anyone who would direct them against the enemy. Knowing the promises of success and the booty it might bring would sway any waverers, Postumius Megellus concentrated the besiegers from their camps around the town to prepare for an all-out assault.

Soon the defenders saw the men they had been used to seeing just manning their lines breasting these earthworks on the way to a barrelling assault. With waves of legionaries rushing the walls and crowding into the narrow, twisting, weaving alleys it took just a 'short time' for the place to fall, with no doubt a familiar pattern of butchery and looting before survivors crawled, dazed and traumatized, out into a landscape of blackened ruin. Despite having stolen a victory to start his campaign, this activity had been incidental to Postumius Megellus' principal concern; the core project had been to devastate Apulia and Hirpini country. So the new consul continued with the main thrust of a war conducted on the eastern flank of the Apennines that is only known about from the scantiest of evidence. It is far from always easy to know what exactly transpired in the Samnite struggle at this time, but what is certain is that the loss of life piled on in years of war had been grinding deep into their population base and left the league with hardly sufficient military wherewithal to face their adversary in the open. They might on occasions be able to mobilize warrior bands to raid vulnerable frontiers and even, as in the case of Fabius Gurges, still give bloody noses to Romans coming too close and being too careless, but not much more. Consular armies that took care of basic security, ensuring that camps were built and that scouts learned what was waiting down the road, did not have too much to fear after 293. We can certainly assume that Postumius Megellus' two legions and numerous allies approaching from the Apulian flank would have wreaked havoc with impunity when they reached the ill-defended communities of the Hirpini, and when this work of destruction was done, construction took over as the consul determined to batten Roman control on the region. Here on the border between Samnite and Apulian country, he discovered an attractive territory highly suitable for settling colonists. This place that would become key to retaining the Republic's Italian hegemony was Venusia, taken from the enemy and founded as a colony in 291 on lands in Samnium's far south in the shadow of Mount Vulture's cone. A real fort built on a defensible ridge, it would become a crucial strategic enclave that in the century to come would be critical, even when Rome's position in the south was threatened by heavyweight outsiders like Pyrrhus and Hannibal.

The mission was a real achievement, and it might have been expected that this and his other feats, Comitium alone was attested to have deducted 16,200 enemy dead or taken, spoke for themselves, but for the man in charge it was not going to be enough. The feathers Postumius Megellus had ruffled over the years were about to come back to bite him. The Fabii, with axes to grind, may have led the way in hounding their old enemy but they found no difficulty in building support with others nursing vendettas against such a recalcitrant character. The process of establishing a new colony was usually a political win-win for the man who took the lead role, but now nobody was in the mood to give him 'any mark of favour or honour by the senate, but even lost the esteem which was his before'. So it was decided that others should take the lead in the foundation, as 20,000 colonists hit the road to fill up the wold country down under the volcanic vestige of Mount Vulture. As might have been expected, Postumius Megellus was deeply angered, though he ought not to have been surprised after he had so recently refused direct senatorial instruction over Fabius Gurges' treatment, but instead of striving to woo back support among the members of an increasingly important institution, he utilized his not yet expired imperium to deny the profits of his marauding to the treasury by distributing all the booty among his soldiers, and then demobbing these same men in a job lot so they would no longer be available as a fighting force to the man taking over. Though undoubtedly these men breaking camp and dispersing to their homes would have soon been telling stories of the profits of their fighting that would undoubtedly embolden others to join any newly-raised legions. This behaviour, while it might suggest the common touch, potentially winning the rank and file to his cause, was surely about personal rancour and not likely to be lauded by chroniclers in hock to an unappreciative elite. So it was hardly a shock that despite past success and popularity with the troops, this did not stop rivals nursing bruised feelings from his past conduct from raising against him the old charge of his misusing his soldiers to work his estates. So on standing down from the consulship, he was finally brought to trial before the 'popular assembly, where he was condemned by all the tribes, the indictment calling for a fine of 50,000 denarii', perhaps one of the severest, if most condign financial penalties ever dealt out in the era.

Habitually the great Roman empire-builders are known to us by their cognomen, a personal nickname that takes on the function of a family appellation. The man who finally defeated Hannibal is generally remembered by the name Scipio, possibly from staff of authority or sceptre, while Julius Caesar's cognomen has been transmitted down the centuries as Tsar or Kaiser and this man, who incorporated so much of modern France and Belgium into the Roman Empire, may have got his name from an antecedent being born with an abnormal amount of hair. Another individual who could almost be put in the same category as these two but is much less well-known was at the helm when the Third Samnite War was concluded. Pliny claims this Manius Curius Dentatus received his name because he was born with teeth already showing, but more probably he suffered from comically prominent teeth or was of a particularly determined character, certainly a characteristic that is well displayed when this member of a plebeian family first appears on the political scene. No respecter of reputations, he tangled with Appius Claudius in 298 when he served a first stint as tribune of the plebs. That contradictory man was acting as interrex when he took him on and trying to use his influence to deny a candidate the opportunity to contest for a consular chair because of his plebeian roots. Though it is possible all this occurred in 291 when he was tribune once again, it is less likely as we know he became consul in 290, so on that occasion he would inevitably have found things complicated by opponents accusing him of egregiously using his sanctified position to push his own candidacy for the highest office.

The new incumbent, after carrying out the requisite religious and municipal functions, took charge of however many levies his officers had been able to raise and joined with those of the men left over after the army had been so cavalierly disbanded by his predecessor. If Eutropius is to be believed, this last year of the third war was not without its excitement, claiming real battles took place that for the Samnites further 'reduced their strength', but these would surely have just been skirmishes or guerrilla actions with little possibility of the consular armies being turned back. As soon as Curius Dentatus approached enemy country, certain things became crystal clear: he was going to be able to march around the high hills and valleys of Samnium virtually at will as no organized armies remained in the field to challenge him. So as his men commenced the campaign, they found most of the locals had taken what they could gather of their goods and chattels and decamped for protection to the hill forts that dotted the landscape, still resolved as far as possible to continue resistance.

Standing in the Biferno valley between the outcrop of La Rocca on one side and the high town of Castropignano where a wonderful castle stands today on the other, it is perhaps possible to get something of an idea of the kind of war being fought in the last years of the 290s. This terrain is extremely difficult and exemplifies perfectly what a task it would have been for the Romans to reduce all the defended places in a country of countless hills and streams. The armed forces of Rome at this time were not yet those of Alesia and Masada that threw up ramps for fun and had artillery trains of ballistas and onagers. The army of the early third century would not have deployed any more techniques than those of basic mining, the use of battering rams and scaling ladders that would not have had a great impact on the massive cyclopean walls, still impressive today, that defended the refuges of these Samnite holdouts. Torsion artillery, using twisted skeins of hair to provide reserves of tension to propel catapult arms, had only been popularized a generation before in the reign of Philip II of Macedon. If his son Alexander had used them widely, both in his great sieges and sometimes as infantry support in battle, while his successors had then increased their size even further, there is no reason to believe that this kind of artillery expertise would have reached central Italy. Even if the knowledge had permeated those Greek communities that the Italians had encountered, like Tarentum and Neapolis, there had been no generations of engineering tradition to ensure there was an expert corps of soldiers capable of deploying them in the wars we are describing.

So when the remnants of defeated armies and populations of the less well-defended centres decamped to their massively fortified retreats, it is impossible to believe that the Romans would have found it easy to get at them. Starvation would have been the main weapon to guarantee reduction and there would simply not have been time in a campaigning season to capture more than a handful of fortresses. The reality was that after Aquilonia and the demise of the Linen Legion, while the reports may have been about the taking of this community and that, it was really a matter of deep and orchestrated reiving of the countryside the invading soldiers could reach. The Samnites would not be brought to their knees by legionaries, carrying by bloody assault the powerfully-walled forts that peppered their country, but because of a patient policy that saw season after season the presence of an occupying army, meaning that the people could not sow or reap their fields nor drive their flocks and herds between summer and winter pastures that was the transhumance lifestyle of so many of them. The whole country was put under siege, agile light troops dispatched to destroy or harvest anything that might sustain the people, while their heavier armed comrades stood guard to ensure they could not be hindered by anybody desperate and active enough to try to intervene. If in the past the war had hibernated for a season, it no longer did and the certainty was that it would only be a matter of time before the locals and their leaders would be prepared to accept any terms to appease their parlous condition. If the establishment of Venusia made particularly manifest the pressure on the Hirpini, the Romans would have directed equal efforts against not just the Pentri and Caudini, the Caracini would not have escaped attention either. If we hardly get any notice of these folk on the east of the mountains, they suffered too as Roman armies marched down the valley of the Sangro, travelling towards the Adriatic, or trashed their fertile acres before cutting over to attack their more powerful brethren in the Pentri. They all trembled with an awful conviction of their own imminent destruction.

Nor could this suffering people, whose entire homeland was being put to the torch, hope for any outside succour, with the Etruscans and Umbrians since 295 largely a busted flush and the Gauls slunk back home. Years of defeat had been a powerful solvent of alliance and Samnium was left to stew, surely abandoned to its fate. More than this, without these distractions it meant that both consular armies were able to concentrate almost exclusively on the peoples of the highland league. The impact of the wreckage inflicted in this dreadful time would not just have consisted of that handed out by Fabius Gurges in 292, but almost certainly his colleague Brutus Scaeva, after his excursion to Etruria, would have been at the task of professional devastation as well. This capable officer is mentioned in the great fight at Cominium in 293; a success in the field that was a factor, on top of a family that contained a master of horse and consuls in the last forty years, in his rising to the top in the following year. He and his men, grimly determined, would have doubled the total of Samnite pain, just as would Postumius Megellus' colleague, lending a hand in the next campaigning season. The same would have been true of Cornelius Rufinus, an ancestor of Sulla, who as the partner of Curius Dentatus, probably with a two-legion army, would have made all of Samnium quake. They brought the blight of war everywhere, advancing from the Sangro to the Ofanto; a proposition supported by the fact that the booty taken over these years, including captives, was estimated at 3 million pounds of bronze, enough of a windfall for the Republic to begin issuing the 'Aes', its first home-minted coinage. Years of this kind of pressure, when no Samnite lands were exempt from devastation, no community that could not observe plumes of smoke and flame on the horizon, could only be endured for so long, and with no option but to look down from their fortified outposts at enemies wrecking everything they valued and with no organized force to counter it, in the end any spirit of resistance was bound to give. For decades these tenacious mountain men might bend without breaking, but with the iron grip of starvation taking hold, the whole scaffolding of life was crashing down.

For years they stiffened their sinews and puffed out their chests, but once all the people were backed into a corner and feeling the pinch in their bellies and the upper crust feeling the tightening in their wallets, the leadership of the Samnite tribes had to listen to what sounded like a death rattle. Crippled enough to consider that resistance to even the loathed Romans might need to come to an end, envoys were sent to ask the inexorable invaders for terms and rough as they were, they had to be accepted. We do not know if each of the four Samnite peoples came to terms individually as they suffered past a bearable point from the roving Roman armies or if the whole league submitted as a job lot, nor are the terms precisely clear. We know that their league was not dissolved at this time and that this was against the general direction of Roman policy towards defeated enemies; perhaps showing the war had not ended in complete surrender, it was not yet even a peace of absolute conquest. Then, with the wraith of resistance finally entombed, demands were punitive, with territory annexed deep into regions that had been held by the Samnites for more than a couple of centuries. Among the places we know they lost were Cominium, Atina, Aquilonia, Casinum Venafrum, east of modern-day Cassino, and nearby Rufrae, all of which probably lay along or near what had long been the invasion route from Sora into the heart of Pentri country. Large tracts of the Hirpini domain we know were lost too; lands required to support the people moving to provide the population of the new colony at Venusia. On top of this loss of great swathes of property, the defeated people also had to accept that as Rome's allies they would in future be required to provide her with soldiers and follow the Tiber city's dictates in foreign policy, and that not to do so would in future be an act of rebellion.

The upshot was that Roman control was brought deep into the heart of the Pentri as far as Aesernia, more than halfway down the road to Bovianum from Sora, which itself had hardly been secure for Rome when the peace was made after the Second Samnite War. Now all that country and more along the Liris River and that commanded the approaches to the Matese massif would be secure, held by farmer soldiers of Latin or Roman stamp who might be expected to sell their lives dearly for the Republic to combat any threats, whether they be from unhappy locals wanting to reverse the realties imposed in recent years or against the kind of threat from dangerous outsiders that would soon become the pattern of the rest of the century. The road east from Sora to Atina and south down the Liris had seen Roman legions and Samnite bands competing for ascendency on an almost annual basis, while the Matese massif and Bovianum had been the great strongholds, birthplaces of resistance, deep within Samnite territory, but after 290 when trouble came again, Roman power was poised within easy reach. On the lower Volturnus, Cales had kept the lands down to the sea tight for decades, but now much of the middle and upper reaches of the river was absorbed as well, making the Republic much better placed to impact on any who might be inclined to disturb a Roman peace. Indeed, in the troubles to come we hear of little action round this area and most significant of all the peoples of the Pentri did not rise, even with the advent of an all-conquering Hannibal when the most pessimistic Roman-hater might have thought there was a good chance of getting out from under their hard-handed occupation.

In the year of his first consulship Curius Dentatus had heralded his arrival by the most welcome achievement. The imperative was to end things and this implacable man had finally accomplished the termination of the great Samnite wars. Finally and dramatically, the conflict was over, and triumphantly he and his men gathered outside the pomerium of Rome, ploughed in legend by Romulus to delineate the city's boundaries in the field of Mars; land confiscated from the last Roman king after he was expelled and prepared to travel a time-honoured route that changed little over the centuries. They would have passed through the porta triumphalis in the Servian walls, under the shadow of the defensive ramparts, by the meat market, circling the Palatine Hill, down the Via Sacra (Sacred Way) and via the Circus Maximus towards the Capitoline Hill. Following on below the ancient citadel where the crude hut claimed as belonging to Romulus still stood, they came to a halt. The litter remaining in the streets from the party was the detritus of glory as they approached the steps that led up to the already old temple to 'Jupiter the best and greatest', a rectangular edifice built by the Etruscan kings with massive pillars and a huge base in the manner of the great temples found further north in Etruria.

None except those with an axe to grind would have doubted that he merited these accolades, but this was only the beginning for Curius Dentatus. He would now contrive to celebrate two separate triumphs in the same year. After his suppression of the old enemy, he hardly faltered in his step before taking up the cudgel against another people whose recent behaviour had drawn the attention of a neighbour's fearsome military machine down on them. His destination was the country of the Sabines, a people who may have involved themselves in the great alliance that was shattered into shards at Sentinum, or perhaps like others had just allowed their young men to be recruited for the fight. Whichever it was, they were going to suffer for it. Curius Dentatus led an army composed of veterans fresh from the recently-ended conflict, many still with triumphal laurels wreathing their brows, heading towards the great Sabine stronghold of Amiternum, deep in the harsh hills of the central Apennines. They came into the bowl of high country where the town lay, near a valley where now the eagle city of L'Aquila, the capital of the Abruzzo, stands and where the theatre and amphitheatre of the later Roman town are still extant. At the heart of the modern city is the brooding, squat sixteenth-century Spanish fortress standing on its hill, built more to intimidate a troublesome population than defend them from external enemies. It would have been the kind of terrain where this fortification stands that the original Sabine city would have been settled; a good defensive post, very different from the level valley where the community was transplanted in a period of Roman peace.

In 290 the mountains looked down on an invading army arriving intent on finally suppressing the independence of a people the Romans had known almost since their own city was founded. Details of the campaign are absent, but it must have been hard fought, with Curius Dentatus surging forward with his men to slash at the heart of the defenders' position; activity that was just his style and that would have led to plenty of casualties, otherwise it is difficult to believe he would have been awarded another triumph. As it was expected that the soldiers involved in the campaign would confirm their general's achievements, these men surely would not have done so unless he had led them to where booty and decorations were available in abundance. These soldiers of the 290s were independent men, yeomen farmers or even blueblood cavaliers, not the legionaries of 200 years later who, as virtual retainers of their commander, anticipated that he would find them land to settle on after their time under arms was up. Curius Dentatus' activity reaped spectacular rewards for his homeland, even before his worth was registered again back home. His men, relishing each and every success, continued to advance against neighbouring holdouts, extending the territory that Rome directly controlled across to the Adriatic and planting a Latin colony at Hadria, modern-day Atri, to pin down this flank of their new central Italian holdings. The town stands on a ridge, today patterned by distinctive erosion, where the consul and his army had climbed to plant the Republican standard and where visitors can still see the remains of another Roman theatre and the early modern defences that largely follow the lines of the ancient ones, occupying country looking out towards a coast with lovely holiday beaches and where it seems atop each promontory running into the sea, an historic town is perched.

In our time many communities sit on the coast itself, but in most of the region's history, the people settled at least a little inland so as not to be exposed as a tempting prospect for seaborne raiders. Over the centuries this pirate-ridden coast, like so many in the Mediterranean, was inhabited by people unable to defend themselves and ruled by powers also seldom up to the job. In this period, apart from Illyrian corsairs making life hell for the residents, there were Etruscan freebooters too, until the Romans finally made the seas safe in the late Republic. Yet Hadria still required an outlet to the sea from the beginning, and down from the hills, along the coast just north of the beaches of Silvi Marina, the running sea breaks over the few remaining stones that show the ruins of this long derelict harbour. The Romans in the very early third century were not proficient seafarers but this colony of Hadria founded on top of the other infrastructural achievements, colonies and roads pushing south-east and north meant from that time, apart from effectively dominating the middle third of the peninsula, their mariners – commercial and military – could start to bring their influence to bear in the lands around the Adriatic.

If much of this had been down to Curius Dentatus, he wasn't leaving it at that. The fasti may not confirm the achievement of a double triumph, but this is no reason not to believe the rest of the evidence, and also this uncommon man would soon complete an extraordinary threesome as only seven years later he added the eradication of the problem of the Gallic Senones to his other achievements. However, this was not accomplished before the Romans were once again sent rocking back on their heels by military disaster and a threat that looked to many like it might be not much less terrible than in the year of Sentinum. In 284 a Gallic army, many probably Senones looking for revenge from that earlier fight, rode out of their country before debouching from the circle of hills surrounding Arretium and settling down in the valley where the River Arno runs. Once one of the most important cities of Etruria, the locals, whose relations with Rome had been good for at least a generation, had had sufficient warning of this imminent and dangerous development to get word to their friends so legions could be dispatched to their aid.

Yet the relieving force found it had entered a lion's den. Bloody encounters ensued and it was skirmish and counter-skirmish until in full-scale battle the army commander, praetor Lucius Caecilius Metellus Denter, fell under the weapons of enemies eager to reverse the decision of just over a decade earlier. The disaster may have reached such a proportion that seven military tribunes and between 13,000 and 30,000 men were remembered as perishing even many centuries later by the likes of St Augustine and Orosius. The dead man's successor called up in time of peril was Curius Dentatus, either as praetor or consul, and unsurprisingly if the reported losses are anything like correct, he was cautious as he assessed his chances in a new situation. So he endeavoured to open negotiations, trying to start talks with the enemy under the pretext of a prisoner trade. However, the Celts were both buoyant and bitter, so they killed the envoys sent to treat with them, ensuring nothing but a proximate bloodletting would be possible. When matters came to a head with both sides deploying in full strength, Curius Dentatus nerved himself and again showed his worth, leading his men, many of whom it should not be forgotten had just suffered a dreadful reverse, in driving the Gallic invaders from the field of battle.

This change of fortune not only allowed the alarmed people of Arretium to return to normal life, but with so many of the Senones' warriors disposed of the victor determined the enemy's own country would now be vulnerable to an immediate strike. This was typical of the man who only a few years earlier had added so much territory to the Republic's portfolio, cut out of country previously occupied by Samnites, Sabines, Marsi, Paeligni and others. Now he decided he would not just bolster the northern border as he had been tasked, but that there was never going to be a better opportunity to solve the problem of the Senones once and for all; to finally pacify this region where these troublemakers had fully settled well over a century before and from where they had so often left to bring terror and grief to the people of Rome and her allies. Again the details are lost but the bloodletting they had already experienced seems to have taken the fight out of the northerners, whose country of foothill fields and coastal lowlands was overrun and their capital secured. Farmers followed the soldiers and a colony was planted on the Adriatic coast, hard by the Senones' own headquarters and named Sena from the defeated people it was intended to keep permanently under wraps.

This formidable man, who had done so much in the decade and a half since he first emerged on the scene, still had one last great shot in his locker, this time as his middle-aged bones were feeling their years. In a final military confrontation near Hirpini Malaventum, he faced the last man standing of those military masters who had earned their stripes in the cauldron of Alexander the Great's successor wars, leading Roman armies now in an age of elephants, beasts that may forever be associated with Hannibal but were first encountered under Pyrrhus, a man who had a far better record of successful use of the giant animals. This unpredictable genius had come back from fighting the Carthaginians in Sicily to take up the cudgel against the enemy he had defeated twice a few years before at the Battles of Heraclea and Asculum, though successes bought at such a cost that these kinds of victories in the future would bear his name. This time it would be different as the consuls for the year 275 weighed in against the returning foe. Lucius Cornelius Lentulus was paired with Curius Dentatus and as the crucial contact approached, they were not far from each other, the former based in Lucania while the latter was in the heart of Caudine country having another thrash at the same enemy he had so severely damaged fifteen years earlier.

Pyrrhus had landed somewhere on the deep south of the Italian coast, Locris is mentioned and certainly that people are reported killing their Roman garrison to let the returning king back in. An attempt on Rhegium fell foul of the Carthaginians, who had far from forgiven him for his troublemaking in Sicily, while he also had problems with some Mamertines from Messana before he could reach the home of his old employers the Tarentines. The garrison he had left there was still in sufficient control to allow him to recoup his strength, though his men's looting of the temple of Persephone near Croton ended up causing more trouble than it was worth, with a shipwreck born of sacrilege soon persuading the king to return what was left of his ill-gotten gains to the goddess. Yet nothing halted the Epirote monarch, who garnered the funds to equip a very considerable army; a return in arms that must have sent a shiver through hearts at Rome, where plague had again been eating at the citizen roll for much of the 270s. Some 16,000 deaths had not only contracted the pool of military men but made many survivors reluctant to risk the precious lives that had been spared to them. So the consuls raising the levy of 275 had to contend with draft-dodging on a grand scale and threats to enslave the offenders were required to even partially fill the ranks.

Pyrrhus moved quickly to take the fight to his enemy and, finding them divided, he first dispatched units to Lucania to bolster local activity that might ensure one consul was fully occupied, while hoping that any weakness caused by this detachment would be more than compensated for by the adherence of Samnites, eager for another chance to drag down the old foe. Unfortunately for his plans, this people had learned to distrust him after he left them in the lurch by decamping to Sicily in 278 and his three years away had not registered a great change in their attitude. They had suffered at the hands of Rome during this time, so when the call came to rejoin the struggle, any response was lukewarm. This attitude did not change significantly, even when he marched in their direction preparing to fight next on Samnite soil, though some more adventurous types must have joined up from the ranks of the Hirpini, who were already suffering at the hands of a Roman army threatening their capital.

Yet even the failure of the Samnites to rush to arms could not suppress a belief that there existed a real opportunity to settle this war. The king's commitment to the offensive remained unshakeable and he was not in a waiting mood. Money was running short and remembering how close he had come to destroying Roman armies in the past, the temptation to try again was just too great. So Curius Dentatus found himself head-to-head with the monarch of Epirus, another man defined by his dentistry,[9] having established himself in a strong hilltop location with an army of something less than 30,000 men. To get at him Pyrrhus split his forces, leading his most dependable elephants and an elite strike force under cover of darkness, intending a surprise attack on the Roman encampment that would drain away the defenders from the ramparts facing his main army, who were then expected to crash through on their front. The inevitable happened; a straightforward turning movement degenerated as lumbering beasts and unguided, heavy-armed soldiers stumbled through thickly-wooded undulating byways and goat tracks. Getting lost in the thickets, they were tired and thirsty when they were noticed by Roman sentries as dawn broke and any element of surprise completely forfeit.

The consul showed that he was up to the challenge of facing this man Hannibal considered to be the greatest general after Alexander the Great and, exhibiting his usual sure touch, rushed to the attack, catching the enemy still strung out on line of march and disorganized, ensuring even the gallant Pyrrhus could hardly stop his men running, exhausted and disorientated by their alarming trek, looking to reach the remainder of their army that was then approaching the Roman position. These men, expecting to find the enemy distracted by the night attack, were disturbed to find the whole defending force emerging from its camp and descending the hill towards them in good order. Now it was a conventional encounter, but with the Epirote army reduced and dispirited by the numbers lost during the night-time raid. Sharp fighting saw Roman success, despite Pyrrhus reinforcing his buckling line with elephants held in reserve. Crushing feet and flailing trunks bolstered the defence until heavy iron-headed missiles punctured even their tough hides and a young wounded animal careened about the field crying out in pain, desperate for its mother. This so disturbed the rest of the beasts that they turned to escape, routing back through their own ranks. It was the tipping-point and, seeing his chance, Curius Dentatus directed an all-out assault, capturing eight elephants and entering the enemy works. So with his colleague, who had also fought the armies in Lucania to a standstill, he was lauded in triumph for their achievements; accolades that would have looked very well-deserved when, as the year ended, word arrived that the Epirote king had decided to depart the peninsula for good.

So in what was surely the apogee of a great career, Curius Dentatus overcame in battle one of the Hellenistic age's greatest generals, though there is a caveat that Polybius and Justin both contend that Pyrrhus was never defeated in decisive battle by the Romans. However, this glowing year of triumph was not quite the end for a man whose commitment to public service remained unshakeable and as censor in 272 he was associated with the construction of Rome's second aqueduct, showing a penchant for public works projects he had previously exhibited back in the 280s when he had begun the draining of Lake Velinus to prevent the flooding of the Sabine town Reate that has left us to this day the extraordinary waterfall of Marmore. If his po-faced compatriots preferred to remember him as a paragon of virtue, eating turnips as he refused corrupting gold from Samnite envoys,[10] what cannot be gainsaid is that his military genius had contributed substantially to the massively increased amount of territory occupied by Rome's growing population since he emerged first as a tribune of the plebs around the turn of the fourth century, and must win for him a place among the Republic's greatest early imperialists.

Epilogue

'No friend ever served me, and no enemy ever wronged me, whom I have not repaid in full.'

Sulla, Epitaph

Crowds were massing on the walls and Roman householders rushing to and fro in the streets near the Colline Gate on the afternoon of 1 November 82, some intent on finding safety, while others more adventurous, perhaps appreciating the fateful moment, were bent on finding a place to witness the extraordinary events unfolding just outside the walls of the capital of the world. There were fine temples nearby, shading suburban plots that were about to become a decisive field of battle, and drawn up in stern resolve were fighting men of a people whose presence sent a tremor down many a Roman spine. Samnites had stood outside the walls of Rome in anger on several occasions since the demise of the Linen Legion; hard men with poisonous intentions from the hills in their bronze war belts had been there when Pyrrhus had approached the city in 280, while even more were present when Hannibal stood in battle array under the walls in a drenching hailstorm in 211 at the height of the Second Punic War. Now these old enemies were back preparing for the bloody climax; a final act in a conflict with extremely complicated antecedents. Chaotic events had brought them there. Civil war had come again to Roman Italy the year before and though strategies were in tatters, great armies had been destroyed or dispersed in Etruria and Cisalpine Gaul and one faction leader had fled to Africa, still the remnants remained. These had not given up hope just yet; instead marching to join up with a people who seemed their last great hope to together go to the rescue of their talismanic principle young Marius, who with his army was holed up, beleaguered in the town of Praeneste, only 22 miles to the east of Rome itself. The troops of Sulla were there in force, dug in behind vast siege lines that the defenders had already tested by sallying out but with no great success and were probably unlikely to be susceptible to similar treatment by any forces marching to relieve the place. So faith was placed in a large force of Sabellian warriors, some Lucanians and Bruttians but mainly Samnites, all under a Samnite general called Telesinus. Once combined, they had tried to relieve the town but the attempt to break through was frustrated when Sulla and his lieutenant Crassus concentrated the armies they had brought from Etruria to join the siege.

If Praeneste was a hard target, finding themselves near Mount Alban, Sulla's enemies realized there was another softer one nearby. Rome, only 12 miles distant, was now under enemy control. Sulla had passed through just a few months before to reach the northern war and put placemen in control, after reassuring the locals what a just and reasonable ruler he would be once the war was won. So the Italian soldiers directed their feet in that direction, trusting to luck that their enemy would have to withdraw most of their strength from the Praeneste entrenchments to come and protect what was still, after all, the place about which the war was being fought. Now it was a culmination; with decks cleared the Samnites were there, part of an army of 70,000 men standing with comrades from all the other peoples of southern Italy and the remnants of the recently-trounced Marians, who had joined them in what was the last gasp of a conflict that itself was the fusion of several different struggles.

The new arrivals must have thought they had won the race for the plum prize and their enemies were thrown into panic when resistance was experienced from an unexpected quarter. Another Appius Claudius, 'a man of high birth and character', descendant of the long-dead Caecus, rode out of the city with other equestrians inclined to the party of Sulla. So with supporters on the walls shouting encouragement, to the music of thundering hooves there was a cavalry encounter before the main armies clashed. Charging at the head of 'the noblest youth of the city', Appius hoped to hold up the tidal wave of invaders descending on the ill-prepared city, but they were ridden over, killed or dispersed by forces that far outnumbered them, though this act of self-sacrifice did at least slow down the advance of the attacking army. They turned out to be not the only hindrance. Sulla had marched with almost all his troops when he received news of the direction his enemies were taking, only leaving Quintus Lucretius Ofella, a character who had been tight with the Marians before jumping ship and joining what appeared to be the winning side, to hold the siege lines. While ahead he had dispatched an advance guard of horsemen. So the invaders' first success could not be exploited, as just as the morning waned: 'Balbus, sent forward by Sulla, was first seen riding up at full speed with seven hundred horsemen. He paused just long enough to let the sweat of the horses dry off, and then quickly bridled them again and attacked the enemy',[1] ensuring that the army arriving with Telesinus could not enter Rome before his opponent had the opportunity to rush forward his main army. The intercession of these cavaliers occupied the confederate army for much of the afternoon, allowing time for Sulla to arrive at the head of the rest of his men.

The memory of past conflicts snapped in the air between the two opposing chiefs. Sulla came from a family of Samnite-haters and he kept up the tradition. His last significant ancestor was Cornelius Rufinus who had been the consul with Curius Dentatus when they brought the Third Samnite War to a victorious end. Also in 277 BC this doughty fighter, whose reputation would be ruined a couple of years after his last consulship when he was caught red-handed with a hoard of illegitimate silver, fought the same foe after they had been deserted by Pyrrhus for the first time. On the other side Telesinus claimed descent from the same family that boasted the victor of the Caudine forks: 'Pontius Telesinus, a Samnite chief, brave in spirit and in action and hating to the core the very name of Rome', a last hero expressing the venom of a people who had suffered so much over almost a quarter of a millennium. He declaimed: 'The last day is at hand for the Romans' and in a loud voice exhorted his men to overthrow and destroy their city, adding: 'These wolves that made such ravages upon Italian liberty will never vanish until we have cut down the forest that harbours them.'[2] All the sources evidence huge antipathy felt by the Samnites against Rome; for Telesinus and his people they were assaulting an enemy town even after 200 years of Roman rule. It was mainly history but geography as well; these Samnites had never been a big city people and always remained wary and resentful of their metropolitan rulers.

The Colline Gate where the battle was fought might have been originally constructed back in the legendary past of King Servius Tullius, but the place had already been huge in the city's story. Brennus had entered there after the Battle of the Allia and in this northern stretch of the Servian walls the Via Salaria and Nomentana left the city and temples to Venus Erycina and Fortuna were well-known landmarks for locals who gave a little shudder when they passed by the site where Vestal Virgins who contravened their oath of chastity were buried alive. In the shadow of these historic monuments Telesinus' thoughts were far from the practices and traditions of his people's blood-deep enemies as he progressed along the ranks of his soldiers, encouraging men who, if not lacking in courage, had been marching for hours to get to Rome and would be going into battle tired, hardly having had time to rest or even grab a few mouthfuls of food and drink.

Yet the same was true of the men in the opposing ranks. Sulla might have breathed a huge sigh of relief that he had arrived in time to defend his capital, but his men were coming up from Praeneste in detachments and he knew it might be late in an autumn afternoon before his veterans were in sufficient strength to hope to take on, with any chance of success, the great lines of confederate troops deployed in the shadow of Rome's Servian Walls. The man who had so recently come from defeating Mithridates himself arrived at noon and had his men put up the most cursory of camps near the Temple of Venus before pushing them into a battle that was well under way. With the walls of the city looming off to his left, Sulla led his legions into the fight just as they arrived, conspicuous on his fine white horse directing the left wing, while Crassus, one of the richest men in Rome and fated in thirty years' time to lose an army in Syria under a hail of Parthian arrows, had command on the right side.

Not all had approved this show of aggression; many of the generals accompanying Sulla, Dolabella and Torquatus that are mentioned did not want to fight that day at all. Pressing round their leader, they stressed there was not enough time to fight a decisive battle and that after a night's march the soldiers would be just too tired; that men with shaky legs, who had trudged night-time miles to get to the encounter, were not fit to face enemies such as the Samnites, Lucanians and their Gallic auxiliaries who, unlike the soldiers they had just been fighting under Carbo and the other Marian leaders, would fight with the desperation of those with their backs to the wall. Yet still the orders to advance were given: 'But he put them by, and commanded the trumpets to sound the charge, though it was now getting on towards four o'clock in the afternoon.'[3] With this musical accompaniment, the lines of men who had chased Mithridates' army out of Greece and Western Asia went forward.

There can be little dispute over the organization and equipment of the soldiers in this epic struggle. The heavy infantry that fought it out that day would have looked almost exactly alike; after all, the allies for well over a century and a half had been almost a mirror of the Roman comrades they fought alongside. Generations would have ironed out any differences in equipment and style of fighting. These two armies, about to clash, were different from the kind that had contended more than two centuries earlier. Both sides were made up of the re-formed legions that the older Marius is given credit for creating a couple of decades before. They were now organized into larger tactical units called cohorts comprising more than 400 men as opposed to the earlier maniple of 140, and Marius' mules all wore mail armour, carried the deadly Spanish sword, body shield, entrenching tools and cooking pots. On Telesinus' side, if they looked the same, the hearts that beat under layers of leather and metal and the brains that nestled beneath a pot helmet pumped and hummed to a very different tune. They hoped to get out from under the sway of the town on the Tiber, unlike the foes they were facing, who had followed their general across half the world and whose vision of the future was a purely Roman one, where the priorities of those in charge would be paying them their due and demobbing them with sufficient land to retire on in comfort.

So when these heavy-handed, iron-bound men with hate in their hearts came together it was appalling. Showers of pila advertised the advance that soon turned into a grinding process of mutual butchery. Many shields were made unwieldy by bent javelins sticking through the wooden planking, opening their owners to the razor stabbing of their opponents' short swords. There could be little subterfuge between men who knew exactly the pattern of each other's fighting, but for the men on the left, even under their general's own eye it turned out too much. They were hungry and tired, all in from the march, and if they bore the brunt for a time, before too long, beside the Colline Gate, Sulla's veterans could be seen cowering dispirited under the lee of the city walls, pushed back by Sabellian warriors with blood in their eyes and generations of bitter resentment to scour. Where they could the men bolted, looking to get back to the gate and behind the walls, until the old men of the gate guard dropped the portcullis, killing not only fleeing soldiers but some senators as well, gone too close to the action in their eagerness to see the outcome.

Sulla himself, on his famous white mount, tried to rally his soldiers, only to find himself attacked with javelins by every enemy in range and only saved by a groom who hustled him out of the way; a brush with death that was famous enough to be recalled by a king of France in a Dumas novel.[4] After this he kept on the move, surrounded by officers and friends who themselves endured considerable casualties for closely following their leader. Kissing a good luck token in the form of a golden Apollo he always carried with him, Sulla alternately entreated and berated his men to rally, but the left wing would not hold, 'at last his left wing was completely shattered' and everyone from commander-in-chief down fell back to try to find asylum in their camp or some fleeing as far as Praeneste, where the man left in charge almost raised the siege on hearing the soldiers' reports. All the while on the other wing, the fight continued.

Sulla, though in despair at the sight of his bolting men, found his fabled luck had not deserted him. The enemy who had battered his followers were worn out too, and failed to press home against the chaos of broken cohorts running away from them. More than this, on the right side of the battle events had fallen out very differently. There Crassus held firm, his finest hour, and his dispirited opposition backed off before lurching in rout from their ranks. Those that were not caught by the pursuing men retreated as far as Antemnae, a town on a hill hardly 2 miles from the city at the confluence of the Tiber and Anio, and there Crassus' troops prepared to besiege them. Soon after the victors on the right brought across reinforcements and supplies to succour their comrades on the other side of the battlefield who had, out of necessity and desperate with fear, fought on under the walls. There the good news and victuals resuscitated beaten men and, together with newly-arrived comrades who had already tasted triumph, there was once more the sound of charging men unsheathing their weapons and cavalry horses champing at the bit as they reopened the combat with opponents who had just bested them.

The ferocity of the encounter is underscored by the fact that even the early onset of darkness did not dampen down the fires. Fighting lasted deep into the evening under a fish-coloured moon, despite the participants hardly being able to see each other. Friend must have cut down friend on many occasions in a scrimmage where even in daylight the warriors on both sides looked so alike. After balancing on a knife edge, the denouement finally came sometime after the first hour of night, as Sulla's men, the breath driven from them and exhausted, were at last able to pause as through the dark they saw the enemy pulling back and moving away, finally accepting defeat and retiring from the field. Whether it was when the news got around that their leader Telesinus had been wounded that broke their will is not known, but that man was discovered the next day, expiring and beaten but not cowed 'with the expression of a conqueror upon his face rather than that of a dying man'. As the battle continued through the night, other senior commanders like Albinus were slain and at the close Lamponius the Lucanian, Marcius, Carinas and the other generals of the confederate faction fled.

There are no details of the pursuit except that Antemnae was certainly taken in a bloodbath and those who got there were not going to have chance to fight again. It was estimated that 50,000 men on both sides lost their lives in this engagement and this was far from the end. The next day Marcius and Carinas were captured and brought in and Sulla did not spare them, despite them both being Roman citizens, but killed both and dispatched their heads to Praeneste to be displayed round the walls. After the Colline bloodletting Sulla's enemies fell apart. Praeneste was not long in surrendering and young Marius committed suicide when he realized he could not escape through the tunnel down which he was hoping to find his freedom, possibly in a pact with Telesinus' younger brother, stabbing each other to avoid the inevitably humiliating end that would follow capture. It was not long before Sulla made evident even further what kind of victor he intended to be. While the conqueror addressed a trembling Senate at the Temple of Bellona, within hearing, 6,000 captives, many Samnites taken at Antemnae, were dragged into the Circus Flaminius and 'cut to pieces' to a man.

* * *

Now the Samnites would really pay the price as their nemesis took total control. When Praeneste fell Sulla could not have made his intentions clearer; all the Samnite men were killed, while the Romans were freed along with the women and children. It had been the 200 years as a defeated people coerced into dependent alliance with her ancient enemy that had brought the Samnites to this pass; a context in which these people under arms remained a massive factor long after the demolition of the Linen Legion, something that perhaps should not have been so much of a surprise considering their history. Defeat at Aquilonia had been a dreadful blow to the fortunes of the mountain folk, yet even for that war it was not the last hurrah, and the few sources we have leave no indication that Rome's enemy was content with their lot after 290. It might be a pared-down Samnite League with colonies established on their frontiers and forced into alliance with Rome and from then on, but they had far from given up the ghost. There had been no real acceptance of defeat among communities of the Pentri, the Caudine, Hirpini or even the Caraceni and certainly no happiness in the face of demands made by a new master that they provide soldiers to fight in her wars. That Roman and Latin settlers tilled their soil around fortress colonies under the very eyes of Samnite neighbours only made things worse, so it is perhaps not very astonishing that the novel relationship did not progress smoothly. Within a very few years the spark of revolt flared and these outbreaks began even before aspirations for independence were animated by the intervention by two of the great adventurers of ancient times.

The Roman thirst for gold, land and glory had been whet by success and the draw to fill the whole south of the Italian peninsula became irresistible to a ruling elite who had so much to live up to. In 286 Thurii applied for an alliance with Rome and inevitably when this was accepted it piled up southern enemies against the Republic, just as had been the case when she had agreed to Capua's request for protection more than fifty years earlier. Their intrusion offended Lucanian and Bruttian sensibilities, not to mention Tarentum, the one Greek city left with ambitions for local pre-eminence and soon the Samnites' old antagonist was at odds with so many of the nations of Italy that the possibilities of taking revenge for Sentinum and the massacre of the Linen Legion became almost irresistible. Expansion south might fill the pockets and burnish the prestige of the Roman nobles involved in far-flung campaigns, but they also involved the Republic in real overstretch. Roman armies were not only still often involved fighting against Etruscans and Gauls in the north, but plenty of Sabellians and Greeks in the south and, after all, the place was still only a city state, able to mobilize just a handful of legions even in the direst of circumstances. Larger territories meant longer frontiers to protect and they certainly did not have the numbers, or even the organization, to patrol the valleys and byways of Samnium, or leave garrisons in the towns. So there was little to stop the active men of the region from looking again at the swords, spears and armour hanging on the walls of their houses. Rome would hardly even hear, never mind hinder, when groups gathered from different cantons, communities and tribes to plot against a master whose hegemony was more oppressive than effective, particularly as resentment was fuelled by their young men being conscripted to fight beside the old enemy, often against people who had been their firm friends just a few years before.

So, barely seven years after they had put their signatures to a treaty, the Samnites refused to keep their heads down, despite what was now perennial weakness, and broke out into revolt; a contest that would rumble on for years before being absorbed in a greater struggle. For much of this time the sources are almost non-existent and only the glamour of a new man arriving on the scene meant that the struggle was tangentially lit by the picaresque career of Pyrrhus, the audacious eagle, King of Epirus. Still, it would have been partly the knowledge that she could hope for active allies like the Samnites that made the Tarentines finally call in the Epirote king to move against a Roman enemy they had long feared and resented. The triumphal fasti suggest fighting against the Samnites had begun by 282, but it was when the Romans, who instead of nipping these rebels' efforts in the bud, decided to press south to face a Tarentine threat exacerbated by the arrival of Pyrrhus' captains Milo and Cineas that we get some flesh on the bones.

Spring of 280 saw the king himself disembark at Tarentum before pushing out to try to eject the Romans from Magna Graecia. If this was of no immediate help to Samnites struggling against intruders in their homeland, it must have given heart to men beginning to wonder if a positive outcome was going to be possible in the war upon which they had embarked. Soon enough real consolations showed; that apart from Roman resources being tied down fighting those inveterate troublemakers the Volsinii and Vulci in Etruria, the other consul Publius Valerius Laevinus was drawn away from Samnite territory, deep down south, to face the invading king. Yet bright hope at what might be the appearance of a potential saviour did not lead the Samnites to send their warriors to join the king straight away. This was not just natural caution; the presence of the proconsul Lucius Aemilius Barbula with forces at Venusia would have made this difficult anyway.

However, with their enemies' discomfiture at the Battle of Heraclea the strategic picture changed and Samnite morale soared as word arrived of the legions falling back in disarray to Apulia. For a time it could have been anticipated that the tower of Roman cards was about to fall; that it might even be possible to rock and remove a detested hegemon. Croton and Locri expelled their garrisons as Lucanians, Bruttium and other Italiot Greeks joined the coalition, headed by the Epirote king. Certainly by this time Samnite emissaries could also have been discovered at the monarch's camp on the instep of Italy's boot. Following them, there arrived bands of warriors from the Pentri, Caudini, Hernici and even the Caracini who had already been in arms at home or had now decided to join what looked like a winning side, mustering with the other southern Italians as military auxiliaries, just as the Greeks offered the services of their navies and the bounty of their treasuries. Yet strengthened though Pyrrhus was, he found after crossing Lucania that the gates were closed against him at Capua and Neapoli and if his Samnite friends had the satisfaction of attacking Fregellae along the Latin Way, the nearest they had got to Rome for a very long time, his main army failed to significantly threaten the city itself. Any hope of joining with the Etruscans was dashed as they heard that Tiberius Coruncanius had suppressed the opposition on that front and was himself marching south. So with these legions pouring down from the north and the remnants of the forces defeated at Heraclea having reached north Campania, Pyrrhus, fearful of being trapped between two fires, aborted the advance and receded towards his south coast base.

That Pyrrhus demanded the Romans give up conquered Samnite lands as part of any peace may have given some comfort, though how much this might count on the ground was bound to be in question with his army now so far away and no agreement sealed. The next year saw the king bouncing back, invading Apulia with many towns joining his cause before another battle was brought on at Asculum. Here both the consuls risked battle and in this two-day affair what transpired was the wounding of Pyrrhus, while his phalanx and elephants won the day. Samnite soldiers certainly battled blow for blow in this hard-fought encounter, though there is disagreement about the position they held; one source has it that they mustered on the right in combination with the Epirote phalanx, while others claim they held firm on the left with not just foot soldiers but a strong contingent of horse as well.[5]

The pleasure of seeing the backs of old enemies flying the flat fields of Apulia did not last long for the Samnites who soon found the attention of their putative saviour straying. Battles against Romans had turned out bloody and strategically indecisive, so the king and his councillors decided a softer target could be found in Carthaginian Sicily, where the African power's Greek rivals were eager to employ a condottiere with both reputation and an army to spearhead their projects. Yet if the rulers of Syracuse saw the up side of this deal, the Italians in general and the Samnites in particular were much less amused. They were deeply angered at what they saw as rank desertion, emotions not at all mollified when the share of campaign booty that was their due was not handed over before the Epirote fleet left to make the short crossing to the island.

As Pyrrhus departed with no agreement with Rome, the Samnites found themselves left in the lurch with a bloodied, embittered and determined antagonist on their doorstep. When their main enemy sailed in 278, the Romans were not only relieved of this pre-eminent menace but discovered an opportunity to punish her most proximate foes. One-eyed Gaius Fabricius Luscinus Monocularis was the man on the spot and was not slow to profit from the new circumstance. This exemplar, whose propriety won him a place in *The Divine Comedy*,[6] took a scattergun approach, flaying Lucanians, Bruttians, Samnites and Tarentines to such effect that the triumph he won name-checks them all. The following year Zonaras records that both consuls concentrated on the Samnite problem, with two armies sweeping through the enemy heartland with little expectation of opposition, but these two were not the first to underestimate an enemy still formidable on home ground. Lack of reconnaissance in perfect ambush country in the Cranite Mountains ended in the Romans suffering a real sucker punch. We don't know where all this took place; that it was rocky and overgrown helps little as so much of Samnium is just such country. What is certain is that the invaders lost a great many dead and prisoners, with the two consuls left blaming each other. Yet now the difference in relative military might was such that even this bloodletting could hardly influence the trajectory of events.

Despite this setback, the Romans still fielded sufficient men that they were able to divide and criss-cross the country, leaving a trail of pillage, destruction and rapine. Indeed, one force even had the resources to push further south, bringing fire and sword down among the Lucanians and Bruttians prior to an attempt on Croton which had recently thrown out their overlords. After that it was just painful repetition, with the peoples of Samnium and further south feeling the pressure of weary years of despoliation and the spreading presence of Roman settlers and soldiery in colonies and garrisons around their mountain heartlands. However, 276 saw Pyrrhus back in Italy again, with the Greeks of Sicily tiring of him and the Italian war looking more of a prospect after he heard of significant Roman losses in Samnium and learned the consuls were squabbling among themselves. As we have already seen, fine weather in 275 saw the Epirote king once more preparing to face an enemy he had fought in two great battles before, this time in the lands of the Hirpini near that people's capital at Malaventum, but few Samnites had been prepared to join him, angry as they were for being deserted in 278. So Curius Dentatus faced limited numbers of these old enemies in the ranks of the army he roughed up sufficiently to persuade the changeable man from Epirus to leave the peninsula and instead challenge for the throne of Macedon. Yet showing no great inclination to chase down the man who had raised what had been such a dangerous coalition against the Romans, he instead stayed put, determined to grind the Samnites into the dust. Curius Dentatus remained to devastate the Hirpini lands after the Battle of Beneventum, while Cornelius Lentulus directed such malevolent attention to the Caudine country that he gained the nickname of Caudinus.

It looked very like hard times for these inveterate rebels, as the Republic looked in 272 to Papirius Cursor and Spurius Carvilius, the same pairing from 293 who now took up the cudgel to finish the job, sharing triumphs over Samnites, Lucani, Bruttii and Tarentines. Eventually it was a wasted people, tired of clutching at broken straws, who bent down under a yoke that was surely not going to be easy to bear. An outcome reported two generations later when they

> sent envoys simultaneously to Hannibal, who addressed him thus: 'We have been the enemies of Rome, Hannibal, from very early times. At first we fought her in our own might as long as our arms, our strength, sufficed to protect us. When we could trust them no more we took our place by the side of King Pyrrhus; when we were abandoned by him we were compelled to accept terms of peace.[7]

The detailed disposal of repeatedly beaten peoples included the Caudini being broken up into fragments. So after this time we hear only of the likes of Telesia, Caiatia, Cubulteria and Trebula Balliensis as communities unrelated to each other, each with independent and submissive arrangements with Rome. The Pentri lost land to the west, with Allifae becoming a colony in 270, Venafrum and Aquilonia were probably annexed and Aesernia remade as a Latin outpost. The Hirpini even had the indignity of their capital Maleventum being colonized in 268 and renamed Beneventum with their tribal headquarters removed to Compsa. Included in this despoliation was the loss of a strip of land from Campania to Apulia that ensured a physical separation from their cousins in the Pentri. Nor was it just dismemberment; on top of this the Republic showed an inclination to an Assyrian disposal when a bunch of Picentes rebels were established on their western border near Alfaterni, a region soon designated Ager Picentius.

Not that it was an easy job to keep these irrepressible enemies quiet; in 270 or 269 a Samnite called Lollius escaped from jail and raised the Caraceni, requiring both consuls to crush a guerrilla uprising based around a camp at Castel di Sangro. Their leaders were killed, the rest enslaved and Caraceni itself reduced to a remnant as most of its lands were annexed with Aufidena never mentioned again. The Lucanians suffered too, with Paestum established as a colony in 264, though unlike the Samnites, at least these people like the Bruttians were allowed to retain a league structure. Since the beginning of the wars, the Samnites had lost half their territory, strategically crucial swathes, much of it the best agricultural land and the key communication nodes of Beneventum and Aesernia were now firmly in the hands of Roman colonists. The Samnite League was finally dismantled, any intra-tribal organization suspended, vital fortifications slighted and a people, long used to agency in the Italian political world, were no longer able to wield anything but local clout. They might have the strength to try to bar the way to enemies breaching their borders or act as auxiliaries to great warlords, but independent action to dominate beyond their own territory was no longer viable for a crippled polity. After Tarentum was forced to terms, Roman authority was virtually uncontested in almost all the peninsula.

Beaten down for two generations, children became men, fathers and even grandfathers before the flame of independence flickered again in the verdant hills of Samnium. The warriors who reached their prime in these years fought, if at all, beside Roman comrades as was expected of all her allies. Though it was far from always an easy relationship, claims are made that in 265 there was some Samnite support for the Volsinii when they again rose against Rome and then in 259 there was almost a mutiny in the fleet at war with Carthage. Many of these 4,000 insubordinate[8] matelots were Samnites, though so was the man Herius Potilius who sold them out by informing the Senate, who had those involved arrested in the dead of night, showing that some at least of that people's leaders had made a commitment to the dominant power. An amount of collaboration was bound to have taken place; certainly members of the wealthy elite would have become real Romaphiles. At Compsa, for instance, the most important town in Hirpini country, the Mopsii[9] had made themselves the leading family with Roman support by the time Hannibal arrived. The young men had fought together and the rich had prospered together with their Roman peers, and the next great crisis would show much that transpired had a class dimension. Over and over again many of the local gentry, who could have jumped in the days of Hannibal's success, stayed loyal to Rome while the common people were often much more intent on a change of rule.

Yet even if some of the elite were inclined to collaboration, there was no great melding of peoples. This was far from a situation where all differences were shrunk, cultural assimilation was always going to be difficult to realize between the hill folk of Samnium and Roman and Latin lowlanders. There were few places they might interact; the great of Rome were generally in a different income bracket to their Samnite equivalents and there are few signs of intermarriage or business partnership in the decades after peace finally settled on lands that had suffered so much from passing Roman armies. Unlike their Campanian counterparts, there was little in the way of joint exploitation of the vast increase in land controlled or the expansion of trade that occurred when successful wars were concluded, first against Tarentum, then Carthage in Sicily.

When that latter city provided the Republic with her greatest test, menaced by the most dangerous man the Romans would ever encounter in their extraordinary protracted history, many subject allies were put in a quandary. Getting behind Hannibal on his appearance in Italy in 218 was far from an automatic reaction, as is made clear by the timing. On an earlier occasion when the Gauls gave Rome a considerable scare in the 220s, there is no hint that any among the Sabellian peoples might come to their aid. If this may be partly explained because all the fighting took place north of their homelands, even when Hannibal arrived in central Italy these people did not straight away rush to side with him in the way so many had when Pyrrhus had appeared. It was indeed partly the memory of that last great captain leaving them in the lurch that meant they had learned caution. The Carthaginians had hoped the Oscan-speaking peoples might rise and join them as they manoeuvred around Campania in 217, but as word of their great victories at Trebbia and Lake Trasimene permeated the mountain cantons, such was the frustration at the lack of response that the Carthaginians even ravaged the Pentri country when their army of invasion marched from Campania to Apulia. It would require even more dramatic events to light a spark eighty years after Aquilonia. So these people did not rush to join Hannibal, even when he demonstrated how defenceless the lands of Beneventum and other Latin colonies were. It was the incredible disaster at Cannae that made the difference, and after that the lead taken by the great city of Capua. When such a major place that had stood so close to Rome went over to the invaders' side, it was bound to influence the long heads in Samnite councils. If the Epirote king had offered hope for just a few seasons, sixty years later events allowed the Caudine and Hernici peoples to really believe it might be possible to squeeze out from under the imposition of a hard-handed rule long imposed by the Republic.

Subservient interdependence battened on by colonies built at Beneventum and Venusia and the Appian Way extending south may have ensured some skin-deep Latinization, but was not enough to keep many of the southern peoples loyal to Rome. When Hannibal exploded into peninsular Italy in 218 and flayed the Romans in three great battles, Samnites across the classes could not help but be deeply affected. Their well-born cavaliers would have faced the ferocious Numidians in some of these encounters, while the yeomen fighters of the allied wings bled with the same ease as their Roman legionary comrades under Carthaginian blows. However, news soon arrived that while Hannibal kept any Roman captives in stern captivity waiting for death or to be sold into servitude, the allied prisoners, high or low, were released without ransom and sent home to their parents, wives and children with no ill treatment to complain of. The invader showed himself very specific in his vitriol. Only Romans needed to fear his bile; every other community in peninsular Italy he only wanted to befriend.

Nor was it just an initial reluctance to jump; one key component never did so at all. The people of the Pentri refused to desert their Roman hegemon and continuing to provide soldiers to fight in the Republic's battles. These loyal Samnites are even reported achieving crucial interventions: 8,000 of their troops under Numerius Decimius of Bovianum saved the Roman master of horse Minucius when he got in trouble at Gerunium by disregarding the dictator Fabius Maximus 'the delayer's' instructions. Also the Samnite cavalry mentioned on escort duty for the consul Nero in 207 were probably bluebloods from this region. It was the people of Caudium and the Hirpini who acted and some of them even showed reluctance; Caiatia for one stayed loyal to Rome. The details of Samnite involvement in the Second Punic War are few and far between, but what was certainly true was that the capacity to provide a large reservoir of military manpower for the great Carthaginian was limited by a determination to keep sufficient men on guard at home to defend against an enemy whose aggression was very soon reignited, despite repeated bloody disasters handed out by the Carthaginian army of invasion. Attention usually concentrates on the contest with Hannibal or the epic, years-long sieges of Syracuse and Capua, though a general picture does emerge. The Romans' response to their allies' insurrection was hard and swift, with early on some forts in the Caudine region falling to the likes of Valerius Laevinus and Fabius Maximus in 215. Marcellus was not merciful either when a year later he recovered Telesia, Cubulteria and Compsa and in 213 the rebels would have suffered more when, with Pentrine Bovianum as a base, the Romans pushed through Samnite lands as they closed in on Capua. As the two-year siege ground to an inescapable conclusion, the Caudine communities in particular would have shivered in dread of Roman retaliation, while after the great city fell, hopes of independence held by any in the Samnite lands must have begun to seem paper thin, even to those still prepared to fight to the bitter end.

It was only a matter of time before the Hirpini suffered as well, first with a couple of important hill forts used by Hannibal as supply dumps taken and razed in 310, before Fulvius Flaccus, the conqueror of Capua, finally ended serious resistance in almost the whole region. The years that followed saw the Carthaginians fading further back down the peninsula at a time they just did not have the resources to help defend their friends so close to the war's front line. Indeed, in some places in nearby Apulia, Hannibal actually destroyed some towns and took the people away to where he could defend them, leaving nothing behind that would sustain the Roman enemy in arms. The great Carthaginian was eventually driven even further back into his last stronghold along the south coast, around the Greek colony of Crotone and the Samnites found just as they had been let down by Pyrrhus, so now this latest great hope had turned out a broken reed. In the last few years of the Hannibalic War, Samnite involvement was confined just to those men who had enlisted in the Carthaginian army and who could expect nothing but death if they tried to return to home towns that had been forced to come to terms with Rome on conditions that had offered even non-combatants hardly anything more than survival, never mind any amnesty for those who had actually spilt Roman blood in the Carthaginian cause.

Three great defeats in succession were suffered by the Romans but the Republic did not fall. It was Capua, Syracuse, Tarentum and finally Carthage whose people the Samnites had fought alongside that were eventually devastated so their troublesome auxiliaries could hardly hope for any better treatment from a master they had troubled for almost a century and a half. As in the wars that ended in the 270s, we do not have much in the way of details on the disposal of land and peoples after the final fires of resistance petered out. Without doubt it would have been brutal; those the Romans were able to find who fought for Hannibal probably paid with their lives, as would many of those municipal leaders who had taken their communities into the Carthaginian camp. Fines were laid and territory confiscated to beef up the landholdings of those colonies that had shown themselves so important in sustaining the Republic's rule in decades of stressful belligerence. It is even known that some veterans were planted in 201 on land conquered during these latest campaigns, though this planting of demobbed warriors would be much more of the Roman future than its past.

That the Hirpini lost land is substantiated by the discovery of Gracchi terminal stones placed a century later near places like Abellinum, modern-day Avellino, but the Caudini endured the most as those independent communities that had survived the earlier defeats were annexed. While the Rome-loyal Pentri may not themselves have suffered from Roman depredations, the loss of land by other tribes meant they were even more isolated from their Hirpini cousins. Communication became increasingly difficult and the road nexus more completely breached by colonies, placed between the different components of what had once been the Samnite League. While the predator from the Tiber, in the decades after the end of the Second Punic War, re-imposed herself first as master of Italy, then as hegemon of the whole of the Mediterranean world, a battered people subsided again and this time it looked like it was going to be for good, as Romanization subsumed so many of those who had once been proudly independent peninsular societies. Nothing of this was complete, yet still a direction seemed set in an Italy-wide phenomenon, with amphorae found at the Mount Vairano hill fort from the years after the Hannibalic War, showing a taste for fine Rhodian wine and the presence of coins for the Greek east indicating the involvement of a local elite in the East Mediterranean world the Romans had just acquired.

The process certainly had less of an impact in Samnium than in many other parts of Italy; the movement of peoples, the establishment of

Romans on captured land, intermarriage and involvement in business arrangements between elites just did not have the same impact on this population of largely impoverished hill people. The populations did not mix a lot; some Samnites went to Rome certainly, but not many, most emigrants travelled to other places in Italy and abroad. Fregellae received a good number of Samnite immigrants in 177, while others migrated to the Po valley and later Spain and Gaul, while some of the municipal elites produced businessmen who found even greener pastures for themselves as tax collectors in the new provinces in the Balkans and Asia.

So Italian traders, who would have included Samnite gentry, benefited, milking the provinces and suffering for it in the Anatolian vespers of Mithridates. However, most remained poor peasants, unlikely to be much influenced when contacts with their conquerors were so limited. Rural Samnites hardly encountered Roman citizens, even as their country was integrated into the Republic's economic system; just gangs of slaves who herded the rich Romans' animals grazing what had once been their own country. Neither would many have been incorporated into the client system that was so fundamental to the political and economic functioning of the Republic. The communities where such arrangements might have been meaningful were few and far between; distance, poverty and lack of urban infrastructures all militated against it. Though while integration was not the norm, this did not mean that the fact that Rome had come to stay as master was not deeply irksome, particularly when other factors rubbed constantly like coarse grains of sand in a sore. Romans utilized an increasing percentage of allied soldiers in their armies during the early imperial days, and more and more, like auxiliaries in the days of empire, these were the cannon fodder and did the dirty work. In the years of expansion beyond Italy, the allies provided more of the men under arms and sustained more of the casualties. They bled at the front of Mediterranean battlefields to a greater extent than their citizen comrades but got nowhere near the benefits. Their leaders did not receive the kudos, the soldiers received less booty, no land and, once demobbed, could not enjoy the free grain and tax relief that their Roman campmates did on their return home.

That Roman attitude is well illustrated by Polybius; a man close to those epitomes of the imperial elite, the Scipios, who hardly ever mentions the huge part played by allied troops in the great imperial onslaught undertaken by Rome to become the Mediterranean power in the second century. It rankled and this outlook was mirrored in action too. The Republic's rulers showed little concern for the economic interests of their allies, happily importing grain from outside the peninsula, so denying Rome to their neighbours as a market for their produce. Also the forbidding of mining to protect Italian natural resources was an awful hit to whatever local industry was beginning to appear in places like Samnium. Latinization had its impact, particularly in Caudium so near Campania and everywhere it was a package imposed by Romans who made little attempt to hide their feeling of superiority and that there was little sign of change in the hegemony's attitude over the decades grated. The year 188 had been the last time citizenship had been widely granted, to the peoples of Arpinum, Formiae and Fundi. Indeed, after this carrot it was all stick, with proposals in 126 that non-citizen Italians domiciled in Rome should be expelled and in 122 schemes to extend citizenship to upper-crust Italians were rejected out of hand. Worse than this, there remained a Roman propensity to exhibit their power in the most brutal fashion. In 125 they obliterated Fregellae; this is the only revolt in the Italian lands that we hear of in the second century and as punishment it was wiped off the map. It was surely also no coincidence that this place was essentially a community of Sabellian immigrants, with most of the original population emigrated to Rome and elsewhere; all grim reminders compounded by the perennial stories circulating of Roman dignitaries visiting allied communities and scourging the local magistrates because of the failure to provide adequate facilities when their wives visited the local bath-house.

This portfolio of grievances fashioned a powder keg ready to explode, that would tear the Italian world apart in the second decade of the first century. The immediate triggers for what became known as the Social War were numerous and convoluted. There was first an ability to fight. Italian allies had been mobilized in huge numbers for the Jugurthine and German wars fought between 112 and 101 and now these demobbed veterans were armed and available to battle for their rights once a leadership arose to deploy them against the Republic for which they had bled so profusely but with so few perceived benefits. Yet if this allowed them to contemplate a successful struggle, it was the impact of radical movements at Rome itself that made the difference. The Gracchi brothers pushed for the distribution of public plots to the landless city proletariat in an effort to recreate the yeoman class that had produced Rome's conquering armies in the past, but had been in decline since the great city set out on the road of first Italian and later world conquest. The reasons for this are much contested and not central to our narrative, but the waves raised by the reforms that were proposed to solve this perceived problem certainly were. The pace of change was torturous and bloody, with both the Gracchi impiously butchered by a Senatorial elite that profited from the status quo, despite their sacred standing as tribunes of the plebs. Yet parts of their radical programme were implemented and the implications of this were a real threat to many of Rome's Italian subjects.

Land commissioners dispatched to effect the distribution of public acres most certainly visited the Samnite country and boundary-markers found from the period make it clear they made a real impact on the ground. What is certain is that in Samnium as well as in the territories of many other Italian allies, particularly in the centre and south of the peninsula, the land to be given to the Roman poor was taken not from those wealthy citizens who profited by exploiting vast stretches of this country but from locals, whether they were peasant farmers scratching a living from the land or larger-scale commercial concerns of Sabellian gentry who had been utilizing these public acres for decades, if not centuries. The particular predicament in these changes in the wind was that these provincials, rich or poor, were without the benefit of Roman citizenship so they could neither appeal against the decisions made to alienate the property on which they lived, nor had the leverage possessed by their peers, whose votes were needed by those who wanted to sit on the consular throne, or secure one of the other magistracies that meant real power in the imperial Republic. Even if they could get their cases heard they would have found the court benches packed with Roman equites who were often their direct commercial rivals. If the Gracchi had done much to feed the fire, they had also recognized the overwhelming desire among Rome's allies for full citizenship and after their deaths another man took over this crusade. It was his fate that provided the final spark in 91. Marcus Livius Drusus, again as tribune of the plebs, proposed another tranche of land reforms but this time one that included the wholesale enfranchisement of most Italians. That would have allowed these peoples to advocate in their own interest when it came to administering the redistribution of public land. Yet once again Rome's great men, most of whom had been exploiting these acres for centuries, would not have it. They lit a fuse when they had Drusus murdered and the whole reform package thrown out.

The Marci reacted first, with a 10,000-man march on Rome along the Via Valeria with proto-civil rights agitation transferred from Washington DC to Latium. Yet non-violence had few takers, particularly when the promises given to persuade the crowd to turn round were not even given a hearing back in Rome. In the rest of Italy military preparations were the order of the day, as allied warriors were readying to fight against ex-comrades who had refused them the political rights they felt they had both earned and badly needed in a changing world. Officials were sent from the capital when word of trouble circulated, but this was an intervention that only made matters worse and when word of Livius Drusus' death reached Asculum on the Apulia-Samnite border, the first of many purges of any Romans found in Italian towns began; a crisis that would see many of Rome's most crucial allies form a federate state. Then when a new capital was proclaimed at old Corfinium it was renamed Italica and the authors of the name change made no bones that their aim was the destruction of their former hegemon. Familiar names like the Marsi, Picentes, Paeligni, Marrucini, Vestini, Frentani and Samnites were all at the heart of the confederacy in these tumultuous times, raising more than 100,000 fighting men between them.

This cousins' war drowned the country in blood, with vicious fighting up around Perusia and south at places like Nola and Pompeii. Rebellion burst out across Campania, Apulia and Lucania where many of the colonies and forts the Romans had placed in these territories were subject to desperate assault. A great siege of Asculum was commenced, but the Romans were lucky that the Latins did not rise against them, with the exception of the colonists at Venusia who clearly had established real empathy with their Sabellian neighbours. This heartland strength ensured the rebels began suffering a number of setbacks on the battlefield as campaigning continued, but their tenacity ensured that the policy-makers at Rome would soon have to concede the key point of citizenship to try to contain what might become a bloodbath out of control. There was a terror of what any failing to suppress or conciliate the allies might mean for the so far unaffected communities in Etruria and Umbria. The Lex Julia was swiftly passed, offering citizenship to those with Latin rights and any others not in arms against Rome that at least ensured the contagion did not spread further.

By 89, though the slaughter had been and continued to be awful, the future was mainly just about mopping up, with the next year seeing most, apart from Samnites and Lucanians, being pacified by a judicious blend of force and promises of citizenship to those who had not revolted or would give up the struggle. By 88 more than a quarter of a million people had perished in this war when the blood-drained Roman polity found it had to face the threat of Mithridates of Pontus, a monarch from Anatolia who had almost pushed Roman power back from Asia to the Adriatic Sea. This was not the worst, as the situation became compounded when civil war broke out over who should command the army sent to fight this menace from the east. The consul Sulla had been harassing Samnites for some time in 89, taking Aeclanum, an important Hirpini town, and suppressing other holdouts from the Italian war in Campania, before he found his command of the army destined to fight Mithridates contested by Marius. This six-time consul and saviour hero against the Germans years before, through intimidation and bodily removal of his rivals, took over the capital and had himself appointed to command in this foreign war. However, Sulla, refusing to take this lying down, took the extraordinary decision to put his veteran army on the road and march on Rome itself, driving out his enemies with hardly any fighting and setting up a congenial regime before he departed to take the fight to Mithridates across the sea in Greece.

Ambition had always been progressed not just by persuasion but intimidation too, but this march on Rome had broken a mould. Once Sulla departed, the year 87 saw his enemies again brutally in control, with another round of butchery between the political factions against the backdrop of a Marian revival. During the years Sulla harried the Pontic armies in the east, though old Marius died, a coalition of his friends continued to run Italy with support from the likes of the Samnites who retained nothing but hatred for Sulla who had hounded them so mercilessly in the Social War. They had been Roman citizens since 87, though registration would not have taken place until the next year, and this new-found status coincided with what must have seemed the springtime of a new independence. While the Republic's leadership, that now included old Marius' son, tried to make sense of a political world ruptured by not just the Social War but a civil war that ended with a consul leading armed soldiers into Rome itself, they were going to have little interest in, never mind the capability, to reassert control in those disparate regions where the inhabitants had been newly granted citizenship. In the years between the end of the Social War and Sulla's return in 83, the Samnites must have been a virtually independent people,[10] despite there being little concrete evidence such as coins to substantiate this state of affairs.

In the period since the first march on Rome and Sulla's return from the East the Marian cause had lost some of its leading lights. Old Marius and Cinna were both gone but those who remained were determined to hang on to power, particularly trying to capitalize on any goodwill that attended the enfranchising of so many new citizens, and with the threat of their returning nemesis they anticipated finding these new Romans eager to join their armies. Into this cauldron Sulla returned in spring 83 with a veteran army honed in victorious if not finally conclusive campaigns in Greece and Asia. This latest civil war appeared unlikely to last as the deliquescent Marian edifice crumbled and the newcomers looked well set on the road to regaining control after landing at Brundisium, marching right through Samnium and finding hardly any local opposition, despite the expedition being undermanned and in a hurry. Sulla's men first encountered real resistance in Campania, when he arrived in person in a region where the Samnites had established themselves, defeating an army near Capua where he was determined to take control, despite the Marian consul Gaius Norbanus being in possession. Then near Taenum, where he spent the winter of 83–82, he enticed another consular army en masse over to his party, while in an attempt to woo as many Italians as possible he confirmed their new-found status as Roman citizens. Although knowing his own loathing of the old Samnite enemy chimed with most of his compatriots, he pointedly excluded them to paint a picture of his programme as something like an anti-Samnite crusade.

In 82 two new anti-Sulla consuls, Carbo and Marius the younger, took up the fight and plenty of Samnites, Lucanians and other Sabellians felt they had little option but to rally to them against the man who had spilt so much of their blood in the past and was certainly intent on continuing in the same vein. The Samnite warriors were commanded by a brother of Pontius Telesinus who had not as far as we know been involved in the Social War but who now committed his people fully after hearing of Sulla's massacre of the Sabellian captives after the Battle of Scariportus (Sacriporto) in the Trerus valley, a defeat that ended with young Marius being bottled up in Praeneste. Nor was this latest mobilization against Sulla an exact equivalent of Samnite involvement in the Social War, as although the Caudinii had not been involved in the early 80s they certainly now enlisted in the fight. It was also at this time that some other famous names appeared, this time on Sulla's side, with Crassus raising armies among the Marci and Pompey among the Picentes.

This was the sequence, with the Samnites as the moving force on the Marian side, that led to the denouement outside the Colline Gate and from that bloodletting there would be no way back as Pontius Telesinus' severed head advertised to young Marius, entrapped in Praeneste, that the end had come, and if this was true of the great Marius's son, it was also true of so much else. The Sulla who had dealt with almost a light touch five years before was no longer in the same mood after years in which his friends and family had been persecuted, often to death, and every effort had been made to undermine his position while he was fighting his wars in Greece and Asia. Now there was no chance of any display of clemency; it would be the heads of young Marius and his lieutenants exposed in the forum in front of the rostra and proscriptions posted that would not only decimate the Roman elite, but leave the survivors traumatized as well. These were also years of agony for the Samnites, as Sulla, always inclined to extirpate beaten foes, exacted brutal revenge on defenceless communities. There was more confiscation of pastures while colonies expanded and Roman carpetbaggers arrived, eager to despoil a ravaged landscape. It was an awful time as the men from Sulla's legions who had butchered their people were planted on their land. As with many other Sabellian peoples, even those including numbers of Roman- and Sulla-loyal Italians, found themselves subject to mass removals. People who had for centuries clung to defensible spurs and hilltops had their homes demolished and found themselves forcibly re-established down from the heights into the valleys. Old Samnite towns like Saepinum, places with great defensive walls looking over the valleys below, soon had their populations moved to low-lying urban centres, replete with all those facilities typical of Roman culture, much of which can still be seen to this day.

The problem of the Samnites had finally been solved; local languages might survive in backward glens or as an archaic art form,[11] but generally Latinizations progressed at such a pace that finding remnants of anything that is definitely Samnite in the rest of the first century and into the imperial age is difficult indeed. Even names that might suggest a Samnite background are not certain, as many might have been non-Sabellians brought onto land taken over during centuries of exploitation. The very name was seldom meaningfully heard as the centuries wore on; the Augustine designation of much of central Italy as the Samnite region had little relation to the old country of the league and that a Lombard invader in the sixth century AD claimed the title of the Duke of Samnium just proved the rule about how completely the reality of this people was lost.

The classical period still provides templates for a modern occidental world in a way that is just not the case from the time before or after, until the mediaeval world fades away. The orthodoxy so often touted is to see the likes of Marathon, Salamis and Alexander the Great at Gaugamela as part of a struggle between East and West to ensure the survival of the kind of democratic individualism seen as being in the very DNA of the modern West, and if this is walking the knife edge between truth and nonsense, it offers some appreciation of why it was important. It all seems so epic because of the size of the theatre where events took place, and perhaps the quality of the sources; a duel between Greece and Persia is performed on a world stage that makes the labours in which Rome was involved in these centuries, culminating in the Samnite wars, seem modest or even provincial. This is not absolutely reasonable; the numbers that were involved at Sentinum or Aquilonia are surely comparable, except in the case of Xerxes' invasion of Greece or Alexander's last battle with Darius III, indeed much greater than those involved at the Battles of Marathon or Thermopylae. In only a very short time, a couple of centuries, the results of these struggles would also reverberate round the world, with Rome becoming a greater player on the world stage than any of the actors who were the direct linear descendants of those who bestrode the globe with Themistocles, Xerxes, Darius, Phillip and Alexander of Macedon.

Greece might have offered high-octane democracy, with barrack-room lawyers arguing the toss on the Pnyx and filling most rungs of their city administration by lottery; the kind of people power that we only now ever recognize in organizations like trade unions. Yet Roman politics mirrors the represented model of our own day, where we can choose between members of a self-selecting, moneyed elite who generally operate within parameters acceptable to the people who vote them into power, and there are meaningful echoes everywhere: some around positive discrimination to allow chipping at the ubiquity of deeply-entrenched establishments; others between ideas of social and ethnic melting-pots or a quilt combining different cultures, communities and colours. This certainly applies in the Republican years when for centuries law, myth and custom contrived to prevent the kind of free play of ambition that finally led to the deluge and the empire that came after. Yet afterwards too Roman power was certainly a function of inclusion and integration; after all, one emperor could laud his Punic roots and on the thousandth anniversary of the founding of the city of Rome the man in charge had the very Greek name of Philip and was labelled by a people who lived on the very edge of empire, the Arabs. Very far from everything in the story of Rome yells that these people had really advanced far in terms of human and social progress, yet still there had been baby steps.

Generally Rome eventually incorporated those she conquered rather than slaughtering them all. It was a unique selling-point that allowed her to grow in a way that was extraordinary, but the Samnites were hardly offered this outcome. They were almost eradicated as a people in a way that was quite unusual. The elimination and exile of the gentry is demonstrated in that hardly any men of confirmed Samnite heritage received significant notice in the generations to come, unlike Marsi and the leaders of other Sabellian peoples who would be noticed in the pages of histories concerning Caesar Octavian or Mark Antony. The Augustine and Diocletian categorization of Italian regions only marks a name and a misty memory, nothing of a recognition of a still existing people. Yet at least if the shades of Gellius Egnatius and Gaius Pontius looked down now and saw that the modern-day town of Benevento, dominated by the Arch of Trajan and Roman baths, when they contemplated nearby Montesarchio it would be with pleasure to see there is a definite feeling in the Castle Museum that this is still Samnite country. On the walls are cartoons of ancient soldiers in typical Sabellian trefoil armour, suggesting a connection at some level with an antique past that probably would not be replicated in some Pennine town with the Briganti or the Iceni in East Anglia. Perhaps too many peoples have passed through and too much has happened in the British Isles for these long-gone ancestors to resonate as their near contemporaries might in the greensward mounts and valleys of Samnium. They might have been trampled by Goths, Lombards and many other intruders in their time, but most country people hardly really moved until a couple of hundred years ago. Since then much more has changed in Britain than that part of Italy; the experience of industrial transformation and flight from the land is of a quantitatively different kind in Manchester and London than in Naples.

Notes

Introduction
1. Nicholas Horsfall, 'The Caudine forks topography and illusion', *Papers of the British School at Rome*, Vol. 50 (1982), pp. 45–52.
2. Livy not infrequently references city records recorded in linen books that clearly survived the sack, as well as mentioning that Augustus had himself seen inscribed temple spoils from the fifth century that presumably were neither destroyed nor taken away.
3. Livy, Book 5, 52 has Camillus persuading his compatriots not to desert a sacked Rome and permanently set up a new home at Veii.
4. Peter Turchin, *War and Peace and War: The Rise and Fall of Empires*.

Chapter One
1. Plutarch, *Romulus*.
2. Livy, 1 11.
3. Livy, 10 23 11 12.
4. Pliny, NH 34 23; Livy, 9 43.
5. Livy, 9 38.
6. Livy, *Periochae*, 11 10.
7. Lorne H. Ward, 'Roman Population, Territory, Tribe, City, and Army Size from the Republic's Founding to the Veientine War, 509 BC–400 BC, *The American Journal of Philology*, 111.
8. J. Armstrong, *Early Roman Warfare*, p. 48.
9. *The Iliad*, Book 2.

Chapter Two
1. Dionysius of Halicarnassus, 6 95.
2. Livy, 6 5.
3. Cicero, *De Officiis*, 1 35.
4. Livy, 8 14.
5. Momigliano, *Alien Wisdom: The Limits of Hellenization*, 1975.
6. Livy, 10 11.
7. This method of holding a large round shield by passing the forearm through a central loop and grasping a grip at the edge of the shield made the tight phalanx the optimum formation, in which each man received protection from the soldier on his right.

8. J. Armstrong, *Early Roman Warfare*.
9. Livy, 10 47.

Chapter Three
1. Athenaeus, *The Deipnosophists*, Book 12.
2. Periplus of Pseudo-Scylax.
3. Livy, 9 1.
4. R. Scopacasa, *Ancient Samnium*.
5. R. Scopacasa, *Ancient Samnium*, pp. 131, 140.
6. Sallust, *The Conspiracy of Catiline*, 51.
7. Livy, 9 21.
8. Paul Orosius, *History Against the Pagans*, 3 15 10.
9. Diodorus Siculus, 19 76.
10. A couple of publications have argued this case: P. Sidnell, *Warhorse* and J.B. McCall, *The Cavalry of the Roman Republic*.
11. Livy, 9 27.
12. Diodorus Siculus, Books 19 and 20.

Chapter Four
1. Livy, 9 29.
2. Diodorus Siculus, 20 35.
3. Dionysius of Halicarnassus, 1 19.
4. Pliny the Elder, *The Natural History*, 3 19.
5. Livy, 9 38.
6. In the fourth century Greek Thebes created a formation of elite soldiers based around pairs of lovers fighting together.

Chapter Five
1. Diodorus Siculus claims forty towns or hill forts were taken, while Livy mentions thirty-one.
2. Livy, 8 25.
3. Livy, 7 10.
4. A first-century historian, who was one of many annalists who wrote yearly chronicles.
5. There is a proviso here in that Livy himself is not convinced that any fighting occurred in Etruria at this time, only that the dictator re-established Rome's protégés, the Cilnii family at Arretium, who had earlier been overthrown by a popular revolt, though against this the fasti confirms that the veteran marshal received a last triumph against the Etruscans as well as the Marsi.
6. Diodorus Siculus, Book 5 24.
7. Diodorus Siculus, Book 5 26.
8. Diodorus Siculus, Book 5 28.
9. Livy, 5 34.

10. This may, in fact, be a title rather than a given name as it seems unlikely that the attack on Rome and a Gallic invasion of Greece 100 years later, the two most famous incursions by this people into the classical world, would have been led by a chief with the same personal name.
11. Plutarch, *Pyrrhus*.
12. Dionysius of Halicarnassus, 16 11.
13. Dionysius of Halicarnassus, 16 14.
14. Dionysius of Halicarnassus, 16 13.

Chapter Six
1. Arthur M. Eckstein, *Rome Enters the Greek East*.
2. Livy, 1 32.
3. Frontinus, *Strategems*, 1 6 2.
4. Itineraria were ancient Roman road maps showing communities and the distances in between, such as the Peutinger Table.
5. Livy, 10 17.

Chapter Seven
1. Livy, 9 29.
2. Diodorus Siculus, Book 20 36.
3. Livy, 10 18.
4. Though much is up for question about the real sequence and personalities involved in these campaigns against Murgantia, Ferentinum and Romulea, with alternative traditions that give credit to Decius Mus or Fabius Rullianus when their commands were extended after their consulships of 297. Still, that the achievements were down to Volumnius Flamma is quite believable.

Chapter Eight
1. Pliny, Book 36.
2. E.T. Salmon in *Samnium and the Samnites* suggests the confederates may have had an eye to bringing the Sabines and perhaps the Marsi into the anti-Roman fold. After all, neither of these tried to stop Samnites moving north and would suffer later from a punitive strike that might have been prompted by a whiff of treachery at this critical time. So Scipio would have moved from Clusium to Camerinum to shadow the main enemy force.
3. Polybius, 2 19.
4. Livy, 10 28.
5. Livy, 10 29.
6. Livy in Book 5 records the patricians who allowed themselves to be killed by the Gauls during the sack of Rome as a form of *devotio* and in Book 8 10 discusses other sorts of *devotio*.
7. Livy, 10 28.
8. Livy, 10 29.
9. Ibid.

Chapter Nine

1. Kyle Harper, *The Fate of Rome: Climate, Disease and the End of an Empire.*
2. Livy, 10 31.
3. Livy, 10 32.
4. The lack of remains of Roman marching camps in central Italy does put a question mark over whether the Roman soldiers were building classic playing card-shaped camps with strong defences this early. It is possible they did not boast significant earthworks until later, which would also fit in with the tradition that King Pyrrhus was the first to use proper fortified encampments.
5. Livy, 10 32.
6. Dionysius of Halicarnassus, 16 15.
7. Ibid.
8. Though there is no record of a triumph in the fasti.
9. A town of this name in Marci country had probably been garrisoned by the Samnites earlier in the year, so it is possible Postumius Megellus was now reversing this incursion.
10. Livy mentions Quintus Claudius Quadrigarius (a first-century annalist who he uses freely) who claims Postumius Megellus captured some places in Samnium before being defeated and driven wounded into Luceria, while it was Atilius Regulus who fought in Etruria and claimed a triumph for it, while Fabius Pictor gives an account that has both consuls fighting first in Samnium and afterwards in Apulia, suffering considerable reverses near Luceria. The triumphal fasti only confuse matters further, with both accredited triumphs in March 293; Postumius over the Samnites and Etruscans and Atilius over the Samnites and the Volsones.
11. Livy, 9 40.
12. Suggested by nineteenth and early twentieth-century German scholar K.J. Beloch.
13. S.P. Oakley, *The Hill Forts of the Samnites*, Appendix.
14. Livy, 10 40.
15. Ibid.
16. Ibid.
17. Livy, 10 41.
18. Ardant du Picq, *Battle Studies: Ancient and Modern Battle.*
19. Livy, 10 41.
20. Ibid.
21. Livy, 10 44.
22. Livy, 10 45.
23. Livy, 10 46.
24. It is also possible that this is referencing Spurius Carvilius' campaigning down in Lucania and Campania years later.

Chapter Ten
1. Macrobius, *Saturnalia*, 3 13.
2. Polyaenus, 8 15.
3. Dio Cassius, fr.36'30.
4. Eutropius, 2 9.
5. Livy, *Periochae*, 11 2.
6. Paulus Orosius, 3 22.
7. Dionysius of Halicarnassus, 17 4.
8. Ibid.
9. Plutarch declares: 'Pyrrhus in the air of his face had something more of the terrors than of the augustness of kingly power; he had not a regular set of upper teeth, but in the place of them one continued bone, with small lines marked on it, resembling the divisions of a row of teeth.'
10. Cicero, *De Senectute* 55, and Valerius Maximus, 4 3 5.

Epilogue
1. Plutarch, *Sulla*.
2. Velleius Paterculus, *History* 2 27.
3. Plutarch, *Sulla*.
4. King Henri III mentions the incident in Dumas, *The Forty-five Guardsmen*, Chapter 54.
5. Frontinus, 2 111 21, and Dionysius of Halicarnassus, Book 20 1.
6. Dante's *Divine Comedy*, Canto XX.
7. Livy, 23 41.
8. Paulus Orosius, 4 7 12.
9. Livy, 23 1 2.
10. R. Syme, *Roman Revolution*, p. 87.
11. Strabo, 5 3 6.

Bibliography

Ancient Sources
Appian, *The Roman History*
Cassius Dio, *The History of Rome*
Marcus Tullius Cicero, *Collected Works*
Diodorus Siculus, *Universal History*
Dionysius of Halicarnassus, *Roman Antiquities*
Eutropius, *Abridgment of Roman History*
Frontinus, *Stratagems*
Herodotus, *The Histories*
Homer, *The Iliad*
Livy, *The History of Rome*
Macrobius, *Saturnalia*
Paulus Orosius, *History Against the Pagans*
Pliny the Elder, *The Natural History*
Plutarch, *Parallel Lives and Moralia*
Polyaenus, *Stratagems*
Polybius, *The Histories*
Strabo, *The Geography*
Valerius Maximus, *Nine Books of Memorable Deeds and Sayings*
Velleius Paterculus, *History*
Virgil, *The Aeneid*

Publications
Afzelius, A., *Two Studies in Roman Expansion* (New York, 1975).
Armstrong, J., *Early Roman Warfare* (Pen & Sword, 2016).
Beard, Mary, *SPQR, A History of Ancient Rome* (Profile Books, main edition, 2016).
Bennett, B. and Roberts, M., *The Wars of Alexander's Successors*, Vol. I (Pen & Sword, 2008).
Black, Jeremy M., *Clio's Battles: Historiography in Practice* (Indiana University Press, 2015).
Bradley, Guy, *Ancient Umbria: State, Culture and Identity in Central Italy from the Iron Age to the Augustan Era* (Oxford, OUP, 2000).
Broodbank, Cyprian, *The Making of the Middle Sea* (Thomas and Hudson, 2015).

Campbell, Duncan B., *Greek and Roman Artillery 399 BC–AD 363* (Osprey, 2003).
Campbell, Duncan B., *Besieged* (Osprey, 2006).
Caven, Brian, *Dionysius I* (Yale University Press, 1990).
Champion, J., *Pyrrhus of Epirus* (Pen & Sword, 2016).
Connolly, P., *Greece and Rome at War* (Frontline Books, reissue edition, January 2016).
Cornell, T., *The Beginnings of Rome: Italy and Rome from the Bronze Age to the Punic Wars (c.1000–264 BC)* (London, Routledge, 1995).
Cowan, R., 'The Clashing of Weapons and Silent Advances in Roman Battles', *Historia 56* (2007).
Cowan, R., *Roman Conquests, Italy* (Pen & Sword, 2009).
Cowan, R., *For the Glory of Rome* (Greenhill Books, 2007).
David, Jean-Michel, *The Roman Conquest of Italy* (Blackwell Publishers, 1996).
Delbruck, H., *Warfare in Antiquity* (University of Nebraska Press, 1990).
Du Picq, Ardant, *Battle Studies: Ancient and Modern Battle* (Windham Press, 2013).
Eckstein, Arthur M., *Rome Enters the Greek East* (Wiley-Blackwell, 2012).
Everitt, Anthony, *The Rise of Rome: The Making of the World's Greatest Empire* (Random House, reprint edition, 2013).
Everitt, Anthony, *Cicero: The Life and Times of Rome's Greatest Politician* (Random House, USA Inc., reprint edition, 2003).
Fields, Nic, *Roman Battle Tactics 390–110* (Osprey, 2010).
Fiske, George Converse, 'The Politics of the Patrician Claudii', *Harvard Studies in Classical Philology*, Vol. 13 (1902), pp. 1–59.
Forsythe, G., *A Critical History of Early Rome* (University of California Press, 2005).
Frank, Tenney, 'Rome's First Coinage', Source: *Classical Philology*, Vol. 14, No. 4 (October 1919), pp. 314–327 (University of Chicago Press).
Fronda, M.P., *Between Rome and Carthage* (Cambridge University Press, 2010).
Fronda, M.P., 'Livy 9.20 and Early Roman Imperialism in Apulia', *Historia: Zeitschrift für Alte Geschichte*, Bd. 55, H. 4 (2006), pp. 397–417.
Garoufalias, Petros, *Pyrrhus* (London, Stacey International, 1979).
Gibbon, Edward, *The Decline and Fall of the Roman Empire*.
Goldsworthy, Adrian, *In the Name of Rome* (Weidenfeld & Nicolson, 2003).
Grant, M., *Myths of the Greeks and Romans* (Meridian Books, 1995).
Greenhalgh, P., *Pompey* (Weidenfeld and Nicolson, 1980).
Griffith, G.T., *The Mercenaries of the Hellenistic World* (Cambridge, 1935).
Hanson, V.D., *Hoplites* (Routledge, 1993).
Harper, Kyle, *The Fate of Rome: Climate, Disease and the End of an Empire* (Princeton University Press, 2017).
Hölkeskamp, Karl-J., 'Conquest, Competition and Consensus: Roman Expansion in Italy and the Rise of the "Nobilitas"', *Historia: Zeitschrift für Alte Geschichte*, Bd. 42, H. 1 (1993), pp. 12–39.

Holland, Tom, *Rubicon* (Little Brown, 2003).
Hubert, Henri, *The History of the Celtic People* (Bracken Books, 1993).
Janssen, L.F., 'Some Unexplored Aspects of Devotio', *Mnemosyne*, Fourth Series, Vol. 34, Fasc. 3/4 (1981), pp. 357–381.
Keegan, John, *The Face of Battle* (Bodley Head, 2014).
Kirkpatrick, James D., 'The Queen of Roads', Source: *The Journal of Education*, Vol. 68, No. 22 (1707) (10 December 1980), pp. 621–622 (Published by Trustees of Boston University Stable).
Kneale, Matthew, *Rome: A History in Seven Sackings* (Atlantic Books, main edition 2018).
Lane Fox, Robin, *The Classical World: An Epic History from Homer to Hadrian* (Penguin Books, 2006).
Lendon, J.E., *Soldiers and Ghosts* (Yale University Press, 2005).
MacBain, Bruce, 'Appius Claudius Caecus and the Via Appia', *The Classical Quarterly*, Vol. 30, No. 2 (1980).
Machiavelli, Niccolò, *Discourses on Livy* (Oxford Paperbacks, new edition, 1997).
Machiavelli, Niccolò, *Art of War* (University of Chicago Press, new edition, 2005).
Malden, H., 'Pyrrhus in Italy', *Journal of Philology*, 10 1882.
Matyszak, P., *Cataclysm 90 BC* (Pen & Sword, 2014).
Mayor, Adrienne, *The Poison King: The Life and Legend of Mithradates* (Princetown, 2010).
McCall, J.B., *The Cavalry of the Roman Republic* (Routledge, 2002).
McCartney, Eugene S., 'The Genesis of Rome's Military Equipment', Source: *The Classical Weekly*, Vol. 6, No. 10 (21 December 1912), pp. 74–79 (Johns Hopkins University Press).
Meiklejohn, K.W., 'Roman Strategy and Tactics from 509 to 202 B.C.', *Greece & Rome*, Vol. 7, No. 21 (May 1938), pp. 170–178.
Messer, William Stuart, 'Mutiny in the Roman Army: The Republic', Source: *Classical Philology*, Vol. 15, No. 2 (April 1920), pp. 158–175.
Miles, R., *Carthage Must be Destroyed* (Allen Lane, 2010).
Millar, Fergus, 'Politics, Persuasion and the People before the Social War (150–90 B.C.)'.
The Journal of Roman Studies, Vol. 76 (1986), pp. 1–11.
Mitchell, F., 'Roman Carthaginian Treaties 306 and 279/8 BC', *Historia*, 20.
Momigliano, Arnaldo, 'Cavalry and Patriciate. An Answer to Professor A. Alföldi', *Historia: Zeitschrift für Alte Geschichte*, Bd. 18, H. 4 (August 1969), pp. 385–388.
Mommsen, Theodor, *The History of Rome*, Book 2 (Cambridge University Press, 2010).
Oakley, S.P., *The Hill Forts of the Samnites* (British School at Rome, 1995).
Oakley, S.P., 'Single Combat in the Roman Republic', *The Classical Quarterly*, Vol. 35, No. 2 (1985), pp. 392–410.

Patterson, John R., *Samnites, Ligurians and Romans Revisited*.
Penrose, Jane (ed.), *Rome and Her Enemies* (Osprey, 2005).
Rankin, H.D., *Celts and the Classical World* (London and Portland, OR, 1987).
Ridley, R.T., 'Notes on the Establishment of the Tribunate of the Plebs', Latomus, T., 27, Fasc. 3 (Juillet-Septembre 1968), pp. 535–554 (twenty pages).
Ridley, R.T., 'The origin of the roman dictatorship: an overlooked opinion', Rheinisches Museum für Philologie, Neue Folge, 122. Bd., H. 3/4 (1979), pp. 303–309.
Salmon, E.T., *Samnium and the Samnites* (Cambridge, 1967).
Salmon, E.T., 'Colonial Foundations during the Second Samnite War', *Classical Philology*, Vol. 58, No. 4 (October 1963), pp. 235–238.
Salmon, E.T., *The Making of Roman Italy* (Thames & Hudson Ltd, first edition, 1982).
Scopacasa, R., *Ancient Samnium* (Oxford, 2015).
Scullard, *A History of the Roman World* (Routledge, 1935).
Sidebottom, Harry, *Ancient Warfare: A Very Short Introduction* (Oxford, OUP, first paperback edition, 2004).
Sidnell, P., *Warhorse* (Hambledon Continuum, 2006).
Spaeth, John William, *A Study of the Causes of Rome's War from 343 to 265 B.C.* (Princeton University, 1926).
Tuck, Steven L., *The Mysterious Etruscans*, The Great Courses (Audible.co.uk, Release date: 8 January 2016).
Turchin, Peter, *War and Peace and War: The Rise and Fall of Empires* (Plume Books, 2006).
Usher, S., *The Historians of Greece and Rome* (Hamish Hamilton, 1969).
Versnel, H.S., 'Two Types of Roman Devotio', *Mnemosyne*.
Versnel, H.S., *Triumphus: An Inquiry into the Origin, Development and Meaning of the Roman Triumph* (Leiden, 1970).
Walbank, F.W. (ed.), Astin, A.E. (ed.), Frederiksen, M.W. (ed.), Ogilvie, R.M. (ed.), Drummond, A. (assistant), *The Cambridge Ancient History*, 7, Part 2 (Cambridge University Press, second edition, 1990).
Ward, Lorne H., 'Roman Population, Territory, Tribe, City, and Army Size from the Republic's Founding to the Veientine War, 509 B.C.-400 B.C.', *The American Journal of Philology*, Vol. 111, No. 1 (Spring, 1990), pp. 5–39.
Ward-Perkins, John Bryan, *Landscape and History in Central Italy* (B.H. Blackwell, 1964).
Wightman, Edith M., 'Topographic Survey in the Liri Valley, Southern Lazio, Italy', *Current Anthropology*, Vol. 19, No. 2 (June 1978), pp. 389–390.
Zhmodikov, Alexander, 'Roman Republican Heavy Infantrymen in Battle (IV-II Centuries B.C.)', *Historia: Zeitschrift für Alte Geschichte*, Bd. 49, H. 1 (First quarter, 2000), pp. 67–78.

Index

Abellinum (Avellino), 33, 273
Abruzzo, 33, 106, 132, 249
Acerrae, 21
Acron, 2
Adriatic, vi, x, xvii–xviii, 17, 33–4, 37, 40, 68, 71, 82–3, 91, 98, 106–108, 111, 117, 119, 127, 151, 153, 246, 250–2, 278
Aedile, 24, 141, 199, 234
Aedui, 97
Aegean, xiii
Lucius Aemilius Barbula, 265
Quintus Aemilius Barbula, 63
Aeneas, 13, 59
Aeneid, 1, 9
Aequi, viii, xvi, 8, 18–19, 22, 29, 31–2, 56, 59, 84–9, 91, 93, 119, 136
Aesernia (Isernia), 122, 191, 248, 268–9
Aetolians, 11
Africa, xviii, 4, 24, 256
Agiads, 109
Aharna (Civitella d'Arna), 153–8, 160
Alba Fucens, vii, 86, 89
Alba Longa, 101
Alban hills, 44
Albinus, 262
Alesia, 145
Alexander the Great, xviii, 88, 108, 120, 209, 245, 253–4, 281–3
Alfaterni, 37, 268
Alfedena, 117
Allifae, 63, 72, 83, 205, 268
Alps, 32, 59, 96–8, 101, 105, 107
Alvito, 213
Ambarri, 97
Ambigatus, 97

Amiternum, 212, 249, 312
Anagnia, 83–4
Anatolia, 88, 108, 157, 274, 278
Ancona, 98
Anio, 19–20, 78, 82, 86–7, 91, 101–102, 261
Antemnae, 261–2
Antigonus Gonatus, 88
Antigonus Monophthalmus, 88
Antium, 21, 73, 103
Anzio, 9
Apaches, 8
Apennines, ix–x, xvi–xvii, 37–8, 45, 60, 68, 71, 82, 98, 107, 127, 129, 153, 160, 164, 202, 205, 212, 242, 249
Appian, xii
Appian Way, ix, 42, 47, 139, 141, 150, 235, 271
Quintus Appuleius Pansa, 94
Apulia, ix–x, xv, xvii, 17, 33, 35, 37, 40, 42, 45, 50, 53–4, 56, 58, 83, 86, 104, 106, 108, 114, 117, 119, 127–9, 131, 151, 173, 205, 242, 265–6, 268, 270, 272, 276–7
Apulia Taenum, 37
Aquilonia, 210, 212–16, 222–7, 231, 245, 248, 263, 268, 270, 281
Arabs, 282
Ardant du Picq, 220
Ardea, vii, 9, 13, 19, 32, 39, 44
Areus, 109
Argive, 26, 28
Aricia, 19
Aristotle, xiii–xiv, 100
Arpaia, xi
Arretium, 60, 63, 70, 92, 252

Arverni, 97
Asensi, 31
Asia, xviii, 59, 108, 260, 274, 278–80
Assēs, 185, 190, 207, 232, 247
Assyrians, 176
Atella, vii, 37
River Aternus, 82
Athenian League, 24
Athens, 11
Atina, 33, 122, 201, 213, 248
Aufidena, 34, 38, 116–17, 268
Augustine inscription, 6
Augustus (Octavian), 13, 136, 282
St Augustine, 252
Aulerci, 97
Quintus Aulius, 42–3
Suessa Aurunca, 52, 92
Aurunci, 20, 31, 37, 42, 45, 53, 91, 151, 178, 191, 230
Ausona, 52
Aventine, 4, 10

Babylonia, 176
Balkans, 274
Barcid, xvii
Bari, 130
Baselice Morcone, 130
Basilicata, 33
Battle of Alalia, 59
Battle of the Allia, 99, 259
Battle of Arausio, 199
Battle of Asculum, 180, 253
Battle of Beneventum, 267
Battle of the Cremera, 8
Battle of Drepana, 135
Battle of Gaugamela, 176
Battles of Heraclea, 253, 265
Battle of Ipsus, 88
Battle of Mars-la-Tour, 220
Battle of Saticula, 123
Battle of Scariportus (Sacriporto), 280
Battle of Silva Arsia, 96
chevalier Bayard, 148
Bellona, 147, 262
Bellovesus, 97

Benevento, ix, 33–4, 127, 130, 283
Biferno River, 123, 127
Bisaccia, 130
Boii, 98
Bovianum (modern Bojarno), 33, 116, 120, 188, 213, 222, 229, 248, 271–2
Brennus, 12, 98–101, 259
Briganti, 283
Britain, xviii, 17, 188, 283
Britons, 175
Brundisium, 142, 279
Bruttians, xvii, 33, 35, 257, 266–8
Brutus, 3, 8, 39
Brutus Scaeva, 224, 234–5
Gaius Junius Bubulcus, 62, 72, 86, 90
Busso, 213
Byzantine, xv, 187

Lucius Caecilius Metellus Denter, 251
Gaius Caedicius, 217, 221
Caeliian Hill, 8
Caeninenses, 2
Quintus Servilius Caepio, 199
Caere, 19, 23, 39, 60, 66, 100–101
Caesar, xv, 14, 98, 140, 175, 244, 282
Caiatia, 33, 192, 268, 271
Caiazzo, 192
Calatia, vii, 37, 42, 83
Cales, vii, xii, 21, 38, 87, 91, 148, 191, 248
Calor River, 33, 127
Camerinum, 68, 71, 82, 92, 107, 160
Furius Camillus, xiii, 9, 28, 100–101
Camillus (son of above), 104
Campania, viii, ix–x, xv–xvi, 1, 4, 5, 21, 29, 31–40, 42, 45–6, 53–4, 56, 59, 86, 91, 102, 106, 108, 119, 121–2, 142, 148, 168, 178, 182, 185, 192–3, 200, 221, 231, 233, 235, 265, 268, 270, 275, 277–9
Campobasso, 130, 202, 213
Cannae, xviii, 199, 220, 270, 199
Canusium, 37
Capena, 18, 66, 103
Porta Capena, 103

Capitoline Hill, 4, 12, 39, 82, 100–101, 249
Capua, vii, xvi, 12, 23, 29, 37, 40, 42, 50, 53, 59, 106, 112, 121, 142, 168, 191, 210, 263, 265, 270, 272, 279
Caracini, 34, 56, 116, 246, 265
Carbo, 259
Carinas, 262
Carnutes, 97
Carthage, xvi, 20, 22, 108, 157, 269, 270, 272
Carseoli, 89
Spurius Carvilius Maximus, 209, 211, 213, 224, 226, 231
Caserta, 191
Casilinum, 37
Casinum, 34, 248
Castel di Sangro, 34, 116, 268
Castola, 70
Castropignano, 245
Catiline conspiracy, 12
Caudine Forks, ix, xii, 39, 57, 123, 141, 239–40
Caudini, 33, 265, 268, 273, 280
Caudium (Montesarchio), vii, x, 33, 110, 240, 271, 275
Censor, xiii, 5, 62, 113, 137–40, 154, 240, 255
River Chiana, 156
Chianciano, 71
Chilonis, 109
Cicero, xii, 13, 18, 22, 132, 135
Cimbri, 199
Cimetra, 126
Ciminian forest, 65–8, 70, 72, 75, 92, 151, 234
Ciminian mountains, 19, 65
Cincinnatus, 198
Cineas, 264
Cinna, 279
Circeii, 19
Circus Flaminius, 262
Circus Maximus, 5, 234, 249
Cisalpine Gaul, 97, 106, 115, 256
Claudii, 22, 136, 141, 236
Marcus Claudius Marcellus, 2, 87, 208, 272

Appius Claudius Caecus, xiv, 15, 62, 133, 135–7, 139–47, 150, 152–8, 191–2, 244, 257
Appius Claudius Crassus, 137
Appius Claudius Sabinus Regillensis, 136
Appius Claudius Crassus Sabinus Regillensis, 135
Emperor Claudius, 8
Claudius Pulcher, 135
King Cleomenes II, 109
Cleonymus 109,110
Cliodynamics, xv
Cloaca Maxima, 60
Clusium, 60–1, 63, 68, 71, 96, 99, 158–60, 186
Cluviae, 34
Cohorts, 14, 30, 38, 222, 260–1
Collatia, 8
Colline Gate, 100, 102, 256, 259, 280
Cominium, 213–14, 225–6, 228, 240, 246
Cominium Ocritum, 240
Compsa, 33, 268–9, 272
'conflict of the orders', 9, 14, 16
Consular tribunate, xiv, 8, 13, 138
Consulship, ix, xiv, 7, 41, 47, 88, 116, 120, 137, 140, 152, 187, 198, 234, 249, 258
Copenhagen, xviii
Corfinium (Italica), 277
Corinth 109
Coriolanus, 8
Cornelius Cossus, 2
Corsica, xvii, 59
Cortona, 63
Tiberius Coruncanius, 265
Cranite Mountains, 267
Crassus, 257, 259, 261, 280
Croton, 108, 253, 265, 267, 272
Cubulteria, 33, 268, 272
Cumae, vii, 59, 142, 168
Manius Curius Dentatus, 152, 244, 249–50, 252–5, 258, 267
Cursus honorum, 41

Darius III, 281–2
Dauni, 31, 115, 131

Decius Mus, 47, 77–9, 118–22, 125, 127–33, 145, 148, 152, 155, 158, 163, 174, 177–85, 191
Decius Mus senior, 119
Delphi, 4, 36
Demosthenes, 132
Devotio, 178, 180
Diana, 167
Dictator, xiv, 12, 41, 43, 47, 53, 57, 62, 72–5, 86, 90, 92–4, 102–103, 116, 137, 139, 151, 240, 271, 209
Diocletian, 282
Diodorus Siculus, xiii–xv, 40, 70, 97, 118
Dionysius of Halicarnassus, 59, 71, 198
Dionysius I of Syracuse, 98, 101
Disraeli, 140
The Divine Comedy, 266
Dodge City, 9
Dolabella, 259
Dresden, xvii
Marcus Livius Drusus, 276
Dumas, 261
Will Durant, xv
Duris, xiv
Duronia, 212–13

East Anglia, 283
Elbe, 59
Quintus Ennius, 100
Eques, x, 31, 48, 75, 137, 139, 171, 174, 221, 278
Etruscan, viii, xv–xvi, 2, 8, 27, 29–30, 37, 56, 59, 61–5, 71–2, 76, 78, 81, 87–8, 90, 96–7, 99, 104, 107, 112, 120, 147, 151, 153, 161, 199, 207, 211, 247, 264–5
Etruria, xvi–xvii, 1, 5, 8, 17, 26, 32, 34–5, 61, 63, 65, 75, 77, 87, 92–3, 95, 99, 105–108, 112, 117–19, 123, 141, 144, 154, 159–61, 185, 190, 193, 201, 206, 228, 231
Etruscan League or Dodecapolis, 59
Eumenes of Cardia, 209
Europe, xviii
Eutropius, xii, 58, 233, 244

Fabii, 8, 73, 99, 119, 207, 237–8, 243
Fabius Maximus 'the delayer', 240, 271–2
Quintus Fabius Maximus Gurges, 124, 234–44
Quintus Fabius Maximus Rullianus, 24, 42–3, 45, 54, 66–7, 69–79, 81, 83, 92, 119, 121–8, 132, 143, 151–2, 154–8, 167–71, 181, 184–6, 205, 237–8
Quintus Fabius Pictor, xiv
Fabrica di Roma, 67
Falernian, 37, 56, 148
Mount Falernus, 54
Faliscan, 18, 66–7, 92, 115, 162, 190, 231–2
Fallerii, 60
Ferentinum, vii, 19, 84, 131
Feritrum 201
Fetial, 114
Fidenae, 99
Fulvius Flaccus, 272
Gnaeus Flavius, 141
Florence, xv
Fondi, 43, 104
Forchia, ix, xi–xii
Forli, 98
Formiae, 21, 190, 275
Forum, 5, 18, 50, 52, 92, 142, 154, 187, 209, 280
Emperor Frederick II, 129
Fregellae, xi, 21, 33, 38, 41, 92, 121, 265, 274–5
Frentani, 31, 34, 85, 117, 277
Frusinum, 84
Fulvia, 135
Gnaeus Fulvius Centumalus, 116–17, 152, 162–3, 185, 190
Fundi, 21, 275

Gabii, 13
Gaesatae, 2
Gaeta, 53
Galates, 97
Gallic, xiii, 18–19, 22–3, 62, 78, 87, 98–101, 104–106, 108, 153, 160, 164, 173–6, 180, 182–3, 251–2, 259

Sena Gallica, 98
Gaugamela, 176, 281
Gaul, xviii
Gauls, xiii, 12, 24, 28–30, 38, 50, 55, 61, 71, 74, 78, 82, 86–7, 96–7, 99–107, 118, 133, 144–5, 150–1, 153, 159–61, 163, 166–8, 173, 175–6, 179, 181–2, 184, 190, 246, 264, 270
Aulus Gellius, xii
Gellius Egnatius, 132–3, 146–7, 161, 172–3, 190, 192, 194, 283
German wars, 275
Germans, xviii, 278
Gibbon, xv
Goths, 283
Gracchi, 15, 273, 276, 278
Greece, 7, 11, 17, 35–6, 61, 140, 157, 260, 278–82
Greek, xiii–xiv, xvi–xviii, 1–4, 20, 26–7, 31, 35–7, 48, 54, 59, 61, 66, 88, 102–106, 108–10, 115, 140, 144, 168, 194, 219, 245, 253, 264–8, 273, 282
Grosseto, 206
Gubbio, 71

Hadria (Atri), 250–1
Hannibal, xvi, 50, 199, 244, 248, 253–4, 256, 269–73
Hannibalic Wars, xv, 9, 28–9, 87, 105, 208, 239, 272–3
Hastati, 26, 30, 124–5, 169–70, 179, 218, 227
Hellenes, 35–6, 108
Hellenistic, xv, xvii, 2–4, 108, 115, 255
Heraclea, 108, 253, 265
Herculaneum, 41, 59, 231
Hercules 3, 97
Herius Potilius, 269
Hernici, 19, 22, 31, 56, 83, 83–5, 112, 151, 188, 205, 265, 271
Herodotus, 59
Hieronymus of Cardia, 88
Hittites, 176
Homer, 13
Hoplite, 26, 39, 61, 168
Horatius, 44

Iberia, xviii, 157
Iceni, 283
Iliad, 11, 153, 175
Insubres, 98
Interamna Lirenas, 33, 92, 204–205, 212
Ionian Sea, 109
Italy, vi–viii, xvi, 2, 13, 17, 19, 22, 27, 32–3, 36, 38, 43, 54, 59, 61, 71, 85, 89, 91, 93, 95, 97–9, 101–102, 105–108, 110, 131, 150, 158, 164, 174, 246, 257, 264–5, 267, 270–1, 273–4, 277, 278, 282–3

Janiculum Hill, 12
temple of Janus, 24
Jena-Auerstedt, 224
Indiana Jones, 117
Jugurthine war, 275
Jupiter, 2–4, 173, 184, 203, 210, 249
Justin, 255
Justinian, 187

Lake Albano, 103
Lake Avernus, 142
Lake Bolsena, 78, 92, 206
Lake di Bracciano, 63–4, 66
Lake di Vico, 63
Lake Fucino, 32, 82, 108
lakes Garda, 82
Lake Maggiore, 82
lake of Fondi, 43
Lake Prile, 206
Lake Trasimene, xviii, 60, 70, 156, 180, 270
Lake Vadimo, 75, 211
Lake Velinus, 255
Lamponius the Lucanian, 262
L'Aquila, 212, 249
La Rocca, 245
Latins, vii, xvii, 8, 17–21, 23–5, 31, 42, 54, 60, 63, 82–3, 86, 92, 101, 103–105, 107, 120, 122, 148, 164–8, 174, 178, 201, 204, 221, 248, 250, 265, 268, 270, 277–8
Latium, xvi–xvii, 1, 9, 13, 17–21, 26, 32, 34–5, 41–2, 44–6, 50, 54–5, 59, 68, 83,

95, 103, 115, 136, 144, 148, 191, 200, 277
Lautulae, 22, 57, 64, 119, 240
Lavello, 131
Lucius Cornelius Lentulus, 153
Le Murge, 130
Leonidas, 43
Lazio, 33, 39, 59
Legions, xi–xii, xvii, 15–16, 23, 28, 30–1, 38, 40, 47, 50, 56, 76, 78–9, 101–104, 108, 121–5, 130, 140–1, 149, 158–60, 164–7, 171–4, 185, 191, 194–8, 202, 210–12, 219, 222, 224, 226–8, 233, 242–3, 245, 247–51, 256, 260, 263–5, 280
Lex Julia, 278
Lex Ovinia, 138
Poetelius Libo, 47–51
Lictors, 60, 73, 136, 145, 181
Ligurians, 113
Ligures Baebiani, 113
Linen Legion, 210–11, 219, 222, 233, 263
Liris River, xvii, 20–1, 33, 37, 40–2, 45, 50, 52, 54, 86–7, 91, 121, 148, 150, 190, 194, 204, 248
Marcus Livius Denter, 179
Livy, xii, 13–14, 24, 30–1, 60, 67, 89, 105, 154, 169, 213
Locris, 108, 253
Lollius, 268
Lombard, 281
London, 6, 283
Longula, 75
Lucania, viii, xvii, 31, 33, 35, 62, 110–12, 117, 122, 127, 129, 142, 145, 151, 195, 231, 253, 255, 257, 259, 262–3, 265–8, 278, 280
Luceria, vii, x, xii, 40, 42, 45, 48, 53–4, 86, 106, 109, 117, 127, 129, 201–202, 205, 212
Lucretia, 8
Lydia, xviii, 59
Lyon, 8
Lysimachus, 88

Macedon, 267
Maddaloni, ix
Gaius Maenius, 53
Magana Graecia, 4
Magnesia ad Sipylum, xviii
Malaventum, 110, 127, 252, 268
Mamertines, 253
Manchester, 283
Maniples, 30, 38, 49, 123, 169, 177, 179, 195, 219
Manlius Torquatus, 29, 72, 87, 104, 178
Lucius Manlius Torquatus, 159
Marcus Manlius Capitolinus, 12
Titus Manlius Torquatus, 94, 107
Marathon, 281
Marcius, 262
Gaius Marcius, 168, 182
Emperor Marcus Aurelius, 187
Mark Antony, 135
Marius, 260, 278–9
Young Marius, 256, 262, 279–80
Marrucini, 31, 82, 85, 151, 277
Mars, 4, 13, 67, 102, 126, 178, 249
Marsi, 82, 85, 88, 92, 151, 252, 277
Masada, 245
Massilia, 4
Matese massif, 33, 50, 189, 229, 248
Mediterranean, xvi, xviii, 2, 25, 108, 240, 251, 273–5
Melfi, 130
Mesopotamia, xviii, 188
Messana, 253
Messapians, 110
Metapontum, 110
Mevania, 79
Middle East, xviii
Milan, xvi, xviii
Milo, 264
Milonia, 199–201
Minturnae, vii, 21, 52, 150, 190, 192
Minucius, 271
Mitanni, 176
Mithridates, 260, 274, 278
Molise, 33
Theodor Mommsen, xvii, 33, 140

Mongols, xv
Gaius Fabricius Luscinus Monocularis, 266
Monte Cassino, 204
Monte Cavo, 103
Monte Sacro, 10
Montesarchio, xi, 33, 283
Mopsii, 269
Mount Taburno, xi
Mount Tifatai, 120
Mount Vairanoi, 213, 273
Murgantia, 129
Museo Pio-Clementino, Vatican, 113

Naples, ix, xvi, 21, 33, 106, 120, 283
Narnia, 95, 105, 107–108, 144
Spurius Nautius, 217, 220
Neapolis, 4, 168, 245
Nepet (Nepi), 19, 63, 95
Nequinum, 93, 95, 105
Nera, 71
Nero consul, 271
New York City, 9
Nile river, 176
Nola, 41, 106, 268, 277
Gaius Norbanus, 279
Norman, ix
Nuceria, vii, 37, 41
Numantia, 22
Numerius Decimius, 271
Numidians, 271

Ocriculum, 71, 94
Odysseus, 11
Ofanto, 33, 129
Quintus Lucretius Ofella, 258
Paulus Orosius, xii, 233, 238, 252
Orvieto, 60, 206
Oscan, 32, 36, 149, 271
Ostia, 4, 21, 45
Ottomans, xv

Ovius Paccius, 210
Paeligni, 31, 34, 82, 85, 133, 192, 252, 277
Marcus Fulvius Paetus, 94

Pagi, 35
Palatine, 4, 82, 249
Palumbinum, 231
Papirii, ix, 236
Papirius Cursor the elder, 40–1, 46, 72–4, 77, 209, 237
Papirius Cursor, 209, 213–14, 216–17, 221, 228–9, 268
Parco di Villa Ada, 102
Paris, xviii, 98
Parthian, 259
Velleius Paterculus, 22
Patricians, 4, 7, 10, 14–15, 53, 57, 136–7
Paulus Orosius, xii, 233
Pedum, 102
Pennine, 283
Pentri, 33, 83, 115, 123, 126, 130, 189–90, 194, 201, 212, 233, 246, 248, 263, 265, 268, 270–1, 273
Perdiccas, 120
Persephone, 253
Achaemenid Persia, 14, 36, 176, 281
Perusia (Perugia), 60, 63, 66–70, 76, 79, 106–107, 144, 147–8, 151, 153–4, 156, 158, 160, 163, 186, 189, 207, 277
Pescara, 83
Gaius Sulpicius Peticus, 103
Phalanx, 26, 28, 30, 61, 167–8, 170, 266
Philip II of Macedon, 3, 245
Quintus Publilius Philo, 3, 40–1, 53, 139
Phocaea, 59
Picentes, 83, 111, 133, 268, 277, 280
Pietrabbondante, vii, 36
Pisa, xvi
Pliny, 71, 244
Plistica, 42
Plutarch, 1, 28
Pnyx, 282
Polyaenus, 233
Polybius, xiii–xiv, 28, 30, 54, 78, 82, 102, 125, 160, 194, 255, 274
Pompeii, 41, 59, 277
Pompey, xv, 208, 280
Pontine Islands, 4, 52
Pontine Marshes, xvi, 32

Pontius Telesinus, 257–62, 280
Gaius Pontius, 233, 239, 283
Lars Porcena, 95–6
Spurius Postumius Albinus, 198
Lucius Postumius Megellus, 162, 186, 190, 197, 199–200, 202, 207, 241–3
Publius Postumius Tubertus, 197
Praeneste, 3, 19, 101–103, 256–7, 259, 261–3, 280
Praetorians, 11
Praetors, 8, 13, 57, 104, 135, 152, 154, 191–2, 251–2
Pro Praetors, 162, 199
Principes, 26, 30, 170, 179, 182
Privernum, 104
Punic War, xviii, 61, 90, 161, 193, 271, 273
Pupinia, 78
Pyrgi, 101
King Pyrrhus, 31, 109, 135, 180, 209, 241–2, 253–8, 265–8, 270
Pyrrhic War, xiv, 4
Pythagoras, 3

Quaestors, 27, 103, 135, 195

Marcus Atilius Regulus, 193–6, 200–205, 207, 212
Remus, 4
Republic, x, xiii–xv, xvii, 4–5, 7, 9–10, 14, 18–27, 30, 32, 38–42, 44–6, 48, 50, 53, 55, 62–3, 74, 79, 83–5, 89–92, 96, 101, 104, 106–10, 112, 115, 117–23, 127, 134–40, 144, 151–2, 157–9, 162–3, 166, 178, 185, 188, 194, 209, 211, 234, 236, 240, 242, 247–52, 255, 263–4, 268, 270–6, 279, 282
Rhegium, 108, 253
Rio Spalla Bassa, 204
Roccamonfina, 52, 122, 148, 190
Roman Empire, xv, 244
Romulea, 130
Romulus, xiii, 1–2, 4, 7, 28, 87, 249
Rotarii, 31
Cornelius Rufinus, 247, 258

Rusellae, 27, 60, 93, 206
Russia, 11
Gaius Marcius Rutilus, 138
Rutuli, 9
Gaius Marcius Rutulus, 75, 224, 258

Sabellians, 31, 33, 35–6, 61–2, 91, 106, 257, 261, 264, 270, 276–7, 280–3
Sabine, 2, 7–8, 22, 28, 31, 35, 68, 71, 82, 101, 136, 151, 212, 249–50, 252, 255
Sabine women, 2
'sacred band', 75
Saepinum, 33, 213, 228–30, 281
Salamis, 281
Sallentines, 143
Sallust, 28
Samnite Wars, xiv, xvii, 9–10, 15, 25, 40, 55, 86, 104, 120
Samnium, 5, 20, 36, 50, 54, 72, 75, 79, 83, 101, 108, 112–16, 126, 131, 143, 145, 147, 149, 158, 188, 192, 197, 206, 208, 212, 228, 231, 233, 242, 244–7, 264, 267, 269–70, 273, 275–6, 279, 283
Duke of Samnium, 281
Sangro River, 33
Sanguerone River, 184
Saracens, 129, 150
Sardinia, xvii, 4
Sarsina, 71
Sassoferrato, 160, 173, 184
Saticula, vii, 33, 40–2, 53, 123
Satricum, 19, 41
Scauri, 148
Scipio Africanus, 113, 208
Lucius Cornelius Scipio Barbatus, 3, 116–17, 159, 168, 182, 222–3
Scotland, xviii
Segovesus, 97
Seleucus Nicator, 88
Publius Sempronius, 84–5
Tiberius Sempronius Longus, 180
Senate, 6, 12, 20, 36, 50, 91, 111, 127, 138–9, 158, 208, 237, 241
Senones, 97–101, 107, 151, 153, 159, 163, 174, 252

Sententiae, 140
Sentinum, xvii, 71, 160, 162–3, 184–5, 187–93, 195, 199, 204, 211, 214, 216, 233–4, 237, 249, 251, 263, 281
Servian walls, 6, 19, 45, 53, 249, 259
Setia, 3
Sibyl of Tibur, 102
Sibylline books, 7
Sicily, xvii ,98, 102, 129, 153, 253–4, 266–7, 270
Sidicini, 31, 37, 121–2, 178
Siena, 71
Sinuessa, 150,192
Social War, 275, 279–80
Solon, 16
Sora, 20, 33, 42, 45, 50–2, 83–4, 87, 120, 122, 194, 197, 200–201, 204, 213, 248
Soviet, 10–11
Spain, xv, 4, 208, 274
Sparta, 109
Spartans, 8, 43, 109, 180
Spoletum, 79
Spolia Opima, 2, 87
Spurius Papirius, 214, 227
Statius Minatius, 149
Strabo, 34, 100, 121
Suetonius, 100
Suessula, 21
hot springs of Suio, 148
Sulla, xiv, 247–63, 278–80
Gaius Sulpicius Longus, 47–51
Sutrium, 19, 63–4, 66–9, 92, 95, 108, 144
Syracuse, 98, 208, 266, 272
Syria, 259

Tacitus, 96
Taenum Sidicinum (Teano), 120, 279
Tarentum, xvii, 168, 244, 264, 269, 272
Tarpeia, 2
Lucius Tarquinius Collatinus, 8
Lucius Tarquinius Priscus, 97
Tarquinius Superbus, 4, 8, 39, 96, 140
Tarquinii, 4, 19, 60, 66, 78, 96–7, 136, 206
Tarracina, 21, 38, 45, 47

Telesia, 33, 268, 272
Terni, 71
Teutones, 199
Themistocles, 282
Theodosius the Great, 120
Theopompus, 100
Thermopylae, 8, 281
Thersites, 11
Thurii, 108, 263
Tiber, xiii, xvi–xvii, 1, 4, 18, 20, 33, 60, 66–8, 71, 74, 78, 82, 92, 96, 98–9, 104, 111–12, 114, 120, 144, 151, 155, 157, 160, 162, 165, 180, 190, 199, 248, 260–1, 273, 281
Tiber island, 2, 4
Tiberius, Emperor, 100, 120
Tibur, 19–20, 22, 83, 89, 101–103
Mont Tifernus, 33, 191
River Tifernus, 83
Timaeus, xiv
River Timia (Topino), 79
Todi, 67
Tolerus River (Saco), 21, 83
Tolumnius, 2
Torquatus, Sullan general, 259
Touto, 35–6
Arch of Trajan, 283
Trebbia, xviii, 180, 270
Trebula, 33, 268
Triarii, 26, 30, 168
Titus Trebonius, 217, 221
Trebula Balliensis, 268
Trerus river, 280
Trigno river, 212–13
tribunes of the plebs, 10–11, 73, 138, 276
military tribunes, 38, 57, 73, 140, 252
Troilum, 231
Trojan War, 128
Troy, xiii, 13
Servilus Tullius, 8, 24, 259
Turin, xvi
Tuscany, xvi, 59
Tusculum, 9, 19
meddix tuticus, 35
Twelve Tables, 3

Wat Tyler, 6
Tyrrhenian Sea, 33, 59, 178

Umbrian, xvii, 56, 68, 70–1, 75, 77–8, 81–2, 86, 98, 104, 107, 111, 119, 133, 144, 147, 150–1, 153, 159, 161–2, 190, 199, 246

Valerius Antias, 90
Valerius Corvus, 29, 87–90, 92–3, 95, 104–105, 107, 116, 118, 124
Publius Valerius Laevinus, 265
Valerius Laevinus, 272
Varro, polymath, 13, 35
Varro, 198
Vatican, 113, 162, 186
Veii, xiii–xiv, xvi, 2, 4, 8, 18–20, 24–5, 60, 62–3, 66–7, 96, 100–102, 104,162
Velia, 231
Velitrae, 19
Venafrum, 33, 248, 268
Venice, xvi
Venus, 234, 259
Venusia, 33, 127, 129–30, 213, 242, 246, 248, 265, 271, 277
Vescia, 52, 148, 230
Vesta, 102
Vestal Virgins, 259
Vestini, 40, 83, 85, 133
Via Amerina, 67
Via Nomentana, 259
Via Sacra, 249

Via Salaria, 102, 259
Via Valeria, 83, 89, 92, 106, 277
Vicus, 35, 71
Villa Gregoriana, 102
Villanovan, 115, 156, 207
Virgil, 1, 13
Viterbo, 75
Volaterrae, 60, 115, 117
Volsci, viii, xvi–xvii, 8, 18–22, 29, 31–2, 34, 41–3, 47, 53, 59, 73, 75, 85, 88, 101, 120, 204, 234
Volsinii, 60, 63, 78, 92, 206–207, 265, 269
Fanum Voltumnae, 59
Colli a Volturno, 121
Volturnus, xvii, 33, 54, 91, 149, 191–2, 194, 235, 248
Volumnius Flamma, 133, 142, 145, 147–52, 158, 191, 211, 217, 222
Mount Vulture, 33, 56, 114, 130, 243

Wales, 117
Washington DC, 277
waterfall of Marmore, 255
Hollywood Western, 7
Dick Whittington, 6

Xerxes, 281–2

Yorkshire, 117

Zonaras, 232, 266